CW01334428

ROMANIA'S HOLY WAR

A volume in the series
Battlegrounds: Cornell Studies in Military History
Edited by David J. Silbey
Editorial Board: Petra Goedde, Wayne E. Lee, Brian McAllister Linn, and Lien-Hang T. Nguyen

A list of titles in this series is available at cornellpress.cornell.edu.

ROMANIA'S HOLY WAR

Soldiers, Motivation,
and the Holocaust

GRANT T. HARWARD

CORNELL UNIVERSITY PRESS
Ithaca and London

Copyright © 2021 by Cornell University

All rights reserved. Except for brief quotations in a review, this book, or parts thereof, must not be reproduced in any form without permission in writing from the publisher. For information, address Cornell University Press, Sage House, 512 East State Street, Ithaca, New York 14850. Visit our website at cornellpress.cornell.edu.

First published 2021 by Cornell University Press

Library of Congress Cataloging-in-Publication Data
Names: Harward, Grant T., 1986- author.
Title: Romania's holy war : soldiers, motivation, and the Holocaust / Grant T. Harward.
Description: Ithaca [New York] : Cornell University Press, 2021. | Series: Battlegrounds: Cornell studies in military history | Includes bibliographical references and index.
Identifiers: LCCN 2020056477 (print) | LCCN 2020056478 (ebook) | ISBN 9781501759963 (hardcover) | ISBN 9781501759987 (ebook) | ISBN 9781501759987 (pdf)
Subjects: LCSH: World War, 1939-1945—Social aspects—Romania. | World War, 1939-1945—Romania. | World War, 1939-1945—Romania—Psychological aspects. | World War, 1939-1945—Moral and ethical aspects—Romania.
Classification: LCC D744.7.R6 H37 2021 (print) | LCC D744.7.R6 (ebook) | DDC 940.53/498—dc23
LC record available at https://lccn.loc.gov/2020056477
LC ebook record available at https://lccn.loc.gov/2020056478

To my beloved eternal companion, Lisa

CONTENTS

List of Figures, Tables, and Maps ix
Acknowledgments xi
List of Abbreviations xiv
Note on Terms xv
Note on Names and Spelling xvi

Introduction 1
1. Ideology of Holy War 17
2. Army Culture, Interwar Politics, and Neutrality ... 36
3. 1940–1941: From Neutral to Axis 64
4. 1941: Holy War and Holocaust 92
5. 1941–1942: Doubling Down on Holy War 131
6. 1942–1944: Holy War of Defense 169
7. Propaganda and Discipline 206
8. Women and Minorities 229
Epilogue 254

Notes 269
Bibliography 315
Index 327

Figures, Tables, and Maps

Figures

1. A chaplain blesses soldiers during an interwar oath-taking ceremony — 49
2. Anti-Judeo-Bolshevism revenge propaganda, September 1940 — 78
3. Anti-Soviet atrocity propaganda, September 1940 — 79
4. Jewish survivors and dead in the Iași police headquarters courtyard, June 1941 — 101
5. Arrested "Jewish snipers" guarded by Romanian soldiers, August 1941 — 105
6. Mass baptism of Soviet peasants by a Romanian chaplain, August 1941 — 122
7. Front page of *Sentinela*'s special Easter edition, April 1942 — 152
8. Romanian soldiers on a road resting next to a German assault gun, December 1942 — 175
9. Near Iași, Romanian soldiers transporting a wounded man, May 1944 — 201
10. Example of *The Misadventures of Private Neață*, November 1942 — 211
11. Execution at the front of probable Romanian deserters, August 1943 — 224

Tables

1. Size of the officer corps and NCO/enlisted ranks, 1924–1939 — 52
2. Romanian military expenditure (in millions of dollars) in comparison with Southeast European states, Nazi Germany, and the Soviet Union, 1934–1938 — 55
3. Sărata Training Center No. 5, 1942–1944 — 221
4. Minorities in the Third Army, May 1942 — 242
5. Situation of labor detachments, December 1943 — 245

Maps

1. Soviet occupation of northern Bukovina and Bessarabia, 1940 — 67
2. Operation Barbarossa, 1941 — 112
3. Spring recovery and Case Blue, 1942 — 145
4. Kuban, Crimea, and Iași front, 1943–1944 — 179

Acknowledgments

Although the researching and writing of this book was a solitary endeavor, I did not do it in solitude. I could not have completed my goal without the invaluable assistance of others along the way. To start, I must thank my mentor, Roger Reese, who provided prompt feedback on chapters and insightful responses to questions. He held my work to a high standard, and I know my skills as a historian markedly improved because of it. Roger represents the epitome of professionalism that I try to emulate as a historian. I am also indebted to Adam Seipp, Brian Rouleau, and Stjepan Meštrović. They each provided important insights that shaped this book. I must thank colleagues in the Texas A&M University Department of History, who helped both at an individual level, in mapping out the chapter organization, and at an institutional level, in generously awarding me multiple research grants. These funded much of my work in archives and libraries in Romania and a visit to battlefields and Holocaust sites in Romania, Moldova, and Ukraine in 2018. I want to thank Michelle Kelso for organizing the Ukrainian part of that tour, offering me feedback on excerpts of manuscript chapters, and being a good friend. Additionally, I received a Fulbright Award funded by the United States Department of State and the Romanian Ministry of Foreign Affairs. I could not have completed the most central part my research without it. I want to specifically thank the Romanian-US Fulbright Commission American program director, Mihai Moroiu. My wife and I appreciate his help facilitating our transition to living in Romania and lending us support during my emergency surgery in country. I also received the Norman Raab Foundation Fellowship at the Jack, Joseph, and Morton Mandel Center for Advanced Studies at the United States Holocaust Memorial Museum, which allowed me to finish researching and writing my manuscript. Moreover, many thanks to Steve Feldman for his assistance during the book proposal stage and the Emerging Scholar Program at the Mandel Center for its generous help publishing this book. I am grateful to all the archivists, librarians, curators, and other staff of the various archives and libraries who assisted me over the years. I want to express special thanks to Sorin Bobîrla and Luminița Dumitru, who kept my table in the reading room of the Romanian National Military Archives piled high with records; Carla Duța, who helped me decipher the handwriting in diaries and memoirs at the National Military Museum Library; and Mirel Berechet, who enabled me to obtain permissions to use illustrations from the Romanian Academy Library despite its closure to the public during the COVID-19 pandemic. I owe a special debt of gratitude to the National Association of War Veterans for its help finding veterans of the Second World War for me to interview and often providing me space to hold the interviews. I am thankful to each of the veterans who made time to meet with me to discuss their experiences in the war. I must remember Victoria Gorzo. This spry septuagenarian provided me room, board, and hours of fun conversation during earlier research trips to Romania when I conducted my first interviews with veterans. I am pleased to have made the acquaintance of Greg Kelley, a retired librarian with a great interest in Romania during the Second World War and a personal collection containing several hundred volumes on the subject. He kindly provided me an annotated bibliography to look for new sources, gifted me several boxes of materials, and loaned me a rare book. Unless otherwise indicated, I translated the Romanian sources quoted in this book, but I did request help with some particularly difficult passages. I especially must thank Ștefan Vizante for always being willing to look over my translations. I cannot forget Stephan Lofgren, my supervisor at the US Army Center of Military History when I was working there, who took me to task about my writing style and grammar. I (re-)learned a lot from him about editing, which came in handy when it was time to work on this book. I also must recognize Răzvan Bolba, Mirel Eugen, Daniel Obreja, and Ioan Dărăbanț, who provided me wartime manuals, documents, and photographs in response to requests for information on the Romanian Army. I greatly appreciate the feedback on my manuscript from my outsider readers, and Cornell University Press's PreBoard and Faculty Board, whose comments allowed me to greatly improve the final version. I am thankful for my editors Emily Andrew, David Silbey, and Allegra Martschenko, who guided me through the complex publication process, and for my copy editors who spotted mistakes in style and helped polish my prose. A host of other friends and colleagues supported me in various ways, and I would like to mention just a few, in no particular order: Dallas Michelbacher, Ștefan Ionescu, Roland Clark, Lorien Foote, Vladimir Solonari, Dennis Deletant, Ionuț Biliuța, Radu Ioanid, Adrian Cioflâncă, and Mioara Anton. Finally, I could not have finished this book without the support of my family, especially my wife. Lisa and I married just before I began this project, so she was with me every step of the way. She worked to help pay the bills, moved across the US, came with me to Romania, and gave birth to two children in the intervening years. I am so blessed to be loved by someone as amazing as Lisa. Of course, any mistakes in this book are my own. Similarly, the arguments and opinions within are mine alone and do not represent the views of the Romanian-US Fulbright Commission nor the United States Holocaust Memorial Museum.

Abbreviations

FNB	Focşani-Nămoloasa-Brăila
GAL	Gruparea Aeriană de Luptă, Air Combat Group
Gestapo	Geheime Staatspolizei, (German) Secret State Police
LANC	Liga Apărării Naționale Creştine, League of National Christian Defense
MCG	Marele Cartier General, Great General Headquarters
NKVD	Narodnyi komissariat vnutrennikh del, (Soviet) People's Commissariat for Internal Affairs
OKH	Oberkommando des Heeres, (German) High Command of the Army
OKW	Oberkommando der Wehrmacht, (German) High Command of the Armed Forces
SS	Schutzstaffel, (German Nazi Party) "Protection Squad"
SSI	Serviciul Special de Informații, Special Intelligence Service
Stavka	Stavka Verkhovnogo Glavnokomandovaniya, (Soviet) Headquarters of the Supreme Main Command

Note on Terms

This book focuses on the Romanian Army; however, because that army collaborated closely with the German Army in combat and SS formations in the rear, the book includes some German terms. Common German terms such as "führer," "Luftwaffe," "Reichskommissariat," or "Einsatzgruppe" have not been italicized. Italics are generally reserved for Romanian words. Furthermore, I use German euphemisms common during the Holocaust, such as the "Jewish Question" and "Final Solution." This book prefers the unhyphenated "antisemitism" over the hyphenated "anti-Semitism" because "Semite" is an outdated term for an imagined monolithic Jewish race.

The book uses the term "Gypsy" to denote the Roma people in the text. I did not do this without careful consideration. Although the term Gypsy [*țigan*] was and is used as a slur by Romanians, some contemporary Roma have reclaimed the term. Moreover, this was the term used in official Romanian reports at the time. Lastly, "Roma"—and any of its common variations such as "Romani" or "Romany"—risk being mixed up with "Romanian" by a reader who is unfamiliar with the history of the Roma or Romania. Consequently, "Gypsy" is used to make it clear who is being referred to. This in no way is meant to denigrate the Roma people. In fact, this book does its best to highlight this group's overlooked role in the Romanian Army.

Note on Names and Spelling

Due to the multiethnic character of interwar Romania's border regions, many places in this book have two or even three name variations. For simplicity, I chose to use the Romanian names officially in use during the Second World War. Additionally, with the exception of Bucharest, I decided to use the Romanian instead of the Anglicized spelling of place names. The same goes for persons, most notably King Mihai I, rather than King Michael I. I did use the Anglicized names for the regions of interwar Romania. Wallachia, Moldavia, and Dobruja made up the so-called Old Kingdom of Romania to which Transylvania, Bukovina, and Bessarabia were annexed after the First World War. Importantly, Transylvania includes not just the historic principality of Transylvania, but all territory Romania annexed from Hungary after the First World War, which included parts of Banat, Crișana, and Maramureș. The names of well-known geographic features retain their Anglicized spellings. If a quotation contained an alternate spelling, however, I left it as it had been written in the original.

Similarly, the USSR had locations with multiple names inherited from the multiethnic Russian empire. Although Soviet policy makers during the interwar period took steps to promote a multilingual society, including recognizing official minority languages like Ukrainian, Russian remained the country's dominant language. Also, German and Romanian soldiers referred to places by their Russian names during the campaign in the Soviet Union. Consequently, again for simplicity, I chose to use Russian names for places in the Soviet Union. I used the common English spelling if one existed and the British standard system of transliteration if one did not. I made an exception for places in Romanian-occupied territory in Ukraine that were too obscure to have a common English spelling. Instead I used the Romanian spelling to reflect the wartime reality. Again, the names of well-known geographic features use common Anglicized spellings.

ROMANIA'S HOLY WAR

Introduction

In 2009, two veterans animatedly discussed Romania's part in the Second World War. At one point, Iuliu Dobrin, a radioman who served only after the "turning of arms" against the Axis, disputed the official number of victims of the Holocaust in Romania. Teodor Halic, a cavalryman who fought alongside German soldiers, interjected, "[Let's] not put blame on the Germans." He believed Jews had "behaved very badly," abusing withdrawing Romanian soldiers in 1940 when northern Bukovina and Bessarabia came under Soviet occupation. "We had a score with them." "When [the Romanian Army] went back, [the Jews] paid it," Dobrin chimed in.[1] This interview was the first of many I conducted with Romanian veterans. While listening to their recollections, I realized Romanian soldiers were far more motivated to fight the Soviets and commit atrocities against Jews than I had been led to believe by previous historians who claimed Romania joined the Axis under duress, Romania's dictator Marshal Ion Antonescu was primarily to blame for the Holocaust in Romania, Romanian soldiers wanted to fight Hungary and not the USSR, and the Romanian Army became easily demoralized owing to a lack of ideological commitment. Yet as I dug through archives, perused diaries and memoirs, and read wartime propaganda it became plain that Romania closely identified with Nazi Germany's purported "crusade" to defend Christian civilization from the supposed threat of "Jewish communism." Of course, a certain amount of Nazi coercion contributed to keeping Romania in the fight after the tide of war turned against the Axis. Nonetheless, common ideological beliefs united Romania, even more than other European nations, under the swastika to battle against the hammer and sickle.

This book argues that Romanian soldiers were highly motivated, primarily by ideology, on the eastern front. Nationalism, religion, antisemitism, and anticommunism fueled Romania's "holy war" from 22 June 1941 to 23 August 1944. "[Marshal] Antonescu said, 'Cross the Prut for the holy war,'" recalled mortarman Marin Ștefanescu. "This was the slogan: against communism until we destroy [it] defensively."[2] He meant to say "definitively," but this slip shows Romanian soldiers believed they participated in a just war against Soviet aggression. Propaganda reinforced ideology. Romanian propaganda incorporated Nazi propaganda because of common beliefs. Indeed, shared antisemitism, anticommunism, and to a much lesser extent anti-Slavism, bound Romania to Nazi Germany.[3] So much so that the Romanian Army closely collaborated with the German Army in Adolf Hitler's "war of annihilation," which included not only destroying the Red Army but also murdering Jews and communists while starving "subhuman" Slavs.[4] While anti-Slav racism was less prevalent than in the German Army, the Romanian Army was anxious to take vengeance on Jews in eastern Romania, whom it accused of treachery, and it was more than willing to back the SS in implementing the "Final Solution" in the Soviet Union. Romania's holy war consisted of two interlinked campaigns: fighting on the front, and slaughtering Jews and communists in the rear. The same ideology that justified sacrifice in battle also predisposed Romanian soldiers toward genocide against Jews. First Lieutenant N. Alexandru Ciobanu was one of a few who found it difficult to reconcile rhetoric with reality. "All the crimes committed impressed me because it was said that holy war was being made when in fact criminal war was made there," he testified later, claiming he only followed orders and did not directly participate in executions or rapes.[5] Most Romanian soldiers, however, saw little contradiction between combat and committing atrocities; both were necessary to destroy "Judeo-Bolshevism." Some commanders not only tolerated but demanded mass murder; and the Antonescu regime harnessed soldiers to "cleanse the terrain" of Jews in northern Bukovina and Bessarabia. In a short period, Romanian soldiers became habituated to the mass murder of Jews and communists, egged on by German soldiers and SS troops, conditioning them to commit atrocities against Soviet prisoners of war, partisans, and civilians. Strict discipline in the Romanian Army played an important but secondary role in motivating soldiers in combat and in committing atrocities on the eastern front.

Romanian soldiers' treatment of Jews was a bellwether of their faith in final victory. The Romanian Army's initial genocidal violence against Jews became mass reprisals targeting not only Jews but also Soviet prisoners of war, partisans, and civilians, and became less frequent as the war turned in the enemy's favor. This closely tracks with the ups and downs of morale among the ranks of Romanian soldiers during the campaign in the Soviet Union. The Romanian Army deeply implicated itself in Axis war crimes in Romanian territory and Romanian-occupied Soviet territory (known as Transnistria). Therefore, even when it became clear the German Army was losing, Romanian soldiers continued fighting alongside German soldiers out of fear of what retribution the Red Army might inflict on them and their families. Propaganda stoked these fears, which were rooted in ideological hatred of Jews and communism. Discipline threatened punishment if soldiers did not do their duty. One cannot understand why Romanian soldiers fought during the Second World War without the perspectives of both military history and Holocaust history.

Missing Historical Debate

Romania became a black box to historians after the war. There were some valiant early efforts to chronicle the Second World War, most notably Matatias Carp's "Black Book" of the Holocaust in Romania published between 1946 and 1948.[6] Upon seizing power in 1948, the Romanian Communist Party restricted access to archives, censored histories of the campaign against the USSR, banned discussion of the Holocaust in Romania, and lionized Romania's part in the "anti-Hitlerite war" between 23 August 1944 and 9 May 1945.[7] Western historians relied on Romanian émigrés to reveal the Antonescu regime's inner workings. These individuals—former diplomats like Alexandru Cretzianu and Raoul Bossy—penned accounts justifying Romania's alliance with Nazi Germany, downplaying Romanian commitment to the invasion of the USSR, and blaming Marshal Antonescu for continuing the war and persecuting the Jews.[8] The only other sources available to Western historians appeared to confirm these claims. German memoirists—former generals like Heinz Guderian, Erich von Manstein, and Johannes Friessner—described Romania as a treacherous ally, claimed Romanian soldiers suffered from poor morale due to insufficient ideological motivation, and scapegoated the Romanian Army for the German Army's defeats.[9] By the 1950s, it was widely accepted that Romania had been a reluctant ally of Nazi Germany.

Little changed during the Cold War. A few more émigré accounts emerged in the 1960s. Platon Chirnoagă, a staff officer during the campaign in the

USSR and then minister of war for a Romanian fascist puppet-state-in-exile established at the end of the war, wrote a history highlighting the Romanian Army's weaknesses in equipment and training but emphasizing high morale until the battle of Stalingrad.[10] His work was never translated into English and languished in obscurity. Prince Mihail Sturdza, an interwar diplomat and later erstwhile minister of foreign affairs for the Romanian fascist puppet-state-in-exile, wrote a memoir claiming an international cabal of Jews had engineered the war to allow the USSR to dominate Eastern Europe.[11] Starting in the 1970s, the Romanian Communist Party pursued a more nationalistic history of the war and even allowed historians to partially rehabilitate Marshal Antonescu, presenting him as a tragic figure caught between Nazi Germany and the USSR who did his best to preserve Romania's sovereignty and territorial integrity.[12] This forced the communist regime to break the taboo of the Holocaust in Romania, but communist historians blamed atrocities on German "occupiers" and a few Romanian fascists.[13] In the 1980s, Jean Ancel, a Romanian-born Israeli, managed to obtain and publish archival documents in Hebrew and English.[14] His pioneering work revealed some details on how the Romanian state persecuted Jews during the Holocaust, and it laid the blame squarely at Antonescu's feet. Nevertheless, historians still knew comparatively little of Romania's holy war.

After the collapse of communism in 1989, two groups rushed into newly opened archives and immediately began talking past each other. Military historians combined anticommunist and antifascist narratives to fashion a new myth of Romanian soldiers' heroic sacrifice and double victimization by the Nazis and Soviets, with Marshal Antonescu as a nationalist martyr.[15] At the same time, Holocaust historians unearthed documents demonstrating the complicity of Romanian troops in the Holocaust at the direction of Antonescu. Military and Holocaust historians worked at cross purposes. It was at this time that the only serious history of the Romanian armed forces was published in English, in 1995. Following military historians' lead (two of whom are cited as coauthors), Mark Axworthy's *Third Axis, Fourth Ally* details Romanian frontline operations and does much to rehabilitate the Romanian Army's maligned reputation. He acknowledges its participation in the Holocaust but cites low estimates of Jewish victims. Axworthy misrepresents the officer corps' politics, claims soldiers lacked motivation after liberating northern Bukovina and Bessarabia, and overemphasizes Romania's contribution to the anti-Hitlerite war. Finally, his history relies on documents collected in Bucharest by communist historians and lacks citations.[16] In Romania, military history and Holocaust history clashed, causing much controversy. In 1998, Alex Mihai Stoenescu wrote *Armata, mareșalul și evreii*

(The army, the marshal, and the Jews). He concedes that the Antonescu regime was antisemitic and that Romanian soldiers murdered Jews, but repeats the myth that Jews persecuted Romanians in 1940, claims that only seventy to eighty thousand Jews died in Romania and Transnistria, blames German troops for the Iași pogrom, and argues that Antonescu saved four hundred thousand Jews.[17] In 2003, after Romania's president made comments also minimizing the Holocaust in Romania, international pressure compelled the Romanian government to create an international commission led by the celebrated Holocaust survivor and Nobel laureate Elie Wiesel. Its report in 2004 provided a basic chronology of events, recognized Romania's guilt, and estimated that between 280,000 and 380,000 Jews died in Romania and Transnistria.[18] The establishment of the Elie Wiesel National Institute for the Study of the Holocaust in Romania in 2005 was a major victory for Holocaust historians.

Since then, despite periodic feuding, Holocaust and military historians have tended to ignore one another, and neither group is interested in Romanian soldiers' motivation. Holocaust historians, often writing in English, take Romanian soldiers' participation in the mass murder of Jews for granted. Vladimir Solonari's *Purifying the Nation* examines policy makers within the Antonescu regime. While he acknowledges "genocidal initiatives" by mid-ranking officers, he depicts rank-and-file troops as mere executioners of policies emanating from Bucharest.[19] Diana Dumitru's *The State, Antisemitism, and Collaboration in the Holocaust* maintains only civilians chose to murder "on their own initiative and without orders from above," so excludes soldiers in her comparative history of the Holocaust in Romania versus Transnistria.[20] Jean Ancel's posthumous *The History of the Holocaust in Romania* claimed Antonescu manipulated every event of the Holocaust in Romania, while depicting Romanian soldiers as murderous automatons.[21] No one has yet investigated atrocities committed by Romanian troops beyond Romania and Transnistria, in Ukraine, Crimea, Russia, and the Caucasus. Similarly, military historians assume Romanian soldiers were willing to fight. Alesandru Duțu's *Armata română în război* (The Romanian Army in war) asserts that Romanian soldiers fought to retake northern Bukovina and Bessarabia from the USSR by force and to return northern Transylvania from Hungary by earning Nazi Germany's gratitude. He ignores or justifies Romanian soldiers' crimes against Jews or Soviet prisoners of war, partisans, and civilians.[22] According to this view, Romanian soldiers fought for God, king, and country, and nothing else. Yet the reasons why Romanian soldiers fought on the front and committed atrocities in the rear are not so simple as either group assumes.

This is the first book to take a detailed look at Romanian soldiers' motivation. It provides a holistic picture of the Romanian Army by integrating military and Holocaust history. It takes a fresh approach and analyzes ideology, army culture, officer politics, propaganda, and discipline—not just operations. The narrative explores the actions of senior military leaders and commanders but focuses on those of common soldiers. It proves that nationalism, religion, antisemitism, and anticommunism pervaded the ranks from top to bottom and motivated soldiers to fight and perpetrate atrocities. It shows how propaganda reinforced ideological beliefs and tried to buoy morale. It also examines how strict discipline kept soldiers in line. Consequently, Romania was Nazi Germany's most important ally on the eastern front, both in the fight against the Red Army and in the mass murder of Jews. Romanian soldiers plugged gaps in the German line and policed the rear (freeing German troops for the front). Additionally, the Romanian Army helped to "cleanse the terrain" in northern Bukovina and Bessarabia, perpetrated massacres in Transnistria, and assisted German troops in implementing the Final Solution elsewhere in the Soviet Union. Romania's holy war pursued different goals from those of Nazi Germany's race war; however, the two complemented each other at the outset. Moreover, even when those goals began to diverge, the Romanian Army kept fighting alongside the German Army out of fear of the "Bolshevization" of Europe.[23]

Motivation

Motivation, according to John Lynn, is "the set of reasons, both rational and emotional, which leads a person to decide to act or to do nothing."[24] While simple to define, motivation is difficult to explain, especially for soldiers. Following Lynn's model, motivation is the result of a motivational system modified by individual interests. Interest comes in four types: coercion that threatens physical punishment; remuneration that promises material reward; normative factors that give or withhold symbolic and psychological rewards or punishment; and self-interest that prioritizes personal survival. Militaries use various combinations of coercive, remunerative, and normative interests; however, since the French Revolution, according to Lynn, soldiers' primary interest became the nation's welfare. Discipline became less harsh and degrading when soldiers became citizens with rights. Remuneration was reduced as soldiers fought to fulfill patriotic duty rather than to profit. Soldiers' self-interest is a hindrance and a boon. A soldier's desire to survive might cause him to shirk duties or desert, but concern for his well-being makes the threat of discipline effective and reinforces his bonds with other soldiers on whom he relies for security in battle.[25] These underlying interests inform the two parts of the motivational system.

The motivational system comprises morale and small-group cohesion. Small-group cohesion is based on "primary groups." A primary group is a "small number of comrades who constantly deal with one another on a face-to-face basis" and who develop relationships that make soldiers willing to risk their lives for each other.[26] Strong primary groups create a more cohesive unit. These primary groups are fragile, however, as casualties in combat tear them apart, which is where morale comes to bear. Morale, again according to Lynn, is the "climate of opinion" in the army.[27] It is divided into five broad categories: basic social and group attitudes ingrained in the soldier in civilian life growing up; opinions and codes indoctrinated into the soldier by the army; wartime opinions of soldiers and civilians (linked through correspondence); reactions to service conditions such as food, shelter, rest, equipment, medical treatment, mail, and casualties; and finally esprit de corps, usually on the regimental or corps level, which convinces soldiers that their unit is unique or elite.[28] The interaction between small-group cohesion and morale causes soldiers to act or not act. Yet the motivational system does not exist in a vacuum. It is shaped by the military system, or, as Lynn phrases it, "the framework in which men act," composed of five parts: discipline, tactics, administration, organization, and command.[29] All these subsystems are important, but discipline is most related to motivation. The disciplinary system should conform to soldiers' expectations of justice, severity, and honor, thereby reinforcing their motivation to follow orders. Contrarily, an abusive disciplinary system damages soldiers' trust in their leaders and undermines morale.[30] Thus, a myriad of factors interact in a complicated manner to shape each soldier's motivation.

Finally, Lynn identifies three types of motivation. First, initial motivation is the decision to answer the call to serve and not try to evade military service. Second, sustaining motivation is the choice to endure army life's hardships rather than desert or commit self-harm. Third, combat motivation is the act of risking one's life in battle instead of cowering, shirking, or surrendering.[31] However, there is another type of motivation not included in Lynn's model that must be added. Fourth, atrocity motivation is the resolve to commit heinous acts—including beatings, thefts, rapes, and murders—against prisoners of war or civilians rather than treating them humanely. The same interaction between small-group cohesion and morale, modified by interest, can result in atrocity motivation under the right conditions, particularly if the military system is geared to make a virtue out of a vice. Since the French Revolution, the raising of giant armies of citizen-soldiers to fight "total wars" against demonized enemies often caused soldiers to see enemy civilians as legitimate targets.[32] Under the guise of "military necessity," armies steal food, enslave civilians, seize resources, and eliminate suspect groups. Isabel Hull argues armies "will tend to value force as the best solution to military-political problems," ignoring other options until "it required the disappearance of any potential enemy."[33] Unfortunately, Romanian soldiers proved to have an abundance of not just initial, sustaining, and combat motivation but also atrocity motivation on the eastern front.

Romanian soldiers' motivation during the Second World War is difficult to measure, but not impossible. Initial motivation is easiest to gauge, as a shortage of it results in widespread draft evasion or draft riots, neither of which occurred in Romania during the conflict. Sustaining and combat motivation are harder to pin down; however, armies are preoccupied about knowing how motivated soldiers are, and one job of the military system is to report on their morale. Alexander Watson points out that the term "morale" is "the common shorthand" for sustaining and combat motivation, so reports on soldiers' morale—or "mood" (*starea de spirit*) in the Romanian case—written by commanders do not evaluate using John Lynn's five categories.[34] Romanian units' reports on morale focus on soldiers' reactions to frontline conditions and soldiers' opinions, but with a decreasing amount of detail for each rank. The average report had a paragraph on officers, a few sentences on noncommissioned officers (NCOs), and just the word "good" for enlisted men.[35] Near the end of the campaign against the USSR, sometimes it had "satisfactory" or "mediocre" instead (bureaucratic understatement for "bad" morale).[36] These reports include anecdotes, although it is unclear how representative they are. Desertion and mutiny are the most obvious signs of poor morale, but shirking is most common.[37] Despite these reports' limitations, Gary Sheffield declares, "the opinion of regimental and even staff officers . . . however subjective, cannot be lightly set aside . . . [because] officers developed close relationships with their men that made them sensitive to changes in mood and spirit among the rank and file."[38] Lastly, atrocity motivation is measured by pillaged property, burned villages, raped women, and mass graves. Romanian reports tend to omit details of theft, rape, and murder, but not always. Court-martial records provide details on such crimes when they were punished. Furthermore, mass reprisals against Jews, Soviet prisoners of war, partisans, and civilians were an accepted practice of antipartisan warfare, meaning such crimes were often recorded. Using official reports, and personal records, this book evaluates the Romanian Army's motivation and morale on the eastern front.

This book marshals an unprecedented array of sources. I am one of the few foreigners (probably the first American) to research extensively in the

Romanian National Military Archives in Pitești. A little off the beaten path, this central repository of military documents is a trove of reports, orders, studies, requests, letters, complaints, and other records. Unlike the more visited Historical Service of the Army in Bucharest, which only has selected copies of certain records gathered by communist historians for their own agenda, the archive in Pitești has all the original documents. Additionally, I examined documents from Marshal Antonescu's Military Cabinet and the Ministry of Defense held at the Central Historical National Archives in Bucharest. As valuable as these official army records are to understanding senior military leaders and commanders' thinking, they leave out soldiers' perspectives about why they reported for duty, endured hardships of frontline life, fought in battle, and committed atrocities. Soldier diaries, witness testimonies, memoirs, and oral histories fill this gap. Soldier diaries are particularly valuable because they offer an individual's experiences, thoughts, and feelings day by day without knowing how things would end. Three soldiers' diaries figure prominently in the narrative. First, Vasile Scârneci was born in Transylvania (then still part of Austria-Hungary) in 1896. He was initially a spy, then a volunteer for the Romanian Army in the First World War. Scârneci worked his way from private to lieutenant by war's end and decided to make the army a career, rising to major during the interwar years. He commanded the 3rd Mountain Battalion headquartered in Brașov. Scârneci's lengthy diary entries from 22 June 1941 to 1 January 1944 comment extensively on combat, frontline life, unit morale, and other subjects. His hatred of communism is palpable, as is his contempt for ethnic Germans and suspicion of Jews.[39] Evsevie Ionescu was born in Wallachia in 1910. He left his village for Bucharest and then Ploiești, where he managed a restaurant-hotel. As a reserve NCO, Ionescu was called up in 1939, serving in the 53rd Artillery Regiment. His diary from 17 July 1941 to 3 January 1944 is filled with the usual concerns, such as food and mail, but also visits to church to pray for victory and excerpts of propaganda from newspapers or radio.[40] Ștefan Cârlan was born in Wallachia in 1918. He was conscripted from his village outside Brăila in 1939 and became a radio operator for the 38th *Infanterie* Regiment. Cârlan's diary between 31 March 1942 and 12 May 1945 often focuses on his diet, but it also contains his reactions to news on the radio, disdain for the USSR, respect for Soviet peasants' faith, and thoughts on rumors circulating on the front.[41] Some soldiers recorded war crimes in their diaries, but most eyewitness testimony of the Holocaust comes from postwar interviews. Investigations into war crimes started immediately once Romania switched sides in the war. The new secret police, known as the *Securitate* (literally, Security), following the communist takeover of Romania, continued investigating war crimes committed by soldiers, gendarmes, and civilians against Jews or Soviet prisoners of war, partisans, and civilians. The interrogations of soldiers arrested for war crimes are not always reliable, since the witnesses passed blame onto others or claimed they had just followed orders; however, these are often the only detailed accounts of atrocities. The records are housed by the National Council for the Study of the Archives of the *Securitate* in Bucharest. The US Holocaust Memorial Museum also maintains copies of records, including war crimes investigations, gathered from archives in Romania, Moldova, and Ukraine. Finally, more soldier voices come from memoirs and oral histories. Memoirs are separated into three groups: written under communism, written in exile, and written after communism. The first group includes those accounts written by senior military leaders and commanders with an agenda to whitewash their wartime record and push blame onto others. Yet they provide an important view from the top.[42] It also includes memoirs by mid-ranking officers who produced sterilized accounts celebrating Romanian soldiers' bravery and sacrifice either for their families or in hopes the communist censor might permit it to be published.[43] The second group consists of remembrances penned by religious or ethnic minorities who fled abroad after the war and usually contain anti-communist overtones.[44] The third group covers memoirs by mostly junior officers and NCOs who could finally tell their story freely. They tend to relate sanitized narratives, with Romanian soldiers as heroes or victims, but some address uncomfortable issues like rape, anti-Gypsy discrimination, flogging, and the Holocaust.[45] Additionally, I carried out interviews with nearly forty veterans across Romania. The passage of time and public discourse about the war influenced the veterans' memories of the war; however, it was still useful to ask them questions relating to my research. The combination of archival records, diaries, witness testimonies, memoirs, and oral histories creates a fuller picture than ever before of the Romanian Army during the Second World War.

In addition, German and Soviet sources provide an outside look at Romanian soldiers. Neither German nor Soviet reports on the Romanian Army are unbiased, especially the latter. Straitjacketed by Marxist-Leninist ideas, Red Army political commissars prophesied that if war broke out with Romania, its peasants would revolt and overthrow the "imperialist bourgeois-landowning class." When this did not happen, the political commissars then declared the German Army coerced the Romanian Army to fight, with a German soldier beside every two Romanian soldiers, the former driving the latter, and claimed "even the smallest Romanian units are led by German commanders."[46] Soviet observers not only discounted Romanian soldiers' motivation but also their morale. Soviet reports on Romanian morale relied on recently captured Romanian prisoners of war, who were often demoralized and anxious to tell Soviet interrogators what they wanted to hear. Consequently, I chose not to use unreliable Soviet reports. German reports about Romanian soldiers are more accurate, but they must be read with more than a grain of salt. Germans viewed Romanians through the lenses of racial chauvinism, Balkan stereotypes, and memory of the previous war. Most Germans believed Romanians were racially inferior "Gypsies" combining Latin decadence with Balkan corruption. Before invading the Soviet Union, German observers arrogantly reported that Romanian officers "almost invariably lacked the will to implement the intentions of the higher command," and their "men's resistance to rumors and moods of panic was not very strong" because of inferior "racial foundations."[47] Moreover, they believed Romania primarily supported Nazi Germany in the hopes of gaining an advantage over Hungary in case war erupted over their rival claims to Transylvania following the USSR's defeat.[48] German commanders were pleasantly surprised when Romanian soldiers performed better than expected during the invasion, but this did not alter their basic assumptions about their ally.[49] German reports on Romanian morale relied on German liaison staffs assigned to Romanian headquarters, from the General Staff down to divisions and brigades. These were small (between ten to eighteen men at army or corps levels and just three men at division or brigade levels), often had only one interpreter, and were overworked.[50] Furthermore, German liaison officers oftentimes did not remain with a Romanian unit for very long. Therefore, German liaison staffs' ability to develop an accurate view of Romanian soldiers' morale was limited by practical factors too. Despite these issues, I decided to employ German sources to evaluate the Romanian Army. These sources' greatest worth is that they compare the Romanian Army with the other Axis armies on the eastern front. Richard DiNardo argues German reports show that poor morale "was more of a problem for the Hungarian and Italian forces" than for the Romanian forces.[51] Additionally, regarding the Holocaust, "behavior here was sharply split between the Hungarians and Italians, on one side, and the Romanians, on the other."[52] This book not only confirms these conclusions but expands on them to demonstrate that Romanian soldiers fought and committed atrocities to a greater degree because they were highly motivated by ideology.

Romanian soldiers' motivation was based on four powerful ideologies that convinced them that uniting with other European states under Nazi Germany against the Soviet Union was in the best interest of the nation. First, nationalism was the predominant ideology at the core of Romania's holy war. Romanian soldiers thought it was imperative to restore the "lost territories" of "România Mare," or Greater Romania, ceded to the USSR, Hungary, and Bulgaria in 1940. Paradoxically, many historians argue that nationalism undermined Romanian soldiers' motivation, claiming that once they liberated Soviet-occupied northern Bukovina and Bessarabia, they saw no point in continuing the war, and their morale rapidly declined.[53] A corollary to this argument is the assertion that Romanian soldiers preferred to fight Hungary for northern Transylvania over the USSR for northern Bukovina and Bessarabia. Holly Case is the most recent to repeat this claim. She reduces the Soviet annexation and later Romanian reannexation of eastern Romania to a few sentences, claiming "the 'Bolshevik menace,' although a genuine concern, was not the primary preoccupation in Hungary or Romania."[54] Her argument incorrectly assumes that Romanians saw Hungary as a greater threat than the USSR and that Romanians did not reckon that if Nazi Germany lost, Romania was sure to lose northern Bukovina and Bessarabia, and possibly bid farewell to southern Transylvania (as the interwar Soviet and Romanian Communist parties opposed the creation of Greater Romania). She correctly argues that many Romanian soldiers were led to believe that if Romania contributed more than Hungary to Nazi Germany's war effort, then northern Transylvania would be returned after victory.[55] Crucially, the idea that Romanian soldiers fought in the east only in order to obtain territory in the west does not hold water once one includes the other ideologies motivating Romanian soldiers. Second, religion legitimized the war as "holy," casting it as an apocalyptic battle to save mankind from "godless atheism." Until recently the Romanian Orthodox Church's support for the holy war was obscured by the Romanian Communist Party to avoid dredging up bitter wartime memories, but now Holocaust historians criticize the church's complicity in the murder of Jews, while military historians celebrate its efforts to boost soldiers' morale.[56] Clergymen from the patriarch in Bucharest to chaplains on the front preached that soldiers were not only fighting to redeem "holy earth" from foreign heathens but also to protect Christian civilization from the twin threats of communism and Judaism. Christian Hungary was far less threatening to Romanian troops than the atheist Soviet Union. Third, antisemitism pervaded the Romanian Army. Military historians try to ignore this pernicious ideology, while Holocaust historians place it front and center.[57] Romanians believed Jews were satanic and both capitalist exploiters and communist revolutionaries at the same time; they were the scapegoat for Romania's social, economic, and political ills. The myth of Judeo-Bolshevism that linked Jews with communism seemed proven when Romanian

Jews allegedly welcomed the occupying Red Army and attacked the retreating Romanian Army in northern Bukovina and Bessarabia in 1940. Thus, Romanian soldiers took revenge on so-called Jewish communists after 1941 and then became fearful of Jewish-communist vengeance if they lost. Antisemitism was the holy war's linchpin.[58] Fourth, anticommunism united Romanians of all classes against the Soviet Union. Romania's decision to join the Axis is usually depicted as a calculated choice of Realpolitik, but it was as much a visceral reaction rooted in fear and hatred of communism.[59] The Russian Revolution's chaos, the Russian Civil War's bloodshed, and the USSR's famine resulting from forced collectivization and breakneck industrialization all occurred just across the border, sometimes spilling into Romania. Communism represented a tangible danger to most Romanians. The Soviet occupation of northern Bukovina and Bessarabia in 1940, and Romanian soldiers' firsthand experience with the Soviet "paradise" after 1941 only heightened rank-and-file anticommunism. Clearly, Mark Axworthy's assertion that the Romanian Army was motivated only by "limited nationalist, not universal ideological, goals" is mistaken.[60]

The Romanian Army used propaganda to reinforce soldiers' ideological commitment to the holy war. Military historians often portray Romanian soldiers as "peasant scapegoats" who did not understand why they were fighting in the USSR because it had not been explained to them.[61] Nothing could be further from the truth. Holocaust historians point out antisemitism in the press, but they have not examined army propaganda.[62] Mioara Anton systematically tackled the Antonescu regime's propaganda effort in *Propagandă și război* (Propaganda and war), which includes a chapter on army propaganda, but she deals only in generalities about its content.[63] This book takes a closer look and incorporates army newspapers distributed for free to soldiers: *Sentinela* (The sentry), the nation's soldierly gazette; *Soldatul* (The soldier), the explanation and information sheet for soldiers; and *Ecoul Crimeei* (The echo of Crimea), the information weekly newspaper for soldiers. It also includes excerpts from *Armata* (The army), the General Staff's official magazine sold to officers, and *Arma Cuvântului* (The weapon of the Word), the Military Bishopric's official organ, purchased by chaplains. These publications are chock-full of articles, poems, songs, illustrations, and even cartoons meant to improve morale. The most popular propaganda piece was *The Misadventures of Private Neață*, a comic strip printed in *Sentinela*. The eponymous Private Neață will be woven into the following narrative because he was so well known to troops. Radio, film, and spectacles augmented print. Officers' speeches, chaplains' sermons, and propaganda missionaries' chats and songs spread propaganda orally. Romanian soldiers were bombarded with propaganda emphasizing holy war, defense of European civilization, anticommunism, and German-Romanian comradeship.[64]

Finally, the Romanian Army employed strict discipline, including corporal punishment, to motivate soldiers. The Romanian Army reintroduced flogging soon after the war started, but it banned beatings, slaps, and kicks—although these practices remained common. Some historians argue that such physical abuse prepared Romanian soldiers psychologically to be defeated in battle, but this is based on supposition, not detailed research.[65] Romanian soldiers accepted corporal punishment as part of army life, although they hated particularly brutal officers. Officers often threatened to shoot cowards, and commanders sometimes even ordered "blocking detachments" to machine gun soldiers who retreated, though this was rarely followed through with. Instead, rehabilitation was the most common fate for men guilty of desertion, theft, or other crimes. Commanders employed strict discipline selectively, severely sanctioning cowardice or insubordination but not punishing theft, rape, or murder. Omer Bartov calls this the "perversion of discipline" and argues that permissiveness in the rear acted as "a convenient safety valve for venting the men's anger and frustration" resulting from draconian discipline on the front.[66] As the war dragged on, the Romanian Army leaned more on strict discipline to counter flagging morale.

Military Effectiveness

Soldiers motivated by ideology reinforced by propaganda and strict discipline increased and prolonged the Romanian Army's military effectiveness on the eastern front. Allan Millett and Williamson Murray define military effectiveness as a country's ability to transform national resources into fighting power to achieve goals set by military and political elites. There are four distinct, if also overlapping, levels of military effectiveness. Political effectiveness consists of the military assessing potential dangers, calculating threats, and obtaining resources from the government to defend against enemies. Strategic effectiveness comprises the military achieving, through its campaigns, strategic goals set by politicians. Operational effectiveness encompasses the military planning, preparing, and prosecuting campaigns. Tactical effectiveness covers large and small units using various techniques to fight battles. A military can be more effective at one level and less at another.[67] Effectiveness at one level can sometimes compensate for ineffectiveness at another. During the Second World War, Romania's military effectiveness was uneven, to say the least, but the Antonescu regime squeezed as many men and as much resources as it could out of the country to contribute to the Nazi war effort.

Below the top tier, Romania's military effectiveness declined at each succeeding level. First, political effectiveness was good. The Antonescu regime's political and military elites generally worked together well, and also leveraged divisions and resources (oil and foodstuffs) to secure deliveries of modern arms and hard currency from Nazi Germany unmatched by any other Axis state.[68] Second, strategic effectiveness was mixed. The Romanian Army needed a powerful ally to achieve its mission of restoring Greater Romania. Once Romania allied with Nazi Germany, the Romanian Army had minimal influence in shaping strategy as the junior partner to the German Army. The Antonescu regime's only other strategic choice was whether to make a maximum or minimum contribution of divisions and resources to the eastern front. Third, operational effectiveness was mediocre at best. At the outbreak of hostilities in 1941, the Mare Stat Major, or the Great General Staff (from now on referred to simply as the General Staff), transformed into the Mare Cartier General (MCG), or the Great General Headquarters, and directed operations for four months before reverting back to the General Staff and ceding operational control of Romanian formations to German commanders. The General Staff again became the MCG to deploy forces to southern Russia in 1942 before dissolving again after five months. The MCG tended toward overambitious planning, poor coordination of combined arms, weak logistical planning, and overall inflexibility. However, Romanian staff work proved satisfactory when under German supervision. Fourth, tactical effectiveness was initially poor, temporarily improved with experience, and then steadily deteriorated owing to mounting casualties, growing matériel problems, and declining morale. Combined, motivational and military systems produce tactical effectiveness.[69] The Romanian Army's shortages of modern weapons and equipment (tanks, antitank guns, heavy artillery, aircraft, motor vehicles, and radios) hamstrung even the most motivated soldiers, however.[70] Elite mountain and cavalry divisions with more training, superior equipment, and better morale demonstrated greater tactical effectiveness than infantry divisions—except for a handful of "model divisions" that received newer equipment and extensive tutoring from German instructors. German reinforcements improved Romanian units' tactical effectiveness, but the German Army could not always prop up the Romanian Army.

The Romanian Army was aware of its weaknesses, especially at the tactical level, but it believed it would fight only a short war of "heroic revenge."[71] The first three chapters explain why Romania joined Nazi Germany's invasion of the Soviet Union. Chapter 1 delves into the ideological basis of Romanian soldiers' motivation. Chapter 2 examines the culture and politics of the interwar Romanian Army. Chapter 3 relates how Romania transformed from

INTRODUCTION

a neutral state into an Axis power united under Marshal Antonescu. The next three chapters, while interweaving analyses of propaganda and discipline, chronicle the Romanian Army's campaigning in the USSR and track fluctuations in Romanian soldiers' morale. Chapter 4 argues that when faith in victory was highest in summer and fall 1941, the Romanian Army perpetrated the most atrocities against Jews. Chapter 5 shows how morale dipped during the bitter winter of 1941–1942 but recovered in the spring before the new summer campaign that appeared to offer a second chance at victory in 1942. Chapter 6 argues that, despite eroding morale following the defeat at Stalingrad during the winter of 1942–1943, Romanian soldiers remained motivated to fight into 1944, but they were less motivated to commit atrocities. The last two chapters take a closer look at how the Romanian Army motivated its soldiers and how it treated women and minorities. Chapter 7 explains how propaganda and discipline functioned. Chapter 8 focuses attention on the long-overlooked role of female volunteers and minority soldiers. Lastly, an epilogue explains how Romania switched sides in late summer 1944 and reluctantly fought alongside the Soviet Union until the end of the war in spring 1945. This book finally provides an accurate account of the Romanian Army on the eastern front from the Romanian perspective rather than through the German or Soviet lens.

Chapter 1

Ideology of Holy War

In autumn 1937, Nicholas Nagy-Talavera, an eight-year-old Jewish boy, traveled with his family from Oradea to a village near Turda in the Transylvanian mountains to visit family. When they arrived, the local "intelligentsia" (mostly ethnic Hungarians and Jews) spoke fearfully about Corneliu Codreanu, leader of the fascist Legion of the Archangel Michael, who was then riding through the countryside electioneering. Nagy-Talavera decided he wanted to see this man who inspired such terror. A friend, the son of a Romanian Orthodox priest, lent him Romanian peasant garb, and then both joined the crowd anxiously awaiting the "Captain" outside a church. Nagy-Talavera, who later survived Auschwitz, never forgot this experience. "A tall, darkly handsome man dressed in the white costume of a Romanian peasant rode into the yard on a white horse. . . . I could see nothing monstrous or evil in him. On the contrary. His childlike, sincere smile radiated over the miserable crowd. . . . An old, white-haired peasant woman made the sign of the cross on her breast and whispered to us, 'The emissary of the Archangel Michael!'"[1] The introduction of universal male suffrage in Romania after the First World War triggered a proliferation of right-wing populist leagues, parties, and movements that radicalized Romanian society and created fertile ideological soil for fascism.[2] Although the Legionary movement was violently suppressed just before the Second World War, the ideologies of nationalism, religion, antisemitism, and anticommunism that had fostered the growth of fascism remained and formed the basis for Romania's holy war.

Nazi Germany and the USSR's titanic struggle has always been recognized as ideological, but Romania's part in it has fallaciously been portrayed as unideological. In truth, centuries of religious tradition, age-old anti-Judaism combined with modern antisemitism, a century of nationalist zealotry, and burgeoning anticommunist paranoia predisposed Romanians to embrace the holy war. These ideological beliefs cut across class boundaries, uniting soldiers horizontally with comrades and vertically with officers. The Romanian Army started mobilizing in 1937, so there was time for soldiers to form primary groups, many of which experienced the humiliating withdrawal from eastern Romania in 1940 that army propaganda blamed on Jews. Romanian units boasted strong cohesion because of these primary groups when they invaded the USSR in 1941, intensifying combat and atrocity motivation. When soldiers lost comrades in battle, they took furious reprisals against supposed Jewish communists. When commanders ordered soldiers to cold-bloodedly "cleanse the terrain" of Jews, members of primary groups pressured each other to shoulder part of this "dirty work" so the rest were not burdened with it; those who avoided participating were mocked, even threatened, by comrades.[3] Yet primary groups were literally shot to pieces in bloody battles. Ideology enabled survivors to create new bonds with replacements and allowed men thrown together as near strangers to risk their lives for each other because they fought for the same cause.[4] Even as Romanian soldiers' morale waned beginning in 1943, nationalism, religion, antisemitism, and anticommunism motivated them to fight well into 1944.

"Scientific" racism did not motivate most Romanian soldiers. During the interwar period a small number of Romanian eugenicists advocated racial ideas that influenced intellectuals and government policy makers to make some public health and education reforms based on eugenics, but they had limited impact on the general public.[5] While Nazis perceived Slavs as subhuman, Romanians viewed Slavs as people, especially as many were fellow Eastern Orthodox Christians, and treated them relatively humanely; German occupation in Reichskommissariat Ukraine was far harsher than Romanian occupation in Transnistria.[6] This is not to deny racism existed in Romania. Of course, antisemitism—a form of racism—existed. Anti-Gypsy bigotry was rife in society. Soon after taking power, Antonescu declared that not only Jews but also Greeks, Armenians, and Gypsies would be interned in camps and made to work "because only this way we will force them to leave."[7] This promise had dire repercussions for thousands of Gypsy soldiers and their families. Romanian officers were more likely than their soldiers to racialize

Slavs as "Asiatic."[8] This helped justify reprisals targeting Soviet prisoners of war, partisans, and civilians. Nonetheless, scientific racism was an alien concept to most peasant conscripts in the Romanian Army.

Nationalism

The first major sign of Romanian nationalism was an uprising in Wallachia in 1821 led by a Russian-trained officer named Tudor Vladimirescu, who, in cahoots with Greek nationalists, sought to throw off Ottoman rule; but the revolt floundered, and he was assassinated by his Greek allies. Ironically, afterward the sultan began choosing Romanian boyars over Greek grandees as princes in Wallachia and Moldavia. The next steps in Romanian nation building occurred under Russian tutelage. After a victorious campaign against the Ottoman Empire, the Russian Army occupied Wallachia and Moldavia from 1829 to 1834, during which time General Pavel Kiselyov promulgated reforms called the Organic Regulations, which created modern state institutions in the principalities.[9] Meanwhile, Romanian priests who joined the Greek Catholic (Uniate) Church in Transylvania, then in the Austrian Empire, traced Romanians back to the Romans and Dacians of antiquity.[10] These ideas quickly jumped across the border and became popular among Romanian nationalists in the Ottoman Empire. Additionally, boyars in Wallachia and Moldavia began sending sons to Paris instead of Constantinople for education, drifting away from Greek culture toward Romanian culture.[11] In 1848, Romanian nationalists orchestrated a revolution in Bucharest in Wallachia (another revolt, in Iași in Moldavia, was nipped in the bud), but the revolution lacked popular support and was crushed by Russo-Turkish forces.[12] In the Crimean War's aftermath, Romanian nationalists engineered elections making Alexandru Ioan Cuza prince in both principalities in January 1859, resulting in de facto unification.[13] Officially known as the United Principalities of Moldavia and Wallachia, but still a vassal to the Ottoman Empire, the Romanian state began a sustained period of nation building.

The Romanian countryside proved resistant to nationalism's allure at first. To create an "imagined community" around shared language, religion, history, and culture requires a literate population.[14] Most Romanians, however, were illiterate serfs who felt little national solidarity with boyars to whom they still owed feudal dues, or to the aloof middle class. In 1864, Prince Cuza implemented land reform, emancipated serfs, and abolished boyar ranks and privileges. ("Boyar" remained a colloquial term for a large landowner.) The great noble families retained much of their land, however, wielding substantial economic and political power; the lesser noble families with little land began assimilating into the middle class.[15] Despite the continued power of the great landowners, serfdom's abolishment facilitated the development of national consciousness in the countryside. Educated village notables—clergy, teachers, civil servants, and well-off peasants—became the flag bearers of nationalism in the countryside. In 1866, a "monstrous coalition" of Liberals and Conservatives frightened by Cuza's reforms launched a coup, forcing the prince into exile. He was replaced with Karl von Hohenzollern-Sigmaringen of Prussia, who became Prince Carol of Romania.[16] After the Russo-Turkish War of 1877–1878, Romania became independent in 1878 and proclaimed itself a kingdom in 1881. Nationalism was ascendant. Mihai Eminescu's *Poems*, equal parts ode to Romania and tirade against foreigners, enjoyed unprecedented popular success in 1883.[17] An economic boom based on grain production and exploited peasant labor under now King Carol I convulsed Romania, modernizing cities but impoverishing the countryside. Peasants lived in small, crowded, and unsanitary houses, subsisted primarily on vegetables and *mămăligă* (polenta), and suffered high rates of disease, alcoholism, and infant mortality.[18] These conditions triggered local peasant revolts in 1888, 1889, 1894, and 1900. Tardily, Romania made some investments in the countryside, like Minister of Education Spiru Haret's programs to construct village schools, train rural teachers, and publish agricultural periodicals for peasant smallholders. This resulted in a spike in rural literacy, which jumped from 15 percent in 1899 to 33 percent in 1912.[19] Nationalism spread among peasants. Village teachers taught students that they were the embodiment of the nation, officers lectured recruits that they were the bulwark of the nation, and politicians speechified to landholding male voters that they controlled the future of the nation. Such nationalist rhetoric clashed with reality.

In 1907, a peasant uprising erupted across Romania. The situation in the countryside had become critical by this point, as almost 32 percent of peasant households owned less than two hectares (about five acres) and were barely able to survive, while in comparison just over 4 percent owned seven to ten hectares and were well-off.[20] Great landowners employed middlemen called *arendași*, or "lessors," to enforce leases and collect rents; many *arendași*, especially in Moldavia, were Jews. A growing number of peasants believed that the absentee great boyars and Jews represented a corrupt alliance exploiting the nation. The uprising started on 21 February when peasants in northern Moldavia protested unfair leases. From the start the revolt had strong antisemitic overtones, as peasants first attacked Jewish *arendași* and merchants who were blamed for high rents and price gouging, respectively. Over the following three weeks, peasant revolts spread throughout Moldavia and even into Wallachia where there were few Jews, becoming a nationwide jacquerie against boyars and *arendași* (regardless of ethnicity). The nature of the revolt varied from place to place, manifesting itself as protests, attacks on manors, pogroms, land seizures, and a few revolutionary committees.[21] The Conservative government was replaced by a Liberal one on 12 March, which declared a state of emergency. Concerned that infantry regiments might sympathize with the rebels, the Romanian Army primarily relied on cavalry and artillery regiments to fire on peasant crowds, leaving thousands dead and wounded.[22] The state brutally restored order by 5 April; however, the peasant uprising of 1907 had shaken Romania to its foundations.

The First World War would act as a catalyst strengthening nationalism in Romania. After the peasant uprising, the Liberal government enacted reforms limiting lease terms, creating a fund to help peasants purchase land, increasing lending to agricultural cooperatives, and limiting how much land could be leased.[23] These reforms mostly benefited well-off peasants and were only halfheartedly enforced. Romania's intervention in the Second Balkan War in 1913, resulting in the annexation of southern Dobruja, garnered little nationalist support. Romania's intervention in the First World War in August 1916 to "liberate" Transylvania was greeted with more nationalist enthusiasm, especially by the middle class. The Romanian Army's advance was halted, however, and then quickly turned into a rout, leaving Wallachia occupied, and only the arrival of the Russian Army allowed it to hold on to most of Moldavia. The conflict transformed from a war of conquest into a war of defense, and soldiers were bombarded with nationalist, religious, and antisemitic propaganda. After news of the February Revolution in Russia, the Liberal government decided it had to act to mend the rift between the peasants and the great landowners and middle class to avoid revolution in Romania. In March 1917, in a speech to soldiers at the front, King Ferdinand I announced that after the war peasants would receive land and equal rights.[24] Romanian soldiers rallied to the cause and fought off Austro-German summer offensives. The October Revolution in Russia left Romania isolated but prompted Bessarabia to vote to unify with Romania in April 1918. Romania was compelled to sign the Treaty of Bucharest with the Central Powers in May, but re-declared war just before the Armistice in November. Bukovina and Transylvania respectively voted to join Romania in November and December. Thus, the Romanian Army snatched victory from the jaws of defeat, nearly realizing nationalist dreams of bringing all Romanians under one state.

Greater Romania's new territories had differing levels of national consciousness. It was strongest among *ardeleni* in Transylvania—Transylvania is also known as "Ardeal" in Romanian—who had resisted Magyarization.[25]

It was weaker among *bucovineni* in Bukovina and *basarabeni* in Bessarabia.²⁶ Many *basarabeni* identified as Moldavians and, radicalized by revolution, preferred independence or joining the Soviet Union.²⁷ Further complicating the situation were large minority populations in each territory. Romania pursued "Romanianization" in these regions. Romanianization meant replacing minorities in administrative positions, developing Romanian-language education, and patronizing Romanian culture. Minority nobles owned most of the land in the annexed territories, so Bucharest expropriated it to redistribute to Romanian peasants as part of land reform in 1921. However, cities were the main targets for Romanianization. Romanians made up only 59 percent of Greater Romania's urban population in 1930 (compared to 72 percent of the total population) and even less in cities in annexed territories. Regardless of region, most cities had large Jewish populations, so, according to a recent historian, Jews were seen as "a kind of elite-urban common denominator" and attracted special ire from nationalists.²⁸ Peasants looking for factory jobs, students going to university, and merchants or professionals in the middle class resented competition from minorities. Student activists demonstrated for more radical Romanianization and even attacked minorities, especially Jews. Less violently but no less radically, economists advocated policies advantaging Romanians over minorities so that the middle class would be quickly Romanianized.²⁹ The Romanian Army was a tool for Romanianization. It had been designated the "school of the nation" after 1859, and now again after 1918. Just as the Romanian Army had helped turn Wallachians and Moldavians into Romanians, it was expected to do the same with *ardeleni*, *bucovineni*, and *basarabeni*. In 1927, an army conference declared, "The army is the school of the people and forms the foundation on which is built the national edifice."³⁰ As part of "moral education," officers lectured enlisted men on Romania's storied past and bright future. Nationalist indoctrination was aided by soaring literacy, which jumped from 33 percent in 1912 to 57 percent in 1930, although it varied by region (highest in Transylvania and lowest in Bessarabia) and gender (69 percent of men versus 45 percent of women were literate, as peasants prioritized educating sons over daughters).³¹ The men who would fight in Romania's holy war were more exposed to nationalism than ever before.

While Romania had nearly doubled in size after the First World War, for some Romanians it was not enough. Ultra-nationalists advocated expanding Greater Romania's borders. The most common refrain was "To the Tisa!" because ultra-nationalists argued Romania's "natural" border was on the Tisa River deeper in Hungary, not the border drawn by the Paris Peace

Conference in 1919. A less common cry was "Across the Dniester!" by ultranationalists who wanted to bring Soviet Moldavians, whom they dubbed *transnistrieni*, into the national fold. Moldavians in the USSR were the largest group of ethnic Romanians remaining outside Greater Romania. Indeed, in the early 1920s, Romania staked a claim to territory across the Dniester, including the important port of Odessa.[32] The Bolsheviks' victory in the Russian Civil War, and the moderating influence of the League of Nations, prompted Romania to mute these slogans. Conversely, the USSR and Hungary never recognized Romania's annexations as legitimate. Romanians saw both Hungarians and Russians as hereditary enemies, but Hungary wanted only Transylvania, while the USSR wanted not only Bessarabia for itself but also the total dismemberment of Greater Romania, as Moscow supported national self-determination.[33] The USSR also threatened that supporting pillar of Romanian nationalism, the Romanian Orthodox Church.

Religion

Eastern Orthodox Christianity was the prevailing religion among Romanians since before Wallachia and Moldavia's formation in the fourteenth century. The churches in the principalities were canonically linked to the Ecumenical Patriarchate of Constantinople in the fifteenth century, and Greek culture increasingly pervaded the Romanian metropolitanates, especially under Greek princes in the eighteenth century.[34] Regardless, the Romanian clergy were the progenitors of Romanian culture in Wallachia and Moldavia. They began printing works in Romanian in 1640, adopting Romanian for church liturgy soon thereafter and translating the Bible into Romanian in 1688. Church educators steadily displaced Greek with Romanian as the intellectual language of the principalities during the eighteenth century.[35] As nationalism spread in southeastern Europe during the nineteenth century, clergies began adopting nationalist views, and churches looked to become more independent from the patriarch in Constantinople, whom they saw more and more as an Ottoman stooge.[36] Yet contemporaneously the churches of Wallachia and Moldavia lost their traditional rights and privileges. The Organic Regulations firmly subordinated the church to the state, prompting the process of stripping clergy of administrative, legal, and judicial powers. After unification, Prince Cuza's reforms included the "secularization" (nationalization) of large monastic landholdings in 1863 and the introduction of a secular civil code in 1864 mandating civil marriages and state recordkeeping.[37] Although the church's secular power over Romanians waned, its spiritual influence waxed.

The Romanian Orthodox Church transformed from a serf-owning and foreign-dominated institution into a unified national church boasting substantial moral authority under Prince Carol. In 1872, parliament united the metropolitanates of Wallachia and Moldavia into the Romanian Orthodox Church and established the Electoral Collegium, which empowered the state to select church leaders.[38] The church blessed the Russo-Turkish War of 1877–1878 as a holy war of Christians against infidels. The Romanian Orthodox Church finally became autocephalous (self-governing) in 1885. Priests preached faith in God, king, and country to congregants. Religion shaped daily life, whether through rituals including baptism, Holy Communion, marriage, and burial, or holidays like saints' days, Easter, and Christmas. The First World War strengthened the Romanian Orthodox Church's authority. Some priests donned uniforms to fight, chaplains ministered to soldiers, and priests tended to wounded and sick. In May 1919, Bishop Miron Cristea of the metropolitanate of Transylvania symbolically blessed the "sacred unity of all Romanians" at the grave of Mihai the Brave—a nationalist icon who was lionized for briefly unifying Wallachia, Moldavia, and Transylvania in 1601.[39] The Bolshevik seizure of power shocked the Eastern Orthodox world as Russia suddenly became an atheist state. Horrific tales about communists persecuting believers quickly spread in Romania; Romanians even saw crosses torn from churches across the Dniester. Greater Romania, now the largest Eastern Orthodox state, became the bulwark against atheism. In November 1925, representatives of the patriarchates of Constantinople, Jerusalem, Serbia, Greece, Bulgaria, Poland, and the Russian diaspora attended Bishop Miron's enthronement as patriarch, raising the Romanian Orthodox Church to a coequal patriarchate.[40] Yet even as the church grew in power, the nation experienced a crisis over faith.

The creation of Greater Romania caused some Romanians to question the centrality of religion in national identity. Bessarabia, Bukovina, and Transylvania had large populations of Catholics, Greek Catholics, Protestants, neo-Protestants, and Jews that diluted the number of Eastern Orthodox from 91 percent of the population in 1912 to just under 73 percent in 1930—and many of these were Russian Orthodox.[41] Even more troubling, only 58 percent of *ardeleni* were Romanian Orthodox; the other 42 percent were Romanian Greek Catholics (Uniates), practicing Eastern Orthodox rites but owing allegiance to the pope, bifurcating Romanians between the Romanian Orthodox and Uniate churches.[42] Consequently, Greater Romania juggled two national churches. Although the large landowning and middle classes were more secular than the peasant class, the granting of citizenship and equal rights to minorities, especially Jews, made religion even more important in defining Romanians' national identity.[43] The religious philosopher Nae Ionescu held a well-publicized debate with a Catholic colleague at the University of Bucharest during 1930 in which he argued Catholics could become "good Romanians" by being respectable citizens, but they could never become true "Romanians" because they were not Romanian Orthodox.[44] He was among the numerous intellectuals who made similar arguments about religion—many of whom were later attracted to the Legionary movement's mystical Romanian Orthodox nationalism.[45] Therefore, most Romanians believed their religion not only set them apart spiritually but also ethnically from other faiths.

The Romanian Army collaborated closely with the Romanian Orthodox Church. In 1921, it created the Military Bishopric, so "the Church will be *in the army.*"[46] The 1923 constitution's minority rights clause obligated the Romanian Army to introduce regulations directing that the chaplain should reflect the faith of the majority of soldiers in each regiment. In practice most chaplains remained Romanian Orthodox priests, but some were Catholic (or Uniate) priests, Protestant pastors, Jewish rabbis, or Muslim imams.[47] Hence the need for the Military Bishopric to offer the Romanian Orthodox chaplains an advantage. Additionally, chaplains were supposed to prevent the military from being undermined by proselytizing sects. Transylvania and Bessarabia had small but growing neo-Protestant and Eastern Orthodox schismatic sects. The Romanian Army was already concerned about the "Adventist danger" in the ranks by 1924.[48] The Military Bishopric was ineffectual under its first two aged bishops, but its third leader was youthful, hardworking, and exacting. A "soldier priest" wounded in the First World War, Partenie Ciopron declared in his inaugural speech in October 1937, "On the front, with [a] weapon I threw out the enemy; from today onward, with the weapon of the word of the gospel—seconded by military priests—I will preach, from one corner of the country to the other, to the Romanian soldiers: faith in God, faith and obedience to the King, love of the fatherland, unconditional discipline."[49] In 1937, the Military Bishopric had thirty chaplains who assisted Ciopron in his mission.[50]

The Romanian Orthodox Church took a direct role in politics during the interwar period. Patriarch Miron was a nationalist, an antisemite, and an anticommunist. He became a member of the three-person regency that ruled Romania between 1927 and 1930 following the death of Ferdinand I. The Romanian Orthodox Church lent great political legitimacy to the Romanian state owing to its moral authority among Romanians. Later, from 1938 until his death in 1939, Patriarch Miron served as the first prime minister under King Carol II's royal dictatorship. While Miron was primarily a figurehead in the post, his government did not rescind recently enacted antisemitic laws depriving many Jews of their rights, citizenship, and ability to work in business or journalism—in fact enforcing these antisemitic laws was at the top of the list in his political program that he sent to the king.[51] Romanian Orthodox clergy did not publicly criticize these actions by the state. While Romanians considered other Christian denominations such as Catholics capable of being good citizens, they believed Jews were bad citizens, trying from within to destroy Greater Romania.

Antisemitism

Modern antisemitism grew out of traditional anti-Jewish hatred rooted in Christian and folk beliefs. Priests taught worshippers that Jews killed Christ and were morally depraved, encouraging Romanians to believe the worst myths about Jews. Peasants believed Jews were demonic because they were not baptized and thus lacked protection from possession by devils. Consequently, with their satanic talents, Jews could mislead and cheat trusting Christians.[52] The most heinous myth was the blood libel, the accusation that Jews needed a Christian child's blood for ritual purposes, such as to make Passover matzo. After the first case in England in 1144, blood libel accusations quickly spread across Catholic Europe but remained rare in Eastern Orthodox Europe for centuries.[53] The first documented blood libel incident in Wallachia or Moldavia was in Târgu Neamț in 1710, which resulted in five Jews being lynched and twenty-two others arrested. Similar accusations multiplied as Jewish immigration to the region increased. In Piatra Neamț alone five Jews were prosecuted for blood libel between 1803 and 1847.[54] The Organic Regulations had opened the principalities to trade and attracted Jewish merchants, with most settling in Moldavia, where the population grew from 30,000 Jews in 1803 to 119,000 in 1859, while in Wallachia there were only 9,200 Jews in 1860.[55] Often blood libel accusations triggered pogroms, such as one in Galați in 1859.[56] Pogroms occurred regularly in the following decades, but with the rise of antisemitism, anticapitalist invective replaced blood libel accusations as the trigger.

"Semite" was a pseudoscientific term coined in Germany to describe Jews as a race, not just a religion; the term became popular across Europe as Jews were denigrated for, as one historian put it, "not what [they] *believed*, but what they *were*."[57] The Romanian middle class was quick to form antisemitic leagues. Prime Minister Ion Brătianu claimed in 1877 that only Jews "of the lowest quality" were immigrating to Romania to avoid military service or paying taxes in Russia, so were "unfaithful citizens."[58] Romania's discrimination against Jews was so notorious that as part of the Treaty of Berlin in 1878 the Great Powers required Romania to add a minority clause to its constitution to protect Jews' rights.[59] Antisemites contradictorily claimed that Jews were capitalist exploiters seeking to suck the nation dry and, at the same time, social revolutionaries aiming to overthrow the natural order. Some Jews had become prominent in capitalist and socialist circles owing to their education, concentration in cities, traditional jobs in lending and trade, multilingualism, and international networks in Western Europe; however, most Jews were poor, conservative, religious, and lived in small market towns in Eastern Europe. Romanian intellectuals adopted German antisemitic concerns about the insidious effect of Jews on the nation's health. In 1880, economist Petre S. Aurelian claimed Romanian population growth was slowing while Jewish population growth was accelerating, especially in Moldavia's cities, which he argued proved that "when the Romanian population decreases, the Israelites multiply."[60] Antisemites warned that Jews would replace Romanians in Romania's cities.

Romanian politicians used antisemitic anxieties to woo the middle class. Romania's 1866 constitution enfranchised large landholders, the middle class, and well-off peasants who owned property. The Conservative Party garnered support from large landowners (who wielded outsize electoral power), while the Liberal Party appealed to the middle class and well-off peasants. A Liberal government provided the venue for the Romanian-European Antisemite Congress in 1886, and politicians or civil servants made up most of the Antisemite Alliance formed in 1895.[61] Antisemites, in newspapers with names like *Strigătul* (The shout), *Antisemitul* (The antisemite), and *Jos jidanii!* (Down [with] the kikes!), accused Jews of siphoning off Romania's wealth through domination of finance, commerce, and industry.[62] All Romania's social ills were blamed on Jews. Student activists launched pogroms in Bucharest in 1897 and Iași in 1899, accusing Jews of economic vampirism rather than literally draining victims of blood. Romanians' fears about cities falling under Jewish domination were heightened by claims of a "Jewish invasion." A combination of population growth, steady immigration from Austria-Hungary, and waves of refugees from Russia caused by multiplying pogroms between 1881 and 1905 meant 240,000 Jews lived in Romania by the turn of the century—but panicked antisemites claimed there were actually 500,000 or even more.[63] The peasant uprising of 1907 indicates antisemitic economic arguments had even penetrated down to peasants, who organized pogroms across Romania during those chaotic weeks.

The First World War intensified antisemitism in Romania. Jews fought on the front and served in the rear, often as doctors risking their lives to treat the wounded and sick (a typhus epidemic ravaged soldiers and civilians in unoccupied Moldavia); nevertheless, Romanians accused Jews of treachery and cowardice.[64] Spymania swept the country even before Romania joined the war. Jews made perfect scapegoats because most were "foreigners" (denied citizenship by the state) and multilingual (Yiddish was viewed as a German code); so when parliament gave the military the power to intern or remove foreigners from border regions, the Romanian Army ruthlessly targeted Jews. The paranoia only increased after Romania joined the war, with army reports and newspapers filled with stories about Jewish spies and saboteurs.[65] A few Jewish soldiers were even executed for espionage on trumped-up charges.[66] Despite such discrimination, by the end of the war some Jews felt they had finally proven their loyalty to Romania, and the Great Powers at the Paris Peace Conference demanded Romania include a minority clause extending citizenship and equal rights to minorities, including Jews, in its new constitution in exchange for recognizing Romania's expanded borders. Many Jews lived in Bessarabia, Bukovina, and Transylvania, and when they were added to those in the Old Kingdom (as Romanians now called Wallachia, Moldavia, and Dobruja), Greater Romania counted one of the most diverse Jewish populations in Europe, with assimilationists, traditionalists, socialists, Zionists, liberals, conservatives, and Hasidim, secular, urban, rural, Sephardic, and Ashkenazi Jews.[67] The Old Kingdom contained Romanian-speaking and Yiddish-speaking Jews. Bessarabia brought Russian- and Yiddish-speaking Jews. Bukovina brought German- and Yiddish-speaking Jews. Finally, Transylvania brought Hungarian-, German-, and Yiddish-speaking Jews. While the percentage of Jews in Romania increased modestly, from 3.3 to 4 percent, the number of Jews tripled, from 239,967 to 728,115.[68] Romanian antisemites were aghast at the thought that so many Jews would be given citizenship and equal rights.

Antisemites quickly organized to oppose the proposed minority clause. Beginning at the University of Iași, students, known as the "Generation of 1922," boycotted classes to try to force the establishment of a quota to limit the number of Jews and other minorities who could attend classes.[69] These students soon turned to intimidation and violence: shouting down professors in class for teaching Jews, carrying weapons on campus, and attacking, beating, or even murdering Jews—sympathetic juries acquitted those accused of several such murders.[70] As student activists organized across Romania, they spread violence without fear of punishment. At the same time, a wave of Jewish refugees from the Russian Civil War (most continuing on to the Americas) temporarily swelled Romania's Jewish population, rekindling antisemitic hysteria about a "Jewish invasion." Yet even after the

Jewish population stabilized, antisemites inflated their numbers, claiming a million or more Jews now lurked in Greater Romania; some demanded "the complete elimination of the kike element in the country."[71] Nationalist activism failed to block the minority clause, which was included in the 1923 constitution. Consequently, Professor Alexandru C. Cuza established the Liga Apărării Naționale Creștine (LANC), or the League of National Christian Defense, that same year. Cuza was a mentor to student activists in Iași, including one of his law students, the future fascist leader Corneliu Codreanu. His LANC had a single platform: antisemitism. However, because eliminating Jews from the economy was supposedly a cure-all for the maladies of poverty and corruption, the LANC attracted many peasants, especially in Bessarabia, Bukovina, and Moldavia, where the greatest number of Jews were located.[72] LANC members attacked Liberals for agreeing to the minority clause and accused them of being controlled by Jews. The new National Peasant Party did so as well. Liberals courting peasant voters, who now made up most of the electorate, blamed social, economic, and political problems on Jews to divert anger away from the party's failure to deliver on promises of a better life in Greater Romania.[73] The reality that many Jews barely eked out a living in rural towns or working-class slums was irrelevant. Antisemitic rhetoric was used extensively by all the major political parties in interwar Romania.

A few Romanian intellectuals tried to fuse their religious beliefs with scientific racism to highlight the danger they believed Jews represented. Professor Cuza argued that Jews were racially inferior because they were "a satanic people."[74] Dr. Nicolae Paulescu, the discoverer of insulin, agreed Jews' "demonic" nature manifested in intellectual and biological inferiority. In 1926, as minister of health and social protection, he wrote a report claiming Jewish men had higher rates of venereal disease because they were sexually depraved. Furthermore, he was convinced Jews purposefully spread venereal diseases to Romanians to endanger the nation. Paulescu believed rich Jewish men impregnated poor Christian women, forced into prostitution because of poverty, to impoverish Romania by requiring the state to care for the mothers and mixed-raced, diseased-ridden children. In *The Lechery of the Kikes*, a pamphlet based on his report, he warned that Jews planned "to exterminate us" by spreading syphilis through miscegenation.[75] Such eugenic ideas were far less popular among Romanian peasants than economic arguments against Jews.

Antisemitic polemics continued to poison Jewish-Christian relations. Student activists organized a pogrom in Oradea in Transylvania in December 1927, but when the authorities sent the local regiment to restore order, the troops stood by, intervening only if Christians or Christian property was threatened.[76] The Great Depression, the effects of which were felt worldwide, worsened the situation as the economy nosedived in 1929.[77] The National Peasant government passed a law requiring small traders, who were usually Jews, to forgive debts for clients, who were usually Christians, hastening the bankruptcy of many Jewish businesses.[78] During the 1933 election, student activists crisscrossed Romania, organizing congresses and conferences that often degenerated into attacks on minorities, particularly Jews. When student activists congregated in cities in Bessarabia, brawls were guaranteed as working-class Jews, often members of socialist or Zionist parties, had established Jewish self-defense leagues (a legacy of tsarist-era pogroms) and were ready to meet violence with violence. Police reports depicted Jews as the aggressors, and civil servants accused Jews of provoking attacks so they could report them to the League of Nations to embarrass Romania.[79] Romanian leaders saw student activists as hooligans at worst and patriots at best, so tolerated their savagery. Even after the economy improved, antisemitic rhetoric worsened. Patriarch Miron attacked Jews as "parasites" in 1937, saying, "One has to be sorry for the poor Romanian people, whose very marrow is sucked out by the Jews. Not to react against the Jews means that we go open-eyed to our destruction."[80] While antisemites presented Jews as the worst example of capitalism, they also linked Jews, especially those in Bessarabia, to communism.

Anticommunism

Anticommunism, also known as anti-Bolshevism, was the midwife of Greater Romania. The first clashes between Romanian troops and Bolshevik revolutionaries occurred immediately after the Soviet seizure of power in November 1917, as the Romanian Army disarmed and escorted revolutionary Russian soldiers out of Moldavia, resulting in skirmishes whenever some refused to surrender arms.[81] In January 1918, the Romanian Army marched into Bessarabia, prompting Vladimir Lenin's Bolshevik government to break off diplomatic relations with Romania and Russian revolutionaries to terrorize Romanian refugees in Odessa. Romanian troops pushed back Bolshevik forces, taking bloody reprisals on civilians, before completing the occupation of Bessarabia in March.[82] Many locals did not welcome Romanian rule. A peasant revolt supported by a Bolshevik force erupted in northern Bessarabia in January 1919, overwhelming several garrisons. "All along the Dniester, from Atachi to Hotin, the victims of the Bolsheviks offer to the terrified onlookers a spectacle of Dantean vision. Bodies of hanged Romanian soldiers dangling from the branches of trees or telegraph poles," one lurid account later related.[83] Reinforcements arrived and viciously crushed the rebellion. Foreshadowing the next war, the chief of the General Staff, General Constantin Prezan, declared the Bolsheviks were not to be recognized as a legitimate enemy: "Consequently, these bands will not enjoy the laws that apply in war to regular troops. All will be treated without mercy, completely and radically exterminated."[84] Romanians had just reveled in the declaration of Greater Romania, but now they feared they could lose everything they had fought for, and more, to Bolshevism.

Bolshevik forces seemed poised to crush Romania with simultaneous attacks from west and east. A Hungarian Soviet Republic was declared in March, and the Hungarian Red Army promised to overrun Transylvania. Then in early April pro-Soviet forces retook Odessa from counterrevolutionary White Russian forces and advanced toward Bessarabia.[85] In mid-April, the Romanian Army attacked in Transylvania, easily pushing back the Hungarian Red Army before halting on the Tisa under pressure from the peacemakers in Paris. Diplomats failed to resolve the conflict, and the Hungarian Red Army attacked in late July. The Romanian Army soon recovered, however, and marched into "Red Budapest" in early August, putting an end to Bolshevism in Hungary. Much to Romania's relief, a Soviet attack against Bessarabia never materialized. General Gheorghe Mărdărescu, who had led the campaign in Hungary, proclaimed, "Anarchy and terror, enthroned in Hungary by this [Bolshevik] regime, ended under the knee of the Romanian Army that brought, through its action, the reestablishment of the previous rights of Magyar citizens, assuring the order, wealth, life and honor of all."[86] When Romania withdrew its last soldiers in March 1920, Hungary was once again declared a kingdom under regent Admiral Miklós Horthy. While Hungary remained hostile toward Romania, the Treaty of Trianon, signed in June 1920, strictly limited the Hungarian Army's size, effectively neutering it. In contrast, the Bolsheviks won the Russian Civil War in October 1922, and the USSR was not bound by any treaty, so the Red Army became the sword of Damocles hanging over Greater Romania.

Refugee crises and peasant unrest kept Romanians' fears of Bolshevism high. A wave of refugees from Russia flooded into Romania between 1918 and 1925 as tens of thousands fled the chaos of civil war, pogroms, and Bolshevik persecution. Romanians viewed most Russian refugees, especially Jews, as potential Bolshevik spies or provocateurs. Bessarabia stayed under martial law because of communist agitation. In September 1924, Russian and Ukrainian peasants from Tatarbunar in southern Bessarabia, led by Soviet agents, revolted and formed a revolutionary committee calling for a

Moldavian Soviet Republic. The Romanian Army crushed the uprising in three days, killing dozens and arresting thousands.[87] Regardless, the USSR established the small, lamb-chop-shaped Moldavian Autonomous Soviet Socialist Republic on the other side of the Dniester to transmit propaganda, entice Moldavians to emigrate to the USSR, and foment revolution in Bessarabia.[88] Another wave of Soviet refugees crossed the Dniester between 1930 and 1934, fleeing famine.[89] In 1929, the Soviet Union had embarked on the rapid industrialization of the country. The communists violently requisitioned grain from peasants to sell abroad to pay for industrialization and forced peasants onto collective farms to industrialize agriculture. Although industry did expand, a man-made famine killed an estimated 3.3 million people.[90] Soviet refugees who slipped past Soviet sentries brought stories—which soon spread among Romanians—of violence, starvation, and even cannibalism. The refugee crisis peaked in the winter of 1931. According to Nichita Smochină, a Moldavian scholar who had escaped the Russian Civil War, "shootings [by Soviet border guards] took place every night, dead and wounded are found daily, because the flight from the U.S.S.R. continues without interruption since the moment the Soviets came to power."[91] Approximately one hundred thousand refugees entered Romania by 1932.[92] In parliament, as senators debated providing famine relief for *transnistrieni*, one senator rhetorically proposed that through the League of Nations "persons who want to cross into the Soviet Union will be exchanged for those who desire to abandon the 'Soviet paradise.'"[93] For Romanians, communism was not an abstract ideology about how to free humanity from capitalism, as it was to sympathizers in Western Europe or the United States, but a concrete regime threatening to despoil, enslave, starve, or shoot them.

Communism attracted few adherents in Romania. When the Romanian Communist Party split from the Social Democratic Party in 1922 it had only two thousand members.[94] If communism ruled Romania, large landowners would lose their land and power, the middle class their property and businesses, and peasants their land and way of life. The working class, which was the most likely to find Bolshevik rhetoric attractive, was very small in Romania. Additionally, the state outlawed the Romanian Communist Party in 1924, discouraging Romanians from joining out of fear of imprisonment. Furthermore, the communists' platform, following the party line from Moscow, advocated Greater Romania's dissolution, which did not endear the party to many Romanians. Consequently, minorities, especially Hungarians and Jews, were overrepresented in the party, which had shrunk to three hundred members by 1927.[95] The composition of the Romanian Communist

Party lent credence to the widespread belief that Bolshevism and Judaism were linked. The myth of Judeo-Bolshevism, or Jewish communism, asserted Jews were responsible for creating and supporting Bolshevism and its crimes. This belief was based on a long Christian tradition of associating Judaism with disorder, modern conspiracy theories about an international Jewish plot for world domination, and bigoted fear of Jewish fanaticism.[96] The ubiquity of Judeo-Bolshevism in newspapers, books, and Russian émigré accounts and the unmasking of "Jewish" revolutionaries in countries across Europe allowed people to think the myth was truth.[97] Romanians believed their country was on the front line of an international battle against Judeo-Bolshevism.

The sizable Jewish minorities in Bessarabia, Bukovina, and Transylvania raised fears that Greater Romania contained a dangerous fifth column in its borderlands. Most Romanians saw the "godless" USSR as the homeland of "atheist" Jews. Romanian Army reports in the interwar period argued Jews in Bessarabia were all communist sympathizers, responsible for all left-wing agitation, and could not be counted on to be loyal in a war with the Soviet Union.[98] The fact that Jews in Bessarabia were less assimilated than those in Wallachia or Moldavia, and more likely to speak Russian than Romanian, deepened suspicions. The authorities also lumped Jewish socialists and Zionists in with communists.[99] The military never completely turned over control of Chișinău to civilian authorities because the provincial capital was perceived as a dangerous center of communist activity, in part due to its large Jewish population; the army retained extralegal powers to censor the press, break up assemblies, and ignore civil rights.[100] Chișinău's jails were filled with socialists and communists, including many Jews. By 1937, the Romanian Communist Party had grown to sixteen hundred members, concentrated mostly in Transylvania's industrial centers.[101] Romanian commanders had posited a "Jewish-Magyar" alliance in Transylvania in 1919 when fighting the Hungarian Soviet Republic.[102] New concerns about this "Judeo-Hungarian" threat revived in 1938 as the possibility of conflict between Romania and Hungary increased.[103] Romanians' flexible antisemitism allowed them to simultaneously see Jews as both pro-communist and pro-Magyar because they believed Jews were intent on destroying Greater Romania.

Fascism

The rise of fascism in Romania demonstrates the strength of nationalism, religion, antisemitism, and anticommunism among Romanians. Right-wing populist groups like the LANC in the 1920s prepared the way for the Legionary movement in the 1930s, which became one of the largest fascist movements in Europe. It appealed to Romanians of all backgrounds: peasants, boyars, intellectuals, priests, professionals, civil servants, workers, officers, and others. Corneliu Codreanu broke away from the LANC after disagreeing with his mentor Alexandru C. Cuza and founded the Legion of the Archangel Michael in 1927. When boiled down, fascism favors employing any and all means to allow the "chosen people" to dominate others and triumph over enemies.[104] The "Captain" Codreanu advocated more violent politics—imitating fascist movements in Italy and Germany—and created the paramilitary Iron Guard in 1930. The Iron Guard's Greenshirts, as they were called, supported the Legionary movement through street violence and became so notorious that the terms "Legion" and "Iron Guard" were used interchangeably. From a handful of followers of Codreanu, the Legion grew to 272,000 members in 1937, with many more supporters or sympathizers, threatening to seize power over the state.[105] Although King Carol II's royal dictatorship scattered the Iron Guard and murdered the Captain in 1938, latent Legionarism remained in many Romanians.

Legionaries believed in a mystical rebirth of the nation through Romanian Orthodoxy.[106] Codreanu had planned to "cleanse" Greater Romania of minorities, especially Jews, and "purify" the nation of communists, selfish aristocrats, or corrupt elites to create a Romanian "new man."[107] The Legionary movement rejected liberalism as "foreign" or "Judaized" and was ready to use violence to create an ethnically homogeneous Romania.[108] Iron Guardists denounced the minority clause for empowering Jews, claimed Jews controlled the country, and argued that Romanianization had not gone far enough. Legionaries accused Jews of being capitalist exploiters and communist revolutionaries. In the Iron Guard worldview, the USSR was controlled by Jews, and Legionaries constantly harped on the threat of Judeo-Bolshevism. The Iron Guard supported joining the Axis. Codreanu declared, "I am against the Little Entente. I am against the Balkan Entente and I have no attachment to the League of Nations in which I do not believe. I am for a Romanian foreign policy with Rome and Berlin. I am with the states of national revolution against bolshevism."[109] Diehard Legionaries in the Romanian Army had to hide their political convictions, especially after Codreanu's assassination, but most Legionaries fit in easily and could pursue interwar goals of national purification, religious worship, antisemitic violence, and even alliance with Nazi Germany against the Soviet Union.[110] The Legionary movement cast a long shadow on Romania's holy war.

Foundation for Holy War

The mere existence of nationalism, religion, antisemitism, and anticommunism—even fascism—during the interwar period did not predetermine Romania's holy war; however, these ideologies made it almost inevitable that Romania would join the Axis. Romania supported the League of Nations during the 1920s in the hope that collective defense would protect its gains from the First World War, but it turned inward when the League of Nations faltered during the 1930s. Now isolated, Romania faced growing threats from Nazi Germany and the USSR; but given Romanians' ideological beliefs, if an alliance had to be made with Nazism or communism, Romania would choose Berlin over Moscow. Romania increasingly drifted into Nazi Germany's orbit, and the Iron Guard attracted more followers as the threat of another war grew. As we shall see, although many officers sympathized with the Legionaries, the Romanian Army backed the monarchy against the Legion in the interest of preserving the status quo. Romania's road to holy war was not a straight line but rather took several sharp turns—however it ran upon firm ideological ground.

Chapter 2

Army Culture, Interwar Politics, and Neutrality

Ioan Manolescu passed the baccalaureate after graduating high school in 1937. Now he wanted to go to university, but his father believed war was threatening Europe and made him go to reserve officer school. He remembered, "I disliked the thought of being a soldier in peace time. Observation confirmed my prejudice as the majority of our officers were unusually stupid."[1] The Romanian Army had trouble recruiting middle-class youths like Manolescu in peacetime, in part because they disliked army culture. The officer corps' aristocratic values, conservative politics, and old-fashioned man management, which often treated soldiers little better than animals, were out of step with the middle class's bourgeois values, liberal politics, and paternalistic treatment of peasants. In wartime, however, the middle class patriotically answered the call to defend the country, and most soon acculturated to the officer corps. After King Carol II introduced a royal dictatorship in 1938, Manolescu, having received his commission as a second lieutenant, trained with other officers in "military legislation, siege-in-law, and so on, just in case of emergency, should the civil administration fail to deal with the growing danger of Fascism."[2] The officer corps backed the monarchy against the Iron Guard, although many officers—especially reservists—sympathized with Legionarism. The officer corps was the army's backbone and played a major role in bolstering morale and motivation through leadership, care, indoctrination, and discipline of soldiers.

The Romanian Army's origins trace back to the Organic Regulations. General Kiselyov created the National Militia in Wallachia in 1830 and the Land Guard in Moldavia in 1831.[3] These militaries recruited officers from boyar families and conscripted enlisted men from free peasant families.[4] Enserfed peasants could not be drafted. Prince Cuza initiated a period of army reform based on the French model in the United Principalities of Moldavia and Wallachia. In 1860, Cuza officially united the National Militia and Land Guard into the Romanian Army.[5] He enacted republican-inspired reforms, like opening the officer corps to non-boyars in 1862.[6] After 1866, Prince Carol pushed to "Prussianize" the Romanian Army, and between 1868 and 1876 he oversaw the introduction of universal military service, merit-based promotion, a general staff, a war council, and a code of military justice.[7] These reforms came just in time for the Russo-Turkish War of 1877–1878, during which the Romanian Army proved its mettle. The Romanian Army continued to modernize and expand under King Carol I, growing from 14,000 soldiers in 1866 to 106,000 in 1914.[8] Romania's nearly unopposed march into Bulgaria during the Second Balkan War in 1913 was over almost before it began, but its invasion of Austria-Hungary in 1916 during the First World War demonstrated how unprepared it was for industrialized warfare.

The First World War transformed the Romanian Army, re-equipping it with the panoply of modern war and acting as a catalyst that increased the officer corps' professionalism. After a devastating Austro-German-Bulgarian counteroffensive, the Romanian Army lost 39 percent of its soldiers killed, wounded, or (in most cases) captured. Shortages in firepower, leadership, and training were the primary causes of defeat, but the large number of prisoners suggests demoralization was a contributing factor.[9] The Russian Army saved Moldavia from occupation. French and British military missions arrived to retrain and rearm the Romanian Army. A terrible typhus epidemic, with half a million reported cases between February and June 1917 alone, decimated Moldavia.[10] Nonetheless, better armed, officered, and trained Romanian troops, backed by Russian soldiers, fended off a major Austro-German summer offensive. The Russian Army collapsed after the Bolshevik revolution, compelling Romania to agree to an armistice and sign a peace treaty. The Central Powers collapsed in 1918, allowing Romania to rejoin the war and share in the Entente Powers' victory. The Romanian Army campaigning in Hungary in 1919 was a radically improved army from the one that had marched off to war three years before. The Romanian Army tried to build upon this progress in peacetime; however, it was frustrated by the social and economic realities of interwar Romania.

The Officer Corps

The Romanian officer corps was small and grew slowly from 1859 to 1890, so boyars and "military sons" filled its ranks. Large landholding families continued to send younger sons into the army. Some middle-class families made military service the family vocation. The state established a "school for military sons" in Iași in 1872, and then in Craiova in 1881, providing subsidized education for sons from military families—although they made up only a quarter of the students. The rest had to pay tuition or win a scholarship. For nonmilitary families the schools offered inexpensive education for entry into the civil service. Romania's middle class disliked the military. Anton Bacalbașa, a police chief's son from Brăila, was disgusted with the conditions he experience when he volunteered in 1883. After leaving the military, he became a journalist, working from 1895 to 1901 for a socialist newspaper, where he invented the character of Moș Teacă, or "Old Man Scabbard," to lambaste officers as stupid and brutal.[11] Old Man Scabbard became shorthand for military arrogance, incompetence, and anti-intellectualism. Additionally, an army career promised dull postings in isolated towns lacking modern comforts. Only a lucky few were garrisoned in cities with theaters, museums, libraries, and clubs.[12] Consequently, when the Romanian Army expanded, the officer corps had to find recruits from elsewhere.

Peasants increasingly joined the officer corps as it more than doubled from fifteen hundred officers in 1890 to four thousand in 1913.[13] The schools for military sons were renamed military high schools as they expanded and military sons made up even a smaller portion of the enrollment; the school in Craiova became a gymnasium in 1902, but another opened outside Târgoviște in 1912.[14] These schools still educated sons from military families, but there were not enough of them or boyar families to meet the Romanian Army's growing need for officers. Peasant families saw an opportunity for their sons to climb the social ladder through the military. Nicolae Dăscălescu testified that he became an officer in 1908 "only for one reason; to pull out my family from poverty."[15] Moreover, peasants were attracted to the social status of an officer and the opportunity to exercise authority over others. They also had less aversion to serving at backwoods posts. Boyars and military sons dominated senior commands in the army, but peasants took over field and company grades. The First World War accelerated the dilution of boyar and military sons in the officer corps.

The officer corps nearly tripled to 11,400 officers after the conflict. Middle-class reserve officers left the army to pursue professions, and large landowners took positions in government or on company boards, leaving behind a "class of modest men," as an article in *România militară* (Military Romania), the General Staff's journal, reported in May 1924.[16] The threat of conscription still induced many middle-class youths to become reserve officers. Those youths who passed the baccalaureate could attend a reserve officer school for two months and serve six months before entering the reserve.[17] They were nicknamed *teteriști*, or TTRs, short for *Trupă cu termen redus*, or "Trooper with reduced term." Few TTR officers reenlisted. Captain Ion Grosu, an artillery officer, remembered that "the youth ran from the army like from fire" during the interwar period.[18] Middle-class youths dreamed of earning a law degree at the University of Bucharest, the usual ticket to the comfortable life of a civil servant in the capital, rather than becoming an officer posted to a podunk town.[19] Therefore, boyars, military sons, and peasants shaped the officer corps' culture.

Culture

The officer corps' culture was rooted in its noble origins under the Organic Regulations. Prince Cuza introduced republican values of meritocracy, egalitarianism, and virtue. King Carol I, however, emphasized aristocratic values of class, honor, and chivalry.[20] Officers from military families often became as haughty as officers from old boyar families; Marshal Antonescu was notorious for his tremendous pride.[21] Military sons also formed nepotistic networks. Cadet Manolescu noted during his training, "Company Commander: Radulescu; Platoon Commander: Radulescu; Tactical Instructor: Radulescu. . . . I soon learnt that the Radulescu family had virtually monopolized the Military Academy."[22] As the officer corps recruited more peasants, it established barriers to keep them from entering the most rarefied military circles, the most blatant of these barriers being the "horse tax." If an officer wanted to join the cavalry or artillery arms, regardless of how meritorious, he had to pay the horse tax, which was 800 lei in 1906 and 12,000 lei in 1932, or roughly a peasant day-laborer's wages for a year.[23] Thus, the horse tax preserved cavalry and artillery arms' social exclusiveness for boyar and military families. Nevertheless, peasants used the military to climb the social ladder, and most assimilated into the officer corps's aristocratic milieu.

Officers were expected to maintain a certain lifestyle, especially once married. They usually lived in town, away from soldiers in barracks. Officers could not marry until age twenty-three and had to find a fiancée with a dowry and a good reputation.[24] Daughters from old boyar families were preferred. Officers often placed ads to find suitable spouses, like this one from 1941:

"Artillery CAPTAIN with foreign post experience, specialized training, owns private automobile, from a good family, brother-in-law a general, seeking to marry a woman up to 35 years old with a house and income."[25] Sometimes officers never married, because of the costs associated with having a family. When asked why he never married, General Dăscălescu responded that a wife "has to be taken to the opera, the theater, to military clubs, and visits with other officers."[26] Senior officers felt entitled to use military funds to pay for patrician comforts. In 1928, one general received an apartment worth 200,000 lei as a "gift" from the corps he commanded, while another used 300,000 lei from the General Staff training budget to renovate his home.[27] Similar misappropriations occurred on a smaller scale at the regimental level, diverting scarce funds from soldiers' training, equipment, and care. Nevertheless, the officer corps felt the Romanian Army's role in creating Greater Romania entitled it to the same prestige and respect in society accorded to German officers before the First World War—revealing grandiose imperial pretentions.[28]

There was a clear pecking order. Cavalry officers were the most prestigious because the cavalry was the most socially exclusive arm, which, according to one general, "provided the model of gestures of honor, loyalty, and generosity in the army."[29] Cavalry regiments were either *roșiori* (literally "reds") or *călărași* ("riders") respectively tracing their lineages back to line and territorial cavalry regiments that fought in the Russo-Turkish War of 1877–1878. *Roșiori* regiments were the domain of officers from large landholding and military families. The cavalry arm also had significant political influence; five prime ministers between 1918 and 1945 were former cavalrymen.[30] *Călărași* regiments transitioned from territorial to regular units in the interwar period. Artillery officers were the next most prestigious, since the artillery arm attracted the most men from the middle class. The infantry arm contained the most officers with peasant origins, so infantry officers were the least prestigious. Infantry regiments were dubbed *vânători* (hunters), *dorobanți* (foot soldiers), and *infanterie* (infantry). The *vânători* and *dorobanți* regiments also traced their lineages respectively back to line and territorial units in 1877–1878, but the *infanterie* regiments were created more recently. By the interwar years there was no difference between them, except that *vânători* regiments were more socially exclusive. The Guard Division, a parade formation formed from two *vânători* regiments, was located in Bucharest and enjoyed favored treatment.[31] The *Grăniceri* ("Frontier Guards") Corps patrolled Romania's frontiers, with eight lightly equipped "groups"—half on the eastern border—and a riverine group. *Grăniceri* served longer and had experience in border skirmishes, so were supposedly more professional.

However, a study in 1939 concluded, "While in comparison to his infantry and light infantry comrades, in most cases, the *grănicer* soldier is better prepared for war, nevertheless, he is not sufficiently formed, neither for combat or guard duties."[32] The Mountain Corps was the most elite in the infantry arm. The *vânători de munte*, or "mountain hunters," had strong esprit de corps (reinforced by regional identity, because most mountain troops were recruited from Transylvania) and attracted the best infantry officers. They wore green berets, golf-style pants, and white socks to advertise their elite status. Cadet Dumitru Teodorescu remembered mountain troops parading in Sibiu in 1937 with "impeccable attire" and "perfect alignment." "You won me mountain hunters! From then began my love for you."[33] The Mountain Corps also did not have regiments, but groups (containing two battalions instead of four). The armored arm was the military's "ugly duckling."[34] Tanks were dirty, noisy contraptions meant for infantry support, so were commanded by infantry, not cavalry, officers.[35] Despite these differences, the officer corps remained united by culture and ideology.

Despite Romania's past as an Ottoman vassal, Christian chivalry became a central part of officer culture. In 1870, every battalion or regiment was authorized a chaplain.[36] Honor became an obsession for officers. Romanians abroad, preferring German codes of honor, had brought back dueling, and duels became so commonplace—over 30 percent of duelists were officers—that the military created "honor councils" in 1908 to settle insults before they became violent.[37] Honor also compelled some officers to suicide.[38] The Romanian Army created a knighthood, called the Order of Mihai the Brave, in 1916. This award for valor, bestowed only onto officers, came with a parcel of land. Officer duels declined in the interwar period because the Code of Military Justice reinforced honor councils, and dueling became less popular in general.[39] Officers patronized the Romanian Orthodox Church by giving donations, collecting funds from their unit, or providing troops as free labor on church projects. After 1918, officers' largesse built and renovated many Romanian Orthodox churches across Transylvania, where Protestant and Catholic houses of worship had hitherto predominated.[40] Chivalry was an important normative interest among officers that motivated them later on the eastern front.

Professionalism

The Romanian officer corps was fairly professional, but it was generally less competent than many other European officer corps of the era. Professionalism requires special knowledge and skills, an impulse to improve standards of performance, strong corporate identity, recognition and articulation of special interests for the institution, autonomy, and voluntarism.[41] Romania's officer training system lagged behind the European standard. The School for Artillery and Engineering and the Superior School of War were created in 1881 and 1889 respectively, but officers still traveled abroad for advanced training.[42] The first staff ride took place in 1888 and the first maneuvers in 1894. Carol I was very critical of the 1903 maneuvers: "The divisions today are nothing but some infantry brigades lacking connection with the other arms."[43] This showed in 1916 as overwhelmed commanders proved unequal to the task of commanding corps and armies, resulting in a slow, poorly coordinated offensive that gave the enemy time to plan a devastating counteroffensive.[44] The officer corps improved with experience and training from the French military mission in 1917.[45] However, critical gaps still existed after 1919. The 1930 maneuvers were criticized for poor coordination, too many counterorders, and micromanaging.[46] Nevertheless, the First World War veterans who commanded during the Second World War were more professional and competent than any preceding generation of Romanian officers.

The Romanian Army improved officer training during the interwar years. The military education system included, in the Old Kingdom, one infantry, cavalry, and engineer officer training school each, plus a health and a chemical institute, and an artillery, an administration, and two infantry officer training schools in Transylvania.[47] These were supported by a number of reserve officer training schools. Officers began being required to pass the baccalaureate, not just finish high school—a result of middle-class unemployment during the Great Depression.[48] Officer training lasted three years. Each day consisted of six to seven hours of lectures (60 percent training, 30 percent military culture, and 10 percent general culture), three to four hours of individual study, and eight hours of sleep, with meals, relaxation, and activities filling the rest.[49] A mechanical training school was created in 1935.[50] Officer training schools taught new doctrine. Before 1914, Romanian Army doctrine copied the French Army's "offensive to excess" of immediate violent attacks to demoralize and overwhelm the enemy.[51] This resulted in France suffering bloody losses in 1914 that Romania repeated in 1916.[52] After 1919, the Romanian Army adopted the French Army's "methodical battle" doctrine of carefully prepared attacks on successive objectives.[53] However, arguments that French doctrine robbed the Romanian Army of offensive spirit are specious.[54] Although military strategists expected to be on the defensive initially because Romania was surrounded by enemies, they planned to go on the offensive as soon as possible. In 1921, *România militară* concluded that the next war in Eastern Europe would be decided by attacking and not defending, because the frontage to cover was far too large. A forward force would pin and slow any enemy attack until reserves could counterattack and encircle the foe, as the Germans had done to the Russians in 1914, the Romanians to the Hungarians in 1919, and the Poles to the Soviets in 1920. "The maneuver and the offensive eternally will remain the means to obtain the decision, whatever will be the shape of war."[55] Romanian officers received better training than ever before in the interwar period.

The most competent officers did not always rise to the top, however. Although laws after 1866 required that officers demonstrate basic competence and serve a specific number of years in each rank before being promoted, those with connections received the best positions.[56] Before 1914, the officer corps was top-heavy with too many generals and colonels and too few majors, captains, and lieutenants.[57] So-called "salon generals" often gambled or attended social events more than soldiered. The catastrophe in 1916 was blamed on such salon generals, but they were often just replaced by royal favorites. General Prezan had been King Ferdinand I's royal adjutant when he was crown prince, which was a major reason Prezan became chief of staff in 1917.[58] After 1919, the senior ranks still contained plenty of salon generals. General Gheorghe Athanasescu (himself Queen Mother Marie's royal adjutant) recorded in 1928 that army inspectors formed a "clique that favors itself reciprocally."[59] After Carol II acceded to the throne in 1930, royal favor became even more important as the king became more authoritarian and promoted cronies over critics. However, the worst of these salon generals were purged once General Antonescu seized power.

Ethnicity

Before the First World War, there were few minorities in the Old Kingdom. The officer corps officially discriminated against Jews and unofficially discriminated against Gypsies, the two largest minority groups. When universal male military service was introduced in 1868, most Jews were excluded as "foreigners" because the new constitution had not granted them citizenship. In 1876, a new conscription law finally extended the requirement to Jews, referred to in the text as "foreigners who do not belong to a foreign nationality." Just prior to this, parliament approved a ban against Jews becoming officers. An 1882 conscription law required Jews to serve as "residents of the country."[60] As more Jews joined the middle class, the military took more steps to ban them from positions of leadership. Jewish doctors and pharmacists served as privates, even though their education qualified them to become reserve officers. Some regiments even banned Jews from being NCOs.[61] No such laws or bans targeted Gypsies. Nevertheless, the officer corps blocked from its ranks the few Gypsies who met the requirements.

Greater Romania's creation dramatically changed the situation. A third of the population were Hungarians, Germans, Jews, Ukrainians, Russians, Bulgarians, or other ethnic minorities. Ethnic Germans and Jews provided the most non-Romanian officers during the interwar years. The Romanian Army gave former Austro-Hungarian and Russian officers their former rank if they joined. Most ethnic Hungarian Austro-Hungarian officers departed for rump Hungary, leaving mostly ethnic German (known locally as Saxons and Swabians) and Jewish Austro-Hungarian officers behind in Transylvania.[62] Romanian politicians saw ethnic Germans as "an element of order and work, having peaceful sentiments," and needed them to counterbalance ethnic Hungarians, so Romanian soldiers were ordered to treat ethnic Germans "like Romanians" in 1918.[63] Consequently, the interwar Romanian officer corps contained many ethnic German officers, including a few generals.[64] Most Russian officers joined the Red or White armies in the Russian Civil War, but a handful remained behind in Bessarabia and joined the Romanian Army.[65] The 1923 constitution forced the Romanian Army to begin allowing Jews to become reserve officers; but the officer corps connived to disqualify Jews from becoming regular officers to keep its ranks "pure and healthy," as the Antonescu regime later put it.[66] Even part-Jewish officers were considered tainted. When Marshal Antonescu was commandant of the Superior School of War, he heard that an officer sitting for the entrance exam was a "kike," so after confirming that the officer's mother was Jewish, he "entered the oral examination . . . [and] screwed him over for two hours. . . . He was well prepared but when a professor wants to fail you, he fails you."[67] Romanian officers most distrusted Jewish officers, but they looked askance at all ethnic minority officers.

Noncommissioned Officers

The Romanian Army lacked a professional NCO corps. Officers selected NCOs from the yearly contingent of draftees—privates could be promoted to corporal after two months and to sergeant after four months—to attend NCO training school for two months.[68] Second Lieutenant Manolescu quipped, "No special qualifications were required, though it was implied that they should be able to read and write."[69] NCOs were promoted quickly so that officers could benefit from their assistance before the draftees completed their two-year service. The handful of NCOs who reenlisted for seven years were called *reangajați*, or "rehires." Corporal Johann Emrich, a Saxon draftee, reenlisted to save up to pay for a house and dowry to get married.[70] Those NCOs who stayed in the army beyond that eventually became sergeant majors who administered the regimental *gospodărie*, or "economy." Other NCOs were less vital—1,434 of 13,790 *reangajați* in 1931 were musicians.[71] Middle-class youths who failed the baccalaureate and working-class youths who graduated trade school qualified as reserve NCOs. After two months of training, they served ten months as TTR NCOs.[72] The Romanian Army's shortage of professional NCOs weakened its institutional knowledge, compromised a stabilizing force between officers and enlisted men, and made it harder to inculcate regimental esprit de corps.[73]

Pressured into leadership, many NCOs decided to use newfound power for personal gain. Anton Bacalbașa depicted NCOs in the 1880s as bullies who hazed new draftees, enforced strict discipline with their fists, and fleeced draftees of valuables.[74] Such behavior remained common in the interwar years. Captain Grosu noted that NCOs "rapidly forget that they had also been privates and flaunt behavior [*mentalități*] unsuitable for a leader, so much so, instead of a help, they were harmful, their comportment being completely contrary to regulations."[75] *Reangajați* were usually more professional, but focused on the regimental economy more than training draftees to a high standard. Private Immanuel Weiss, serving in a territorial *călărași* regiment in Bessarabia, recalled, "The sergeants were always finding little ways to force us to give them money."[76] His polyglot troop, which numbered ethnic Ukrainians, Bulgarians, and Germans along with Romanians, needed to have pristine uniforms at roll call, so when small stars on their boots went missing, as they were wont to do, privates paid sergeants ten or twenty lei for replacement ones to avoid punishment. Abusive NCOs were common in peacetime; however, the quality of NCOs improved in wartime.

Enlisted Men

The relationship between officers and enlisted men was like that of "lords and vassals."[77] The fact that nearly 77 percent of Romanians were serfs in thrall to boyars in 1859 and 82 percent were peasants laboring on smallholdings or large landholders' estates in 1939 illustrates why.[78] Despite significant social changes over the course of eighty years, military culture lagged behind. Officers treated enlisted men like serfs even after emancipation in 1864. Although universal military service was introduced in 1868, the Romanian Army was small, so few men needed to be drafted. In general, peasants saw military service as a misfortune. Anton Bacalbașa described induction as a shock to draftees. Soldiers halfway through their two-year commitment, watching the barber cut off hair and beards, shouted, "Go get your haircut, newbie [leat]! . . . When you get home, they'll believe that you escaped from prison."[79] Soldiers had to quickly learn unfamiliar military jargon or be beaten. As the Romanian Army expanded, more men were drafted, and military service became a normal routine of life. In 1893, Romania created the Rural Gendarmerie, a paramilitary police force, to maintain order in the countryside, and whose duties included collecting and delivering draftees to regiments each spring. A 1908 law established the requirements of military service for men between twenty-one and forty: seven years of eligibility to be drafted into the regular army, five in the reserve army, three in the militia, and four in the territorial army. Draftees served two years, except cavalrymen, who needed an extra year to master horsemanship.[80] This remained the norm through the interwar years.

Enlisted men used to the grinding poverty and tedium of village life often discovered that army life was not just tolerable but sometimes enjoyable. Soldiers got steady pay and saw more of Romania than the nearest market town. Food was monotonous but regular: a cup of sweet tea and a slice of bread for breakfast, vegetable or bean soup three days and *mămăligă* four days a week for lunch, and leftovers for dinner. Soldiers augmented these rations; Private Weiss and fellow ethnic Germans pooled cash, since they "always had to buy extra food to survive."[81] The infamous "cauldron soup" of beans with meat or vegetables was sometimes watered down to cut costs.[82] Garrisons had "military gardens" to grow vegetables for the pot. A chronic shortage of infrastructure meant soldiers often slept in tents.[83] Barracks had common beds, lacked bathing facilities and heating, and were often unsanitary.[84] Draftees sometimes received "old rags" instead of new uniforms.[85] These conditions prompted different reactions depending on class. Second Lieutenant Manolescu noted, "The ranks were treated like animals. Beatings, torture and deliberate underfeeding were part and parcel of a soldier's life during his military training."[86] However, Corporal Emrich concluded, "In the Balkans, to be a soldier in a time without conflict between nations was a blessing."[87] What seemed intolerable to a middle-class reserve officer was not so bad or even good to a peasant draftee.

Discipline

The Romanian Army's discipline was harsh. Flogging remained an official punishment, but it was not as common as unofficial slaps, kicks, and beatings. Anton Bacalbașa described brutal punishments in the 1880s. If a soldier responded incorrectly, instructors sometimes ordered another soldier to spit on him or give "this dumbass a slap," but more often commanded the soldier to hold a length of wood outstretched in front of him until told to stop.[88] Drill included slaps and blows for missteps; one officer even "filled his pockets with stones and threw them at soldiers. He regularly beat them with [the flat of his] sword, until he had to unbend it with [his] foot."[89] Most armies had officially banned corporal punishment by the First World War, although some continued practicing it surreptitiously, like NCOs in the German Army.[90] Entente observers were appalled by the Romanian Army's use of corporal punishment. A French officer witnessed a Romanian officer beat two NCOs, who "stood upright, unmoving," with an iron-handled walking stick. "In France the victims would have jumped on him."[91] The 1923 constitution granting equal rights to peasants prompted the Romanian Army to eliminate corporal punishment from *The Regulation on the Interior Service for Troops of All Arms*, which set out soldiers' rights, obligations, and punishments. Punishments like extra duties, revoking leave, confinement, and half rations remained. In 1939, *România militară* warned officers to be careful, as punishments instead of being "a means of education, many times degenerate into abuse, on a whim and arbitrary."[92] Yet officers still held NCOs responsible for enlisted men's poor performance, so, as Teodor Halic recalled, "[NCOs] were worse than officers. . . . [They] were still knocking, were still cursing."[93] Enlisted men could report officers or NCOs who were abusive, but slaps, punches, and kicks remained part of army life throughout the interwar period.

Misuse

Many officers saw enlisted men as a source of free labor. It was not unusual for officers to equate soldiers and horses as beasts of burden. Soldiers were leased to large landholders to work their fields, with profits going to the regimental economy, a practice officially endorsed during the Great Depression.[94] These funds often paid for officers' lifestyles as much as they filled the coffers of the regimental economy. Regiments leased soldiers in spring and fall, when extra hands were needed for planting or harvesting, and often sent them home on extended leave in winter to save on caring for them. Consequently, soldiers trained only in summer. In 1925, *România militară* admitted that soldiers received a "maximum of 7 months of training" over two years because of extended leave, guard or service duties, and "endless drudgery" in fields, vegetable gardens, and forests.[95] Soldiers often returned from extended leave almost raw draftees. Misuse of soldiers undermined the Romanian Army's military effectiveness.

Moral Education

The Romanian Army, "the school of the nation," prioritized indoctrinating troops through "moral education." Regimental commanders speechified on patriotism, sacrifice, discipline, duty, and monarchism on special occasions, such as induction or holidays.[96] Officers read *Words to Soldiers* regularly. These pamphlets contained poetry, songs, and lectures on subjects like "To Love Country, King, and Nation."[97] Chaplains' blessings, sermons, and ceremonies contained a heavy dose of moral education. Medical officers taught classes on hygiene and health, a first for many soldiers because of a lack of village doctors.[98] Sanitary lectures focused on disease prevention, including against venereal disease, but also addressed issues like alcoholism.[99] In 1923, *România militară* ordered, "The [hygiene] training, which you give to soldiers, must be serious, orderly, methodical and heated with sacred fire, so it not only perfects the soldier, but throws light also in the depths of the villages, still remaining darkened."[100] Moral education reinforced draftees' ideological upbringing and elementary education.

Interwar Army Politics

The 1866 constitution made Romania a constitutional monarchy, but the electoral system empowered large landowning and middle-class men who generally backed the Conservatives or Liberals, respectively. Officers were supposed to be apolitical and not allowed to vote; however, most favored the Conservatives. While some historians argue that Romanian officers had "pro-French, and by extension pro-Western, sympathies," few in fact believed in Western liberal democracy.[101] Some Romanian officers attended military schools in France, but few returned as convinced republicans, because French officers were nearly all staunch monarchists.[102] The 1923 constitution radically redrew Romania's political map. The Conservative Party collapsed following the introduction of universal male suffrage.[103] Populist parties sprang up in the vacuum, like the Peasant Party under Constantine Stere and the People's Party under General Alexandru Averescu. The Romanian National Party of Transylvania under Iuliu Maniu was a powerful new political force. While some officers gravitated toward populist leagues, most turned to the de facto establishment party, which was the Liberal Party led by the venerable Ion I. C. Brătianu.

The Liberals' policies matched the military's goals. After the First World War, inflation and cheap American agricultural products depressed Romania's economy, but the military supported investment in industry over

FIGURE 1. The annual induction of new draftees each spring was one of the highlights of the army calendar in peacetime. Like all such military celebrations, it consisted of speeches, prayers, and parades. These special events, along with routine lectures by officers on moral education and sermons by chaplains about "holy" Romania, reinforced the indoctrination of soldiers to fulfill their duty to God, king, and country in wartime. Courtesy of Daniel Obreja; photographer unknown.

agriculture. In 1921, *România militară* pointed out, "Military industry was, then [in 1916], in [an] embryonic state, and private industry could not satisfy the army's needs, from lack of preparation."[104] Therefore, the Liberals' efforts to industrialize under the motto *prin noi înșine*, or "by ourselves," was music to the military's ears.[105] The Liberal government also made sure to keep the officer corps happy. Inflation had eroded officers' pay. Captain Grosu was ordered to use "local resources," often meaning his "own pocket," to feed and shelter soldiers.[106] Although the cost of living rose seventeen-fold, and spending on soldiers and horses twenty-fold, officer pay only quadrupled. In 1923 *România militară* huffed, "The officer is not paid for his work and even more again: he is not provided for."[107] The Romanian Army's solution: a drastic pay raise or subsidies, access to military services and stores for officers' families, and an "extra-military activity" stipend.[108] Liberals doubled the military budget between 1924 and 1927, much of it going to officer pay.[109] A 1925 law expanded two munitions factories and established the Romanian Aeronautical Industry in Brașov. Over the next five years 2.3 billion lei were spent on armaments: 100 million lei on munitions, 1.2 billion lei on aeronautics, and 1 billion lei on arms ordered from France.[110] There were difficulties, and the munitions factories were soon in debt.[111] These and other Liberal priorities did not resonate with peasant voters.

In 1926, the Liberal Party lost to the People's Party led by retired general Averescu. This ambitious war hero was credited with saving Romania from being totally overrun in 1916 and inflicting a defeat on the enemy in 1917. Averescu quit the military to enter politics, where as prime minister in 1918 and 1920–1921 he was seen as an island of virtue in a sea of corruption. His vague promises of a brighter future allowed voters to project their hopes on his candidacy. For many officers he was a possible authoritarian strongman to fill the void left by a royal crisis. Ferdinand I was dying from cancer, and Crown Prince Carol (whose amorous past already included an unacknowledged child and annulled elopement) had renounced his claim to the throne in 1925 to divorce his wife Princess Helen of Greece and enter exile with his mistress Elena Lupescu, the daughter of baptized Jews.[112] Prime Minister Averescu's third tenure was plagued with problems and unable to change economic policies to help the peasantry, so he had to resign in less than a year—but not before considering bringing back the exiled prince or even becoming a dictator to stay in power.[113] Carlism, support for restoring Carol to the line of succession, was quickly becoming a powerful movement. The new Liberal government under Ion I. C. Brătinau, however, passed a law requiring a three-person regency to rule for Ferdinand I's grandson Crown Prince Mihai if the king died, as it was deemed unacceptable for Carol to return, especially as the exiled prince insisted on bringing his "Jewish" mistress with him. In July 1927, Ferdinand I died, succeeded by five-year-old King Mihai I's regency, but then Ion I. C. Brătinau died four months later. As the People's Party had proven incapable, and the Liberal Party was in disarray, the National Peasant Party (a fusion of the Romanian National and Peasant Parties) won the 1928 election.

Officers disliked the National Peasant Party since it advocated social reform, investment in agriculture, and was supposedly soft on communism.[114] While the Hungarian and Bulgarian armies were limited to 35,000 and 20,000 men respectively, the Red Army had 585,000 men in arms. In 1928, *România militară* argued, "We must be careful, war is being prepared on the borders of the nation in the East, and the Bolshevik doctrinaires want to impose their utopian ideas through Red Army force, for which [purpose] they make every sacrifice and spend over 100 billion lei annually!"[115] In 1929, at the same time Joseph Stalin announced the Five-Year Plan and the Wall Street crash occurred, *România militară* published an anonymous article titled "The Need for the Introduction of Pre-regimental Training at Home." It claimed Hungary had formed "a II-nd army" by establishing militaristic youth sports groups, and the USSR had ordered youths "to attend sessions on military training, target practice, maneuvers, campaigns, etc."[116] The article proposed pre-military training comprising four months of "national-patriotic-religious" training and four months of weapons and technical training spread over two years, starting at age nineteen. Those who finished would only serve eighteen months if drafted.[117] The article triggered a firestorm. The National Peasant Party argued that pre-military training risked encouraging militarism, limiting education, harming health, and extending military service.[118] The Great Depression meant there was no money for pre-military training, as the National Peasant Party even had to renege on its campaign promises, causing support for it to quickly ebb.

As Iuliu Maniu turned to austerity measures, Carlism grew in popularity, including in the military hit hard by budget cuts. Captain Grosu recalled his artillery regiment did not receive pay for months, fostering "a situation of total demoralization."[119] On 27 March 1930, during an anniversary celebration of Bessarabia's annexation attended by Constantin Stere, three generals walked out. Stere was despised for his left-wing, pro-peasantist politics and collaboration with the occupiers during the war. Liberals claimed the National Peasant Party had created the conditions for a military coup, so Maniu dismissed Stere.[120] Support for Carlism continued to grow. Vintilă I. C. Brătinau, who took over the Liberal Party after his brother's death, confronted a revolt led by Gheorghe I. Brătinau, his nephew, over supporting the exiled prince. Maniu negotiated Carol's return (dependent on Elena Lupescu remaining behind), which occurred on 8 June.[121] Carol II wooed the officer corps. Within weeks, he established the rank of field marshal and promoted Generals Prezan and Averescu to that elevated position: however, the army budget continued to be slashed, over 50 percent in 1932 alone.[122] To cut expenses, fewer men were drafted, shrinking the enlisted ranks from 171,306 in 1930 to 120,602 in 1932; but the officer corps grew from 14,387 to 15,724 as unemployment drove middle-class youths into the military (see table 1). Enlisted men were used as labor or sent on extended leave, receiving even less training.[123] Meanwhile, the Red Army grew to 885,000 soldiers.[124] Rumors began spreading that the economic depression alone was not responsible for weakening the Romanian Army—the corrupt monarch was also to blame.

A camarilla had formed around Carol II and Elena Lupescu, subsidizing the couple's lavish lifestyle in exchange for favors.[125] The king had broken his promise to leave his mistress behind, prompting Iuliu Maniu's resignation and replacement with Alexandru Vaida-Voevod. Tales of Carol II and Lupescu cavorting around Bucharest depicted them as more debauched with each retelling.[126] General Athanasescu often referred to "the kike woman," and heard that "at the Palace are happening things like in Sodom and Gomorrah, as the King is led by the nose [like a bull] by lady Lupescu."[127] According to an insider, "If a person approved of their relationship, he was the King's friend; if he opposed it, he was his enemy."[128] Lupescu wielded immense power and became an object of near-universal opprobrium. Carlism's reputation

Table 1. Size of the officer corps and NCO/enlisted ranks, 1924–1939

YEAR	OFFICERS	NCOS/ENLISTED	TOTAL
1924	11,379	135,564	146,564
1925	12,344	127,483	139,827
1926	12,293	128,483	140,776
1927	13,436	136,333	149,769
1928	14,658	170,968	185,626
1929	14,725	171,414	186,139
1930	14,387	171,306	185,693
1931	15,334	158,941	174,275
1932	15,724	120,602	136,326
1933	16,596	124,789	141,385
1934	16,478	124,921	141,399
1936	15,296	115,643	130,939
1937	14,890	149,635	164,525
1938	13,613	147,946	161,559

Source: League of Nations, *Armaments Year-Book*, Eighth Year, 266, and Fourteenth Year, 717.

of corruption and immorality triggered the rise of anti-Carlism. Meanwhile, the Romanian Army crushed worker demonstrations. Beginning in 1931, the National Peasant–led government implemented successive "sacrificial curves," cutting state employees' salaries by 10–12 percent at a time, totaling nearly 50 percent by 1933 and causing increased left-wing activism.[129] States of siege were declared in Bucharest, Ploiești, Iași, Galați, Timișoara, and Cernăuți. When state railway workers in the capital (many of whom had been temporarily laid off because of bad weather) found out they would not be paid unless they could prove they had paid taxes, they went on successive strikes, on 28 January, 2 February, and 15 February. Vaida-Voevod sent in soldiers on 16 February. When "communist" workers allegedly opened fire, soldiers machine-gunned the strikers, killing three and wounding forty before arresting twelve hundred workers.[130] This heavy-handedness caused a small outrage, but it was soon overshadowed by a scandal of epic proportions.

The Škoda affair revealed corruption at the highest levels of the military. On 10 March, army investigators entered Bruno Seletzki's Bucharest office. He represented Škoda Works, a Czechoslovak arms manufacturer. There they found a bonanza of top-secret Romanian military documents: letters, reports, ciphers, statistics, plans, projects, and personnel files.[131] The prime minister ordered a cover-up and allowed Seletzki to burn many incriminating documents. On 22 March, the scandal leaked. An inquiry revealed civilian and military leaders had been bribed to secure lucrative contracts for Škoda. Liberals turned the affair into a witch hunt, during which General Dumitru Popescu, secretary to the minister of defense, committed suicide.[132] A growing number of officers pointed the finger of blame at the monarch. Marshal Averescu railed against the king's camarilla "in which the kike woman plays the principal role" and argued that Carol II should be deposed in favor of his son.[133] The Škoda scandal was the final straw for the National Peasant Party, which soon collapsed.[134] Legionaries brawled in the streets during the election, but the Liberals won handily. On 10 December, the new prime minister, Ion Duca, outlawed the Iron Guard, and on 29 December three Legionaries assassinated him in revenge. They did not try to escape, declaring at their trial that they had acted to save the nation from corrupt politicians.[135]

Before his murder, Duca appointed General Antonescu as chief of staff, with a mission to renegotiate arms contracts. Antonescu was born in Pitești in 1882 into a well-connected military family.[136] He attended the School for Military Sons in Craiova, became a cavalry officer in 1904, and received a plum assignment in Galați in a *roșiori* regiment. During the peasant uprising of 1907, Antonescu instructed his troop to disperse a peasant mob in Galați, killing or wounding twenty to thirty people.[137] He attended the Superior School of War, became royal adjutant to Crown Prince Carol, and served as Fourth Army chief of staff under General Prezan. He was a competent staff officer but rode Prezan's coattails. Royal patronage landed Antonescu a job as military attaché to Paris from 1922 to 1926. There he met and married Maria Niculescu. Antonescu commanded the Superior School of War from 1927 to 1930 and 1931 to 1933, distinguishing himself as the only commandant to never lecture or publish.[138] His reputation for irascibility and difficult exams earned him the nickname *roșul*, or "the red one," referring to his thinning red hair.[139] Not coincidentally, folk superstition held that "ruddy men" were Jews, descended from Jews, or demonstrated negative traits associated with Jews.[140] Some have suggested Antonescu's mercurial temper was due to syphilis; but while evidence exists that he was probably treated for the disease during the Second World War, there is little to indicate that syphilis could explain his personality or might have impaired his mental capacities.[141] His oft commented-upon "extreme" chauvinism and xenophobia were unremarkable in the officer corps.[142] Surprisingly, Antonescu's disingenuous claim that he "was neither a politician nor diplomat" but "a soldier" is often still repeated uncritically by historians.[143] Although his path to power was unlikely, depending on several contingencies, it was not accidental. Antonescu should be seen not as a naïve soldier who dabbled in politics but as an opportunistic politician with a military background. Without him it is less likely Romania would have later committed itself so fully to Nazi Germany's war effort on the eastern front. Antonescu's promotion to chief of staff, jumping ahead of more senior officers, was a key step on his path to dictator.

General Antonescu soon clashed with Carol II over rearmament, earning him a reputation for incorruptibility. The Nazi takeover in Germany in January 1933 had triggered a European arms race. Antonescu opposed "useless throwing away of billions over the frontier" to replace outdated French artillery with modern Czechoslovak artillery because it meant buying expensive new shells, which he claimed was an underhanded Czechoslovak business trick.[144] Romanian industrialists lobbied for lucrative vehicle contracts. Antonescu opposed procuring trucks, declaring that they were not useful or urgently needed.[145] While the chief of staff resisted what he saw as the camarilla's corrupt meddling, other officers contemplated more direct action. In April 1934, a plot by nine officers to assassinate the king was uncovered. The conspirators claimed they had only planned to kill Elena Lupescu to remove her corrupting influence over Carol II.[146] General Paul Angelescu became minister of defense in July. He quickly butted heads with the chief of staff, ostensibly about rearmament policy, but Antonescu informed an acquaintance that "the divergences between him and P. Angelescu began from when he had found out that Angelescu had been brought to power thanks to connections with lady Lupescu."[147] In December Antonescu resigned, ironically because Angelescu blocked an order for small arms from Czechoslovakia.[148] Antonescu was not a progressive "Romanian Cassandra" frustrated by corrupt or hidebound officers as some historians claim, but the epitome of an old-fashioned cavalryman.[149]

In April 1935, with the economy improving, the Liberals passed a ten-year rearmament plan to modernize and expand the military to twenty-two infantry divisions, three cavalry divisions, three mountain brigades, and one armored brigade.[150] The Liberal government also enacted pre-military training. While some arms contracts went to local manufacturers, large numbers of heavy weapons could only be obtained from abroad. France was unwilling to sell to Romania because it was rearming itself (in reaction to Nazi Germany's rearmament), nor was France willing to subsidize Romania's purchases of modern weaponry, because the French Army judged the Romanian Army as inept and not worth the investment.[151] Czechoslovakia was willing, so in 1936 an agreement was signed worth 2.5 billion lei; Czechoslovak investors bought Romanian bonds to help finance the deal, and soon 70 percent of Romania's heavy weapons came from Czechoslovakia.[152] In 1936, the Ministry of Air and Navy was established, but the Romanian Aeronautical Industry produced mainly training or reconnaissance aircraft.[153] Military expense was 29 percent of the budget in 1935, peaked at 35 percent in 1936, and hovered at 33 percent thereafter.[154] Romania outspent local rivals but could not match Nazi Germany or the USSR (see table 2).

Table 2. Romanian military expenditure (in millions of dollars) in comparison with Southeast European states, Nazi Germany, and the Soviet Union, 1934–1938

YEAR	ROMANIA	HUNGARY	BULGARIA	YUGOSLAVIA	GERMANY	USSR
1934	27	13	6	36	546	10,461
1935	66	19	8	35	723	13,882
1936	62	21	10	36	1498	17,449
1937	48	25	11	42	2090	20,045
1938	56	30	12	48	4675	23,404

Source: For Romanian, Hungarian, Bulgarian, and Yugoslavian expenditures see League of Nations, *Armaments Year-Book*, Nineteenth Year, 718, 426, 215, 906; for Romanian, Hungarian, Bulgarian, and Yugoslavian exchange rates in 1938 see S. D. Zagoroff, Jenö Végh, and Alexander D. Bilimovich, *The Agricultural Economy of the Danubian Countries, 1935–1945* (Stanford, CA: Stanford University Press, 1955), 91; for German and Soviet expenditures and exchange rates see Steiner, *Triumph of the Dark*, 331, 441, 1069.

Note: US dollar equivalents are rough estimations using 1938 exchange rates (172.4 lei, 5.1 pengő, 114.0 lev, 54.9 dinar, 2.4 deustche mark, and 5.3 rubles to the dollar respectively).

Romania now navigated between the Scylla of the USSR and Charybdis of Nazi Germany. In 1934, the USSR joined the League of Nations and reestablished diplomatic relations with Romania, so it appeared less threatening.[155] Nazi Germany needed Romania's oil, food, and raw materials and was willing to pay with manufactured goods, so in 1936 Romania adopted a position of neutrality between the Western Allies and Nazi Germany in an increasingly bellicose Europe. Soon half of Romania's trade was with Nazi Germany.[156] In 1937, *România militară* argued that the League of Nations made war more likely, since collective defense encouraged states to mount surprise attacks to win quick victories before allies could mobilize.[157] Romania's web of overlapping and contradictory alliances (the Little Entente of Czechoslovakia, Yugoslavia, and Romania; the Polish-Romanian anti-Soviet alliance; and the Balkan Pact of Greece, Turkey, Yugoslavia, and Romania) frayed. Hungary, supported by Nazi Germany, now seemed the likeliest external threat, so Romania began fortifying its border in Transylvania.[158] At the same time Romania also faced an internal threat in the Legionary movement.

The Legionary movement expanded steadily after its breakout performance in the 1933 elections and began infiltrating the ranks of the officer corps. The outlawed Iron Guard continued campaigning under the guise of the Totul pentru Țară, or "Everything for the Country," Party led by retired general Gheorghe Cantacuzino, the scion of a princely family and a war hero. Cantacuzino lent the Legion respectability, but he was a figurehead, and the Captain, Corneliu Codreanu, pulled the strings.[159] Most officers saw Legionaries as hooligans and did not use deadly force against them. For example, in 1935, soldiers fired shots in the air and used rifle butts to disperse a student mob attacking Jews and Jewish shops in Bucharest.[160] The Everything for the Country Party attracted more supporters from the LANC.[161] Consequently, officers began to take the Legion more seriously, although most still believed that Iron Guardists were naïve patriots. An intelligence report of a speech by the Captain extolling the Legionaries' lack of political platform caused Antonescu to harrumph, "Not serious. It is not possible to improvise the program of the simplest family farm in a single night, let alone that of an organism as vast as the modern state."[162] Most officers were from the elite or aspired to join it, so they found the Legion's egalitarian rhetoric unpalatable. However, they liked other Legionary values like discipline, hierarchy, organization, sacrifice, oaths, patriotism, monarchism, Christianity, and anticommunism.[163] Mid-ranking and junior officers angry at self-interested senior officers were the most likely to harbor Legionary sympathies.[164] They also had a material incentive. Iron Guardists promised to end nepotism and to remove "Judaized" officers, which would open a path to rapid promotion. Despite growing anti-Carlism and Legionarism among officers, most remained loyal to Carlism.

Carol II embodied the social order, supported the Liberal establishment, and showered the military with honors, so the officer corps backed him when he seized dictatorial powers. The Liberal Party lost an election in December 1937 despite garnering 37 percent of the vote, because a 1926 law required the winning party to obtain at least 40 percent to receive a premium of half the parliamentary seats, granting it a supermajority.[165] The National Peasant Party received 21 percent, and the Everything for the Country Party received 16 percent, meaning together they could form an anti-Carlist coalition; they already had agreed to an electoral truce.[166] Iuliu Maniu and Corneliu Codreanu both hated Carol II, and the National Peasant leader sympathized with the Captain's goals, even though he disliked Legionary methods.[167] Carol II asked Octavian Goga and Alexandru Cuza's National Christian Party to form a government despite garnering a mere 9 percent of the vote, to preempt the possibility of an antagonistic National Peasant–Legionary government. The National Christian Party was the union of the LANC and the National Agrarian Party facilitated by Nazi ideologue Alfred Rosenberg a few years earlier.[168] Octavian Goga, an ultranationalist poet, chose his close friend General Antonescu as minister of defense. Carol II was unhappy that Antonescu had jockeyed his way into the position: "This is the last attempt [to cooperate] with this unstable and ambitious man."[169] Antonescu had cultivated a relationship with Corneliu Codreanu as well, so he did not have his eggs all in one basket. The Goga-Cuza government was as chaotic as it was antisemitic, issuing during its short rule a slew of laws stripping Jews of their rights. On 10 February 1938, Carol II proclaimed a royal dictatorship when it appeared the National Christian Party might ally with the Everything for the Country Party. The new 1938 constitution made him *conducător*, or "leader," and outlawed political parties except for the hurriedly established Front of National Rebirth, the pro-Carlist party whose members wore military-style uniforms. Patriarch Miron became prime minister.[170] General Antonescu was immediately replaced as minister of defense. Few officers lamented the failure of democracy; in fact, most believed an authoritarian monarchy was preferable, especially since war threatened Europe.

Nazi Germany annexed Austria on 12 March, and then Hitler demanded Czechoslovakia cede the Sudetenland, triggering a crisis. At the same time in Romania, Carol II ordered Corneliu Codreanu arrested. He was found guilty of libel and sentenced to six months in prison, but then he was tried for sedition, again found guilty, and sentenced to ten years' hard labor.

Antonescu was a character witness on Codreanu's behalf at the trial.[171] With the Legion muzzled, the king focused on uniting all Romanians, even minorities, behind him in defense of Greater Romania as war threatened to explode in Europe. The Front of National Rebirth offered minorities a stake in Carlism through the General Commissariat for Minorities, which granted minority rights within the limits of approved segregated minority cultural organizations.[172] Patriarch Miron did not rescind the Goga-Cuza government's antisemitic laws, and 225,222 Jews lost their citizenship.[173] On 19 September, at the height of the Sudetenland crisis, the General Staff took the precaution of extending the service obligation of soldiers finishing their two-year stint, in order to maintain the Romanian Army's strength.[174] The Munich Agreement eleven days later averted war; however, the First Vienna Award forced Czechoslovakia to cede territory to Nazi Germany, Hungary, and Poland on 2 November. Britain and France appeasing Nazi Germany by sacrificing an ally raised fears that Romania might be next.

Carol II now decided to put an end to the Legionary movement for once and for all. On 30 November, he ordered Corneliu Codreanu and thirteen Legionary leaders taken from Jilava Prison and "shot while trying to escape."[175] Vice–Prime Minister Armand Călinescu arrested other Iron Guardists. The Legion went underground and broke into factions, arguing over who was to be the Captain's successor. General Antonescu criticized the anti-Legionary crackdown, playing on anti-Carlist disquiet about the harsh treatment of perceived misguided patriots. Now the III Corps commander, he toured Chișinău's prisons and claimed Iron Guardists were being tortured, but his report was rejected, and he was fired.[176] Many officers privately supported Antonescu because of their anti-Carlist and pro-Legionary sentiments, but others were not displeased. When Second Lieutenant Manolescu revealed his socialist leanings by speaking approvingly of Codreanu's assassination, he later noted, "My life became a misery. Lieut.-Colonel Procop had his eye on me . . . and the other officers imitated him. Instead of consolation or tacit sympathy, I got cold looks, harsh commands, and the worst jobs. . . . Worse of all was the fact that even the soldiers took liberties with me."[177] He recalled that officers planned to "lose rifles" to pass to Iron Guardists, sung Legionary songs, hung a portrait of Codreanu in the regimental office, handed out Legionary pamphlets to enlisted men, formed a segregated company of Jews, beat Jewish soldiers out of hand, and discriminated against *basarabeni* and *ardeleni* in the ranks.[178] Manolescu later deserted abroad, his situation became so bad. Nevertheless, officers continued to back Carol II as another crisis threatened European peace.

Nazi Germany's recent annexations rang alarm bells in Romania. In early 1939, *România militară* proclaimed, "The war has already begun. Austria and Czechoslovakia were invaded. Although they did not defend themselves, the act of war was consummated."[179] On 15 February, Hungary reintroduced universal military service. Then, on 15 March, Nazi Germany occupied Czech lands, and Hungary occupied Transcarpathia after Slovakia declared independence from rump Czecho-Slovakia. Four days later Carol II approved partial mobilization, expanding the Romanian Army to five hundred thousand men. The General Staff, fearing revanchist Hungarian or Bulgarian attacks, concentrated the First Army in Transylvania and the Second Army in Dobruja. Garrisons were overcrowded as peasants misread mobilization orders, overzealous gendarmes grabbed all military-age men, and patriotic reservists appeared without orders.[180] There was little draft evasion, even among minorities. Second Lieutenant Teodorescu recalled, "Near midnight, the city [of Sibiu] and barracks were 'flooded' with reservists. A single cry stirs the city barracks, 'Weapons, weapons! Give us weapons!' "[181] Nazi Germany now demanded the so-called Polish corridor. In March, Britain and France gave Poland a guarantee to defend its sovereignty, and in April Greece and Romania got a similar pledge.[182] Nazi Germany's bluff seemed to be called, but then the jaw-dropping announcement of the Nazi-Soviet nonaggression pact on 24 August reshuffled the deck. On 1 September, Nazi Germany invaded Poland, causing Britain and France to declare hostilities and plunging Europe into war.

Neutrality

Romania suddenly found itself caught between Nazi Germany and the USSR, with no allies nearby. On 4 September, Carol II ordered general mobilization, adding the Third Army in Bukovina and the Fourth Army in Transylvania. The First and Fourth Armies formed Army Group No. 1. The Soviet invasion of Poland on 17 September altered plans. Armand Călinescu, now prime minister after Patriarch Miron's death, declared, "The Russians' advance changes the situation. The German danger recedes. Now, at the forefront is the Russian threat."[183] Yet he would not be a part of what was to come. On 21 September, nine Iron Guardists ambushed and killed Călinescu; they in turn were executed on the spot of his assassination and left for days in the street in Bucharest as a warning to others.[184] Carol II also ordered three Legionaries shot in each county, but scores of others were tortured and executed.[185] The Fourth Army started reconcentrating in Moldavia the next day. Army Group No. 1, now comprising the Third and Fourth Armies, planned to defend on the Prut, conceding Bessarabia if the Soviets attacked, but the king ordered it forward to the Dniester, because not doing so risked demoralizing the public, encouraging pro-Soviet uprisings, and signaling lack of resolve to Moscow.[186] The Romanian Army now numbered 1.1 million soldiers, but the General Staff knew it could not hold off the Red Army for long, especially if the Hungarian and Bulgarian armies attacked at the same time.

The USSR's invasion of Finland convinced many Romanians that Romania could resist if attacked, however. The Soviet-Finnish War, starting on 30 November, gave a "glimmer of hope" to Romanian diplomats like Alexandru Cretzianu because outrage across Europe "made us think that the Russia of Stalin had at long last been seen in its true colors, and that henceforth the Soviets could never again benefit from the trust or support of the great Western democracies."[187] Although the General Staff was privately skeptical the Romanian Army could repeat the Finnish Army's success against the Red Army in the "Winter War," it publicly encouraged this belief through its propaganda. The first issue of *Sentinela* appeared Christmas Day to inform and entertain the eight hundred thousand troops guarding the borders that winter. The newspaper's name was defensive, referring to a sentry, and it printed soldiers' letters, poetry, and songs expressing their determination to fight. *Sentinela* lionized the Finns: "For 45 days, in a very small country, about which almost nothing is known, although it is not far from us, a war is being carried out that is amazing the whole world. . . . The example of the Finns proves to the whole world that when a people is imbued with love for country and nation, any attempt to destroy it fails."[188] On 13 March 1940, Finland finally sued for peace, surrendering part of its eastern territory to the Soviet Union. It soon became clear Romania would be next. The Soviet minister of foreign affairs Vyacheslav Molotov revived Soviet claims to Bessarabia just sixteen days later, and Soviet newspapers began condemning Romanian oppression of Bessarabia's inhabitants.[189] If Romania was to have any chance to repeat Finland's feat against the Soviet Union, it needed a fortified frontier like the celebrated Mannerheim Line.

Although propaganda encouraged faith in the so-called Carol Line, Romania's eastern frontier was practically unfortified. The General Staff belatedly began construction of defenses in the spring, using labor detachments consisting primarily of minorities. Minorities were divided into three groups. Category 1 was Romanian neo-Protestants or Eastern Orthodox heretics and schismatics. Category 2 was ethnic minorities deemed friendly, like Czechs, Poles, Yugoslavs, and Turks. Category 3 was ethnic minorities considered unfriendly, like Hungarians, Russians, Ukrainians, Bulgarians, and Jews.[190] Labor detachments were commanded by reserve officers, assisted by Category 1

NCOs and filled with Category 2 and 3 enlisted men.[191] By April, sixty-three labor detachments with seventy thousand troops were laboring on various fortifications.[192] On paper the Carol Line was impressive: casemates, antitank ditches, observation/command posts, protected passages, minefields, and barbed wire. In reality, "Carol's dike," as some mockingly nicknamed it, was mostly unfinished. Construction had started earliest and progressed most in Transylvania, with 316 of 510 casemates completed by June, compared to 127 of 1,033 in Bessarabia and 24 of 498 in Bukovina.[193] Some civil servants and officers reportedly embezzled funds or sold off construction materials.[194] The officer corps' old habit of skimming from the regimental economy died hard.

The Romanian Army also needed to be as large as possible to fend off the Red Army, not to mention the Hungarian and Bulgarian armies, so it expanded to 1.2 million soldiers by summer.[195] It included twenty-one infantry, eight reserve infantry, two guard, one *grăniceri*, three cavalry, and one reserve cavalry divisions; four mixed mountain brigades and one territorial cavalry brigade, plus two fortress, one coastal, and one moto-mechanized brigade; five *grăniceri* regiments, sixty-three labor detachments, and a smattering of other units. Infantry divisions had two artillery regiments with older French guns, plus one battery of antitank guns. Mixed mountain brigades had two to four mountain artillery batteries. Cavalry brigades had one horse cavalry regiment, plus one antitank squadron. The moto-mechanized brigade had one motorized artillery regiment. Corps had one motorized heavy artillery regiment with new Czech guns. Armies controlled a reserve of horse-drawn heavy artillery, with a mixture of old and new guns.[196] The General Inspectorate of Gendarmerie had been transferred from the Ministry of War to the Ministry of Internal Affairs in 1931, but it still provided gendarmes as military police for the army. The Operational Gendarmerie boasted thirteen gendarme battalions, one railway gendarme legion, and one (socially exclusive) "dismounted" gendarme regiment in Bucharest. The Operational Gendarmerie assigned one gendarme battalion to each corps' praetoral service.[197] A praetor was a civil servant with police and judicial authority. The military praetors of the Praetoral Service maintained order in the rear and oversaw courts-martial. The General Staff mobilized seven times as many men as had ever served in the Romanian Army during the interwar years, but only at great cost and by cutting corners.

The General Staff had difficulty equipping, sheltering, and feeding this massive force. A British journalist observed, "Those privates who could afford it hired beds in peasants' cottages; the rest slept in stations, in barns, in cowsheds or in the open. No facilities were provided for washing; they were nearly all covered with lice. Few outside Bucharest had complete uniforms. One would have army boots, another a cap, a third trousers, and a fourth a rifle."[198] She believed troops were "discontented and unhappy," but Army Group No. 1 reported soldiers' morale was "excellent." The report praised a sergeant for refusing a bribe to not break up a Zionist meeting, the 56th *Infanterie* Regiment for feeding needy children, and the 8th Artillery Regiment for donating 2,500 lei to build a school.[199] General mobilization was very costly, adding to special taxes levied since 1935 to pay for rearmament. Officers expected enlisted men, particularly Jews, to make up for the budget shortages. Private Mihail Sebastian, a Jewish writer in Bucharest, noticed the "military rapaciousness" of officers. "If the company is missing a bridle, we buy one ourselves. If there is need of three hundred plates and three hundred sets of cutlery, we buy them ourselves."[200] The General Staff upbraided commanders when it was discovered that some neglected to distribute copies of *Sentinela* to soldiers to make sure they understood the necessity of leaving their homes, paying extra taxes, and enduring shortages.[201]

The General Staff's most difficult challenge may have been finding officers. Not all Category 1 minorities were assigned to labor detachments. George Crișan, a Baptist bank employee in Arad, trained as a TTR sergeant in the winter, and his unit guarded the Yugoslav frontier during the spring. "I had the most unusual experience—living in a ditch or in the fields of wheat or corn. It was a rainy spring. . . . There were hundreds of frogs underfoot. . . . I remember the place in the Bible where I read of God's sending frogs on the Pharaoh's land."[202] He was encouraged to attend an artillery reserve officer school and received his commission in the summer, just eight months after being drafted. Second Lieutenant Crișan's case was not unique, as the Romanian Army rushed to identify and train potential officers. Despite months of mobilization, Romanian troops were in good spirits and expected to defend Greater Romania.

On the Eve

Almost a year into the Second World War, Romania remained neutral, surrounded by threats on all sides. Britain and France were far away and had done little to prevent Poland from being partitioned between Nazi Germany and the USSR and disappearing from the map of Europe. Romania feared it might suffer the same fate. Romanian soldiers were prepared to fend off any threat, but they hated and feared communism much more than fascism. The General Staff expected a Soviet attack, like the one against Finland, and deployed the bulk of the Romanian Army in Bukovina and Bessarabia. Carol

II's royal dictatorship enjoyed widespread support. The Legionary movement had been crushed. General Antonescu was out of favor. The citizenship of a third of Romania's Jews had been revoked, but Jews still served in uniform, and the only camps at this time in Romania were internment camps for Polish soldiers or refugee camps for Polish civilians who had escaped across the border. The German blitzkrieg into France on 10 May put in motion a series of decisions culminating in the Soviet occupation of eastern Romania. This event would change everything and set Romania down the path to holy war.

CHAPTER 3

1940–1941: From Neutral to Axis

On 6 January 1940, King Carol II arrived in Chișinău on Epiphany as part of a three-stop tour of the threatened frontiers to reassure Romanians that the army was ready to defend Greater Romania. His automobile was escorted by cavalrymen with drawn swords to the cathedral, where Romanian Orthodox clergy blessed the waters. The king reviewed a military parade with infantry jogging at double time, cavalry trotting, and vehicles whizzing past to show an aggressive spirit. In full battle dress, Carol II delivered a speech laying claim to Bessarabia, expressing solidarity with minorities, and promising "an enemy will never be able to set foot on what is holy and eternally Romanian!"[1] Yet within six months he ordered the Romanian Army to withdraw from northern Bukovina and Bessarabia without a fight, and two months after that he had also ceded southern Dobruja and northern Transylvania. While the subsequent loss of territory to Bulgaria and Hungary was galling, the unexpected abandonment of lands to the USSR was traumatic. During the withdrawal, Romanian soldiers felt misled and betrayed by leaders, were ridiculed and even assaulted by some civilians, and were harassed and humiliated by Soviet troops. The Romanian Army immediately accused Jews of being ardent communists, and during the withdrawal it targeted Jews for reprisals, although the General Staff intervened when antisemitic violence threatened to spiral out of control. Once the evacuees were safe over the new border, the public reproached the military for its shameful retreat. The General Staff shifted blame onto Jews. Carol II turned to Nazi Germany to salvage the situation, but the price of joining the Axis cost him his crown. In retrospect, the Soviet occupation of northern Bukovina and Bessarabia was the de facto start of Romania's holy war against the supposed threat of Judeo-Bolshevism.[2]

Romanians united under a new monarch, King Mihai I, and a new *conducător*, General Antonescu, who promised to eventually restore Greater Romania, but until then he declared "we must clean wounds, gather strength, pick up honor, and ensure the future."[3] Initially it appeared Romania might become a fascist state, but Antonescu carefully walked a political tightrope and outmaneuvered Legionary efforts to seize power. Under his direction, Romania joined the Axis. Antonescu hated Hungary and was determined to regain northern Transylvania, even by force if necessary, but he despised Judeo-Bolshevism even more and intended to rescue the Romanian Army's sullied honor by reconquering northern Bukovina and Bessarabia. He bet that a war between Nazi Germany and the USSR was inevitable and would allow Romania to take revenge on the Soviets and earn Hitler's support against the Hungarians. Antonescu was far from alone in thinking this way. The men—including former Carlists and former Legionaries—who made up his regime, many leaders of the still outlawed Liberal and National Peasant Parties, and practically the entire officer corps believed in this course of action. Most average Romanians also accepted the Antonescu regime's prioritization of the Soviet threat, given their ideological beliefs, which were reinforced by propaganda. Allying with Nazi Germany radicalized antisemitic policies in Romania, setting the stage for antisemitic violence on a scale greater than ever before. If Carol II and not Antonescu had been the *conducător*, it is possible Romania would not have committed itself so fully to Nazi Germany's war effort, including Hitler's Final Solution, but following the Soviet ultimatum, such a path was not the one likely to be taken.

Soviet Ultimatum

France's surrender prompted the USSR to act on a secret protocol in the Nazi-Soviet nonaggression pact that assigned Bessarabia to the Soviet sphere of influence. Soviet Foreign Minister Molotov delivered Ambassador Gheorghe Davidescu an ultimatum at 10 p.m. on 26 June 1940. Predictably it demanded Romania "return Bessarabia to the Soviet Union at any price," but unexpectedly it also required "the northern part of Bukovina, with its frontiers, according to the adjoining map."[4] The thick pencil line marking the new border left the exact fate of many towns unclear.[5] Molotov insisted on a response in seventeen hours, or the Red Army would invade. At 4 a.m. on 27 June, the General Staff alerted Army Group No. 1, following agreed-upon orders, that "our firm decision that we will fight if we are attacked must come off clearly to the Soviets."[6] Army Group No. 1's twenty infantry and three cavalry divisions, plus one mixed mountain brigade, faced the Soviet Kiev Military District's forty-six infantry (including three motorized) and ten cavalry divisions, plus eleven tank brigades, not to mention overwhelming Soviet air superiority.[7] Despite the odds, some Romanian leaders believed Romania, like Finland, could stymie a Soviet invasion. Davidescu proclaimed, "I do not doubt for a moment that our resistance could paralyze the Soviet forces, which rest in large part on legend and are led by incompetent 'officers.'"[8] At an emergency Crown Council meeting, however, Minister of Defense General Ioan Ilcuș and Chief of Staff General Florea Țenescu emphasized Soviet numbers, incomplete Romanian fortifications, German pressure to accede to the Soviet demands, and probable Hungarian and Bulgarian intervention to argue that resistance was futile.[9] Reconvening, nineteen cabinet ministers voted to accept the Soviet ultimatum, with six opposed and one abstention.[10] Molotov gave Romania just four days to evacuate, even as Soviet forces advanced.

After months of bellicose speeches, Carol II's decision not to fight shocked Romanians. General Nicolae Ciupercă, commanding the Fourth Army in Bessarabia, explained that no withdrawal plans had been made because "there was no indication, however vague, of a possible retreat."[11] At 2 a.m. on 28 June, the first Soviet units crossed the border, fired on by Romanian units in some places. The General Staff issued orders at 4 a.m.: Army Group No. 1 was to evacuate Bessarabia by 12 p.m. on 2 July and establish a defense along the Prut; Cernăuți, Chișinău, and Cetatea Albă should be evacuated by 7 p.m. and surrendered (by mayors not commanders) at 8 p.m. on 28 June; and Romanian commanders must coordinate with Soviet commanders to avoid incidents. The vague orders left much to be improvised and resulted in chaos.[12] Major Nicolae Ciobanu, a III Corps staff officer, recalled that the order "fell among us like a bolt of lightning."[13] Moreover, many commanders did not receive the orders until midday, and it took units hours to pack, meaning many did not start retreating until afternoon.[14] Private Weiss remembered waking up to the noise of wagons and automobiles. "Normally it would be quiet in Ismail [a city on the Danube]. Our landlady, a Romanian officer's wife, told us, 'The Russians crossed the border. Our army had four days to clear out of Bessarabia.'"[15] Constantin Mihalcea, a second lieutenant on the Dniester near Soroca, received orders that his battery would be the

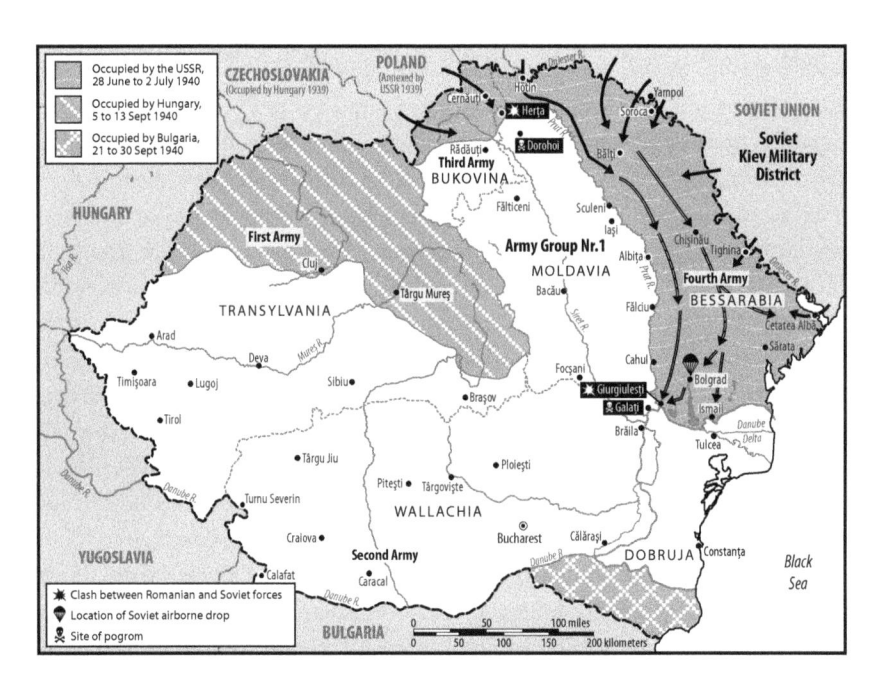

Map 1. Soviet occupation of northern Bukovina and Bessarabia, 1940

rear guard of a cavalry troop, causing him to joke he was "making history," since artillery were protecting cavalry instead of vice versa. His heavily laden column finally departed around 2 p.m.[16] Romanian units grabbed what they could, often looting local businesses, and then stampeded toward border crossings in a race with advancing Soviet units.

The Soviet Kiev Military District's initial objectives were to occupy northern Bukovina and northern Bessarabia while also securing bridgeheads on the Dniester in central and southern Bessarabia. Soviet units simply marched or drove over the border into Bukovina, causing the Third Army, under General Iosif Iacobici, to backpedal southward. In Cernăuți, refugees crowded train stations, Soviet sympathizers celebrated, and soldiers started looting and drinking. When someone scaled the town hall and ripped down the Romanian tricolor to hoist the communist red banner, a soldier shot him dead.[17] Captain Epifanie Cozărăscu recalled, "After the lunch hour the sinister rumbling of Soviet tanks, coming closer and closer, began to be heard."[18] The last overcrowded train left Cernăuți at 2 p.m., and Soviet forces occupied the city three hours later. Meanwhile, Soviet units had crossed a bridge at Hotin and constructed two pontoon bridges at Mogilev and Yampol over the Dniester to seize a bridgehead in northern Bessarabia.[19] The Fourth Army initially retreated west toward Moldavia, but Soviet motorized units began seizing key bridges over the Prut at 12:30 p.m., so at 1 p.m. Army Group No. 1 ordered it to turn south toward Dobruja. Soviet forces secured small bridgeheads on the Dniester all the way down to Cetatea Albă on the Black Sea coast, where pro-Soviet demonstrations started in the afternoon. Concurrently, Soviet columns converged on Bălți in northern Bessarabia.[20] Still heading west, Constantin Mihalcea's column arrived at Bălți at 4 p.m. "Luck had it that I knew the city Bălți very well." His battery navigated city streets without an incident, but once on the highway they encountered "a line of population that beat on me," wounding some horses as they galloped away.[21] Mihalcea arrived at Sculeni to find Soviet tanks blocking the bridge. He ordered his men to gallop straight at the enemy, playing a game of chicken, which his battery won, as they passed unmolested. Other Romanian units were not so lucky and were disarmed before being allowed to continue to retreat.

Incidents between Romanian and Soviet units began to multiply. By evening, the Third Army had halted, and the situation became tense, because no one knew the exact position of the new border in Bukovina. Romanian soldiers fired on Soviet tanks wandering toward Rădăuți, turning them back.[22] At 4 a.m. on 29 June, Soviet armored cars entered Herța, but Romanian soldiers believed it was a mistake because the town and surrounding region, jutting toward Cernăuți, was part of the Old Kingdom. Soviet troops, supposedly guided by local Jews, ordered Captain Ioan Boroș, commanding a battery from the 16th Artillery Regiment, to surrender.[23] He, Second Lieutenant Alexandru Dragomir, and two enlisted soldiers approached to parley. A report claimed they had their hands raised, but an eyewitness said Dragomir fired in the air with a pistol to intimidate the Soviets, as had been done elsewhere, but this time the Soviets shot back, killing both officers and Private Iancu Solomon.[24] Ironically, the Romanian Army's first casualties resisting the Red Army included a Jewish soldier. As the day progressed, the Soviets ignored Romanian proposals to create "evacuation zones" to avoid similar incidents. Soviet motorized units reached Chișinău in the morning, occupying central Bessarabia, and Soviet airborne troops landed around Bolgrad in southern Bessarabia—the twelve-hundred-man Gudarevici detachment landed at airfields or dropped by parachute.[25] The sudden appearance of Soviet airborne troops spooked General Athanasescu then the Cavalry Corps commander, who scurried across the Danube to Galați, where he related wild tales about "terrorist threats."[26] General Ciupercă angrily ordered him to return, to persuade the Soviet airborne commander Colonel I. I. Gudarevici to reopen rail traffic through Bolgrad, so that more soldiers, refugees, and goods could be evacuated. These incidents added to the growing panic among Romanians about a communist fifth column led by Jews in the rear.

Romanian units reported attacks by communist bands consisting of Jews, minorities, and "delinquent Romanians."[27] General Ciupercă claimed, "The population of the cities and towns is completely hostile to us in contrast to that of the villages, sad and benevolent."[28] Although this report was colored by his prejudices against ethnic Russians and Jews, who were concentrated in urban centers, cities and towns full of workers were generally more dangerous for the withdrawing Romanian Army than villages full of Romanian and Ukrainian peasants. A convoy of buses in Soroca had been ambushed on 28 June, leaving four dead; a later biased investigation blamed a communist band of Jewish lawyers.[29] Elvera Reuer, an ethnic German from the town of Arciz in southern Bessarabia, witnessed an attack on retreating Romanian soldiers. On 30 June, she and a friend, along with other ethnic Germans watching "out of curiosity," found ethnic Russians and Jews waiting with flags to welcome Soviet soldiers at the Arciz train station after rumors spread of the Red Army's imminent arrival.[30] Romanian soldiers were loading carts with goods looted from German and Jewish shops. A train arrived; however, only a few "partisans" jumped off, who handed out rifles and then disappeared. As the disappointed crowd dispersed, a sniper shot and wounded a Romanian soldier.[31] By evening Red Army soldiers finally arrived, crowding

Arciz's streets with tanks and trucks, plus carts filled with items seized for themselves after intercepting the Romanian wagon train.[32] Romanian reports quickly embroidered such pinprick attacks by a few disgruntled locals into ambushes by large communist bands.

Romanian units also reported being disarmed and humiliated by Soviet motorized units. Soviet soldiers targeted Romanian officers as capitalist exploiters but treated Romanian enlisted men amiably as downtrodden peasants, even encouraging them to join in humiliating Romanian officers by mocking and spitting on them and tearing epaulets from uniforms.[33] Such degradation was particularly disgraceful to regular officers. After Captain Ioan Iepure's troop from the 3rd *Călăraşi* Regiment was surrounded and disarmed, he and a lieutenant were demeaned by enemy soldiers and locals. Iepure committed suicide upon his release.[34] Captain Arnold Hansenhöhrl of the 10th *Vânători* Regiment also shot himself due to similar "vexations" after his company was disarmed.[35] These suicides were propagandized by the General Staff to inflame fury against the Soviets. Romanian units that had been recruited from Bessarabia experienced high rates of desertion whenever they were intercepted by Soviet columns. The III Corps instructed that "commanders of all regiments will arrange the withdrawal of ammunition distributed to Bessarabian soldiers" because it distrusted their motivation.[36] Officers promised soldiers that they would be allowed to return home after helping to evacuate, but many deserted anyway. Private Weiss, loading boats in Ismail, found excuses to avoid evacuating until he finally decided to desert on 29 June. He and eleven other ethnic Germans sneaked away at dawn, crawling through fields until feeling safe enough to walk. "We didn't feel proud to be deserters from our country."[37] If a Romanian unit was halted by a Soviet motorized unit, Soviet officers urged Romanian enlisted men to go home. An officer reported, "All Bessarabian soldiers, who threw down their weapons, took with them all equipment with which they had been equipped, even taking carts with horses, loading the baggage of officers and soldiers from [the Old] Kingdom, they put it in the carts and all left for their homes in Bessarabia."[38] The 6th *Roşiori* Regiment's soldiers, after reaching Moldavia, demanded to be released, leaving just officers and a handful of enlisted men from the Old Kingdom.[39] For others, the choice between home or nation was more difficult. First Lieutenant Ştefan Airinei recalled, "Every one of them, I believe, had to decide alone if they were going to remain or cross the Prut with us. . . . I almost physically felt the pain of my heart breaking. What historical moment was I living . . . that of 1812, when Bessarabia was torn [from Romania by Russia] the first time, did it feel the same then?"[40] Romanians often expressed much sympathy for *basarabeni* who stayed behind, but little for minorities, especially Jews.

Soldiers' belief in the threat of Judeo-Bolshevism meant they singled out Jews for special opprobrium and began shooting Jews as alleged communists. Army reports depicted mournful *basarabeni*, passive minorities, and actively hostile Jews.[41] Jews supposedly acted like communists "even before" the Soviets arrived: wearing red cockades, blocking trains, degrading the Romanian flag, desecrating churches, attacking Romanian civil servants, and terrorizing *basarabeni*.[42] Indeed, a few Jewish self-defense groups sported red ribbons, and some Jews joined the crowds humiliating Romanian officers.[43] However, antisemitic fantasy fueled by anticommunist hysteria coalesced into a myth of Jewish-communist treachery embraced by Romanians. Commanders reported encounters with Jewish communists beginning on day two of the retreat. The 11th *Călărași* Regiment claimed it fought off a communist band outside Bălți, leaving "a few dead and wounded Jews."[44] General Constantin Pantazi reported that when the 3rd Cavalry Division turned west to avoid Soviet parachute infantry in Bolgrad, it was ambushed by "communists/ terrorists" while crossing the Prut and returned fire, resulting in ten to fifteen dead locals.[45] General I. Mihail Racoviță believed that, as the 2nd Cavalry Division passed through southern Bessarabia, "enclosed trucks were probably transporting terrorist bands, which together with Jews, agitate the population in villages through which we must pass and prepare attacks and looting of columns and trains."[46] The Romanian Army had requisitioned horses and carts from locals, which were often laden with looted goods, so peasants (often including *basarabeni*) organized to reclaim what they felt was rightfully their property. The 6th *Roșiori* Regiment commander reported, "[Peasants] gathered on the margins of the road and on the edges of the forest; as a beast lying in wait for his prey, they waited for the Soviet tanks to come and to disarm our units."[47] Soldiers comforted themselves by blaming Jews and communists for displays of disloyalty on the part of minorities and especially *basarabeni*. Following the withdrawal, the General Staff ordered commanders to gather evidence about the "abuses committed against elements of the army, State, and civilian population by the Jewish and communist population under the protection, or at the urging of the army of the USSR."[48] Commanders were only too eager to tell the General Staff exactly what it wanted to hear.

On 30 June, Ambassador Davidescu convinced Foreign Minister Molotov to delay the evacuation deadline by a day. General Ciupercă ordered the Fourth Army to save as much matériel as possible and form strong rear guards under bold officers to enforce the agreed timeline. Also, he emphasized, "Any attempt at rebellion by the population will be sanctioned as such," thus authorizing summary execution of alleged rebels.[49] Romanian units had limited success slowing Soviet progress the next day. Second Lieutenant Ion Iliescu, leading a company from the 2nd *Dorobanți* Regiment, set up a roadblock and halted a Soviet column by sheer bravado.[50] Yet this was an isolated success, and Soviet motorized units could quickly find alternate routes around such obstacles. Additionally, Soviet commanders were uncooperative. General Athanasescu slunk back from Galați to Bolgrad to negotiate the release of trains. Colonel Gudarevici claimed ignorance of any deadline extension, and then reneged on a promise to unblock some trains.[51] The Fourth Army started mining bridges on the Prut and Danube, as Ciupercă feared the USSR might attempt to overrun Moldavia. Romanian fears that Soviet troops might not stop and reports of communist bands of Jews contributed to an explosion of antisemitic violence in Moldavia.

Massacre and Pogrom

Pogroms usually break out when the state is weak.[52] The situation in frontier cities like Rădăuți, Dorohoi, Iași, and Galați, which all had large Jewish communities, rapidly spun out of control. Gheorghe Ioniță, a high school student in Iași, which was now fifteen kilometers from the frontier, remembered, "The news that the Russians crossed the border before the deadline established even by them aroused indignation and panic. Will they stop at the Prut? Or will they cross further to the Siret? Skepticism and fear wreaked havoc."[53] Furthermore, frustrated soldiers and frightened refugees crowded into cities, bringing with them lurid stories of Jews raping women, communist bands attacking refugees, Jews torturing priests, and other Soviet atrocities. Newspapers reported that Jews led pro-Soviet celebrations, threw stones at retreating soldiers, and perpetrated other perfidious crimes.[54] Additionally, these cities were flooded with people from northern Bukovina and Bessarabia who had suddenly become émigrés and wanted to reach their home country before the border closed. Angry soldiers, panicked locals, fearful refugees, and anxious émigrés made for a volatile mixture that threatened to overwhelm city authorities in Moldavia and southern Bukovina as antisemitic violence escalated.

On 30 June, a massacre erupted in Galați, where General Ciupercă had established the Fourth Army headquarters. The Danube port city of one hundred thousand people, including thirteen thousand Jews, had become crowded with refugees, a mixture of Old Kingdom civil servants, local wealthy landowners or professionals (including minorities), and humble *basarabeni*, heading west, and émigrés, mostly Jews and other minorities but also *basarabeni*, heading east.[55] The authorities viewed the émigrés, especially

Jews, as communists. Soviet parachutists' seizure of Bolgrad had created a backlog of two thousand people at the Galați train station.[56] The station gendarme commander, citing security concerns, ordered Jews separated and marched to an empty field nearby to be guarded until rail traffic resumed. Accounts are contradictory, but approximately one thousand men, women, and children were left exposed without food or water in stifling heat until late afternoon. The crowd became tense and demanded to be released. Suddenly, a pistol shot rang out, perhaps fired by an officer to intimidate the Jews, causing nervous gendarmes to shoot indiscriminately.[57] The shots panicked people in the nearby station, and the situation worsened when another officer decided to shoot his pistol into the air to calm the crowd.[58] Meanwhile, some Jews escaped, pursued by gendarmes shouting about Jewish-communist snipers firing on them from nearby houses, who were soon joined by civilians. One merchant caved in the skulls of several Jews who had ducked into his shop to hide.[59] The initial reports described the hour-long massacre as an attempted Jewish-communist uprising, so Ciupercă diverted two infantry battalions already en route to quell another reported Jewish-communist disturbance across the river in Reni, where soldiers also killed dozens of Jews.[60] A postwar investigation cited 400 dead, but at the time, Radio Sofia reported 280 Jews killed in a "battle" in Galați.[61] Even as that broadcast went out on 1 July, a pogrom unfolded in another city far to the north.

The day in Dorohoi began somberly because Captain Boroș and Private Solomon were to be buried after their bodies arrived from Herța. The city of 15,800, including 5,800 Jews, now lay twenty kilometers behind the border in Bukovina. It had been an interwar LANC and then Legionary stronghold.[62] The 8th Artillery, 3rd *Grăniceri*, and 29th *Infanterie* Regiments (the last the local regiment, with many Jews in its ranks) were all crowded in the city. Soldiers and refugees spoke darkly about communist fifth columnists. Witnesses later claimed that soldiers had marked Christian homes with the letter *C* or told Christians to display crosses or icons in windows, but this seems to have been a rumor spread after the fact.[63] Dorohoi was calm until 2 p.m., when the honor guard's salute at the Jewish cemetery rang out. The 29th *Infanterie* Regiment had sent ten Jewish soldiers under a Christian NCO to Solomon's burial. Some later claimed Legionaries fired the shots as a prearranged signal, but this seems unlikely. The noise attracted the unwanted attention of some 3rd *Grăniceri* Regiment troops nearby. When the Jewish soldiers exited the cemetery, they were halted by an officer commanding a platoon of *grăniceri* who ordered the Jews disarmed and shot as communist snipers. *Grăniceri* began searching for and killing other supposed Jewish communists, starting with eight women, three children, and an old man in the funeral parlor.[64] The pogrom spread as frenzied soldiers attacked Jews, looted stores, broke into homes, and murdered anyone deemed suspicious. Dentist George Brăilescu-Gotlieb, while seeing a patient, heard isolated shots, which soon became more regular. Suddenly, soldiers burst into his office and dragged him into the street, driving him with rifle blows to a headquarters set up in a Jewish school, where he joined twenty-five other Jews gathered for interrogation.[65] They were accused of firing on soldiers. A machine gun squad, awaiting the order to shoot, stood outside, with corpses already splayed before it; but after a search uncovered no weapons "or something compromising," the captives were released.[66] Brăilescu-Gotlieb was lucky, as proof of fifth-column activity could be mundane objects: a radio, "communist" books, red cloth (allegedly to signal Soviet pilots), or wire (construed as an improvised radio).[67] A 29th *Infanterie* Regiment patrol sent to investigate the disturbance nearly had its Jewish soldiers murdered too, but its officer prevented more military fratricide. Bestial crimes occurred over the next three hours: beards ripped out, ears sliced off for jewelry, breasts slashed, and genitals mutilated. A sudden storm drove soldiers from the streets around 5 p.m., momentarily halting the violence, but it took several more hours to restore order.[68] Officially fifty-two Jews were killed and seventeen wounded, but other records estimate two hundred victims.[69] The Dorohoi pogrom was just the worst case of antisemitic violence being spread by retreating soldiers in Bukovina.

A pogrom atmosphere spread along routes of retreat and railroads, resulting in scores of victims. A few atrocities were later investigated. On 30 June in Costănaț, two soldiers murdered a Jewish soldier; on 1 July in Șerbăuți, a gendarme shot four Jews; on 2 July in Gărurani, soldiers executed a Jewish couple; the same day in Comănești, 14th *Infanterie* Regiment soldiers killed five Jews; and again the same day in Solonet 1st Military Police Company gendarmes murdered two Jews.[70] Jewish soldiers on trains were particularly vulnerable. If lucky, they were disarmed, beaten, and turned over to the authorities; but if unlucky, they were thrown from moving trains, shot, and even bayoneted—the violence often urged on by civilians.[71] "We have saved them from reserve duty," some joked after shooting two Jewish soldiers thrown from a train.[72] For days, injured, dying, and dead Jews were discovered along railways in southern Bukovina, Moldavia, and even Transylvania.[73] Most antisemitic violence was spontaneous, but in some cases it was directed by mid-ranking officers. Major Valeriu Carp, leading a battalion in the 16th *Infanterie* Regiment as they withdrew through Bukovina, ordered troops to round up "suspicious" Jews from towns, beginning in Storojineț. On 30 June, in Ciudei, a town about to fall under Soviet occupation, his soldiers arrested Jews accused of being snipers, interrogated them, and executed eight on the spot.[74] The General Staff grew alarmed by multiplying reports of soldiers engaging in antisemitic violence.

The General Staff feared future pogroms could become "true uprisings."[75] Senior officers recalled how quickly local antisemitic mobs had transformed into a national peasant uprising in 1907. A pogrom threatened to break out in Iași, where more than a third of the one hundred thousand inhabitants were Jewish, after soldiers at the Prut crossing in nearby Ungheni started assaulting Jews. Soviet troops had started stripping refugees of goods at the border, so Romanian soldiers began doing the same to émigrés, but shakedowns easily turned into beatings.[76] The antisemitic violence soon spread from Ungheni to Iași, where soldiers and civilians attacked Jews and Jewish businesses. The Fourth Army warned on 2 July, "In general, the army and the population evacuated from Bessarabia are expressing revolt against the Jews. More serious anti-semitic demonstrations on the part of the army not excluded."[77] In response, General Țenescu ordered "severe measures in order to stop these actions [pogroms], which could have unfavorable effects in the current situation."[78] The General Staff acted as a brake on antisemitic violence, not to protect Jews but to preserve order. After learning of the 3rd *Grăniceri* Regiment's murderous rampage in Dorohoi, Țenescu declared, "Even if these excesses on the part of the *grăniceri* soldiers might be justified, as a reaction to the violent events [*bruscările*] suffered during the withdrawal from Bukovina, nevertheless they cannot be tolerated under any condition because such events can degenerate into actions with grave nature and consequences, the first being the weakening of military discipline in units."[79] The Romanian Army needed to maintain discipline to resist the Red Army if it crossed the Prut. Additionally, Romanian leaders believed Soviet leaders might use pogroms as a pretext to occupy Moldavia. The previous year, the Soviets justified occupying eastern Poland by arguing the "Polish Government has disintegrated" and claiming "kindred Ukrainian and Belorussian people" needed Soviet protection.[80] The USSR's "friendship of peoples" included Jews. Moreover, army intelligence claimed Jews from Moldavia were in Bessarabia trying to coax Red Army commanders to intervene and cross the Prut to halt pogroms.[81] The General Staff ordered commanders to rein in soldiers and organize an investigation into the Dorohoi pogrom.

Meanwhile, the last Romanian troops withdrew from southern Bessarabia. On 2 July, a midday skirmish between Romanian and Soviet forces occurred at Giurgiulești. The Fourth Army had established a defensive perimeter outside the town, located on the Danube near Galați, to hold on to the road and rail bridges until the extended withdrawal deadline the next day, so that more refugees and matériel could be evacuated. Soviets commanders were determined to respect the original deadline, however. Soviet tanks panicked Romanian infantry, capturing a company. Still holding the bridges, the Cavalry Corps negotiated the turnover of prisoners (including two wounded) and then dynamited both bridges at 6:30 p.m.[82] General Ciupercă informed the Soviet commander this was "a regrettable mistake" but at the same time pleaded for permission from Army Group No. 1 to demolish bridges on the Prut.[83] Ciupercă's fear that Soviet Kiev Military District forces might advance into Moldavia were overblown, but this was not clear at the time.

The Romanian Army set to work reasserting control over scattered and demoralized units following the withdrawal from northern Bukovina and Bessarabia. Some commanders requested permission to reintroduce flogging to restore discipline, but General Țenescu argued the situation did not yet merit this, and moreover "ten days of effectively executed incarceration constitutes . . . a physical punishment much greater than 25 lashes."[84] On 3 July, the Mountain Corps ordered round-the-clock gendarme patrols "to prevent possible disorder in Vatra Dornei as well as attacks against Jews."[85] The same precautions were taken in Iași, so on 5 July, gendarmes intervened when soldiers attacked a Jewish innkeeper.[86] Commanders' efforts to restore discipline prevented more spontaneous pogroms, but sanctioned reprisals did not stop. On 6 July, after reaching Zaharești, Major Carp ordered thirty-four Jews who had been arrested in various villages and dragged off by his unit during the withdrawal to be executed as communists.[87] They were tortured to elicit confessions, or simply out of sadism, and two Jewish soldiers joined the firing squad, likely as a loyalty test.[88] Isolated attacks continued for days, as individual soldiers roamed the countryside and rode the rails. Many soldiers resented efforts to restore discipline, and some even prevented comrades from being punished for attacking Jews; some of Carp's soldiers, for example, sprang three fellow soldiers from the Comănești gendarme post who had been jailed for "antisemitic activity."[89] General Constantin Sănătescu, commanding the VIII Corps, led the investigation into the Dorohoi pogrom. He pinned the blame on two captains, neither of whom was seriously punished, and reprimanded the 3rd *Grăniceri* Regiment. "I am surprised by these acts of banditry committed by what I thought were elite units," Sănătescu remarked with feigned outrage.[90] With discipline more or less restored, the Romanian Army turned to improving morale.

Wounded Honor

The Romanian Army suffered losses during the withdrawal from northern Bukovina and Bessarabia, but the greatest damage was to its pride. Army

Group No. 1 counted nine killed, five wounded, and 62,503 missing (nearly all locals who deserted), plus 67,079 rifles, 6,134 pistols, 1,080 light machine guns, 277 machine guns, 43 mortars, 147 artillery pieces, and mountains of ammunition lost.[91] Greater Romania shrank by 59,762 square kilometers and 3,776,000 inhabitants, although 200,000 refugees fled across the border.[92] Soldiers now had to confront accusations of panicked flight and dereliction of duty.[93] Iași teenager Gheorghe Ioniță recalled, "Soldiers spilled onto the streets with weapons, cannons, vehicles, horses and carts. People looked at them with rebuke. Why were they not allowed to fight? Perhaps they would have died under the folds of the tricolor flag, but [dying for one's country] has been the soldier's mission since the beginning of time. How will they, and their posterity, bear the burden of abandoning the holy Romanian earth . . . without a fight?"[94] The Romanian Army's dishonor was even greater in light of the Red Army's recent rough handling by the Finnish Army, which led most Romanians to view the Soviet colossus as having feet of clay and to expect that their own countrymen should fight like the Finns.

The General Staff tried directing soldiers' anger toward Judeo-Bolshevism instead of at Carol II. In the first issue after the retreat, *Sentinela*'s editors reassured readers that the decision to abandon the Herța region, northern Bukovina, and Bessarabia without a fight was not "from cowardice," because the Romanian soldier "was not and never will be cowardly."[95] A week later, in the comic strip in *Sentinela*, Private Neață asks his friend Private Stan, "What is this thing communism?" Stan directs Neață to hand over his cap, shirt, and pants. "Why are you making me do this Stan," Neață protests; "you are not a doctor!" With Neață stripped nearly naked, Stan replies, "Look, this is communism Neață, you get it? What is mine is mine and what is yours is also mine. So now we are comrades." "Now I understand brother Stan, so if my old lady [*muierea*] would be here, you would take her too!"[96] Most army propaganda was not so lighthearted. Flyers were posted in barracks with drawings of Jews directing Soviet soldiers to loot Romanian homes, Romanian children being kidnapped by Soviet soldiers to raise them as communists, a Jewish-communist vampire bat flying over a devastated city, a demonic-looking Jew instructing a Soviet soldier to hack apart a cross, a Jewish capitalist leading a chained Soviet bear into Bessarabia, and a well-dressed Romanian soldier mocking a disheveled Soviet soldier across the Prut that Soviet tanks "were old and re-painted . . . and even more . . . you don't know how to drive them."[97] Army propaganda fueled hatred for Jews and communism, but Romanians did not unite under the king because they increasingly blamed him, his "Jewish" mistress, and his camarilla for the cowardly decision to withdraw, especially once he surrendered more territory.

FIGURE 2. "Quickly they came and quickly they will leave. Have patience!" So urges this flyer that, along with others with similar messages, was posted in soldiers' quarters after the Romanian Army's flight from northern Bukovina and Bessarabia ahead of the Red Army. Army propaganda already promised vengeance against Jews and communists. Courtesy of Arhivele Militare Naționale Române.

Royal Dictatorship to Military Dictatorship

Carol II desperately attempted to woo Nazi Germany to shield Romania from the Soviet Union. On 4 July, he appointed Ion Gigurtu, a pro-Nazi industrialist, as prime minister. A week later Romania left the League of Nations. Hoping to rally popular support for the king, Gigurtu persuaded Horia Sima, who had claimed leadership over the Legionary movement, and two other Iron Guardists to join his government, but they resigned within days, saying they could not work with the king.[98] Both longtime opponents and former supporters hurled abuse at Carol II. Iuliu Maniu and Gheorghe I. Brătinau wrote to the king, "The Romanian people . . . cannot understand why, when the army had to defend the country's frontiers, it was ordered to withdraw in haste and give the enemy a free hand to occupy the two provinces, leaving

1940–1941: FROM NEUTRAL TO AXIS 79

FIGURE 3. "I'm leaving everything! God is great! . . . and He will make good in time . . . the day of reckoning will come!" says a Romanian peasant watching his homestead being looted as a Soviet soldier gruffly yells "Move!" (in Russian) and grabs him to be deported or forced into the Red Army. Meanwhile, two Jews watch mockingly, one holding a whip. Army propaganda quickly spread such atrocity propaganda about the fate of Romanians in Soviet-occupied northern Bukovina and Bessarabia. Courtesy of Arhivele Militare Naționale Române.

three million Romanians to the mercy of the USSR."[99] General Antonescu penned a letter condemning the king's decision too, while also trying to obtain a ministerial appointment. Unsuccessful, he started scheming with Sima, resulting in his own arrest on 9 July.[100] His allies persuaded German diplomats to warn the king that the general's "accidental death" could harm German-Romanian relations.[101] Therefore, two days later Antonescu was put under house arrest in the isolated Bistrița monastery in Wallachia. He resigned from the military on 12 July. Meanwhile, Carol II pleaded for Hitler to send a German military mission to Romania. On 9 August, Gigurtu's government introduced new antisemitic laws, based on the Nazi Nuremberg Laws, using a "biological conception of the nation" to define who was a Jew and forbidding intermarriage between Jews and Christians.[102] Nazi Germany delayed allying with Romania despite Carol II's initiatives because Hungary and Bulgaria, which Hitler also desired as allies, revived respective claims on Transylvania and Dobruja. Romania had to make territorial concessions to join the Axis. Negotiations with Bulgaria progressed, but talks with Hungary deadlocked, requiring Nazi Germany and Fascist Italy to intervene.[103] On 30 August, the Second Vienna Award gave a swath of northern Transylvania to Hungary. Hitler and Benito Mussolini threatened to give Hungary even more if Carol II did not agree, but they also promised, if he cooperated, to guarantee Romania's revised borders and send Axis military missions to Romania to deter the Soviet Union. Carol II felt he had no choice but to accept the Second Vienna Award.

The announcement that half of *Ardeal*, won at such great cost in the last war, would also be surrendered without a fight caused protests across the region. Large demonstrations of *ardeleni* occurred in Brașov, Cluj, Oradea, Sighișoara, and Bucharest, causing Prime Minister Gigurtu to resign on 4 September.[104] Protesters accused Carlists of embezzling or squandering the military budget, shouting, "Where are the planes for which we paid [special tax] stamps? Where are the arms for which we paid the [army] endowment tax? Where are the munitions for which we paid the rearmament taxes?"[105] Carol II now summoned General Antonescu from house arrest and asked him to form a government.[106] The general's reputation for honor and incorruptibility stood in stark contrast to the king's reputation for self-interest and corruption. Additionally, Antonescu could command the respect of the military, which was increasingly mutinous, as some anti-Carlist officers openly denounced Carol II while others clandestinely armed Legionaries.[107] Antonescu refused to be a figurehead and demanded dictatorial powers. Carol II agreed, on the conditions that he needed to cosign any fundamental changes to the structure of the state and that he remained head of the army. On 5 September, Antonescu became prime minister.[108] Almost immediately, however, he demanded that Carol II abdicate, citing an alleged assassination plot against himself by the king and Carlist officers.[109] General Dumitru Coroamă, whom Antonescu had just appointed commander of the Capital Military Command (controlling police and military forces in Bucharest), refused to disperse demonstrators outside the palace who were baying for Carol II's head.[110] Antonescu again requested that the king abdicate, saying he could not assure his safety if the king remained.[111] Early on 6 September, Carol II succumbed and left for exile with Elena Lupescu and a few other intimates. Mihai I succeeded to the throne, but Antonescu became *conducător*. Ironically, his first major action was enforcing the Second Vienna Award.

The evacuation from northern Transylvanian beginning on 5 September was much more organized than the retreat from northern Bukovina and Bessarabia. First, the withdrawal was not unexpected, coming after weeks of negotiations. Second, the Hungarian Army lacked armored and motorized units, so it could not outpace the Romanian Army. Third, Romania and Hungary agreed to a phased occupation, with evacuation zones (Hungarian aircraft could not even fly over Romanian routes) designed to prevent incidents between Romanian and Hungarian soldiers. Officers also preemptively disarmed and dismissed local soldiers so they could not desert with equipment or goods; any demobilized *ardeleni* who wanted to could follow their unit later and rejoin the colors in the Old Kingdom.[112] Fourth, few *ardeleni* joined pro-Hungarian celebrations; in fact they organized pro-war protests in cities like Cluj, shouting "We want war!"[113] Fifth, to most Romanians, the prospect of Romanians living under Hungarian rule was much less disturbing than Romanians living under Soviet rule. A Ukrainian women who fled Soviet-occupied Bessarabia reported a topsy-turvy nightmare of crosses and icons destroyed, summary executions, shortages of food and goods, Jews in prominent positions, Jews seizing abandoned Romanian property, and Jewish women operating businesses "free to do whatever they want."[114] In contrast, Hungary respected class, religion, and property and discriminated against Jews. Plus, Romanians had lived under Hungarian rule once before, and could do so again. Sergeant Ioan T. Lungu, a gendarme with a military police unit, visited his family near Oradea before leaving for southern Transylvania. He told his parents, "Be calm, because the Hungarians won't stay long around here and again we will be together!"[115] (He would not see his parents again for seventeen years after surviving the fighting, a prisoner of war camp, and a communist prison.) The Romanian Army preserved its honor during the withdrawal. Captain Alexandru Ionescu Saint-Cyr remembered when he observed Hungarian flags replace Romanian flags in Cluj: "Then I was overcome by [a] thought which I had to give voice: 'Do not worry, now we leave, but surely we will return.'"[116] Amid such drama, Romania's agreement with Bulgaria on 7 September ceding part of Dobruja barely registered with the public. Dobruja had been part of Bulgaria until northern Dobruja was granted to Romania in 1878, and southern Dobruja had been seized by Romania in 1913 after the Second Balkan War. Thereafter Dobruja was briefly reoccupied by Bulgaria from 1916 to 1918, before Romania reclaimed ownership. By giving up southern Dobruja, some 6,921 square kilometers and 425,000 people, and implementing a population exchange, Romania hoped to permanently end any border dispute. Army propaganda never told this to soldiers. On 8 September, *Sentinela* printed a new version of an old First World War song: "Land, you still seek neighbor, Land! / You want us to give you our land, / Because we have enough... and Lord! / If we don't have enough [land] to make you a grave!"[117] All "lost territories" were marked in black on the map of Greater Romania in every subsequent issue, but southern Dobruja was always a distant third to northern Transylvania and northern Bukovina and Bessarabia. The withdrawal from northern Transylvania was not without difficulties: the military had to abandon much matériel, refugees crowded highways, and rumors of Hungarian atrocities swirled. Romania lost another 42,243 square kilometers and 2,628,238 people, while 234,714 refugees evacuated over the frontier.[118] Momentarily, it seemed General Antonescu might not survive the loss of northern Transylvania.

The new *conducător* quickly consolidated his hold on power, however. Iuliu Maniu and Gheorghe I. Brătianu attacked General Antonescu for accepting the Second Vienna Award.[119] "I did not have the whole army on my side," Antonescu admitted later.[120] Therefore, he moved to put a trusted comrade in charge of his safety. General Pantazi, a fellow cavalryman from an old military family, had stood by Antonescu when Carol II's ire caused other officers to treat him as a pariah.[121] The day Antonescu drove Carol II into exile, he made Pantazi sub-secretary to the minister of defense and commander of the Capital Military Command.[122] With his loyal lieutenant on guard against a Carlist countercoup, Antonescu moved to form a government. He invited Maniu and Brătianu, but both refused to work with Horia Sima.[123] The *conducător* wanted the Legion for popular support and to prove his fascist bona fides to the Axis. On 9 September, he declared the National Legionary State. Sima became vice–prime minister. Iron Guardists held the ministries of Internal Affairs (shared by Antonescu and retired general Constantin Petrovicescu), External Affairs, Public Instruction, Communication, and Health. Antonescu also held the post of minister of defense, but Pantazi performed the day-to-day work. Legionaries replaced Carlists as prefects in Romania's fifty counties.[124] Thus, Antonescu maneuvered the Legion into backing his decision to accept the Second Vienna Award.

The loss of territories to the USSR, Hungary, and Bulgaria significantly reduced the Romanian Army's strength. The withdrawal from northern Transylvania was completed on 13 September. The turnover of southern Dobruja began on 21 September and ended ten days later without incident. During the following month, most of the Romanian and Bulgarian populations in Dobruja were exchanged, although negotiations over the remaining Romanians and Bulgarians dragged on for over a year.[125] The Romanian Army lost nearly 378,000 soldiers who remained behind in northern Bukovina and

Bessarabia, northern Transylvania, and southern Dobruja. As one historian wrote, "A major defeat had been inflicted on the Romanian Army without it being able to fire a shot."[126] Once the withdrawals were completed, the General Staff moved to consolidate and reorganize the reduced Romanian Army. Three infantry and reserve infantry divisions were disbanded. Additionally, every remaining infantry or reserve infantry division was reduced by up to three battalions. The four cavalry divisions and cavalry brigade were reorganized into six cavalry brigades. There was a silver lining. The Romanian Army became more ethnically homogeneous because many of the soldiers who stayed behind were minorities, thus increasing primary group cohesion. Romanian soldiers united under General Antonescu in preparing for a confrontation with Judeo-Bolshevism.

The *conducător* vowed to redeem Greater Romania, but he urged patience until after he purified the country of Carlist corruption. In *Sentinela*, General Antonescu told soldiers they had to bear the burden of the Second Vienna Award not only for the good of Romania but of Europe, because Christian states needed to unite against Judeo-Bolshevism and not fight each other.[127] He demanded iron discipline of them, calling it his regime's "first law," and inveighed against the "inner enemy" of disorder.[128] *Arma Cuvântului* instructed chaplains to preach to soldiers that "the providential General [Antonescu]" would soon "create another country, another soul, another Romanian conscience."[129] Queen Mother Helen returned from exile to join Mihai I. The National Legionary State celebrated cleansing the monarchy of Carol II and Elena Lupescu, and *Sentinela* extolled Legionary virtues of discipline, duty, self-sacrifice, and order.[130] Antonescu purged Carlist senior officers from the Romanian Army, claiming, as General Pantazi recalled, "[They] contributed through their stance to the moral state that caused the turning back [*carmirea*] of the country's borders, without the army firing so much as a shot."[131] He knew, however, that banishing Carlism alone would not be enough fulfill his promise to return the lost territories.

General Antonescu believed Nazi Germany would soon defeat Britain and thus become the sole arbiter over Europe. The *conducător* asked the führer to send a German military mission soon after implementing the Second Vienna Award. He trusted that the presence of German soldiers would deter further Soviet demands. He also wanted German advisers to train the Romanian Army for a future conflict. Teodor Halic was in Arad when the German 13th Motorized Infantry Division arrived after entering Romania on 12 October. Halic associated these Germans with local ethnic Germans— who he believed were honest, clean, educated, and pragmatic—and his initial impression was "very good."[132] A British journalist attributed Romanians' lack of animosity toward the Germans to apathy, as the former were "past feeling anything or caring about anything" following recent events.[133] Actually, Romanians were comforted by the presence of each German tank, gun, truck, and man. Another British observer in Bucharest noted that "Rumanians were certainly not too depressed about the arrival of the German armored might," and Romanian army intelligence smugly reported that Soviet plans "were thwarted" and Soviet commanders "were no longer talking about crossing into Moldavia."[134] On 10 November, after arriving in Bucharest, German soldiers had a chance to earn Romanian goodwill by helping in rescue efforts after an earthquake struck the country. Of course, Nazi Germany's role in the loss of northern Transylvania prompted some averted gazes or thrown bottles, but few Romanians were ardent anti-Nazis.[135] As a peasant in Transylvania explained, "We chose Germany because we hate and fear Bolshevism and want to continue to have our own plots of land to till."[136] Consequently, on 23 November, Romania signed the Tripartite Pact.

While the two dictators cemented an alliance between their countries, General Antonescu and Horia Sima's National Legionary State was fraying at the seams. Sima had begun building a fascist dual state, with parallel Legionary police, courts, press, charities, and other organizations that competed with the state, fostering confusion and chaos.[137] Antonescu was not pleased: "If everyone interferes, if everyone gives orders and intervenes—according to one's own free will and time—the collapse, under the present internal and external circumstances of the country, will come most rapidly."[138] Iron Guardists had also become increasingly indiscriminate in employing violence against other Romanians. Initially, Legionaries mostly targeted Jews as part of extreme Romanianization, taking over businesses, extorting cash, stealing goods, and seizing property.[139] Legionary violence against Jews was supported, or at least tolerated, by most Romanians, but an influx of opportunists into the Legion meant it became increasingly arbitrary and greedy as many sought to profit from their membership. Moreover, Iron Guardists began attacking non-Jews like Carlists, beggars, liberals, gamblers, socialists, drunks, minorities, anyone deemed suspicious, and of course communists.[140] Legionary anarchy alienated the public, particularly the middle class, civil servants, and the officer corps. On the night of 26 November, Legionaries enraged by the approaching anniversary of the murder of Corneliu Codreanu broke into the Jilava Prison outside Bucharest, killing sixty-five prominent Carlists, while other groups murdered Nicolae Iorga, a respected historian, and Virgil Madgearu, an accomplished economist, in their homes—both were ardent nationalists but had been leaders of the Front of National Rebirth.[141] Now no one seemed safe from Iron Guardist violence. Antonescu and Sima appeared publicly together for the last time four days later, at Codreanu's reburial ceremony.

Signs of a coming Nazi-Soviet war started appearing in Romania after the *conducător* and the führer's first meeting the day prior to Romania joining the Axis. On 1 December, *Sentinela* proclaimed, "The German soldier knows he fights for a new order of honesty and work, not just for [his] nation, but for the many. The victory that he achieved over those corrupted [nations] also caught in the nets of Judaism—is the victory for honor and [the] happiest country in [the] world."[142] The next day Marshal Wilhelm Keitel, the chief of the German High Command of the Armed Forces (OKW), held talks with General Antonescu. Keitel wanted information on the Romanian Army's capabilities, ostensibly for defensive reasons but actually for offensive plans already in the works by the German High Command of the Army (OKH) to invade the USSR, so he was pleased when Antonescu suggested an Axis preemptive attack and claimed that the Romanian Army, with the help of a couple of German motorized divisions, could break through Soviet defenses and march on Kiev. On 5 December, an OKW conference agreed that Romania's participation in Nazi Germany's attack on the USSR was no longer a question of if but to what extent.[143] On the same day, the Romanian Army banned Jews from military service. On 18 December, Hitler commanded the OKW and OKH to begin final preparations; his order assumed that Romania would act as a base for the German Army on the southern flank, and that the Romanian Army would support the invasion. German planners did not believe the Romanian Army capable of much offensively, so they decided against having it join in the initial attacks.[144] Hitler sent the German 16th Panzer Division to safeguard Romania's vital oil fields, which increased the German Military Mission to twenty-two thousand soldiers.[145] *Sentinela*'s Christmas and New Year's issue told soldiers that while 1940 had passed "like an ugly dream," 1941 brought "resurrection's light" to redeem Greater Romania.[146] Teams from the Todt Organization (a Nazi paramilitary engineering organization) reinforced bridges in northern Moldavia to support German panzers. General Erik Hansen, commanding the German Military Mission, requested the General Staff use its resources to do likewise throughout the remainder of Romania. He also organized war games with Romanian commanders to familiarize them with German operations.[147] German advisers started training the 5th, 6th, and 13th Infantry Divisions, which were dubbed the "model divisions." Nevertheless, these developments did not indicate to Romania that a gigantic invasion of the USSR by Nazi Germany was just months away.

A second meeting between the *conducător* and the führer on 14 January 1941 went well, convincing General Antonescu he did not need Horia Sima any longer.[148] On 20 January, after a German officer was shot in Bucharest by a Greek assassin (who may have been a British agent), Antonescu accused General Petrovicescu of incompetence and removed him as co-minister of internal affairs.[149] Legionaries took to the streets in Bucharest and other cities in protest of the decision. In the capital, three thousand Legionaries occupied police headquarters, seized the radio station, and threw up roadblocks. Iron Guardists believed Antonescu's move against the Legion was a "Judeo-Masonic plot," so they also invaded Jewish neighborhoods and seized two thousand Jews, who were tortured, raped, or murdered. Additionally, they ransacked 25 synagogues, 616 shops, and 547 homes.[150] A battalion of tanks and six infantry regiments arrived with orders to shoot anyone who failed to stay far enough away from the Ministry of External Affairs (where Antonescu had his offices). Alexandru Cretzianu remembered, "The Presidency had been transformed into a general headquarters. A swarm of Staff officers, red-eyed and unshaven after a sleepless night, were poring over large-scale maps of the city or speaking on the telephones." He heard telephones ringing endlessly as the pogrom peaked on 21–22 January. When Cretzianu asked why appeals for help were ignored, he was informed the military was not going to disperse soldiers into penny packets rushing from place to place; instead, the "proper thing to do" was to concentrate troops "that seized the town by slowly spreading like an oil stain."[151] The German Military Mission sat on the sidelines. German panzers drove through Bucharest in a show of support for Antonescu, but other than that did nothing.[152] The Capital Military Command mopped up the last pockets of Legionary resistance on 23 January. The pogrom left officially only 118 dead; however, other estimates counted 630 dead and 400 missing.[153] The military suffered twenty-one dead and fifty-three wounded, while the Legionaries lost at least double that—plus casualties on both sides in other cities.[154] On 26 January, *Sentinela*'s front page ran an illustration of a soldier holding the hand of a worker and the hand of a peasant flanking him to either side, declaring, "The Romanian soldier ensures the union and tranquillity of the country."[155] The message was clear that the military, not the Legion, was in charge.

Following the Legionary rebellion, General Antonescu dissolved the National Legionary State. Army propaganda blamed the Legion's leaders for leading its followers astray. General Gheorghe Băgulescu, a well-known Legionary sympathizer, wrote an article in *Sentinela* that defended the officer corps' anti-Judeo-Masonic credentials, accused Legionaries who supported Horia Sima of being communists, and warned that Romania might share

Poland's fate of partition if Iron Guard anarchy continued.[156] Antonescu treated Legionaries leniently. Most Iron Guardists arrested during the Legionary rebellion were released. Some Iron Guardists went underground, and a few, including Sima, fled into exile, but most accommodated to Antonescu's new regime.[157] Army propaganda depicted Legionaries as misguided patriots who only needed light punishment. In *Sentinela*'s comic strip, Private Neață sees his wife among Legionary demonstrators. He halts the mob, shouting, "Stop! I am the country and no one gets by me!" Neață berates his wife for neglecting chores, reminding her that whenever "she makes food it's always burned and now she does politics," and proceeds to spank her with his rifle. "I will teach you to behave! You won't be able to sit on a chair for six months!"[158] Coincidently, many of the Legionaries who were still imprisoned six months later were released to fight the Soviets. Antonescu replaced Legionaries in his government with soldiers. On 27 January, General Constantin Voiculescu had only an hour's notice before being sworn in with other generals as ministers, and he initially was not sure what post he held. "How I came to be Minister of Labor, I don't know!"[159] (He accepted assignment as military governor of liberated Bessarabia six months later in like manner.) The *conducător* selected the minister of justice, Mihai Antonescu (a friend, not a relation), to be the vice–prime minister. Officers replaced Iron Guardists as county prefects. Antonescu trusted the officer corps because it was trained to follow orders and shared his worldview. Antonescu often spoke in messianic terms about destiny "forcing" him to become *conducător*, a sentiment shared by many officers who believed the army had been compelled to step in to save Romania from weak liberal democracy, a corrupt monarchy, and Legionary anarchy.[160] Officers agreed an alliance with Nazi Germany against the USSR was the best way forward. Nicolae Staicu, son of a well-off peasant family near Tecuci, was attending a military high school "when Romania was crucified." "The country was obligated to go with the Germans because France was occupied, England was being bombed by German aircraft and they did not have the ability to help us," he argued later. "The Germans were the only ones that promised that they will give us the provinces taken in summer 1940."[161] Most Romanians backed Antonescu's military dictatorship for the same reasons.

Gathering Storm

General Hansen was ordered to keep Nazi Germany's plan to invade the USSR secret from the Antonescu regime even as the German Military Mission stepped up its preparations for war in Romania. A long, snowy winter hampered German advisers from training Romanian soldiers. Furthermore, the Romanian Army had shrunk to 378,000 men after many were sent home on extended leave. Those soldiers who remained, some of whom had been mobilized for over a year, showed signs of demoralization. Discontent among NCOs and enlisted men increased when they heard of difficulties facing their families at home. Romania's territorial losses, exacerbated by the Legionary Romanianization campaign, had wreaked havoc on the economy, creating shortages, especially in border cities cut off from normal markets.[162] In some places soldiers launched hunger strikes because "they have been concentrated too long and their families were dying of hunger," while others went absent without leave. The 58th Pioneer Battalion refused to board a train when it did not get Christmas leave.[163] The Romanian Army imprisoned protest ringleaders, but also increased financial aid to soldiers' families. German reports on the Romanian Army from this time were not flattering. German 16th Panzer Division commander General Hans Hube concluded on 7 February that the Romanian Army would be "worthless" in offensive operations because enlisted men were brave but lacked initiative, NCOs were corrupt and incompetent, and officers were good for nothing except maintaining a semblance of order in the country.[164] The Antonescu regime weathered the difficult winter. It attacked the Iron Guard for the "parallelism of methods on procedures between Legionarism and Communism" and blamed the Legionaries for having caused the country's economic woes.[165] Antonescu felt confident enough that he ordered a plebiscite on 2–5 March. The simple yes or no vote without a secret ballot resulted in 2,960,298 in favor and 2,996 against Antonescu and his policies. While the plebiscite's result was obviously skewed, the fact voters turned out in numbers comparable to interwar elections instead of staying home to protest suggests Romanians backed Antonescu.[166] The *conducător* knew his regime's legitimacy depended on reclaiming lost territories, so he was disappointed when Hitler suddenly attacked south instead of east.

German campaigns against Greece and Yugoslavia distracted the Antonescu regime from spotting German preparations to invade the Soviet Union. The German Twelfth Army's five hundred thousand men traversed Romania to stage in Bulgaria to invade Greece after British forces landed, which also brought British aircraft within range of hitting Romania's vital oil fields. German troops bought up goods wherever they went, benefiting from an advantageous exchange rate, causing massive inflation that exacerbated Romania's economic problems.[167] German soldiers also got drunk, caused fights, drove recklessly, and even helped local ethnic Germans evade the draft, keeping the German Military Mission and the General Staff very busy smoothing over incidents.[168] The two German panzer divisions in Moldavia were transferred south and replaced by seven German infantry divisions. The German Military Mission was instructed that this German buildup was to be "strictly disguised from the Romanians as nothing more than a precautionary measure to meet a possible Russian attack."[169] Some Romanians showed coolness or hostility toward German soldiers, so the Third Army ordered mayors to establish "citizen committees" to welcome German units, visit with German officers, and minister to German sick.[170] Locals soon became accustomed to the increased German presence in Moldavia. An army intelligence report summarized, "Romanian intellectuals consider the presence of German troops as necessary, being convinced that in the current international situation, through them we can guarantee calm and the borders of the country, against the danger from the east."[171] Events in Yugoslavia complicated German plans. On 27 March, Serb officers within the Yugoslav military ended the pro-Axis regency of Prince Paul and installed the pro-Allied King Peter II on the throne. The new Yugoslav government refused to ratify Yugoslavia's joining of the Tripartite Pact and negotiated a nonaggression pact with the Soviet Union. Hitler furiously ordered a last-minute invasion of Yugoslavia. The OKW did not ask the General Staff for help because it wanted to preserve the Romanian Army for the invasion of the USSR; moreover, the Romanian Army was not fully mobilized and lacked sufficient mobility for the lighting campaign.[172] Hitler wanted the fighting in the Balkans over as soon as possible so Nazi Germany could focus on defeating the Soviet Union.

Bad weather and logistical difficulties delayed the campaign against the USSR, but the German Military Mission started nudging the Romanian Army to prepare. On 3 April, General Hansen suggested the General Staff bring units in Moldavia up to two-thirds strength. German advisers began training two more infantry divisions and the recently established 1st Armored Division. Romanian officers busied themselves whipping new draftees into shape, focusing on drill so that soldiers would march handsomely in parades on 10 May (Romania's national day). On 7 April, new chief of staff General Alexandru Ioanițiu wrote a scathing report on the Romanian Army's unpreparedness. Officers blamed the upheavals of the previous year for interrupting their training schedules. Ioanițiu dismissed these excuses, upbraided officers for squandering time on drill, ordered practical field training increased, and emphasized a focus on offensive tactics.[173] He overlooked another issue. With limited manpower, the Antonescu regime chose to prioritize spring planting over training. Commanders had to provide men, horses, and carts to prefects to help peasants plow fields and transport seeds; even elite mountain and cavalry troops spent much of their spring laboring out in the countryside instead of training at post.[174] Even had the Antonescu regime known how close war was, it is likely it would have made the same decision so it could feed its hungry citizens.

Twin blitzkrieg campaigns in Greece and Yugoslavia seemingly confirmed the wisdom of General Antonescu's decision to join the Axis. On 6 April, German troops supported by Italian, Hungarian, and Bulgarian forces simultaneously invaded Greece and Yugoslavia. Within just eleven days Yugoslavia surrendered and was soon occupied and broken up. The Antonescu regime used Yugoslavia's fate as a warning to any officers who disagreed with accepting the Second Vienna Award and allying with Nazi Germany. Minister of defense General Iacobici (Antonescu finally had felt secure enough to assign the position to someone else) declared, "The recent events in Yugoslavia demonstrate to us what misfortune can be produced if the army conducts its own politics. . . . From now on officers who manifest [animosity] in any way against comrades from the German Army, will be considered practicing politics and will be removed."[175] Antonescu's worries about a countercoup led by disgruntled Carlist officers were overinflated because the officer corps had united behind him by this time. On 30 April, mainland Greece fell to German forces. These fresh German conquests also reinforced Romanian soldiers' belief in the German Army's invincibility, which contributed to their motivation later.

The Antonescu regime was finally alerted to the coming invasion of the Soviet Union. On 24 May, General Eugen von Schobert arrived in Piatra Neamț to take command of the German Eleventh Army. Two days later General Hansen requested General Antonescu to mobilize units in Moldavia to full strength and move them to the frontier by 10 June.[176] Antonescu visited von Schobert, who claimed the preparations were defensive, and then left to set up the General Headquarters (MCG) in Odobești. On 31 May, Vice–Prime Minister Mihai Antonescu chaired the first Council of Ministers meeting focusing on war preparations.[177] On 12 June, Hitler and Antonescu met in Munich, where the *conducător* was the first foreign leader the führer sounded out about invading the Soviet Union. On the record, Antonescu insisted Romania should join in the invasion from day one and put its military and economic forces at Hitler's disposal for "the great event that was approaching." Hitler offered Antonescu command of an army group to liberate eastern Romania. Hitler was vague about the exact date of the invasion, but Antonescu argued that any delay worsened Axis chances of victory.[178] Off the record, Hitler probably informed Antonescu about plans to execute Red Army political commissars, Soviet civil servants, Jewish communists, and all "radical elements" captured during the invasion—the so-called Commissar Order. They also most likely discussed plans to deport Soviet Jews east of the Urals following victory.[179] While the dictators chatted, commanders warned of communist fifth-column activity in Moldavia and ordered units to take precautionary measures. The 8th Infantry Division evacuated twenty "communists" from a town and proposed deporting all Jewish men ages eighteen to fifty to concentration camps in Wallachia. The Mountain Corps banned Jews from possessing telephones, traveling, or working in telegraph or telephone exchanges.[180] The threat of war greatly increased officers' paranoia about Jewish-communist treachery.

Countdown

The traumatic occupation of northern Bukovina and Bessarabia had united Romanians under the Antonescu regime in an alliance with Nazi Germany against the Soviet Union. Now Romania stood on the brink of war, prepared to make as great a commitment as possible to the destruction of the USSR, not only to liberate northern Bukovina and Bessarabia but also hopefully earn Nazi Germany's support to return northern Transylvania. In the grander scheme, Romanians saw themselves as part of a pan-European alliance intent on safeguarding Christian civilization forever by ridding the world of Judeo-Bolshevism. Additionally, the Romanian Army was anxious to assuage its wounded honor and take revenge on Jews and communists for the humiliating withdrawal from northern Bukovina and Bessarabia. The antisemitic violence during the withdrawal from eastern Romania foreshadowed what was to come during the advance into the USSR; however, the *conducător* did not begin planning to "cleanse the terrain" in northern Bukovina and Bessarabia until after his meeting with the führer. Distracted by political and economic crises in Romania, and German campaigns in the Balkans, the Antonescu regime had missed the signs of an invasion of the USSR and now rushed to prepare Romania for war. The Romanian Army was also caught flatfooted, but its soldiers were anxious for an opportunity to finally fight for their country.

Chapter 4

1941: Holy War and Holocaust

"Soldiers, I order you: Cross the Prut!" General Antonescu's laconic command was part of a grandiloquent declaration, the rest of which was promptly forgotten, but army propaganda repeated this order ad nauseam, soldiers excitedly recorded it in journals, and veterans still recite it like a mantra because it encapsulated the Romanian Army's desire to expunge the shameful retreat from northern Bukovina and Bessarabia a year earlier. In Bucharest, Vice–Prime Minister Mihai Antonescu, running the government while the *conducător* was at the front heading the MCG, emerged with King Mihai I to greet an ecstatic crowd outside the palace.[1] "The war, this war, is a great battle of Christian civilization in opposition to the new barbarians," he proclaimed. "I believe that since the sacred wars of the Crusaders, not a battle was holier, greater, and more epic than that which Adolf Hitler, the apostle of our new civilization, began today."[2] He then led a prayer for victory. Alice Voinescu, a theater critic and anti-Nazi, was one of the few unmoved by the "bombastic" declaration, writing, "This war is immoral. We should only take what is ours. Lord help us! At the least we should wash away the shame of being brothers with bandits, through a soldierly conduct without fault."[3] She was soon disappointed, as Romanian soldiers proved as depraved as German troops. Soldiers' confidence in victory greatly increases their motivation.[4] Nearly all Romanian soldiers believed the German Army would easily defeat the Red Army, so morale was extremely high. In this heady atmosphere, the Romanian Army gave soldiers free rein to take revenge on Jews for supposedly humiliating them in 1940 or aiding the Red Army in 1941, and the Antonescu regime decided to "cleanse the terrain" in northern Bukovina and Bessarabia of Jews. Romania's holy war began with liberating battles and genocidal massacres.

The atrocities against Jews perpetrated by the Romanian Army went beyond what could normally be expected in war. Soldiers commit two varieties of atrocity, either "hot-blooded" or "cold-blooded."[5] A hot-blooded atrocity occurs when soldiers come under fire, especially if they suffer casualties, triggering a primal reaction of fear and anger resulting in the criminal murder of civilians or prisoners of war. In 1941, the myth of Jewish betrayal in 1940 contributed to a paranoia among Romanian soldiers of guerrillas—known in Romanian military parlance by the French term *franc-tireur* (literally "free shooter")—lurking in the rear. As a consequence, Romanian troops targeted alleged Jewish communists for reprisals after losing comrades or experiencing a defeat. A cold-blooded atrocity results from a policy to brutalize and kill those who resist the occupier, in order to deter others or any who were members of a group deemed a threat by the occupier. The MCG believed reports of Jewish-communist *francs-tireurs* and legitimatized atrocities by ordering hostages be taken from the local Jewish population and authorizing mass reprisals targeting Jews and communists.[6] Additionally, the Antonescu regime sent gendarmes following in the wake of soldiers with orders to round up Jews, execute all deemed guilty of communist outrages, and then expel the survivors from northern Bukovina and Bessarabia. Crucially, each commander's character influenced how murderous soldiers and gendarmes were, because if he was pitiless, then his unit became cruel.[7] Some commanders pushed soldiers, or gendarmes, to kill as many Jews as possible, while others merely passed on orders leaving subordinates to decide how they would act. Once in Ukraine the situation changed somewhat, but the Romanian Army continued to commit atrocities as it advanced into the Soviet Union.

War Preparations

The Antonescu regime still did not know when the German invasion would start or what the Romanian Army's role would be in it, but it excitedly began to prepare. On 16 June, General Ciupercă crowed to the Fourth Army, "*I feel that the moment approaches to make [the Soviets] pay the price [for 1940,] dear soldiers.* With the help of God, and our great ally [the German Army], I have unshakable faith that we will succeed in returning the borders of the

Country to the *Dniester*."⁸ The next day, in a Council of Ministers meeting, Mihai Antonescu emphasized that Romania faced "a historic moment" to "effect purification of the population" in liberated territory.⁹ At the same time, the state intelligence service—the Serviciu Special de Informații (SSI), or Special Intelligence Service—helped the General Staff compile lists of scores of Jews, other minorities, and *basarabeni* who "did evil" during the Soviet occupation and were to be arrested.¹⁰ On 18 June, Hitler finally officially informed General Antonescu that the invasion, code-named Operation Barbarossa, would begin four days later. Romania received three missions: first, Army Group Antonescu—the Third, German Eleventh, and Fourth Armies—would protect the Ploiești oil fields and other vital infrastructure like the Cernavodă bridge and the port of Constanța from Soviet counterattack and seize bridgeheads on the Prut to distract the Red Army; second, the Romanian Air Force, with help from the German Luftwaffe, would defend against Soviet air or airborne attack; and third, once German Army Group South advanced, Army Group Antonescu would attack and pin down Soviet forces for encirclement.¹¹ Antonescu would be titular commander, but General von Schobert would actually direct Army Group Antonescu's operations. Romania's role in Nazi Germany's war effort after liberating northern Bukovina and Bessarabia was left unclear.

Both dictators and their respective staffs, however, clearly assumed the Romanian Army would continue to support the German Army into Ukraine. On 19 June, the MCG issued its first offensive plans, which turned over operational control of the Third Army, now commanded by General Petre Dumitrescu, to the German Eleventh Army, while it only commanded the Fourth Army.¹² The MCG also ordered all civilians to be evacuated within three or four kilometers of the border in southern Bukovina and Moldavia. The next day, the order was amended to instruct gendarmes to escort all Jews from towns but "only the suspects" from cities in this evacuation zone to train stations for transport to and incarceration in Târgu Jiu in Wallachia.¹³ On 21 June, the Ministry of Internal Affairs clarified that "all able-bodied Jewish men" from towns should be loaded onto trains, but Jewish women, children, and elderly should be directed to the nearest city in Moldavia.¹⁴ The Antonescu regime lacked sufficient gendarmes, trains, and camps to deport and intern all Jews. The MCG's orders reinforced commanders' belief that Jews represented a dangerous communist fifth column. Meanwhile, the Romanian Army expanded to 686,000 men as the Third and Fourth Armies moved to the frontier; the First Army remained in reserve.¹⁵ Soldiers who had been humiliated a year earlier would now have a chance to strike back.

Commanders began informing subordinates of the invasion the afternoon before the predawn attack. In Botoșani, the 7th *Roșiori* Regiment commander Colonel Gheorghe Carp called his officers together to announce the invasion and issue combat orders. Then, according to a postwar interrogation, he explained that "a verbal order was given that when we cross the Prut we will exterminate Jews who mocked Romanian units during the evacuation of Bessarabia in 1940."[16] This seems to indicate the MCG ordered soldiers to take revenge on Jews, but there is reason to doubt this account's veracity. The officer who provided this testimony was under investigation for war crimes and had every incentive to point the finger up the chain of command and claim that he himself was just following orders from Carp (who was by then conveniently dead). While there is much evidence that Antonescu issued orders for soldiers to carry out mass reprisals against Jews and communists and for gendarmes to round up and drive Jews into Ukraine after the war started, there is little indication he gave orders to exterminate Jews before the war started. Soldiers, particularly honor-obsessed regular officers, needed no such order to initiate atrocities against Jews. Soldiers' ideological worldview convinced them that Jews were communists, and many soldiers had already proved willing to attack and kill Jews the year before. Army propaganda blamed Jews for soldiers' humiliation, and soldiers soon discovered commanders were not likely to discipline them for crimes against Jews. Around midnight on 22 June, officers informed their men that Operation Barbarossa was about to begin, and at 3:15 a.m. Army Group Antonescu joined in the massive bombardment unleashed by the Germans against the Soviets from the Baltic Sea to the Black Sea.

Bridgehead Battles

Artillery fire and aircraft engines announced the war to citizens in Rădăuți, Dorohoi, Iași, Galați, and Tuclea, but there were no celebrations like those in Bucharest, since these border cities were almost within range of Soviet guns. *Sentinela* trumpeted, "Comrades in battle, the German soldier elbow to elbow with the Romanian soldier . . . threw themselves upon the greatest enemy of the world: Bolshevism. . . . [They fight to free] the earth of Bessarabia and the mountains of Bukovina from the communist yoke. Forward, brave comrades! The God of righteousness is with you!"[17] Army Group Antonescu fielded 326,000 Romanian and 136,000 German soldiers and formed a backward S-shape: the Third Army facing north in Bukovina, the German Eleventh Army and the Fourth Army facing east in Moldavia, and the II Corps facing north in Dobruja. The Grupare Aeriană de Luptă (GAL), or Air Combat

Group, and German Luftflotte 4 provided air support. The Third Army probed forward, the German Eleventh and Fourth Armies seized bridges and ferried troops over the Prut, and the II Corps engaged in artillery duels on the Danube. Cartoons on *Sentinela*'s "Cheerful Page" showed Stalin kicked out of Europe by a boot to his hindquarters and a Soviet skeleton with the caption, "Land he wanted, land he got!"[18] The Soviet Odessa Military District had only 320,000 soldiers, but it had plenty of tanks, heavy artillery, and aircraft.[19] It immediately prepared counterattacks to take the fight onto enemy soil and launched a strategic bombing campaign against Romania.[20]

Soviet air attacks caused little damage to key targets but created massive panic. Axis antiaircraft units were concentrated around Ploiești, Bucharest, and Constanța, leaving border cities exposed; moreover, most cities lacked air raid shelters, effective air raid warning systems, and disciplined blackout procedures.[21] Prefects anticipated numerous civilian casualties and ordered mass graves dug, often by Jewish forced laborers. Frequent air raids and even more frequent air raid alarms fostered paranoia that Jews were signaling Soviet pilots with red cloths at day or fires at night. It was even rumored that Jewish émigrés from Moldavia were piloting Soviet aircraft.[22] Reports of "red rockets" fired from Jewish neighborhoods in cities as far away as Bucharest flooded in after air raids, but investigations determined these were tracers from antiaircraft guns, not signals by Jewish communists.[23] Soldiers were not immune to panic. On 22–23 June, the 3rd *Călărași* Regiment in Siret, a border town in Bukovina, reported being fired on by civilians, so a military praetor was assigned to investigate. He ordered gendarmes to look for snipers, investigated reports of local Ukrainian or Lipovan (Russian Orthodox schematics) snipers in other nearby villages, arrested a Romanian lawyer concealing a Jewish family from deportation, and oversaw the evacuation of civilians. Fortunately, the military praetor concluded that Soviet soldiers had fired the shots, although nervous Romanian soldiers were likely responsible, and no one was executed.[24] Any air victories were celebrated to bolster morale. On 23 June, First Lieutenant Hoira Agarici downed three Soviet bombers over Constanța, and his feat became a popular song, "Agarici has gone to hunt *bolșevici*."[25] However, a constant flow of warnings from the MCG about saboteurs, spies, and parachutists in the rear kept soldiers, and civilians, on edge.

Soviet counterattacks reduced Axis bridgeheads on the Prut; one Romanian toehold was described as a "nest of projectiles," and in some places Axis forces were forced to evacuate back over the river, triggering the first mass reprisals against Jews.[26] One of the worst massacres occurred after Axis troops evacuated the Sculeni bridgehead. The town had changed hands four times in the previous three days, when Axis troops finally evacuated twenty-five hundred civilians, including a thousand Jews, also joined the exodus to escape the carnage. Colonel Ermil Matieș, commanding the 6th *Vânători* Regiment, ordered his intelligence officer "to arrest and execute all the suspected Jews" blamed for directing Soviet artillery fire onto his men. On 26 June, officers began to "classify" Jews with the help of soldiers and civilians from Sculeni. Soldiers marched Jews who had been fingered as communists into the hills around the village of Stânca Roznovanu and forced them to dig mass graves before being shot. German soldiers and Romanian civilians arrived to watch, sometimes joining in to beat men to turn over valuables, and to rape women. Over the next several days soldiers became increasingly indiscriminate, killing women, children, and the elderly, totaling around six hundred people.[27] Shocked civilian authorities reported the soldiers' atrocities, prompting an investigation, but Matieș justified the crimes as legitimate reprisals, and no one was punished.[28] The Stânca Roznovanu massacre shows how mass reprisals quickly turned into genocidal massacres as permissive officers allowed soldiers—joined by civilians—to do whatever they wanted to Jews.

Meanwhile, Soviet troops had even crossed the Danube, establishing bridgeheads near Ismail, which increased Romanian commanders' fears of Jewish uprisings in the rear to support Soviet attacks at the front, especially in Iași.[29] The city had come under regular air attack because it was an important rail hub on the frontier. On 26 June, bombs killed two hundred citizens, including thirty-eight Jews.[30] Some people fled to the countryside, but most lacked the means; Jews were not allowed to leave. Some Romanians blamed corrupt or incompetent authorities for inadequate air defenses, but even more told stories about Jewish communists signaling Soviet pilots.[31] The press contributed to hysteria with stories about Jewish agents. Iași garrison commander Colonel Constantin Lupu, Prefect Colonel Dumitru Captaru, Police Superintendent Colonel Constantin Chirilovici, and two others formed an emergency committee that ordered a search leading to the arrest of 207 Jews for possessing flashlights or red cloths and the provisional arrest of 317 other Jews. The few women rounded up were immediately released. The men were beaten during interrogations at police headquarters, but many were soon freed, owing to lack of evidence.[32] Certain that police interrogators were blind or bought off, soldiers took matters into their own hands. Sergeant Mircea Manoliu, a former Legionary, first started shooting released Jews instead of escorting them home, then shooting newly detained Jews instead of taking them to police headquarters.[33] Iași city authorities were losing control, in part because of institutional confusion. There was an array of groups within the city operating independently and often at cross purposes, including police, gendarmes, garrison troops, units heading to the front, SSI agents, and German soldiers.[34] Police lacked authority over soldiers; 14th Infantry Division soldiers were mostly spread out in the countryside; Romanian military police had no control over German soldiers; German 198th Infantry Division and Todt Organization troops had their own missions; and SSI agents operated clandestinely. On 27 June, after hearing gunfire, Colonel Chirilovici found a group of Romanians in a Jewish cemetery singing Legionary songs while receiving rifles from two men who said they had orders from army intelligence to arm volunteers in case of a Jewish-communist uprising. He discovered later they were SSI officers.[35] German patrols prowled the streets as well. Colonel Lupu began preparations to deport "suspect" Jewish men to prevent "rebellious actions in Iași on the part of the Jews" that army intelligence had been predicting for a year.[36] Hundreds of Jewish men from towns in the evacuation zone had already been deported, and now the *conducător* wanted to do the same thing on a far grander scale in Iași, since by now nearly half the city's population was Jewish after having been swollen by ten thousand Jews—refugees from Bessarabia the year before and deportees from surrounding towns in recent weeks.[37] Colonel Captaru requested the 6th *Vânători* and 13th *Dorobanți* Regiments to organize patrols to help the overstretched municipal police after reports of looting during the blackout. Unintentionally, these orders destabilized Iași even further and set the stage for a pogrom.

On 28 June, the situation in the city deteriorated, and inflammatory army propaganda did not help. An article in *Soldatul* reminded soldiers it had been a year since Soviet troops entered northern Bukovina and Bessarabia, calling the day a "black page in the calendar of the Romanian nation," but rejoiced that soon Romania would be "reborn in all its ancient virtues, under the correct leadership of a great soldier and Romanian, General Ion Antonescu."[38] At 10 a.m. soldiers from the 13th *Dorobanți* and 24th Artillery Regiments, including Sergeant Manoliu, entered the Tătărași neighborhood to search for radios but quickly began ransacking Jewish homes. Police arrived to find soldiers holding Jews, many beaten and bleeding, at gunpoint as civilians shouted encouragement. When the police tried to intercede, those on the scene "screamed that [the police] belonged to the Jews and had been bribed by them."[39] Manoliu told a passing German patrol "the police were protecting the Jews."[40] The German troops let the Romanian soldiers continue searching for radios and did nothing to stop the abuses. Only when Colonel Lupu and a military praetor came with gendarmes was the looting stopped and Manoliu temporarily detained.[41] Calm was not restored for very long. An air raid alarm at 9 p.m. put the city on edge, then antiaircraft gunfire was misidentified as blue or green "flares" (actually different-colored tracers indicating different antiaircraft guns), and by 10 p.m. Romanian and German patrols reported being fired upon. The patrols shot back and searched homes but never found any snipers.[42] German patrols reported casualties; it took days for Romanian authorities to confirm that this was false.[43] At 11 p.m. General Antonescu phoned Lupu, ordering him to restore order and deport all Jewish men in the city at once.[44] Soon afterward, two Romanian columns passing through Iași on the way to the front reported being fired at by snipers. By 3 a.m. soldiers across the city were grabbing Jews from buildings they thought were the sources of fire and summarily executing them. A report recorded three hundred dead and fifty wounded during the night.[45] As the sun rose, civilians joined soldiers, turning reprisals into a pogrom.

"That Sunday," as locals subsequently referred to 29 June, soldiers, gendarmes, civilians, and some Germans killed thousands of Jews, mostly men, but women and children too. At dawn city authorities realized that, despite all the gunfire, not a single soldier had been killed; nonetheless, soldiers and gendarmes pulled Jews into the streets, sorting out military-age men, to be arrested. Anyone who resisted was shot. Romanian and German patrols marched "convoys" of Jews to various collection points or directly to police headquarters.[46] Those who fell behind or lowered hands from over their heads were shot, and streets were quickly littered with bodies. The cells at police headquarters were already crammed, so its courtyard was used as overflow, and by 9 a.m. it contained perhaps two thousand Jews.[47] Civilians began looting Jewish properties. City authorities believed Jewish communists and "very weak Romanian communist elements" had attacked to hinder troop movements by purposefully triggering a pogrom to spread disorder, so commanders made feeble attempts to restore order.[48] General Gheorghe Stavrescu, commander of the 14th Infantry Division, visited police headquarters several times. At 11 a.m., he gave a speech to the Jews under guard in the courtyard, saying not all Jews were communists, promising to release women, children, and the elderly, and warning men would be shot if proven guilty.[49] The freed Jews found Iași's streets a dangerous place. Crowds had gathered along routes taken by convoys to spit on, throw things at, beat up, and even murder Jews.[50] People from all walks of life, laborers to tax collectors, guided troops to Jewish neighbors and encouraged their execution. Romanians who shielded Jews were accused of being "sold to the kikes" and sometimes murdered, like an engineer shot by an officer shouting, "Die you dog, with the Jews you're protecting."[51] By 1 p.m., some Todt Organization personal had gathered at police headquarters to watch Jews being beaten during interrogations.[52] Despite hundreds being released, and given papers with the word *liber* or "free" written on it, the police headquarters courtyard now held perhaps three or four thousand Jews. Some Jews had heard of the free slips and came to obtain one to prove their innocence, although many soldiers did not recognize the papers as valid and rearrested Jews who possessed one.[53] At 3 p.m., air raid sirens wailed again. In the police headquarters courtyard terrified Jews sought shelter, and the sheer press of humanity crushed some to death while provoking others to jump the wall. Soldiers fired machine guns, rifles, and even pistols into the crowd, killing or wounding hundreds. Thereafter, joined by German troops and Romanian civilians, soldiers and gendarmes hunted down Jews who had escaped, executing on the spot any that they caught.[54]

The military finally enacted strict measures to end the pogrom after this bloodbath. In an order posted around Iași, signed by General Stavrescu, he declared a curfew between 7 p.m. and 5 a.m., ordered all firearms be turned in by 5 p.m. (after which anyone caught with one could be shot on the spot), required citizens to lock out strangers, authorized soldiers to shoot everyone in buildings from which snipers fired, and demanded that ten hostages be taken from the "terrorist-communist movement" to be shot for each wounded soldier.[55] Despite these draconian threats, Colonel Captaru feared "grave disorders" could continue, since German soldiers were "stubborn" in trying to round up Jewish snipers, who were said to be well hidden.[56] Stavrescu's curfew cleared civilians from the streets by 6 p.m., but soldiers continued to roam the city, killing Jews. Colonel Lupu decided to deport the survivors at police headquarters, including hundreds of women, children, and the elderly. At 11 p.m., Stavrescu asked German patrols to withdraw from Iași, but disorders continued.[57] After trains were assembled, soldiers, gendarmes, and railway workers violently crammed Jewish survivors, including the wounded, into unventilated freight cars, with 120 to 150 people in spaces unsuitable for 40. A first train, with twenty-five hundred Jews aboard, left after midnight, and a second, with nineteen hundred, departed before dawn.[58] Iași remained dangerous for Jews. Another air raid alarm on 29–30 June triggered rumors that Soviet parachutists had been dropped into the city, keeping everyone on edge. In the morning, workers at the trolley car factory and power station murdered scores of Jewish coworkers who showed up to work. Later, in the afternoon, soldiers murdered eighteen men, women, and children found in an apartment above a Jewish pharmacy that they claimed was the source of sniper fire.[59] Shots continued to be heard for days. Meanwhile, Jews in the two "death trains" died of hunger, thirst, and exhaustion as the trains meandered through the countryside for days, often pausing for hours to allow

FIGURE 4. The aftermath of the massacre in the Iași police headquarters courtyard in June 1941. The Iași pogrom was the first large-scale atrocity perpetrated by Romanian soldiers and civilians, and a few German troops, against Romanian Jews. Although the Antonescu regime acted to prevent any more pogroms in the rest of Romania west of the Prut, it condoned pogroms east of the Prut in northern Bukovina and Bessarabia. Romanian soldiers tended to execute Jewish men, leaving Jewish women, children, and elderly to be deported by Romanian gendarmes later. United States Holocaust Memorial Museum, courtesy of Serviciul Român de Informații.

military trains to pass. Gendarmes kept the freight cars under tight guard, but some allowed railway workers to sell water to the Jews at astronomical prices.[60] One survivor remembered, "My fellow passengers, many of whom were exhausted from the beatings and the suffering they had undergone . . . collapsed onto the floor of the boxcar in which they were standing, and many of them never got up again. They suffocated because of the overcrowding and because of the unbearably high temperature."[61] Finally, the first train halted at Podu Iloaiei, disgorging 1,200 bodies, and the second at Târgu Frumos, unloading 650 corpses.[62] Some of the survivors died soon after.

The Iași pogrom remains controversial. For decades Antonescu was held responsible for manipulating what occurred in an attempt to exterminate the city's entire Jewish population; but he did not order the massacre. Nor did city authorities try to murder all Jews. The death toll is still hotly contested. Rumors soon afterward among Jews in Bucharest claimed ten thousand dead.[63] Since then, estimates ranging from 3,200 victims (tabulating only the dead from police headquarters and the two trains) to 13,200 (subtracting between censuses) have been proposed.[64] The truth lies in between these extremes. A year after the pogrom, the Iași Jewish community reported it lacked death certificates for some seven thousand Jewish men who "disappeared" during the violence.[65] With slain Jewish women, children, and elderly added, the total figure was probably close to eight thousand dead. Although the number of victims may not be as high as commonly assumed, this does not lessen the depth of depravity plumbed by Romanian soldiers and civilians.

The Iași pogrom stunned the MCG into action—not to protect Jews, but to maintain order. Colonel Lupu blamed German soldiers and German interference, but General Ioanițiu identified panicked Romanian soldiers and bad Romanian leadership as the primary causes. On 30 June, he instructed that patrols should be led by regular officers, kept close together, and only fire on clearly identified targets.[66] Ioanițiu ignored what role his own repeated warnings of Jews supporting the Soviets in the rear had in the pogrom. In fact, the same day, he announced Soviet aircraft had dropped spies and "terrorist agents" (supposedly including an émigré Jewish baker) into Iași to provoke more disruptive pogroms with the help of local Jews. Therefore, the MCG ordered a curfew for Jews from 6 p.m. to 7 a.m. across Moldavia, during which time Jewish men were concentrated into a few buildings, and it instructed garrisons to hold Jewish hostages during the day to deter communist attacks.[67] Constanța was an exception, because an attempted Soviet amphibious landing four days into the war convinced authorities to deport all Jewish men in the city to camps in the countryside.[68] The Fourth

Army passed on Ioanițiu's orders and authorized commanders to summarily execute Jews helping communists in the rear.[69] Ironically, the precautions taken to prevent "rebellions by the Jewish population," such as increased patrols, assigning police to patrols, and requiring greater fire discipline, actually prevented more pogroms in Moldavia.[70] On 2 July, General Dimitru Carlaonț replaced Lupu as Iași garrison commander. He had a mission from Antonescu to stamp out disorder, but continued antisemitic disturbances prompted the *conducător* to personally intervene. On 4 July, in a special order, he began by blaming Jews for impoverishing Romania and mentioning the shame of 1940, but then he declared, "The shame is even greater when isolated soldiers on their own initiative, and many times only with the purpose to rob or maltreat, attack the Jewish population and randomly kill as was the case in Iași."[71] Antonescu argued the state would "legally" implement antisemitic laws and bemoaned the chaos in Iași because it proved Romanians were undisciplined and uncivilized. He ended by threatening soldiers with court-martial if they kept maltreating Jews. While this may seem surprising, Antonescu worried that popular antisemitic violence could spiral out of control and disrupt operations to liberate northern Bukovina and Bessarabia.

The MCG did not halt the deportation of Jewish women, children, and elderly from towns in the frontier evacuation zone to nearby cities or of "suspect" Jewish men to internment camps in Wallachia.[72] Approximately seven thousand Jews from Moldavia and southern Bukovina were interned over the next month in camps across Wallachia in Călărași (including eleven hundred survivors from the first "death train"), Caracal, Craiova, Calafat, Turnu Severin, Lugoj, and Târgu Jiu. The majority were men. Hundreds of other minorities were also interned, mostly Lipovans from Dobruja. In September, all except one thousand communist, socialist, or Zionist Jews imprisoned in Târgu Jiu were sent back to cities in Moldavia and southern Bukovina.[73] The Antonescu regime prioritized law and order in Moldavia and southern Bukovina in grudging benefit to Jews; however, it used the chaos of war in northern Bukovina and Bessarabia to "cleanse the terrain" of Jews.

Cleansing the Terrain

The Soviet Odessa Military District's counterattacks delayed Army Group Antonescu's main attack from 25 June to 2 July.[74] German Army Groups North, Center, and South had already blasted through Soviet defenses in the Baltic states and Poland. *Soldatul* proclaimed, "Christian armies penetrate deep into the land of hell."[75] Now Army Group Antonescu was expected to do the same. The Third Army would execute a left hook into northern

Bukovina to seize Cernăuți on the way to Hotin. Simultaneously, the German Eleventh Army, reinforced with the 1st Armored Division, most of the Cavalry Corps, and the IV Corps (including the three "model divisions"), would spearhead the offensive attacking into northern Bessarabia, heading for Mogilev. Next, the Fourth Army would advance into central Bessarabia to liberate Chișinău before taking Tighina. Finally, the II Corps would cross into southern Bessarabia, aiming for Cetatea Albă. The MCG emphasized the need for strict discipline right before the offensive, and General Antonescu ordered that any soldier caught abusing civilians or prisoners be "sanctioned on the spot." He argued, "The Romanian Army must appear as a civilized army and not repeat that which the uncivilized hordes of the Soviets do."[76] Yet, on 2 and 3 July, Mihai Antonescu gave two public speeches in Bucharest promising "radical purification" and "very severe" administration in northern Bukovina and Bessarabia.[77] *Soldatul* published a piece titled "Kikes: The Tools of Bolshevism" at the same time.[78] Throughout the attack there was tension in the Romanian Army between the need to enforce strict discipline to maintain combat effectiveness and brutal occupation policies toward Jews that fostered indiscipline by giving soldiers cover to loot, rape, and murder.

Army Group Antonescu's attack initially went like clockwork. The German Eleventh Army lunged across the Prut. Second Lieutenant Radu Vueric's company crossed in pneumatic boats "strongly supported by our artillery, as well as fire of machine guns," supporting a German attack at Sculeni that cracked Soviet defenses.[79] Soviet forces retreated from northern Bukovina and northern Bessarabia to escape encirclement by German Army Group South. The Third Army was slowed more by soldiers pausing to commit atrocities in liberated towns than enemy resistance. When First Lieutenant Nicolae Dan's mountain battalion entered Adâncata, ten kilometers over the border, soldiers started shouting about Jewish communists after hearing gunfire, and scattered down streets to search homes. "The troops were inflamed with a kind of madness and only very few soldiers remained calm." Some Jews were shot on the spot, while the rest were rounded up to be sorted before execution. Dan took pity on a Jewish woman and her child being led by a corporal and ordered them turned over. The mutinous NCO nearly refused. Dan soon had six more terrified captives, whom he tried to keep out of sight, but then a major arrived and took them. Dan followed to a courtyard where Jews were being interrogated and shot. He could not stand to watch, so another lieutenant accused him of being a "kike" and said he ought to be shot "together with them."[80] Most commanders did not question reports of Jewish snipers. On 3 July, General Mihail Lascăr, the 1st

1941: HOLY WAR AND HOLOCAUST

Mixed Mountain Brigade commander, authorized "the most energetic measures" against *francs-tireurs*.[81] Romanian units often recklessly pushed into towns without clearing surrounding Soviet positions but then blamed Jewish communists for casualties inflicted by Soviet fire and butchered Jews in revenge. Second Lieutenant Ignat Timaru boasted of dodging "kike bullets" in the corpse-strewn streets of Storojineţ. On 4 July, the *conducător* and General Ioaniţiu arrived in the captured town and saw the chaos and carnage.[82] General Antonescu ordered commanders to detour around towns filled with "malevolent foreigners" to speed the advance.[83] Additionally, he complained that units bunched up (thereby presenting easy targets for enemy air attacks or ambushes), launched costly frontal attacks, did not inventory captured matériel, caused traffic jams, left antiaircraft guns too far in the rear, fed troops poorly, did not mark soldiers' graves, stole tractors, and left "Jewish or Ukrainian snipers (francs-tireurs)" in the rear.[84] Some brutal commanders used the fear of *francs-tireurs* as cover to murder all Jews in the towns they passed through.

FIGURE 5. Photograph taken somewhere in Ukraine shows a Romanian soldier guarding a group of Soviet Jews, mostly men but also a few women, arrested in August 1941 on suspicion of being *francs-tireurs*. Those Jews that were not shot immediately by Romanian soldiers or gendarmes were held as hostages to be executed in reprisal for any casualties blamed on Soviet partisans. Bundesarchiv, Bild 183-B11501 / photo: o.Ang.

Soldiers depended on help from local civilians to identify Jews and communists. Axis troops were joyfully greeted by many *bucovineni* and *basarabeni* who had become thoroughly disillusioned with Soviet rule. Three months earlier the Soviets had begun deporting well-off peasants, and Soviet border guards shot anyone who tried to cross the border—the most notorious incident had occurred at Fântâna Albă, where scores were killed when a large group of Romanian peasants tried to march over the frontier.[85] News of Soviet atrocities, real and imagined, quickly spread among Romanian soldiers, stoking anger against Jews and communists. Local Ukrainian nationalists hoped to establish an ethnically pure, independent Ukraine, laying claim to swaths of Bukovina and Bessarabia, and soon formed militias with weapons provided by German units. In places, former LANC/Legionary activists or Ukrainian nationalists organized pogroms even before Axis troops arrived.[86] These opposing groups used the invasion as an opportunity to cleanse villages and towns of Jews (and sometimes of each other); other locals were motivated by greed or a chance to settle old scores.[87] Usually, soldiers' arrival triggered violence, beginning as mass reprisals against Jews (or other minorities) identified as *francs-tireurs* by soldiers and turning into pogroms as emboldened civilians joined in attacking any Jews, or in some places Ukrainians, and looting their property. Major Carp's battalion with the 16th *Infanterie* Regiment immediately took up where it had left off in Cuidei a year earlier and shot most of the remaining Jews in the town with local help.[88] Romanian soldiers had plenty of time to commit atrocities because Soviet troops were in full retreat.

The Third Army soon liberated northern Bukovina. On 5 July, mountain troops reached the Prut. General Gheorghe Avramescu, commanding the Mountain Corps, unlike many other commanders investigated reports of *franc-tireur* ambushes and spent that day "crossing all over" the rear, but in every case the gunfire was "only from panic-stricken soldiers."[89] Consequently, he ordered that soldiers should not fire unless expressly ordered to by an officer. When his unit was shot at outside Cernăuți, Major Scârneci sent a patrol to a Jewish cemetery on a hill, and it reported they "found a Jew who was praying at his mother's grave and that this [man] said that other civilians had fired the gunshots."[90] How his soldiers reacted is unknown, but others attacked Jews, as well as Ukrainians, after entering the city. SS troops arriving six days later reported, "Action against Jews until the arrival of the Einsatzkommando spotty. Romanian soldiers looted all the houses. Above all, Ukrainians were ill-treated. [Cernăuți] is destroyed."[91] The Mountain Corps crossed the Prut the next day, reached the Dniester on 7 July, and then tuned toward Hotin. The Romanian attack was stopped for a day by Soviet soldiers dug in on the hills around the city, and artillery on the far bank, until it found an open flank.[92] The Third Army cleared the last Soviet troops from northern Bukovina, while the German Eleventh Army drove into northern Bessarabia.

While German infantry focused on reaching Mogilev, Romanian cavalrymen took time to take revenge on Jews. Cavalry officers were more likely to be particularly vengeful because they were most concerned about besmirched honor; moreover, elite units were more contemptuous of what were viewed as dishonorable enemies.[93] Captain Leon Ostrovschi in the 7th *Roșiori* Regiment gave a speech to his soldiers after crossing the Prut on the need to take revenge on Jews and communists for the events a year prior and requested "worthy, courageous, and determined men who will not give up for anything. To kill without mercy from babes in swaddling clothes to [elderly men with] white beards."[94] Only nine men volunteered, so he chose seven others and formed an "execution team" that shot Jews in groups of five to fifty. Initially, many soldiers found killing women and children distasteful, so they tended to single out men, whom they saw as legitimate targets. In addition to Jews, they targeted village leaders and others accused of collaborating to be interrogated and executed. Between 4 and 6 July, successive cavalry regiments passed through Edineț, leaving behind a growing number of bodies in the streets, looting, and imprisoning some thirty-four hundred Jews. A soldier later testified, "In Ediniț they drank a good wine, shot Jews, and raped women."[95] Soldiers raped not primarily from lust but from a need to humiliate. A few days later, in Secureni, Michael Stivelman discovered his teenage neighbor had been gang raped by soldiers who forced her parents to watch, and then she bled to death.[96] Soviet counterattacks temporarily stopped the Cavalry Corps' sadistic ride.

The Soviets abandoned northern Bukovina but fought fiercely to hold on to Bessarabia. On 4 July, Fourth Army attacks from bridgeheads at Albița, Fălciu, and Cahul immediately ran into trouble because of waterlogged terrain, poor logistics, and lack of artillery; moreover, Soviet troops dug in along hills dominated the bridgeheads. Meanwhile, the German Eleventh Army faced strong Soviet counterattacks led by tanks. Romanian units were particularly vulnerable because they had fewer antitank guns than German units. On 6 July, Second Lieutenant Vasile Stănescu, commanding a scout platoon outside Bălți, spotted an enemy tank. "I froze! I knew what disaster it could cause us. Sergeant-Major Nicolae Marin, commander of two Bofors 37 mm caliber guns, opened fire. Suddenly, to the right and to the left of the tank appeared another two and in back of them two other tanks. The battle was unequal. At some point the guns ceased firing, because they had run out of ammunition."⁹⁷ His unit was nearly overrun. Axis soldiers entered Bălți the next day, reporting street battles "with armed bands," but a Soviet counterattack soon expelled them from the city.⁹⁸ The 6th *Vânători* Regiment was repulsed at Mărculești. After the regiment regrouped and took the town on 8 July, Colonel Matieș had four hundred Jews rounded up, separated and interrogated, stripped of valuables and cash, and shot.⁹⁹ The same day, the 35th Reserve Infantry Division, which was supposed to maintain contact between the Fourth Army and the German Eleventh Army, suffered a stinging defeat. Its two columns, ignoring proper security as inexperienced reserve officers tried to keep up with the Germans, were surprised by a Soviet battalion that emerged from the wooded hills, cut the road, and caused a panicked retreat. General Antonescu publicly castigated the unit, and several officers were court-martialed for cowardice. Despite performing well afterward, the 35th Reserve Infantry Division was broken up at the end of the next month and cannibalized to provide replacements for other divisions.¹⁰⁰ The Soviet defenders inflicted heavy losses on the Fourth Army and temporarily stymied the German Eleventh Army.

The Antonescu regime had no doubts about the war's final outcome, however, pressing full speed ahead in its plans to "cleanse the terrain" in northern Bukovina and Bessarabia. The Romanian press, following the German press's lead, was extremely optimistic in its reportage of the war; German successes were such that predictions that the war would be over by Christmas seemed realistic.¹⁰¹ General Antonescu, Mihai Antonescu, and others in the government did not want to waste the opportunity to "purify" the liberated provinces. The Ministry of Internal Affairs sent General Constantin "Piki" Vasiliu, chief of the Gendarmerie, to hold conferences with gendarme officers between 2 and 6 July: in Galați for the Fourth Army, in Roman for the German Eleventh Army, and in Fălticeni for the Third Army. General Ioan Topor, the "great praetor of the army" who controlled gendarmes assigned as military police, attended the conference in Roman, where the MCG was also now located. Vasiliu told gendarme officers it was their sacred duty to "cleanse the terrain" of Jews and communists and explained that this meant liquidating Jews in the countryside, establishing ghettos for Jews in cities, and executing all non-Jewish collaborators.¹⁰² These brutal orders were influenced by Hitler and Antonescu's talks before Operation Barbarossa. It was not a coincidence that Einsatzgruppe D arrived at the German Eleventh Army headquarters in Piatra Neamț on 4–5 July.¹⁰³ Heinrich Himmler had created three "task groups" of approximately nine hundred SS men to police the German Army's rear, designated Einsatzgruppen A, B, and C and assigned respectively to Army Groups North, Center, and South. At the last minute, he also cobbled together a smaller Einsatzgruppe D to attach to Army Group Antonescu. In addition to carrying out the Commissar Order, the Einsatzgruppen encouraged local allies to initiate "self-cleansing efforts" of Jews and communists "without leaving a trace."[104] Romanian soldiers did not need to be pushed to murder Jews or communists. In fact, SS troops believed they brought orderly methods to the Romanian soldiers' chaotic rampages.[105] Einsatzgruppe D collaborated closely with the Eşalon Operativ, or Operational Echelon, a group of 100 to 160 SSI agents attached to the Romanian Army to help gather intelligence, report on morale, and secure the rear.[106] They were not fascists (indeed many had arrested, tortured, and executed Legionaries) but hated Judeo-Bolshevism and imitated SS tactics. On 11 July, the Operational Echelon informed the Fourth Army that it had recruited agents to create "an unfavorable atmosphere for Judaic elements" behind enemy lines.[107] Gendarmes, SSI agents, and SS troops following behind frontline soldiers began systematically cleansing the terrain in the rear of Jews.

Territory had to be conquered from the enemy first, however. The Fourth Army was stuck on the Prut, and nowhere worse than at the Fălciu bridgehead, where infantry advanced through marshy ground to attack uphill near a village called Țigancă. On 9 July, the 11th *Dorobanți* Regiment took nearly 50 percent casualties to advance a handful of kilometers. General Ciupercă considered evacuating, but commanders rebelled at abandoning the blood-soaked gains.[108] Private Ioan Popa wrote home, "Papa this war ain't like nothing since creation, that's going on between Romania and Russia. . . . Know that we've barely gone seven kilometers, advancing without tanks, artillery, or planes, only with infantry fire, while the Russians got casemates."[109] Frontline troops sang a tune that went, "O'er in the valley at Țigancă, / the Russians sat in casemates, / and they hit us with grenades, / with grenades and shrapnel, / and with light machine guns."[110] The Fourth Army could not break out of its bridgeheads, so the German Eleventh Army came to its rescue. Once footbound infantry caught up with motorized spearheads, the German Eleventh Army reoccupied Bălți on 10 July. Romanian soldiers ran amok, sorting out "not dangerous" Jews and shooting hundreds of others, and used survivors to clean up the damaged city.[111] With the path open to the Dniester, General von Schobert diverted the 1st Armored Division south to outflank enemy defenses, and soon Soviet forces withdrew from central Bessarabia.

Axis troops occupied towns and cities that were increasingly empty and devastated. The Soviet withdrawal and civilian evacuations created a wave of refugees, including approximately 124,000 Jews, trying to escape over the

Dniester.[112] While northern Bukovina fell so quickly that few had time to flee, northern Bessarabia took longer, so towns and cities were noticeably deserted; and municipalities in central and southern Bessarabia were the most desolate. Soldiers believed Jews who fled were communists, but they accused any who remained of hiding from them out of guilt for 1940.[113] Each successive echelon's arrival unleashed a new wave of atrocities in towns and cities.[114] First, soldiers looted goods, raped women, and shot alleged *francs-tireurs*. Next, gendarmes under the Praetoral Service arrived, enacting a semblance of order as military police tried to halt looting, took custody of Jews and communists, arrested more suspects, and shot hostages in reprisal for attacks.[115] Finally, gendarmes under the Ministry of Internal Affairs took over and established ghettos. Einsatzgruppe D's four Einsatzkommandos rushed from city to city trying to direct the efforts of Romanian soldiers and gendarmes, and in some places prevailed on Romanian authorities to require Jews to wear yellow stars.[116] On 13 July, after the MCG moved to Iași, General Carlaonț evacuated Jews from the downtown and required them to wear yellow stars for a short time.[117] At first, some military police escorted Jews back over the border to be deported to Wallachia. Then, on 16 July, the Third Army passed down the decision that gendarmes should intern Jews in ghettos in northern Bukovina and Bessarabia controlled by the Ministry of Internal Affairs.[118] General Topor chided gendarmes in Soroca the following day: "The country has no need of Jews and must be cleaned of Jews. . . . It is banned to keep sending Jews into the interior."[119] The Antonescu regime believed the ghettos were a temporary expedient and planned to start deporting Jews into Ukraine as soon as Axis forces held the other bank of the Dniester.

The German Eleventh Army had already begun crossing the river. General von Schobert had transferred General Racovița's Cavalry Corps back to the Third Army and tasked it to secure the rear during the crossing. Racovița was pleased to report civilians had reacted "very violently" against Jews, "the second and even more dangerous enemy," and suggested deporting survivors to "the interior" in Wallachia. He recorded that the brutality of the Romanian Army "frightened" Jews, but argued it was necessary to "annihilate" Soviet propaganda.[120] The MCG complained that soldiers were treating liberated Bessarabia more like occupied enemy territory, looting anything not nailed down, and General Antonescu noted that booty-laden units resembled "true Gypsy caravans."[121] One medical NCO shipped an entire dental office home, and NCOs driving a captured Soviet truck chock-full of soap, sugar, and leather fired on sentries in Buzău before being arrested in Ploiești.[122] On 16 July, the 1st Armored Division, accompanied by motorized German units, entered Chișinău. Overall, German observers were pleased with Romanian units. German liaison reports criticized the Romanian officers' command ability and the NCOs' lack of professionalism but praised the enlisted men's bravery and endurance. Hitler attributed the Romanian Army's good combat performance to Antonescu's presence at the front.[123] As the German Army encountered growing enemy resistance, the OKW reconsidered the limited role it had originally envisioned for the Romanian Army, requesting that the MCG provide even more troops for operations across the Dniester.

Advance into Ukraine

The Third Army had paused on the Dniester, but now it joined the German Eleventh Army in pressing forward into Ukraine, and in a few more weeks so would the Fourth Army. Subsequently, the Romanian Army's brief logistical pause on the Dniester metamorphosed into a crossing of the Rubicon when General Antonescu singlehandedly overrode commanders, politicians, and the public, who all supposedly were against continuing onward—so that in the view of many, the *conducător* alone was to blame for what followed.[124] In fact, senior officers did not oppose crossing the Dniester at the time. Mihai Antonescu and the other ministers in the government supported fighting in Ukraine to win German support to revise the Second Vienna Award; moreover, they planned to use Ukraine as a dumping ground for Jews deported from northern Bukovina and Bessarabia. Even the opposition was split. Iuliu Maniu privately protested the decision, but Gheorghe I. Brătianu joined the Third Army headquarters, translating German documents. Most Romanians believed Axis propaganda promising the USSR's annihilation by Christmas. Antonescu even began thinking of annexing Ukrainian territory with a large ethnic Romanian population. The *conducător* proactively ordered the MCG to intensify propaganda efforts after the crossing of the Dniester, to include messages about bringing *transnistrieni* into Greater Romania and liberating Ukrainian Christians from communist persecution.[125] Romania's holy war continued deeper into the Soviet Union.

The German Eleventh and Third Armies joined German Army Group South's assault on the so-called Stalin Line. Hoping to halt the Axis advance, the Red Army had retreated to these fortifications on the old 1939 border, which had mostly been stripped of equipment after 1940.[126] Marshal Gerd von Rundstedt commanded German Army Group South, which he later referred to tongue in cheek as a "League of Nations Army" because by now it had been reinforced with Romanian, Hungarian, Italian, Croatian, and Slovak forces. He recalled, "The Rumanian divisions were not bad then,

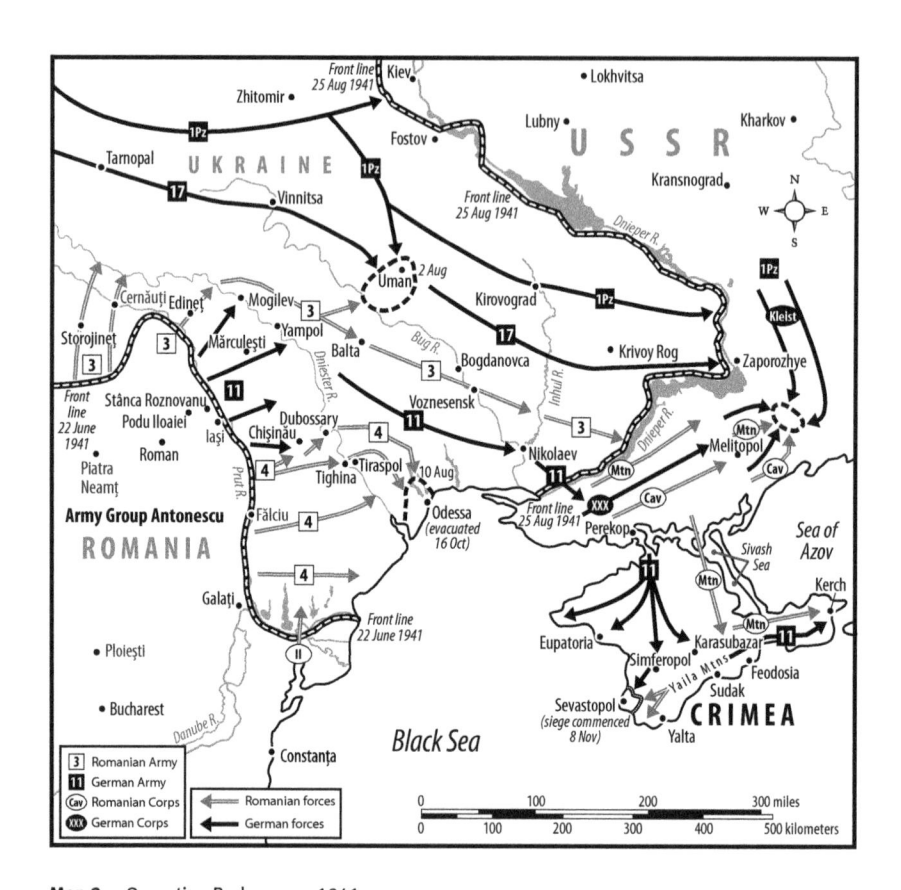

Map 2. Operation Barbarossa, 1941

although they were afterwards. The mountain divisions in particular were good and the cavalry brigades. But the leadership was beyond description. The officers and NCOs . . . !"[127] On 16–17 July, the Third Army also began crossing the Dniester near Mogilev and initially encountered scant resistance. Major Scârneci discovered Soviet officers locked inside casemates by subordinates who had deserted or surrendered. "In some I even found them tightly bound. These facts increased the morale and the trust of my soldiers a lot."[128] The Mountain Corps ran into trouble as the swollen river, insufficient bridging materials, and a shortage of heavy artillery and antitank guns made its bridgehead vulnerable. A Soviet counterattack supported by tanks turned triumph into panic. "My soldiers, who had only seen tanks of cardboard on the firing range, cocked ears and begin to look back." Scârneci rallied his men, "'At them, brothers, 'cause they don't have bullets!'"[129] His mendacious bravado saved the day, as did poor Soviet infantry-armor coordination. The Mountain Corps pierced the Stalin Line in two days, its unit journal trumpeting "the Victorious Crossing of Romanian troops across the Dniester and decisive battle for the destruction of Bolshevism."[130]

The Cavalry Corps now took the lead pursuing the Soviets, while the Mountain Corps trudged in the rear. Just before saddling up, General Racovița ordered that he "didn't want to see a kike" in the rear so that *francs-tireurs* could not attack his supply columns.[131] Gendarmes swept refugees from crowded highways in northern Bessarabia. Jews, and to a lesser extent ethnic Ukrainians and Russians, were imprisoned in concentration camps (often next to prisoner of war camps) on the Dniester; soon the camps were bursting with mostly women, children, and the elderly. On 17 July, General Topor reported to General Antonescu, "We cannot guard them. We cannot feed them. I beg you to give an order concerning what to do with them."[132] The same day, Chișinău fell to Axis troops. The city had been devastated. Sergeant Lungu was appalled by the damage to the cathedral that his military police company discovered, but inside "on the wall of the burned iconostasis, there is the icon of the pure Mary, untouched by the flames of fire!"[133] Some of the destruction was purposeful Soviet demolition, to leave the city a flaming wreck for the Axis occupiers. Romanian soldiers blamed Jews for the Soviet actions, prompting reprisals, but no one counted how many Jews were killed in Chișinău before General Voiculescu arrived a few days later to restore order. On 19 July, the 1st Armored Division reached Tighina, having cleared the way for the Fourth Army to occupy central Bessarabia and for the II Corps to cross into southern Bessarabia.

Gendarmes were much more murderous in Bessarabia than in northern Bukovina. First, fighting had ended very quickly in northern Bukovina but was drawn out in Bessarabia, intensifying antisemitic violence, especially as army propaganda highlighted Soviet destruction of cities and atrocities against Romanians. Second, the gendarme commanders' starkly contrasting attitudes to General Vasiliu's orders resulted in divergent efforts. In northern Bukovina, Colonel Ioan Mânecuța passed along to his subordinates orders to "cleanse the terrain" but did little else. In contrast, in Bessarabia, Colonel Teodor Meculescu repeatedly pressured his subordinates, threatening them with all manner of punishments if they did not shoot as many Jews as possible.[134] Additionally, although Cernăuți had the largest Jewish population in liberated territory, Mânecuța did not establish a ghetto, so instead Chișinău soon boasted the biggest ghetto because Meculescu ruthlessly concentrated surviving Jews from the countryside into the city. Most of Chișinău's sixty to eighty thousand Jews had fled, but four thousand returned because Axis troops blocked their escape, and a ghetto was established on 22 July. Soon gendarmes brought in more Jews, increasing the population to 11,500.[135] Third, Einsatzgruppe D operated more extensively in Bessarabia than in northern Bukovina and encouraged Romanian soldiers and gendarmes to kill more Jews. Overcrowded ghettos in cities and overcrowded camps on the Dniester became centers of starvation and pestilence, but the Antonescu regime made no effort to supply food or medicine to Jews it was preparing to expel over the river.

In the meantime, the II Corps crossed the Danube into southern Bessarabia. Officers reported that "Jews and communist elements" in Ismail had blown up infrastructure and burned stores, while the NKVD (the Soviet secret police) had shot twenty-seven Romanians in the Jewish cemetery. The Jews who had not evacuated were put in a "camp" (a commandeered synagogue) for men and a ghetto for families; later SS troops arrived and shot 105 Jews in the camp.[136] The Soviet Odessa Military District was in full retreat; nevertheless, Soviet rear guards easily checked Romanian advances, giving the Soviets time to set villages and fields on fire after evacuating whatever they could to Cetatea Albă.[137] On 26 July, even though the Soviets still held on to Cetatea Albă, General Antonescu declared Bessarabia liberated, because the Fourth Army had reached the Dniester. The next day, after the German Eleventh Army made a second crossing at Dubossary, gendarmes started deporting Jews from camps in northern Bessarabia into Ukraine. Second Lieutenant Ioan Manu, whose military police unit was guarding a bridge near Mogilev, became alarmed when 10,200 women, children, and elderly were dumped nearby over two days. He warned of "imminent danger" because "10,000 provocateurs" might arm themselves with weapons discarded on the battlefield.[138] Simultaneously, in southern Bessarabia, soldiers entered Cetatea

Albă to adulating crowds. The *Grăniceri* Division looted mounds of goods abandoned by Soviet forces, broke into a wine factory, and hunted for Jews and communists. Civilians reported mined buildings and communists hidden in basements waiting to ambush soldiers.[139] Drunken *grăniceri* murdered scores of Jews. Bartu Buzea saw a lieutenant in the 2nd *Grăniceri* Regiment who was from Cetatea Albă shoot "all the Jews on his street."[140] The Romanian Army now had 402,700 soldiers on the front and had suffered 5,011 dead, 14,898 wounded, and 4,487 missing during the liberation of northern Bukovina and Bessarabia—over a third at Țigancă.[141] At this juncture, Army Group Antonescu dissolved as the Fourth Army paused on the Dniester and the Third and German Eleventh Armies pushed deeper into Ukraine.

General Dumitrescu could no longer permit indiscipline to slow the Third Army's march, because German Army Group South was poised to encircle several Soviet armies at Uman but needed the German Eleventh Army to link up with the German Seventeenth Army. Since crossing into Ukraine, soldiers had broken into homes, pocketed valuables, devastated beehives, rustled animals, and even profaned churches. The day Bessarabia was declared liberated, Dumitrescu rebuked officers for tolerating soldiers' abuse of Ukrainian peasants who were "not guilty of the communists' outrages." He ordered more gendarme patrols and authorized them to punish "with the greatest severity, up to and including the shooting of those who committed acts of banditry."[142] A growing number of officers started flogging soldiers to keep them in order, despite regulations banning corporal punishment. Dumitrescu was not inclined to tolerate Romanian soldiers abusing Soviet civilians for several reasons. First, Ukrainians were Russian Orthodox believers. Additionally, German commanders pressured him to treat Ukrainians better because the OKH wanted to win Ukrainian support.[143] Finally, most importantly, to keep up with the front, soldiers needed to be marching and not pausing to loot. Dumitrescu did not rescind orders to root out Jews and communists. Yet reprisals no longer became pogroms, because Romanian officers were less permissive of indiscipline, and Soviet civilians remained bystanders, not perpetrators. Soviet patriotism, belief in communism, and decades of *anti*-antisemitism propaganda convinced most Soviet civilians not to denounce neighbors or attack Jews when Axis troops arrived—although some collaborated.[144] The Third Army protected the German Eleventh Army's left flank during the advance into Ukraine.

Soldiers spent each day tramping through hot dust until enemy air attacks forced them to march at night. Soviet counterattacks slowed the Axis offensive. Major Scârneci's mountain battalion was shelled before being attacked by infantry and tanks. "Three [tanks] rushed over us to crush us, because

CHAPTER 4

we had just begun to nest ourselves in individual foxholes. Among my soldiers, some panic, but quickly they recoil and, here with bottles with gasoline, there with [armor-]piercing bullets, in less than 15 minutes these three tanks are completely immobilized and begin to burn." Romanian artillery finished off the Soviet infantry. After another day of Soviet bombardments, Scârneci awoke on 28 July to silence. "Have the *ciolovecii* hightailed it?"[145] The "bumpkins" had indeed retreated in a vain attempt to escape encirclement by the German First Panzer Army at Uman. Again, the Third Army marched eastward, soldiers feeling like liberators of downtrodden Ukrainian peasants. Whenever the soldiers paused to rest or wait for supplies, Ukrainians took icons out of hiding places, brought children to be baptized, organized mass weddings, and joined in other ceremonies. On 30 July, Scârneci noted during a burial, "The women look at Captain-Father Manu with a kind of ecstasy. Too bad they are old ladies!"[146] After the ceremony, he held a moral education session while his soldiers deloused. The Cavalry Corps trotted ahead of the Mountain Corps, rounding up Jews, executing in groups of fifty or sixty those deemed dangerous, and keeping the rest as hostages in synagogues and schools.[147] The Third Army quickly outran its supply lines. General Ioan Dumitrache, commander of the 2nd Mixed Mountain Brigade, had to employ soldiers, hostages, and civilians to reap, grind, and bake wheat into bread at a collective farm to feed his men.[148] The German Eleventh Army's lunge to the Bug River left it vulnerable to Soviet counterattacks from Odessa.

General Ciupercă now also became concerned about discipline in the Fourth Army. Hitler had asked General Antonescu if the Fourth Army would cross the Dniester to secure the German Eleventh Army's overextended right flank, and on 31 July, he responded, "I will go to the end of the line."[149] The Fourth Army needed to put its rear in order first. Colonel Dumitru Tudose, Chișinău military commander, reported that officers and NCOs permitted, even participated in, looting, and authorized military police (including German gendarmes) "to execute on the spot any offender."[150] The MCG's arrival in the city probably influenced this hard line. On 2 August, General Ciupercă reissued Tudose's order to all the Fourth Army. The same day, after several vehicles had been ambushed, five "proven" communists began to be executed in each village along the road from Chișinău to Tighina on Ciupercă's order.[151] Bartu Buzea recalled one case of summary execution for indiscipline. A sergeant who had been ordered to shoot a Jewish family instead let them go after raping the daughter. After finding out, the 2nd *Grăniceri* Regiment commander assembled the unit and, after some words about discipline, shot the sergeant.[152] Soldiers still got away with looting under the cover of authorized reprisals. Cetatea Albă's few remaining Jews were held in a synagogue, while Jews from nearby towns were imprisoned in another. On 3 August, Major Virgil Drăgan, commander of the city market; Captain Olimpiu Mihailescu, assistant gendarme commander; and Major Horia Olteanu, an SSI officer, met with two SS officers. Einsatzgruppe D now ignored the Commissar Order's limits and murdered Jews indiscriminately.[153] The Cetatea Albă garrison commander was absent, but these low-ranking officers went ahead, without orders, with plans to liquidate the Jews in the city. When Captain Alexandru Ochișor reminded them at dawn of recent orders instructing suspected communists be sent to Chișinău, they woke Colonel Marcela Petala, the Third Army chief praetor who happened to be visiting the city, to obtain permission to shoot the Jews. Petala was angry to be disturbed. "In Chișinău all Jews are imprisoned in a ghetto and in every night they pull out hundreds of Jews f[or] executions!"[154] Under Ochișor's eye, groups of forty were driven to the maritime railway station, where in two days some one thousand Jews were interrogated, stripped of valuables, and shot in a quarry.[155] A month later, 150 Jews from Chilia Nouă who stopped in Cetatea Albă were murdered for their belongings.[156] Soldiers were almost never punished for crimes against Jews.

While the Fourth Army crossed at Dubossary, gendarmes pushed twenty-five thousand Jews across the Dniester at Mogilev.[157] General von Schobert complained that Jews clogged roads and bridges, threatened telecommunications, consumed rations, spread disease, and should be kept for labor. On 6 August, General Ciupercă issued an order repeating these points and banning gendarmes from pushing Jews over at Dubossary.[158] General Antonescu met Hitler that day too. He received a Knight's Cross and orders for the Fourth Army to capture Odessa.[159] During the meeting, the crisis at Mogilev worsened. German troops pushed three thousand Jews back into northern Bessarabia and shot thousands of others who were too exhausted to move.[160] The following day Romanian gendarmes stopped German troops from sending back more Jews; nevertheless, within a week 12,500 Jews, not counting 4,000 dead, had been returned. Antonescu whined that this was "contrary to the guidelines which the Führer had set forth to him in Munich regarding the treatment of eastern Jews."[161] On 15 August, gendarmes guarding twelve hundred Jews at the Tătărești labor camp in southern Bessarabia shot hundreds when they became "aggressive."[162] By now soldiers and gendarmes had killed an estimated 43,500 Jews in northern Bukovina and Bessarabia.[163]

German Army Group South closed the Uman pocket but needed more men to strengthen the encirclement, so the Third Army lengthened its stride while tightening its belt. Sergeant Ionescu noted, "During the advance into Ukraine we were without bread five days continuously, because the field bakeries had fallen behind. . . . Many times we eat soup without bread, *mămăligă* or potatoes."[164] General Avramescu urged on his soldiers "to avenge thereby our dead comrades" and "[deliver] a people from slavery." He promised, "Just one more week of fresh efforts and the triumph will be great."[165] German units crowded Romanian troops off the roads, Major Scârneci angrily noted. "We admire, however, their way of marching: without excitement, without racket and Gypsy-ness [*țigănie*]."[166] His mountain troops passed Jewish refugees from Balta. "They are in an unimaginable squalor: scared, starving, dying of thirst, dirty. Of what little they have left they are robbed everywhere by villains. All the sins from Moses onward they are atoning now, in spades."[167] Taking pity, he gave them some water and bread before moving on. On 8 August, Soviet resistance in the Uman pocket ended, resulting in one hundred thousand prisoners. The following day, as the Mountain Corps began crossing over to Voznesensk, the Hungarian Rapid Corps holding the opposing bank became alarmed, and the Hungarians threatened to attack the Romanians if they did not turn around. German liaisons intervened and decided to keep the river between the two rivals.[168] The Third Army took up a defensive position on the Bug for a rest.

Battle of Odessa

Meanwhile, the Fourth Army advanced into the teeth of Soviet defenses outside Odessa. The city proved a tough nut to crack, as its six hundred thousand citizens, a third of whom were Jews, had constructed four concentric fortified lines. Two estuaries divided the battlefield into western and eastern sectors. Odessa's factories produced mountains of weapons (enough to export some to Crimea), including mortars, grenades and incendiary bottles, and armored tractors nicknamed "Odessa tanks." The Soviet Independent Coastal Army only had eighty-six thousand soldiers and 247 field pieces but could call on coastal artillery, warships, and aircraft. Crimea acted as an unsinkable Soviet aircraft carrier. The Soviet Black Sea Fleet dominated the sea, so the Soviet Headquarters of the Supreme Main Command (Stavka) could still quickly reinforce Odessa.[169] The German Military Mission pressured the MCG to seize Odessa as soon as possible, to use its port to supply German Army Group South; General Franz Halder, chief of OKH, wrote in his diary, "No Odessa, no Crimea."[170] The Fourth Army's hundred thousand men overwhelmed Odessa's outer fortified line by 10 August and captured seven thousand prisoners.[171] The 1st Armored Division broke through the second and third defensive lines in the eastern sector. Sergeant Lungu saw the carnage left behind: "The field was dotted about with dead, Romanian and Russian.

Some had died with weapons in their hands, others with a telephone at their throat, others on houses, swollen like barrels and eaten by flies in the heat of summer."[172] Soviet counterattacks halted Romanian infantry divisions in the western sector. First Lieutenant Gherghe Petrescu in the 6th *Dorobanți* Regiment recalled, "An enemy counterattack supported by tankettes caused us great losses. Many soldiers were crushed by tankettes, lacking shelters. Houses and trees in orchards were burned."[173] The Soviet defenders finally stopped the 1st Armored Division in the narrowing isthmus between the estuaries and sea in the eastern sector, creating a small killing field. The Fourth Army's piecemeal rush to take Odessa in a single stroke had failed.

As the Fourth Army prepared a proper assault against Odessa, the Third Army crossed the Bug. The renewed advance shocked the Third Army, because General von Schobert had bid farewell to General Dumitrescu and thanked Romanian commanders for fulfilling the mission, creating the impression in the ranks that their role in the invasion was finished.[174] The Red Army was fighting harder than ever, however, and the OKH was desperate for reinforcements for the German Army.[175] On 14 August, Hitler again turned to General Antonescu, who acquiesced to sending the Third Army eastward on the condition that German Army Group South supplied it.[176] The same day, perhaps not coincidently, the MCG officially reintroduced flogging to maintain discipline. Major Scârneci wrote, "Illusions shattered. . . . Many among the soldiers are steamed." He reasoned the chances of the Second Vienna Award being revised had just increased, however. As for his soldiers' morale, "Anger, like joy too, is passing."[177] After reports of soldiers' lack of enthusiasm, the MCG ordered the Third Army to remind its disappointed troops that so long as the USSR resisted, Romania was imperiled: "Every drop of blood shed across the Dniester is thus an absolutely necessary sacrifice, a sacrifice made only for our cause and not for any other."[178] Dumitrescu again pushed his troops forward in long marches.

General Antonescu believed German triumph was weeks away, so he was anxious to win a Romanian victory at Odessa to impress Hitler.[179] General Ciupercă ordered a general attack on 18 August without artillery preparation, to try to surprise the defenders, but it met with little success. His forces penetrated to the second line in the western sector and reached within fifteen kilometers of the port in the eastern sector in six days but could not advance any farther. The Fourth Army suffered 27,307 casualties.[180] The MCG blamed Romanian cowards and Soviet Jews for the failure. Antonescu believed soldiers had demonstrated insufficient élan. On 20 August, General Ioanițiu threatened to revoke decorations, land grants, and financial aid to families of cowards and ordered blocking detachments to fire on panicked troops. On 26 August, he ordered soldiers with self-inflicted wounds to be executed, but commanders uncovered few cases and shot even fewer. The III Corps executed two soldiers, but the XI Corps only sentenced twenty-three soldiers to twelve years' hard labor.[181] Antonescu blamed Soviet resistance on Jews. Army intelligence claimed a Soviet unit formed from Jews called "the death battalion" policed Odessa, "Jewish" Red Army political commissars used terror to get Soviet troops to fight, and all Jewish men over fifteen in the city had been mobilized.[182] Under pressure from the MCG, Ciupercă launched a second assault in the western sector on 28 August—this time with twenty to twenty-five minutes of bombardment—which nearly overwhelmed the second line.

As the Fourth Army clawed its way forward, the MCG made a land grab. A month earlier the *conducător* had informed the German Military Mission that Romania was interested in annexing part of Ukraine, so when Hitler, as part of another request for the Third Army to advance (this time beyond the Dnieper River), suggested the Romanian Army secure southern Ukraine between the Dniester and the Dnieper Rivers for the German Army, General Antonescu assumed—mistakenly or shrewdly—that the führer offered the whole territory as a prize. Romania could police the whole area, the *conducător* responded, but it could only administer and economically exploit the smaller region between the Dniester and the Bug. Antonescu had maneuvered Hitler into giving Romania not just territory to occupy but to govern.[183] On 30 August, eight days after Mihai I promoted Antonescu to marshal, deputy chief of staff General Nicolae Tătăranu and General Arthur Hauffe (who had replaced General Hansen as commander of the German Military Mission) signed a deal in Tighina. The Tighina Agreement granted the MCG authority over the territory between the Dniester and the Bug, required the Romanian Army to provide rear security between the Bug and the Dnieper, granted the German Army some key concessions, including control over railroads, and clarified that Jews should be held in ghettos and camps west of the Bug until after final victory.[184] The Antonescu regime dubbed Romania's new territory Transnistria. On 1 September, the Third Army reached the Dnieper, having taken 19,861 casualties since crossing the Dniester, and fended off Soviet counterattacks.[185] The Romanian Army now fought not just to hold on to newly liberated northern Bukovina and Bessarabia or for the possible return of northern Transylvania, but also to aggrandize Greater Romania with Transnistria.

The Fourth Army's bloody attacks at Odessa continued unabated. Romanian soldiers satiated their need for revenge for lost comrades on Soviet civilians: on 2 September, fifty people were shot in recently occupied Bilyaivka for supposedly having weapons and participating in the defense of the village.[186] The Fourth Army now had two hundred thousand soldiers and three times the field guns of the Soviet Independent Coastal Army, which had half as many troops, but Soviet trenches and heavy coastal or naval guns negated the Romanian numerical advantage. Moreover, Romanian artillery was primarily light 75 mm guns, ineffective at blasting infantry out of trenches (eventually 1.3 million 75 mm shells were fired, compared to just two hundred thousand 105 mm and 150 mm shells), and it coordinated poorly with infantry.[187] Supply lines relying on horses or oxen created shell shortages. A captured Soviet officer reported that Romanian infantry advanced in dense formations, lacked fire discipline, were timid in pursuit, and attacked "by template."[188] The departure of German Luftflotte 4, leaving only the GAL to support the Fourth Army, did not help either. Soviet reinforcements arrived on 5 September, just in time to prevent a Romanian breakthrough as fresh Soviet troops blocked exhausted Romanian soldiers.[189]

Although the battle at Odessa paused, the campaign against Jews in Bessarabia restarted. On 7 September, General Topor ordered gendarmes to prepare to deport Jews from camps on the Dniester into Transnistria, starting with twenty-three thousand Jews held at Vertujeni near Soroca. They would be deported in groups of one thousand, and any who resisted would be shot.[190] The ghettos in Bessarabia would be emptied once Odessa fell. Transnistria was to be a dumping ground for unwanted Jews, but at the same time a place where Soviet Moldavians could be reclaimed for Greater Romania. The Fourth Army claimed that Soviet Moldavians welcomed Romanian soldiers with "greater warmth" than *basarabeni* because these ethnic Romanians had suffered great oppression under communism. In the village of Buhai, the Moldavians celebrated by baptizing children at a well because the Soviets had demolished the local church. Chaplains contributed to the evangelical fervor. Chaplain Sever I. D. Husariu wrote a letter to the *conducător* petitioning for funds for a Romanian Orthodox Church youth program in Transnistria because the "first measure that we need to occupy ourselves with, is the religious culture problem and formation of the youth."[191] The Antonescu regime eventually embarked on such imperial projects in Transnistria, but at the moment it was focused on ridding northern Bukovina and Bessarabia of Jews and finishing the conquest of Odessa.

After taking another 31,522 casualties in two weeks, General Ciupercă believed the Fourth Army was bled white, but the MCG ordered another assault, believing Odessa was near collapse.[192] On 9 September, Marshal Antonescu sacked Ciupercă for insufficient offensive spirit, replacing him with General Iacobici, but publicly claimed Ciupercă was physically

Figure 6. An evangelical fervor pervaded the Romanian Army during its advance into the Soviet Union. Scenes like this mass baptism of Soviet peasants by a Romanian chaplain in August 1941 during the Odessa campaign were repeated wherever Romanian soldiers went in 1941, and even in 1942. Romanian soldiers admired the piety of older Soviet civilians, easing tensions between the occupiers and the occupied. Photo by Ioan Todor, courtesy of Ioan Darabanț.

exhausted. He was not the only one who was worn out. Major Virgil M. Protopopescu, an artillery battalion commander with the 13th *Infanterie* Regiment, scribbled, "For 19 days we don't move except on our bellies and the same number of days unwashed we take meals at night 'once a night' and then only cold. The only entertainment is bombs, aircraft, whistling of bullets, etc. We don't get bored of them but the dirty rat life that we endure for so many days constantly wears us down."[193] Antonescu took over Iacobici's job as minister of defense in Bucharest and left General Ioanițiu at the MCG in Tighina. Ciupercă's departing message argued that Romanians would not be "true masters" of Bessarabia until the Soviets were defeated. "At the gates of Odessa, we are now only a step away from this goal. Country and Nation ask from you to make the ultimate efforts to smash the gates of Odessa and squash our bitter enemy.... Forward with God.... Righteousness is with us!"[194] Antonescu asked General Hauffe for German soldiers, tanks, and aircraft, but only two infantry, one heavy artillery, and four engineer battalions could be found.[195] On 12 September, the Fourth Army's third assault began after a ten-to-fifteen-minute barrage and soon succeeded in capturing two thousand prisoners. After two days, the Soviet Independent Coastal Army abandoned the second line, pulling back to the third line anchored on Dalnik. This town atop a slight hill lying perpendicular across the direct road to Odessa had been heavily fortified. A hastily prepared Romanian attack spearheaded by recently arrived German battalions was repulsed by the Soviet defenses at Dalnik on 17 September.[196] Romanian units were bombed heavily by Soviet aircraft, especially because the Romanians often neglected camouflage.[197] Meanwhile more Soviet reinforcements arrived, preventing collapse. Soviet resistance only seemed to increase as Romanian soldiers advanced. The German Army also found the Red Army a much tougher enemy than expected, making the Romanian Army's continued support essential for operations farther east.

As the Fourth Army dug in outside Odessa, the Third Army crossed the Dnieper. The day before the failed attack at Dalnik, General Avramescu told his mountain troops, "Today, as we expand the field of battle against the Bolsheviks across the Dnieper, we win the right to enlarge the truncated borders of Transylvania."[198] After German Army Group South's crushing victory at Kiev, the German Eleventh Army was free to attack Crimea, but it did so under a new commander, because General von Schobert was killed when his plane landed on a Soviet minefield at Nikolaev. Bad luck struck again as General Ioanițiu died when he accidently stepped into an aircraft propeller after landing near Odessa. An intelligent, hardworking, and calm chief of staff, he was sorely missed. "[Ioanițiu] was the best complement possible for the volcanic temperament of the Marshal," General Pantazi recalled.[199] General Iacobici became chief of staff but also retained command of the Fourth Army. The Third Army followed the German Eleventh Army, now under General Erich von Manstein, into the Nogay Steppe north of the Azov Sea. He broke up the Third Army and put the Mountain and Cavalry Corps to the left and right of a German corps to form a line from the Dnieper to the seashore, gambling that this amalgamated force could hold the rear while the main force broke into Crimea. The OKH vaguely hoped that if the German Eleventh Army could take Crimea it would somehow compel the Soviet Independent Coastal Army to surrender Odessa.[200]

The MCG had no more troops or matériel to reinforce the exhausted Fourth Army with, so it focused on trying to buoy morale with propaganda. The Fourth Army had difficulty supplying itself. Soldiers drank from scummy pools and gathered vegetables from nearby fields. Hunger and casualties sapped Romanian soldiers' spirits. Corporal Constantin Iancu munched on fresh vegetables between attacks that devolved into hand-to-hand combat. "After [one] cruel attack, at the sight of mangled corpses and so many puddles of blood, for a long time I could not tolerate tomatoes, I only saw blood before me."[201] To discourage troops from surrendering, army propaganda accused Soviet troops of torturing and murdering captured Romanian soldiers; these claims also stoked hatred against Jews, who were blamed for these alleged atrocities.[202]

Romanian soldiers had been told for weeks that the Soviet defenders were on their last legs, so the Fourth Army was unprepared when the Soviet Independent Coastal Army launched a major counterattack in the eastern sector on 21 September, which was supported by a small amphibious landing and a tiny air drop into the Romanian rear. Panicked Romanian troops fled ten kilometers, abandoning vital artillery positions overlooking the port, and Soviet soldiers took thirteen hundred prisoners.[203] To explain away the defeat, *Soldatul* published an article on 30 September titled, "Why Are the Bolsheviks Resisting?" The answer: Jewish communists. It claimed that 90 percent of Red Army political commissars were "kikes" practicing "animalistic" propaganda and prosecuting a "subhuman" war by terrorizing Soviet soldiers. The article described Odessa as a "nest of Bolsheviks" prepared to fight to the bitter end.[204] After the Soviet Independent Coastal Army's show of force, the MCG abandoned any plans for another assault until the Fourth Army was reinforced with German forces.

Odessa's fate would not be decided at Dalnik, but at Perekop. German forces had begun battering Soviet defenders blocking the entrance to Crimea, causing two Soviet armies to attack the German-Romanian line on the Nogay Steppe, trying to break through before the German Eleventh Army smashed through the Perekop isthmus. Soviet artillery and aircraft pummeled the Axis line between attacks by infantry and tanks for eight days; General Dumitrache remembered that one night there were four air attacks every hour.[205] The Third Army had to keep its reserves far to the rear.[206] The unceasing bombardments inflicted psychological as well as physical damage. Major Scârneci recorded, "Many are shocked. Second Lieutenant Arsenie—a worthy soldier—babbles. I return bitterly to my den, I slowly nest myself next to comrade Second Lieutenant Pitiș, who sleeps deeply and shakes abundantly."[207] The German-Romanian line started buckling on the flanks as the 4th Mixed Mountain Brigade had to pull back along the Dnieper bank and the 8th Cavalry Brigade lost contact with German troops near Melitopol.[208] General von Manstein halted the attack in the south and rushed forces to the north. Then, on 1 October, German Panzer Group Kleist encircled the attacking Soviet armies, and the German Eleventh and Third Armies went on the attack. The Cavalry Corps' motorized regiments kept in reserve charged forward, linking up with the German panzer divisions, and helped capture one hundred thousand Soviet troops.[209] The Stavka ordered the Soviet Independent Coastal Army to evacuate from Odessa to Sevastopol as nothing now prevented the German Eleventh Army from breaking into Crimea.

Romanian soldiers began showing signs of deteriorating morale as summer turned to autumn and victory seemed no closer. The Third Army's morale had been fairly good despite long marches and tough combat, because it had participated in encirclement battles without taking heavy casualties; even German liaisons admitted the Romanian units had fought well. Nonetheless, its soldiers were exhausted.[210] The OKH planned to only use the Third Army to secure the Azov Sea coast.[211] The Fourth Army's morale was satisfactory at best. An artillery officer reported soldiers saying, "Why don't the Germans come? Why not bring one or two PANTZER [sic] Divisions? Why don't the Stukas come? Until the Sea is closed . . . nothing can be done." The SSI reported a few soldiers muttering mutinously, "Why were we brought through these parts?" "Should we not fight?" "We don't have any business here."[212] Soldiers faced all the horrors of trench warfare. Movement brought down withering enemy fire, soldiers dug "Tartar holes" that were just wide and deep enough for a man to shield from tanks and mortar blasts, rations ran short, and tainted water caused diarrhea (army intelligence blamed poisoning by Soviet agents).[213] Some soldiers cracked under the pressure. After an officer in the 15th *Dorobanți* Regiment lost his composure, Major Gheorghe Rășcănescu threatened to punish him for cowardice, and then "I gave him two powerful slaps. 'What is this First Lieutenant Velicov?' 'You hit me!' 'You see that you know what's happening now? But what you did earlier you didn't know? Go, get yourself healthy and after four days come back.'"[214] On 5 October *Sentinela* ran an article titled "Why Do We Fight?" It answered this question with a question: "What would happen if we do not fight?" If the Red Army was not defeated, it would return ten times stronger to "break all the borders, from Finland to the shores of the Dniester," bringing class warfare, destroying the family, destroying churches (but sparing synagogues), and forcing peasants onto collective farms.[215] Even though morale had dipped, soldiers remained committed to Romania's holy war.

Odessa's sudden fall seemed an omen of final victory and raised spirits on the front and in Romania. Romanian air reconnaissance and Soviet prisoners informed the Fourth Army of the Soviet Independent Coastal Army's preparations to evacuate, but General Iacobici could do little but occupy vacated positions, since his troops were exhausted and enemy fire remained deadly.[216] The Soviets evacuated 86,000 troops and 150,000 civilians by the time the last ships left on 15–16 October.[217] At dawn Romanian units warily advanced. Major Răşcănescu led his battalion through suddenly vacant trenches. "The telephone wire that the battalion's team of telephonists was extending arrives. I report that I arrived at the Russian railway and I made the fire plan. Not a gunshot fired. . . . Joy, but they still did not believe me!"[218] Patrols captured prisoners, eventually over six thousand, and navigated hastily laid minefields. Romanian troops reached the city's outskirts that afternoon. Răşcănescu hesitated until a passing general yelled at him to get a move on. His battalion picked its way through barricaded streets to the Potemkin Steps and dug Tartar holes on the bluff in expectation of partisan ambushes.[219] The Fourth Army had suffered 63,280 wounded, 17,891 killed, and 8,849 missing during the battle for the city.[220] Soldiers who began pouring into Odessa the next day were anxious to celebrate their survival and avenge fallen comrades.

Commanders believed that Odessa represented a dangerous Jewish-communist center. The German Military Mission warned the MCG that Soviet partisans had mined Kiev a month earlier, killing many German soldiers, so General Ionel Glogojanu, the 10th Infantry Division commander, was put in charge of the Odessa Military Command to clear the city of threats. He had authority over all military forces in Odessa and was responsible for maintaining order, but this was difficult to do from his headquarters on the city's edge.[221] General Iacobici told Glogojanu that Odessa was "teeming" with Jews and Soviet soldiers disguised as civilians, so he ordered "radical searches."[222] Soldiers entered homes looking for weapons but also demanded food, especially sugar, with multiple groups visiting the same place if well stocked. Citizens later mockingly nicknamed these "sugar patrols," but they were deadly serious, especially for Jews. Over seven thousand people were arrested as partisans, and some were executed.[223] A few fires broke out each night in the city, which army intelligence immediately blamed on Jews. On 21 October, a Jewish "ringleader" and fifteen "communist terrorists" were shot.[224] In *Sentinela*'s comic strip, Private Neață walks into Odessa after neutralizing Soviet soldiers by spraying vodka into a machine gun nest, causing the defenders to fall into a drunken stupor.[225] Odessa's occupation did involve alcohol, but consumed by Romanian troops who began looting, raping, and murdering. Looting occurred on an epic scale, and the Odessa Military Command resorted to severe measures to keep order. Major Rășcănescu recalled finding a sergeant shot dead with stolen shoe leather all about him outside a warehouse turned over to a German unit.[226] The Odessa Military Command ordered all male residents to register with authorities. Some four thousand Jewish men were held for interrogation. Israel Adesman recalled, "Some were taken to gallows or trenches, while others were jailed. A few were allowed to return to their looted homes, but only for the time being."[227] There were a handful of partisans hiding in Odessa, and in the catacombs beneath the city, but Romanian security measures mostly targeted innocent Jews.

The Antonescu regime prepared to establish ghettos and camps in Transnistria while it emptied ghettos and camps in northern Bukovina and Bessarabia. The MCG issued deceptively detailed orders on how to deport Jews that did not include providing sufficient gendarmes, carts, or food and demanded that women, children, and the elderly march thirty kilometers a day.[228] Gendarmes started emptying the Chișinău ghetto a week before Odessa fell, as it became clear the Soviets were evacuating, and finished by the end of the month. Jews in Bessarabia were marched to the border. The Cernăuți ghetto, with 49,500 Jews, was finally established. Jews in northern Bukovina, plus those in southern Bukovina (despite not having been under Soviet occupation), were deported by train to the Dniester before continuing on foot.[229] Gendarmes robbed, raped, and murdered thousands as convoys traveled to the border; not counting those who died along the way, 86,000 Jews from Bukovina and 56,000 Jews from Bessarabia arrived in Transnistria.[230] The recently established Governorate of Transnistria started herding the 100,000–150,000 Soviet Jews that remained in Transnistria into ghettos and camps as well.[231] Romanian Jews displaced Soviet Jews who were deported farther east to make room for the new arrivals.

An act of partisan sabotage intervened in Odessa, triggering vicious retaliation against local Jews. On 22 October, General Glogojanu moved the 10th Infantry Division and the Odessa Military Command headquarters into the former NKVD headquarters near the port to better enforce order in the city. Civilians warned that the building was mined. German and Romanian pioneers had already searched the headquarters; and now Romanian pioneers who rechecked it for a third time again found nothing.[232] Then, at 5:35 p.m., the building exploded, killing seventy-nine soldiers and sailors, including Glogojanu, wounding forty-three others, and leaving thirteen missing.[233] General Constantin Trestioreanu, the 10th Infantry Division's second in command, had been elsewhere and appeared an hour later to direct rescue efforts and reprisals. "I took measures to hang in public squares in Odessa Jews and communists," he reported.[234] Troops hanged Jews from lampposts along the central thoroughfares and shot others. General Iacobici informed Marshal Antonescu that he had ordered "severe reprisals," including executing one hundred or two hundred communists for each soldier or officer killed, respectively, and displaying the corpses to deter further partisan attacks. A warehouse caught fire in the night, heightening fears of further sabotage. Iacobici sent General Nicolae Macici, the II Corps commander, to take control. He was disgusted with Trestioreanu and his staff. "You're a bunch of cowards and scaredy cats, by now Odessa should've been turned inside out!"[235] Macici initiated a new wave of atrocities that convulsed the city.

Commanders directed soldiers' pent-up anger at the departed Soviet troops, who had inflicted so many Romanian casualties, against the Jews of Odessa. Soldiers shot thousands of Jewish men in a square by the port near the smoldering ruins of the Odessa Military Command and escorted Jewish women, children, and elderly to the city jail that held over twenty thousand Jews. Marshal Antonescu added fuel to the fire by confirming General Iacobici's orders, and adding, "All Communists in Odessa will be taken as hostages as well as a member of each Jewish family."[236] On 24 October, soldiers marched Jews from Odessa's jail two kilometers down the road toward Dalnik, shooting any who fell behind. After reaching antitank ditches, which were used as improvised mass graves, they machine-gunned groups of forty to fifty Jews at a time. Other soldiers shoved thousands of Jews into four warehouses near the jail, two with men and two with women and children, and set them ablaze.[237] They shot or threw grenades at anyone who tried to escape. Major Gherman Pântea, a bilingual *basarabean* recently appointed as the city's mayor, was appalled. He prevailed upon Macici to turn back the convoys of Jews being marched to antitank ditches on the edge of the city. Pântea also refused to move the mayoral offices outside Odessa when ordered to by General Nicolae Ghineraru, acting commander of the 10th Infantry Division. Pântea believed the civilian administration could not do its job to restore the city to functioning order from so far away, and the move would only increase panic and suffering for locals because he would not be on the spot to challenge the military authorities. Ghineraru scoffed, "I don't need the city, nor your citizens. If I was in the Marshal's place, I would set alight this infected city with all your citizens in 24 hours." Pântea wrote Antonescu, begging him to intervene. "I am not the Jews' defender, but I am convinced Mister Marshal that these hasty and unjust measures will later make [things] worse for us."[238] Antonescu instead ordered Macici to kill all Romanian Jewish refugees in Odessa and put communists "inside a building that will be mined and detonated" on the day that Glogojanu and the other casualties from the headquarters were buried.[239] Macici had already stopped reprisals by the time he received these instructions, but he blew up one of the burned, corpse-filled warehouses the next day to fulfill the letter of Antonescu's order.

The Odessa massacre's total number of victims has been the subject of wild speculation. At the time, Einsatzgruppe D reported ten thousand dead.[240] Postwar investigations claimed nineteen to twenty-three thousand victims, and some today suggest forty thousand.[241] Trial records indicate hundreds hanged, five thousand shot near the port, hundreds machine-gunned at the antitank ditches on the road to Dalnik, five thousand burned in the warehouses, and hundreds more killed elsewhere. Hundreds of Jews killed after the city fell but before the headquarters exploded should be added. The Odessa massacre likely claimed the lives of twelve thousand of the eighty to ninety thousand Jews not evacuated from the city.[242] Some Jews were released following the massacre, but the SSI reported, "The return of the evacuated Jews has led to deep dissatisfaction among the Christian inhabitants who took over their abandoned houses in the belief that the explosion in the military headquarters would result in a radical purge of Jews."[243] The Antonescu regime decided to deport "suspect" Jews from Odessa to camps on the Bug. Soon convoys of ten thousand to twelve thousand Jews were trudging along muddy roads in freezing rain. Gendarmes robbed, raped, and shot Jews along the way. By November forty thousand Jews had been expelled from Odessa, but forty thousand remained.[244] These were herded into a ghetto in the Slobodka industrial zone to be deported over the Bug after German victory.

Victory?

Romanians believed the holy war was nearly over, and the *conducător* thought the Romanian Army would only need to help the German Army mop up the defeated Red Army. The Antonescu regime celebrated not only the reconquest of northern Bukovina and Bessarabia, but also congratulated itself for cleansing the terrain of Jews. Romania had fully committed itself to Nazi Germany's final victory. Marshal Antonescu had seized Transnistria and now envisioned not only restoring Greater Romania's interwar borders by convincing Hitler to force Hungary to return northern Transylvania but also expanding them to encompass *transnistrieni*. Furthermore, the Romanian Army's war crimes in the USSR bound it tightly to the German Army's fate. Indeed, after the Odessa massacre, Romanian soldiers engaged along with German troops in warfare that increasingly targeted not just Soviet partisans but also Soviet civilians and prisoners of war, in addition to Jews. Thus, when the USSR did not collapse, Romania kept fighting alongside Nazi Germany.

CHAPTER 5

1941–1942: Doubling Down on Holy War

Sergeant Ionescu stood guard near Eupatoria in Crimea on Christmas day. Two days later he attended holiday Mass, where the 38th *Infanterie* Regiment's colonel said, "In winter we will keep watch so that we don't lose what we conquered here . . . yet in spring, the German Army, together with the Romanian Army, will continue to fight until the annihilation of the Bolsheviks, and [I believe] that in two months, in spring, the battle against the Bolsheviks will be finished."[1] Soviet troops had actually already disembarked on the opposite end of the peninsula at Kerch a few days before, part of a gargantuan Soviet winter counteroffensive along the entire eastern front. The German Army's failure to defeat the Red Army seemed to herald disaster. Romanian soldiers confronted probably the worst conditions of the war, because overstretched Axis logistics failed to deliver winter gear, supplies, replacements, and even mail. The Romanian Army's morale plummeted, although a combination of propaganda, strict discipline, devotion to comrades, and self-preservation, plus German support, kept it fighting through the winter. The crisis at the front in Crimea caused the Antonescu regime to adopt genocidal policies in the rear in Transnistria. The German Army's near-miraculous recovery during the spring and apparently successful offensive in the summer raised the Romanian Army's morale, increasing its combat motivation. Romanian units helped Einsatzgruppe D exterminate Jews, especially in Crimea, proving atrocity motivation was also still strong. Furthermore, Romanian troops increasingly committed atrocities against Soviet civilians, prisoners of war, and partisans. Even when the campaigning continued into the autumn, soldiers remained committed to Romania's holy war and still believed in Nazi Germany's final victory over the Soviet Union.

Conquest of Crimea

The Romanian Army partially demobilized after Odessa fell. On 15 October, the MCG ordered the Fourth Army to start sending home units mobilized the longest, leaving just four infantry divisions and two cavalry brigades for occupation duties, so the Romanian Army soon shrank from 750,500 to 410,500 soldiers.[2] The German Army needed as many men as possible for its final push, so the Romanian Army's continued contribution was a huge help, with 104,000 soldiers occupying Transnistria and 23,000 securing southern Ukraine between the Bug and Dnieper Rivers, as agreed to in the Tighina Agreement, plus 50,000 more guarding the Azov Sea coast.[3] Every Romanian soldier committed to securing the rear freed a German soldier for the front. Autumn storms turned roads into mud, slowing the German Army Group Center's advance into Russia, but better weather allowed the German Army Group South to continue forward in Ukraine and Crimea.[4] General von Manstein approached Marshal Antonescu requesting Third Army units to support the German Eleventh Army's attack into Crimea. As von Manstein would lead more Romanian soldiers for longer than any other German commander, his evaluation of the Romanian Army is particularly valuable. He identified the same weaknesses as other German observers, such as brave but poorly trained soldiers, lack of professional NCOs, poor man management by officers, lack of experience, outdated French doctrine, obsolete weapons, and tendency to panic owing to "their terrific respect for 'the Russians.'" "Despite all the defects and reservations mentioned above, however, the Romanian troops performed their duty as best they could. Above all, they always readily submitted to German military leadership and did not, like other allies of ours, put matters of prestige before material necessity."[5] Antonescu immediately agreed to provide von Manstein with several Romanian brigades.

Final victory seemed tantalizingly close, with Leningrad besieged, Moscow threatened, and Kiev captured. The MCG drew up lists of soldiers to receive land in northern Bukovina and Bessarabia for winning medals, and soldiers spread rumors that once Crimea fell, they would go home.[6] On 18 October, the German Eleventh Army again began to attack at Perekop. The

Korne Detachment (the 6th Motorized *Roșiori* Regiment reinforced with a mechanized cavalry squadron) and some German motorized units were combined into the Ziegler Motorized Brigade—von Manstein's sole mobile unit—and held in reserve. On 21 October, the MCG naïvely cabled the OKW, "We ask if you could please communicate to us how long it will be necessary for III Army units to remain East of the Dnieper, both to secure the Azov Sea littoral and eventually in Crimea."[7] In Bucharest even staunch anti-Nazis believed the end was near. Jewish writer Mihail Sebastian recorded, "[Alexandru] Rosetti tells me that the Germans have won the war, that the Russians can no longer put up any resistance, that Britain has no option other than to reach a compromise peace. I try to raise his spirits, but without success."[8] On 24 October, the remaining Fourth Army units in Transnistria were subordinated to the Third Army headquarters.[9] Then the MCG reverted to the General Staff and returned to the capital. Wilhelm Filderman, the leader of Romania's Jewish community, publicly begged for an end to the deadly deportations of Jews to Transnistria. On 26 October, Jewish doctor Emil Dorian overheard an old man haranguing other streetcar passengers, "Imagine that! The kike's general, this Filderman, dares to call General Antonescu for killing kikes! Doesn't he know that the kikes spat on our soldiers? They're only getting what's coming to them. It's either them or us!"[10] Romanians anticipated the destruction of Judeo-Bolshevism in a climatic final battle between Nazi Germany and the Soviet Union.

As General von Manstein's troops battered against Soviet defenses, General Dumitrescu settled into rear-area operations. The Third Army headquarters was next to the German Eleventh Army and Einsatzgruppe D headquarters in Nikolaev. General Dumitrescu ceded control of brigades sent to General von Manstein, but he retained responsibility for administration, supply, and discipline of Romanian units spread across nine hundred kilometers from Tiraspol on the Dniester to Taganrog near the mouth of the Don River. He was also responsible for securing this area from Soviet guerrillas, called partisans. The partisan movement began in July when the Stavka instructed Soviet stragglers to form guerrilla groups to fight in the rear after being overtaken by German spearheads. Initially an inchoate mass, the sheer number of Soviet stragglers was a serious threat to Axis logistics, and became even more dangerous as they became organized.[11] In September, the NKVD reported 21,530 partisans operating or training in Ukraine.[12] Partisans replaced *francs-tireurs* as the bête noire of Romanian soldiers. Teodor Halic remembered, "[The Soviets] fought very well. . . . With great courage they fought on, in particular the civilian population too. . . . Very many troubles there were with partisans."[13] Soldiers used the term "partisan" loosely. True partisans were organized along military lines, but civilians accused of supplying partisans and even enemy soldiers who did not immediately surrender were often labeled partisans and summarily executed. Of course, Romanian soldiers assumed all Jews were partisans.

Romanian units played a supporting role in overrunning Crimea. On 28 October, German infantry broke through at Perekop, and the next day the Ziegler Motorized Brigade began moving down the west coast toward Sevastopol.[14] Romanian brigades joined another attack across the Sivash Sea under pressure to reach the southern and eastern coasts as soon as possible. "Here comes the staff [officer], with all the retinue from division," Major Scârneci noted. "A kind of council of war is made. We must, *volens nolens*, move, attack, penetrate into Crimea. The Germans . . . order this." The 8th Cavalry Brigade rode east to Kerch, and the 1st Mixed Mountain Brigade marched south to Karasubazar (Bilohirsk), cleared the Yaila Mountains, and secured southern coastal cities like Yalta, Alushta, Sudak, and Feodoisa. General Avramescu noticed that General von Manstein diverted Romanian units away from cities at the last moment.[15] He believed this was to hoard the glory, but likely the Germans wanted to prevent the Romanians from looting cities. The German Eleventh Army had recently ordered looting to stop in Ukraine, so the Third Army organized more patrols, set curfews, and restricted access to buildings in cities like Kherson, Melitopol, and Mariupol.[16] The mountain troops captured thousands of Soviet stragglers in the Yaila Mountains while suffering only eight hundred casualties in eight days. Scârneci's mountain battalion beat a motorized SS unit to the coast by three hours. "We dip our fingers in seawater, we wipe our eyes of tears of happiness. With eyes up to heaven, we thank the Omnipotent God that rewarded so greatly our endeavors."[17] Axis troops now converged on Sevastopol, hoping to arrive before the Soviet defenses solidified and take it off the march without need for a prolonged battle.

The Soviet Independent Coastal Army blocked the German Eleventh Army's first attempt to seize Sevastopol on 8 November. The same day, in Bucharest, the Fourth Army marched in a victory parade celebrating the liberation of northern Bukovina and Bessarabia and the fall of Odessa. On 9–12 November, the *conducător* organized another plebiscite, with 3,446,889 yes and 68 no votes for his regime.[18] Even soldiers on the front participated, and if they voted yes they had to sign a form declaring, "I . . . covenant to support our Marshal by thought and deed to the fulfillment of his program to reorganize the State and Nation and I stand ready [any] place and time for [whatever] duty that I will receive."[19] Meanwhile, the Mountain Corps hunted partisans in Crimea. General Avramescu warned that villagers who did not turn in weapons or partisans would "be treated according to the laws of war."[20] General Lascăr ordered the 1st Mixed Mountain Brigade to shoot thirty civilians for each wounded soldier.[21] Soviet stragglers who put up resistance were labeled partisans and shot in groups of twenty, fifty, and even two hundred prisoners.[22] Reports noted female enemy soldiers' presence. Major Scârneci described one with revolted fascination: "A woman with a mop of coal black, curly, tangled hair. She seems completely wild."[23] In one of his comic strips, Private Neață shoots down a Soviet plane but discovers that the pilot floating down on a parachute has a buxom figure and exclaims, while looking up her billowing skirt, "Oleoooo! A female Bolshevik! What is there to do 'cause she is taking photos of military objects? To shoot or take her prisoner?"[24] Reports indicate the women were often shot along with the men. General von Manstein requested more Romanians, to free Germans to attack Sevastopol, and Marshal Antonescu agreed, diverting the 4th Mixed Mountain Brigade that was supposed to follow the 2nd Mixed Mountain Brigade to Romania to refit. Soldiers were not happy when they found out. On 15 November, Sergeant Ionescu recorded that the colonel read out the order to the regiment and then gave a speech saying Romania must help destroy the USSR, since "if Germany is defeated we are also defeated." As he promised that there would be plenty of opportunities to win medals in Crimea, a chant of "home, home, home" drowned him out. The colonel demanded those who had participated step forward; the seven or eight who did were court-martialed, while the rest continued on to Crimea.[25] Obviously, these soldiers resented being sent to battle while others were heading home, but this does not mean they did not support the crusade against Bolshevism.

Romanian soldiers initially did not play much of a role in the Holocaust in Crimea. The Third Army had been too busy marching and fighting since crossing the Bug into Ukraine to murder many Jews, and the German Eleventh Army captured the important cities, so by the time Romanian soldiers arrived, SS troops had already initiated massacres and created ghettos in Nikolaev, Kherson, Melitopol, Mariupol, Taganrog, and elsewhere. The SS troops believed that Romanian soldiers and gendarmes were "very corrupt," "very incompetent," "take bribes from all sides," "plundered," and "[do] not regard this war as ideological," so SS commanders assumed Jews could manipulate Romanian gendarmes.[26] Consequently, when the VI Corps took over security between the Bug and the Dnieper, General Karl Kitzinger, military commander of Reichskommissariat Ukraine, told General Corneliu Dragalina that Jews were "exclusively reserved to the 'S.S.' troops."[27] Dragalina ordered the VI Corps to surrender Jews, including hostages in Kirovograd, to Einsatzgruppe D. After Axis troops overran Crimea, SS units established ghettos for up to forty-five thousand Jews still in the peninsula.[28] The USSR had resettled Jews as collective farmers in Crimea, so the 8th Cavalry Brigade created a rural ghetto in Voikovstat, a village near Kerch, imprisoning one hundred Jews.[29] Einsatzgruppe D teams of twenty SS men, supported by German and sometimes Romanian troops, organized massacres beginning on 23 November, peaking on 9–13 December, and ending on 18 December, killing between eleven thousand and seventeen thousand Jews in Eupatoria, Kerch, Feodosia, Bakhchysaray, and Simferopol.[30] German policy, not Romanian reluctance, minimized the Mountain Corps' involvement.

The German Eleventh Army's second assault on Sevastopol began just as Einsatzgruppe D wrapped up its terrible work. General von Manstein's soldiers faced three concentric lines of fortifications, the Soviet Independent Coastal Army's fifty-two thousand soldiers, coastal guns, and warships.[31] The German Eleventh Army was spread across southern Ukraine and Crimea and could only commit two German corps, with the Korne Detachment and the 1st Mixed Mountain Brigade on either flank. German soldiers made good progress in the center while Romanian troops cleared the south, but only by pushing forward relentlessly. When Major Scârneci reported his men's path was blocked by mines, "General Lascăr calls me on the telephone and begins to scream like he was out of his mind: 'Attack immediately, pass over the Germans, over mines, I don't want to know anything, 'cause if not, I'll shoot you all etc. etc.'" A new route was found, but his soldiers had to infiltrate through neck-deep water without artillery support while being fired on from casemates. "Who the devil taught them tactics, put nooses (general-staff aiguillettes) and cuckoos [golden badges] on the chest of these dumbasses of command?" Scârneci recorded. "If I will not be killed by the Russians, I will surely go insane."[32] On 20 December, German attackers almost broke through, but Soviet defenders managed to hold.[33] Suddenly, Soviet landings around Kerch on 25–26 December forced von Manstein to call off future attacks.

Winter Crisis

Stalin had launched a massive counteroffensive against German Army Group Center outside Moscow at the beginning of the month that had expanded to the whole front. News of a German reversal broke in Bucharest three days before Christmas. Mihail Sebastian recorded, "Hitler has taken personal command of German land forces through a proclamation that is also a call to fight on, drafted in an unexpectedly alarmist style. . . . All day, everyone you meet speaks of nothing else."[34] The General Staff became concerned about morale as soldiers complained about infrequent mail, no leave, and poor rations. In Transnistria, a labor unit in Tighina collectively demanded Christmas leave. The General Staff sent packages of coffee, rum, cigarettes, and soap to soldiers in Ukraine and Crimea (only coffee and cigarettes for troops in Transnistria) as a Christmas gift from Marshal Antonescu to try to raise spirits.[35] Second Lieutenant Crișan and two Baptist NCOs in Balta in Transnistria studied the Bible together on Christmas. One wondered if the war was a sign of the Apocalypse and asked when it might end. "We found maps of Russia.... I ventured to say, 'If the Germans along with us move forward in Russia at the pace we were doing at the time then maybe in fifty years we will arrive at the other end of Russia at the eastern coast of Vladivostok.'"[36] Crișan was threatened with court-martial for defeatism when someone reported his joke. Antonescu issued a declaration that recognized the Mountain and Cavalry Corps for their continued sacrifice and reminded soldiers that "their precious fruit" of liberated northern Bukovina and Bessarabia "could be easily lost."[37] The Axis winter crisis ended the Antonescu regime's plans to deport Jews in Transnistria across the Bug.

The Antonescu regime's policy to use Transnistria as a holding pen for Jews had resulted in predictably nightmarish conditions that caused some mid-level officials to embark on genocide in the rear even before the winter crisis on the front. Most Soviet Jews were imprisoned in camps without food, medicine, or shelter on the Bug, but most Romanian Jews were held in ghettos with access to the black market and opportunities to work on the Dniester. The Governorate of Transnistria had fewer than six thousand gendarmes, too few to effectively guard three hundred thousand Jews (even with help from local Ukrainian police), raising fears that camps and ghettos would become centers of partisan activity.[38] The Tighina Agreement gave the SS authority over ethnic Germans in Transnistria, even letting them establish ethnic German militias that sometimes clashed with Romanian gendarmes, and Himmler sent the two-hundred-strong Sonderkommando R in September.[39] SS commanders unhappily watched Romanian gendarmes march Jews from Odessa through ethnic German towns to camps on the Bug in November. The SS worried that Romanian gendarmes would let Jews in the camps spread disease to nearby ethnic German towns. Additionally, Sonderkommando R wanted to do its part to realize the Final Solution, so it decided to persuade the Romanian authorities to exterminate the Jews in the camps.[40] SS commanders approached Lieutenant Colonel Modest Isopescu. Before being assigned prefect of Golta County in central Transnistria, Isopescu had served in the Fourth Army's Praetoral Service in central Bessarabia, so he was accustomed to working with the SS to murder Jews. Moreover, he was annoyed with having to care for forty thousand Jews from Odessa crowded into camps in the villages of Bogdanovca, Domanovca, and Acmecetca. Typhus soon broke out among the Jews. Shortages of soap, hot water, and uniforms for soldiers raised fears of an epidemic like that in Moldavia after 1916.[41] Therefore Isopescu was amenable to Sonderkommando R's overtures, especially since the SS promised to provide ethnic German militiamen to help out.[42] On 21 December, seventy Romanian gendarmes and Ukrainian police, plus sixty ethnic German militiamen, began killing a thousand Jews a day in Bogdanovca.[43] Soon after, Romanian gendarmes and Ukrainian police at Domanovca and Acmecetca began shooting Jews, although at a much slower pace.[44] The multiethnic group of shooters in Transnistria took a break from murdering Jews to celebrate Christmas, even as Soviet forces landed in Crimea.

Soviet troops established a firm bridgehead at Feodosia by 27 December, accelerating the Antonescu regime's plans to deport the remaining Jews in Odessa to camps on the Bug. Ten days earlier, the governor of Transnistria Gheorghe Alexianu told Marshal Antonescu he wanted to keep ten thousand Jews as workers, although he lacked supplies to feed them; but he did not know what to do with the others. Antonescu ordered him to get rid of the Jews in any way possible, even suggesting packing them into the catacombs under Odessa or throwing them into the sea. "But get them out of Odessa. I don't want to know. A hundred can die, a thousand can die, all of them can die, but I don't want a single Romanian official or officer to die."[45] Alexianu decided on mass deportation, not mass execution, but it took weeks to organize the operation. On 28 December, Antonescu reiterated the need to deport "all kikes" from Odessa, because "we could expect a disagreeable surprise" in the event of a Soviet landing, so "to keep [Jews] there is a crime. I do not want to stain my activity with this lack of foresight."[46] The Antonescu regime believed 40,000 Jews (mostly women, children, and the elderly) in Odessa were a major threat to 112,000 soldiers occupying Transnistria. The General Staff's worries of a Soviet amphibious assault against Transnistria were overwrought. Soviet landings in Crimea were poorly organized, lacked amphibious landing craft, and were hindered by bad weather.[47] Regardless, on 2 January 1942, Alexianu ordered the expulsion of Jews from Odessa. Jews were expected to sell all but twenty-five kilograms of possessions to pay for their exile to Berezovca and Oceacov Counties.[48] Although the Governorate of Transnistria carried out the deportation of Jews, the General Staff contributed significantly to the decision.

Meanwhile, the Mountain Corps cajoled and threatened soldiers to hold on in Crimea. The German commander at Kerch had panicked, ordering a retreat, but General von Manstein took things in hand, transferred a German corps from Sevastopol (the Grodeck Motorized Brigade rushing ahead), and ordered the 8th Cavalry and 4th Mixed Mountain Brigades to immediately counterattack. Soviet troops steadily consolidated control over the Kerch peninsula and freed Jews from ghettos, including eighty at Voikovstat.[49] On 4–5 January, Soviet commanders landed a diversionary force on the western coast to divert Axis reinforcements, but German infantry and Romanian artillery on the spot quickly responded. Sergeant Ionescu recorded, "We changed position and put a battery on the seashore next to the city port Eupatoria. During the night of 5 toward 6 January t.[his] y.[ear] they destroyed an enemy steamer. Our guns stay in position, day and night.... [Talk] says that our army in Crimea will be changed with another, but after finishing with the Russian debarkations."[50] After retaking Eupatoria, German and Romanian troops shot twelve hundred civilians accused of supporting the landing.[51] On the eastern coast, Soviet attacks threatened to overwhelm Axis defenses and drove back the 4th Mixed Mountain Brigade at Feodosia. General Avramescu accused "cowards" of causing others to retreat. On 6 January, he encouraged, "The defense of CRIMEA at any price is more necessary for us Romanians because only maintaining this region can we keep far from our country the danger of Bolshevism and defend our cities from aerial bombardments." He also warned, "All those who will abandon the front and will desert from duty, will be sanctioned on the spot with shooting, indifferent of their past. If constituted units abandon positions without orders, the guiltiest will be executed, choosing a number, in relation to the unit's effectives."[52] On the Azov Sea coast, the Cavalry Corps helped defeat several smaller Soviet landings probing for weaknesses. In Transnistria, gendarmes finally began emptying the Slobotka ghetto in Odessa on 8 January. Back in Crimea, the next day, Soviet bombardments caused "stupefied" Romanian troops to abandon foxholes in part of the 4th Mixed Mountain Brigade's line. General Gheorghe Manoliu blamed the retreat on a machine gun battalion that had become "an element of panic" after its original commander had been killed. "There are officers that respond, hit me, shoot me, I cannot do anything more."[53] He dissolved the machine gun battalion and dispersed it among other units. Despite some shell-shocked soldiers, most fought ferociously. On 12–13 January, when Soviet commanders tried to outflank the Axis line with a landing at Sudak, the 4th Mixed Mountain Brigade threw it back into the sea, then contained a second landing nearby three nights later to a tiny beachhead.[54] Without Romanian soldiers' determination, Axis forces could not have delayed Soviet attacks until German reinforcements arrived.

The continued precariousness in Crimea contributed to genocide in Transnistria. Civilian authorities rushed to empty Odessa of Jews, who were inspected for hidden valuables before they were marched under guard to the train station, and each day dozens froze to death waiting for a train in freezing cold, and dozens more died in overcrowded freight cars before being unloaded in Berezovca and Oceacov Counties.[55] Romanian gendarmes and Ukrainian police marched groups of fifty to a hundred Jews from train stations along the most direct route to the Bug, happening to pass through ethnic German towns along the way. Einsatzkommando R was surprised by the unannounced appearance of these convoys, but SS commanders, citing the possibility of Jews spreading typhus, quickly decided without consulting the Romanian authorities to intercept and annihilate arriving convoys, with the help of ethnic German militiamen, before they entered ethnic German towns. Governor Alexianu did not know about the ongoing massacres of Jews in the camps in Golta County. He did not sent Jews through Berezovca and Oceacov Counties knowing the SS was going to murder them, but it is unlikely he would have changed his orders if he had known.[56] Romanian gendarmes and Ukrainian police usually turned Jews over to SS-led ethnic German militiamen with no questions asked. The deportations from Odessa continued through the end of the month. On 15 January, the massacre at Bogdanovca concluded after fifty thousand Jews had been killed; however, the executions at Domanovca and Acmecetca continued. On the same day, after enough soldiers had arrived from across Crimea, the German Eleventh Army launched a counterattack to retake Feodosia.

The Soviet winter counteroffensive had also triggered a political crisis in Bucharest that shook up the Romanian Army's leadership. The OKW was already planning another summer offensive meant to finish off the USSR that would have to rely heavily on Romanian, Hungarian, and Italian manpower to make up for German losses, so after sending Marshal Antonescu a Mercedes automobile as a New Year's gift, Hitler requested Romania make a large commitment to the coming campaign.[57] Antonescu offered ten divisions, plus more, if Hitler promised the German Army would equip them and the Hungarian Army would contribute an equal number.[58] General Iacobici opposed this decision; along with his deputy chiefs of staff, Generals Tătăranu and Nicolae Mazarini, he wrote a report against fielding too many Romanian divisions, because they had proved to be outmatched by Soviet divisions. On 17 January, ignoring the General Staff report, Antonescu promised General Hauffe to remobilize the entire Romanian Army and provide fourteen divisions. He also signed an economic agreement to supply oil and grain to the Nazi war economy.[59] The next day, Soviet armies broke through

1941–1942: DOUBLING DOWN ON HOLY WAR

in Ukraine at Izyum, and German Army Group South pleaded for the Romanian divisions dispersed in the rear to be rushed to the front. This was the final straw for Iacobici. He penned a letter of resignation that argued the war was unpopular, that the Romanian Army was being ground down while the Hungarian Army was avoiding significant losses, and that only eight divisions should be fielded in the summer.[60] On 20 January, Antonescu accepted Iacobici's resignation, citing the recent plebiscite as proof of public support for the war and calling him a defeatist. Tătăranu and Mazarini also resigned, but they were retained for "continuity," although both were soon demoted.[61] Iacobici had few other supporters, and many were happy to see him go, because they resented that the former Austro-Hungarian officer (who spoke with a German accent and fought against Romania in the last war) had been elevated over Old Kingdom officers owing to his assumed pro-German sentiments.[62] General Ilie Șteflea, commander of the 3rd Infantry Division and a former deputy chief of staff, became the new chief of staff. General Pantazi was promoted to minister of defense. The military triumvirate of Antonescu, Pantazi, and Șteflea endured until the end of the regime. Antonescu was sure the best course of action was not to hedge his bets by sending the minimum number of divisions but instead to double down, sending the maximum, because if Nazi Germany lost, then the USSR would again menace Romania. Antonescu's view represented the majority view of the officer corps, including the generals and colonels who served as his ministers and prefects.

The German Eleventh Army stabilized the front in Crimea, but the German Seventeenth Army in Ukraine, according to the OKH, was "in a terrific mess," so the General Staff's fears about a Soviet attack on Transnistria did not abate.[63] In Crimea, Axis forces faced fierce Soviet resistance. The 4th *Roșiori* Regiment had rushed from Simferopol, slowed by horses slipping on the highway's icy asphalt, and immediately launched a night attack after arriving at Feodosia. Second Lieutenant Vasile Bumbu advanced through knee-high snow, and when weapons jammed from the cold, "then we engaged in hand-to-hand combat, using weapons and Linemann shovels, not having another option; only 60 mm mortars still functioned."[64] Soviet tanks temporarily drove his unit back, but on 19 January, Axis troops again captured Feodosia. In Ukraine, on 21 January, the 1st Infantry Division's forward units arrived from Kirovograd, joined five days later by the Rotta Ski Detachment (two mountain ski battalions), and were thrown into the fray to protect the key railway hub at Dnepropetrovsk. In Transnistria, the following day, the II Corps, now commanded by General Dăscălescu, took control of all military and police forces in Odessa and kept its soldiers guarding the coast on high alert, as concerns of a Soviet amphibious landing had faded, only to be replaced by new fears about a Soviet airborne drop.[65] Axis forces implemented harsh measures to secure the rear from the partisan threat.

Einsatzgruppe D resumed its murderous work in Crimea with a vengeance, and Romanian soldiers were now directly involved. This second wave of massacres began in recaptured cities. German commanders could no longer divert Romanian troops away from cities at the last minute, because they needed them to drive out the Soviet defenders. Soldiers immediately began looting and shooting Jews and other civilians accused of aiding the enemy during the Soviet landings. The remaining small Soviet beachhead near Sudak was eliminated on 28 January, and Romanian soldiers massacred Jews left behind on the shore by the evacuating Soviet troops.[66] SS troops, often working in conjunction with Romanian soldiers and Tatar police, proceeded to organize massacres in ghettos across the rest of Crimea, liquidating the surviving Jews in Karasubazar, Simferopol, and Dzhankoy. In the months to come, Romanian soldiers assisted SS troops in searches for Jews still hidden in Crimea.

The Mountain Corps did its best to shore up morale during a pause in the fighting, as the outmatched German Eleventh Army waited for reinforcements to destroy the bottled-up Soviet forces in the Kerch peninsula. Chaplains preached sermons, held conferences, and passed out propaganda. One issue of *Soldatul* from this period declared "Odessans [were] thankful for [the] liberating Romanian brothers" who had delivered fellow Christians from Soviet bondage.[67] Reports from the field to the Military Bishopric indicated that there were too few priests on the front, and many of them were old, so a call went out for young priests to minister to frontline regiments. Chaplain Ioan H. Popescu organized lectures for soldiers titled "Patience in Suffering," "The Holy Cause—the Holy War," "Soldiers' Sacrifice—Pleasing to God," "Espionage—Holy Silence—Consequences" (on the need to avoid careless talk that might harm the war effort), and "Spiritual and Bodily Cleanliness—Debauchery, Danger, and Sin."[68] General Avramescu informed soldiers, "By defending Crimea, we defend the borders of the country. . . . For as long as the enemy will be held far away from the borders of the country, our families will be able to work, to give us the necessities of war."[69] After seven months of intense operations, the Mountain Corps had been ground down. General Lascăr reported that the 1st Mixed Mountain Brigade was at 60 percent strength, and that its troops were "totally demoralized."[70] He had received the Knight's Cross a month earlier, and the Order of Mihai the Brave a couple months before that, but now the General Staff replaced him. Major Scârneci commented that "[Lascăr], after he was laden with the most distinguished decorations, abandoned us."⁷¹ This humiliating demotion for lacking grit probably explains Lascăr's later steadfastness outside Stalingrad. The General Staff took extra steps to improve reserve officers' morale. With the breadwinner gone, reserve officers' families were struggling, so families of reserve officers with the "expeditionary corps" in Crimea received the same rights as families of regular officers to access food and goods from military warehouses.⁷² Mountain Corps morale was shaky, but troops dug in and held on in Crimea.

While the Soviets were quiescent for the moment in Crimea, they were extremely active in Ukraine. Axis forces knocked back the Soviets from Dnepropetrovsk by 2 February, but the Soviets soon pushed back against the brittle Axis line. Second Lieutenant Aurelian Stoica with the 5th *Vânători* Regiment recalled how Soviet forces on skis cut off a battalion. He was tasked to take a radio to the encircled troops. Stoica helped the battalion break out by "directing sub-units on the road on which I had infiltrated . . . some hours before."⁷³ In Transnistria, gendarmes wrapped up deportations in Odessa around this time after expelling thirty-three thousand Jews from the city, leaving a few thousand still in the Slobodka ghetto. In Ukraine, the rest of the 1st Infantry Division's units had arrived by 13 February, except for its artillery that was still in Mariupol; but the German Seventeenth Army threw the Romanians into the icy maelstrom of the Izyum salient anyway. In Transnistria, Romanian gendarmes and Ukrainian police finished mass executions of Jews at Domanovca and Acmecetca in Golta County around this time, having killed approximately fifteen thousand at each camp. Ethnic German militias under SS command continued seizing Jews from Romanian gendarmes and Ukrainian police in Berezovca and Oceacov Counties, eventually shooting twenty-five thousand.⁷⁴ In Crimea, on 20 February, the 10th Infantry Division carried out "a cleansing action" in Eupatoria in coordination with some German troops, capturing seven partisans and shooting twenty-six Jews.⁷⁵ In Ukraine, on 22 February, a Soviet counterattack hurled the 1st Infantry Division back. General Emanoil Bârzotescu personally led a counterattack halting the retreat the next day, for which the Germans awarded him an Iron Cross. General Dragalina, who seemingly disliked Bârzotescu, described the retreat as a panicked rout resulting from command incompetence, and an inquiry was opened.⁷⁶ The ugly truth was that such incidents were inevitable as long as the General Staff sent poorly equipped divisions into battle against enemy divisions supported by tanks, heavy artillery, and aircraft.

By now reports of massacres in Golta, Berezovca, and Oceacov Counties and mass starvation in Balta, Tulcin, and Mogilău Counties had begun trickling in to the Governorate of Transnistria in Odessa, and the Third Army sent investigators to ascertain the situation. An inspection of the Domanovca camp found unburied bodies being eaten by dogs as sick or dying Jews watched. Ukrainian policemen who were found shooting Jews in scores said they were acting on orders but could not produce any proof. Starvation, disease, and exposure killed tens of thousands more Jews in ghettos; in just the Obodovca and Berşad ghettos five thousand Jews died from disease. Army doctors visited ghettos, curious to observe the effects of epidemic diseases.[77] Romanian gendarmes, Ukrainian police, and SS troops had shot nearly one hundred thousand Jews. Romanian civilian and military apathy allowed additional tens of thousands of Jews to die from insufficient food, shelter, and medicine. The first winter of Romania's holy war was the deadliest for Jews in Transnistria.

The Germans and the Soviets both raced to build up forces in Crimea to break the deadlock at Kerch, but the three Soviet armies there beat the German Eleventh Army to the punch. The Soviet Independent Coastal Army, which had been reinforced by sea to eighty thousand men, sallied out of Sevastopol on the western coast, trying to distract General von Manstein from the Kerch peninsula on the eastern coast. Just three German infantry divisions, plus the 1st Mixed Mountain Brigade and the 10th Infantry Division, ringed Sevastopol. The Soviet Independent Coastal Army first hit the Romanian units on the flanks. Major Scârneci's soldiers fought off waves of enemy infantry supported by heavy bombardments. "We are at the limit of powers. Lord, help us! . . . My soldiers overcame with worthiness and manliness. They waited grinding together teeth until the Russians approached to a small distance and then opened a murderous fire. In some places, with bayonet, and clashed chest to chest, they took [enemies] by the throat. The machine guns' and light machine guns' barrels turned red."[78] After these attacks failed, the Soviet Independent Coastal Army attacked the German corps in the center the following day. At the same time, three Soviet armies attacked from the Kerch peninsula on the other side of Crimea, but only won an eleven-kilometer bulge on the northern end of the Axis line where the 18th Infantry Division, newly arrived after being force-marched hundreds of kilometers in freezing weather, cracked under tank and artillery attacks and retreated. German reinforcements rescued it.[79] On 28 February, the Soviet Independent Coastal Army pulled back into Sevastopol's defenses when it became clear its efforts were in vain, as the three Soviet armies in the Kerch peninsula could not break the German Eleventh Army's line.

Meanwhile, at Izyum in Ukraine, Soviet armies continuously smashed against German Army Group South, with heavy casualties inflicted on both

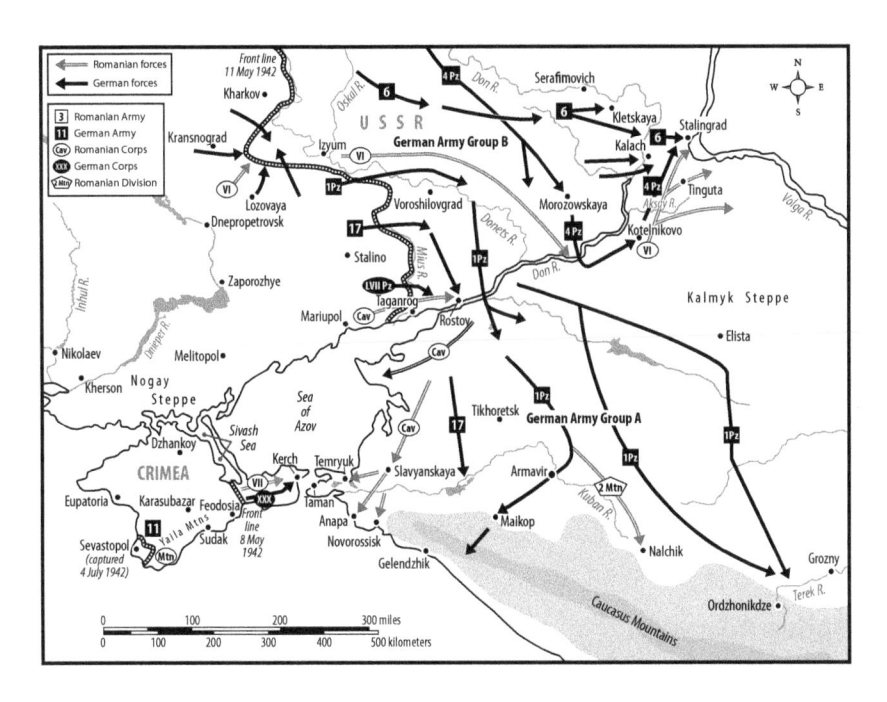

Map 3. Spring recovery and Case Blue, 1942

sides. The 2nd Infantry Division, which had taken over rear security from Nikolaev to Kirovograd, was ordered to join the 1st Infantry Division reinforcing the battered German Seventeenth Army. Some units marched 450 kilometers in intense cold and through deep snow, with 40 percent of the horses dying and 30 percent of the soldiers suffering frostbite.[80] On 9 March, the 2nd Infantry Division joined a counterattack at Lozovaya, suffering two thousand causalities (half from cold) in ten days.[81] A demoralized General Ghineraru, bypassing the VI Corps and Third Army, wrote alarming reports directly to the General Staff, saying Soviet tanks were too strong, German units did not provide enough support, and his division was utterly spent. He repeatedly asked for leave too.[82] General Dumitrescu's response to these reports, forwarded to him by General Șteflea, provides insight into the mindset of most senior officers at the time. He dismissed Ghineraru's concerns, exhorted that as an officer he should be the first to embolden and encourage, not to complain or doubt, and reprimanded him for anti-German comments. "The vital interest of our country is to give as much support as possible to the German Army to crush the common foe. It is your duty to cooperate most sincerely and in the best manner [*condițiuni*] with the German Army."[83] In another letter addressed to "Beloved Șteflea," Dumitrescu complained to his friend, "The general interest forces us to sacrifice [deficient commanders], but we don't really have anyone to replace the sacrificed."[84] Consequently, the General Staff waited to fire Generals Bârzotescu and Ghineraru until May and June respectively, when replacements were found. Soviet attacks grew weaker but did not stop, leaving the Axis line at Izyum bent but not broken.

Spring Recovery

As the German Army prepared for spring counteroffensives in Crimea and Ukraine, the Romanian Army started remobilizing for the summer offensive. Mihai Antonescu launched a new propaganda campaign focused on final victory to increase support for the war.[85] General Pantazi ordered the Ministry of Defense to expand efforts for "education in the army through images—photographs, cinema."[86] Films celebrated previous victories, highlighted Soviet atrocities, and emphasized the need to defeat the Red Army to hold on to northern Bukovina and Bessarabia. The Mountain Corps began printing *Ecoul Crimeei* for soldiers in Crimea. During the winter, the Third Army had rounded up stragglers and deserters in Ukraine, a few of whom had formed bandit groups; by springtime, thousands of soldiers arrested for theft, desertion, and other crimes were locked up in prisons in Romania or jails on the front.[87] The General Staff decided these imprisoned soldiers could not be left kicking their heels in confinement when it was desperate for manpower. General Order No. 240 instructed that deserters, instead of being imprisoned or shot, would be reassigned to a frontline infantry or cavalry regiment for rehabilitation by showing bravery in combat.[88] Even soldiers accused of self-inflicted wounds qualified for rehabilitation; only men caught "in the flagrant act of self-mutilation" were to be executed (within forty-eight hours).[89] Most Romanians still believed there was a good chance Nazi Germany might defeat the Soviet Union.

The Romanian Army reequipped and retrained divisions for the summer offensive, which now had been code-named Case Blue. On 15 March, mixed mountain and cavalry brigades were redesignated divisions because Marshal Antonescu did not want Hitler to underrate Romania's (compared to Hungary's or Italy's) contribution to Case Blue.[90] The General Staff split divisions into two groups. Echelon I divisions fighting in Ukraine and Crimea included the 1st, 2nd, 4th, 10th, 18th, 19th, and 20th Infantry; the 1st and 4th Mountain; the 5th, 6th, and 8th Cavalry. Echelon II divisions remobilizing in Romania and Transnistria included the 5th, 6th, 7th, 9th, 11th, 13th, 14th, and 15th Infantry; the 2nd and 3rd Mountain; the 1st, 7th, and 9th Cavalry; and the 1st Armored. The General Staff reduced the number of battalions from nine to six in infantry divisions because of heavy losses during Operation Barbarossa but increased the firepower of Echelon II divisions with Romanian arms, captured Soviet matériel, and German deliveries. Echelon I divisions would be reequipped later.[91] Worryingly, Marshal Keitel pointed out to General Șteflea that the German Army was having trouble equipping its own divisions so might not be able to fulfill all the Romanian Army's needs. He requested Echelon II divisions to be ready to depart from Tighina within a month.[92] Echelon II divisions simplified training for new recruits, as reserve officers and NCOs with recent combat experience focused on combat tactics.[93] Echelon II divisions actually had nearly four months to train because Case Blue was repeatedly delayed.

The morale of Third Army soldiers fighting in Ukraine and Crimea remained satisfactory. On 17 March, General Constantin Vasiliu-Rășcanu, who had taken over the 1st Mountain Division outside Sevastopol, reported that his companies took fifteen to twenty casualties daily, reducing some to just sixty to seventy soldiers, so they could not rotate men off the line to rest for even a few days, and most were covered in lice. Nevertheless, he reported morale was "pretty good, even at its best, [considering] the situation we find ourselves in."[94] Major Scârneci recorded a rash of self-mutilations in his mountain battalion. Soldiers employed various methods: injections of urine or gasoline, knife cuts, burns from boiling water, and cutting off fingers. He blamed new replacements "not raised in the spirit of the mountain hunters."[95] German officers worried whether Romanian troops would fight and sometimes tried to motivate them through threats. Constantin Mihalcea, now a captain with the 3rd Horse Artillery Regiment, was reassigned from regimental headquarters to a battery after its commander was killed by enemy artillery fire on the Kerch peninsula. During one Soviet attack a German officer appeared and asked, "Who commands the artillery battery?" He drew his pistol, pointing it at Mihalcea, and said, "What is the mission? Are you thinking of retreating?" Another Romanian officer leveled his own pistol at the German officer. Mihalcea defused the situation, saying the Germans and Romanians had different tactics. "Leave me to resolve mine first and after the fighting sit down for a talk." The German did not return.[96] The arrival of fresh Romanian and German divisions in Ukraine and Crimea strengthened confidence and improved morale.

Half of Echelon I divisions were now in Crimea, creating supply shortages that triggered a spat between the Mountain Corps and the Third Army. General Avramescu complained of insufficient food, replacements, and matériel; demanded that the battle-worn 1st Mountain Division be replaced; and accused the Third Army, now headquartered in Odessa, of being distant and unresponsive. General Dumitrescu argued he was well aware of conditions on the front; blamed logistical problems on distance, bad roads, and railroad shortages; and emphasized that the German Eleventh Army had agreed to supply the Romanian divisions in Crimea, leaving the Third Army responsible just for discipline.[97] Avramescu also criticized Dumitrescu for a backlog of Mountain Corps deserters and miscreants waiting for trial by the Third Army. The few courts-martial were in Ukraine, gendarmes could not be spared to escort accused soldiers, and transport of course was limited, so military jails in Crimea were full of potential rehabilitation soldiers needed as replacements.[98] The General Staff concurred with Avramescu and created the Mountain Corps and Romanian Troops in Crimea Command that was in charge of liaising with the German Eleventh Army, administering discipline, and overseeing local propaganda efforts. These included operating a Romanian-language radio station, printing *Ecoul Crimeei*, building churches, and holding moral education. To help alleviate food shortages, on 24 March Avramescu ordered Romanian soldiers to help Soviet peasants with the spring planting in Crimea.[99] The same day, the General Staff established agricultural work labor detachments consisting of five hundred raw draftees (usually minorities) in Romania.[100] Axis propaganda blamed the food crisis on Soviet scorched-earth tactics, but the OKH had implemented a harsh economic regime prioritizing soldiers over civilians in food distribution; one hundred thousand people would starve to death by the end of the year in Crimea.[101] The Tatar minority received favorable treatment, however: as General von Manstein had informed Avramescu, Axis forces needed local assistance, particularly from "Mohammedans," in antipartisan warfare. Romanian commanders therefore established canteens to feed Tatar orphans with soldiers' leftovers, officers participated in Islamic ceremonies, and an imam from Constanța carried out missionary work.[102] Army propaganda presented this as spontaneous Romanian goodwill, but it was a German scheme to divide and conquer using ethnicity and food to convince starving Soviet civilians to betray partisans hiding in the peninsula. Avramescu developed an excellent working relationship with von Manstein while coordinating the details of operations, supply, administration, propaganda, and occupation in the Mountain Corps's new little fiefdom in Crimea.

The Third Army collaborated with the Governorate of Transnistria to secure the province from imagined and real threats. Over 150,000 Romanian and Soviet Jews had survived the winter. Civilian and military authorities agreed that Jews needed to be put to work, watched closely, and fed sufficiently. An SSI report argued, "Aside from the fact that it is inhuman to leave them in the current living conditions, this also constitutes a permanent danger [of disease]," imperiling the "security and the health of the population and soldiers, which means the purpose for which these camps were created is not achieved."[103] Some commanders, however, disliked civilians' supposed coddling of Jews. On 1 April, General Traian Cocorăscu, commanding the 9th Cavalry Division, claimed that the number of Jews in Mogilev had grown from eight thousand to fifteen thousand, and that thirty thousand more lurked in the countryside. He considered it scandalous that Jews walked freely in the streets, and demanded that Jews be deported to the Bug.[104] Under military pressure, civilian leaders occasionally deported Jews deemed unproductive. Commanders also blamed corrupt civil servants, gendarmes, and police for the thriving black market that developed in Transnistria, even though many soldiers also smuggled goods to sell "at speculation prices" on the black market.[105] Ironically, such "Jewish" behavior by Romanians allowed many Romanian Jews to survive through black-marketeering. General Dumitrescu's primary concern was Odessa. The NKVD had left behind partisans hidden in fourteen hundred kilometers of subterranean stone quarries and catacombs beneath the city and surrounding area, with some one thousand openings; criminal gangs had used the system of tunnels as hideouts for decades. The SSI estimated that seven to eight hundred partisans sheltered in the catacombs. Groups of desperate Jews also hid from Romanian persecution under the earth. Partisans occasionally organized attacks or gathered intelligence, but mainly focused on surviving in the dark tunnels. The II Corps had blocked up all the cave openings it discovered. Some partisan groups in the catacombs had fallen into infighting during the winter, and even practiced cannibalism.[106] A smoke company (trained to obscure ground attacks or targets from air attack) arrived to literally smoke out the partisans after the OKW had vetoed General Staff requests to use poison gas.[107] Smoke generators were employed periodically between February and May but proved ineffective. Those living in the dank underground quarries developed skin ailments, however, that could betray them to police. Five Jewish "partisans" caught exiting the catacombs were in a deplorable state, thin and sickly.[108] The Third Army was certain that Jews and partisans also lived "camouflaged" aboveground in Odessa, hiding their true identifies using false papers, so it demanded new deportations to secure the city for good. On 11 April, Dumitrescu reestablished the Odessa Military Command, under General Trestioreanu, to root out Jews and partisans in the city, leaving the II Corps to concentrate on guarding the coast. First on Trestioreanu's list were the few hundred Jews still in the city jail; second, members of the Communist Party (factories with between one thousand and five thousand workers were closely surveilled); thirdly, "suspicious" people in seaside towns.[109] Many Soviet civilians at this time accommodated or even collaborated with the Romanian authorities and helped track down Jews and partisans above and below ground.

The Soviet armies had apparently exhausted themselves, and the OKH used April to ready counteroffensives, committing to the effort German Luftflotte 4, the German 22nd Panzer Division, and a German infantry division in Crimea. Furthermore, after the 18th Infantry Division shifted to Sevastopol, the 19th Infantry and the 8th Cavalry Divisions formed the VII Corps to support General von Manstein's planned attack. Meanwhile, in Ukraine, the square-shaped Izyum salient, roughly one hundred kilometers in length and width, offered the Stavka a jumping-off point for another attack and the OKH a target to pinch off.[110] The 4th and 20th Infantry Divisions reinforced the 1st and 2nd Infantry Divisions with the German Seventeenth Army. The OKW released the VI Corps from security duties between the Bug and Dnieper and assigned it to command Romanian forces at Izyum, totaling sixty-four thousand soldiers.[111] German Army Group South, under Marshal Fedor von Bock, was also reinforced with the Hungarian Second Army. Meanwhile, deserters, political prisoners, and even common criminals released from prisons began training at Training Center No. 5 in Sărata in Bessarabia to be formed into rehabilitation infantry battalions. Army propaganda encouraged Romanian soldiers to be optimistic, claiming that the Red Army would be unable to resist the German Army. "General-Winter has gone into retirement," a caption read in a cartoon in *Soldatul* showing a melting Soviet snowman revealing Soviet soldiers' bones, while drowning others who shouted, "Our last hope has also gone to hell!"[112] An article in *Ecoul Crimeei* prophesied "Germany's Victory" and urged one final effort: "Jewish-Communist hopes placed in General 'Winter' were shattered. . . . The breakdown of the Red Army approaches."[113] The OKH planned two staggered counteroffensives. The German Eleventh Army would clear the Kerch peninsula, and then German Luftflotte 4 would move north; and the rest of German Army Group South would encircle and destroy the Izyum salient, seizing a better jumping-off point for Case Blue.

The OKH's plan initially appeared to run like clockwork. On 9 May, General von Manstein worked a military miracle in Crimea as the VII Corps attacked the northern bulge to pin down Soviet forces, and the German 22nd Panzer Division penetrated Soviet defenses on the southern part of the line before wheeling north to encircle two Soviet armies. The masses of Soviet forces squeezed into the Kerch peninsula meant that German pilots found it difficult to miss Soviet vehicles crammed on narrow roads.[114] Corporal Cârlan, outside Sevastopol, wrote, "Around 25 German airplanes loaded with bombs of all calibers leave from the aerodrome here toward Kerch. This repeated five times in the course of the day. . . . Evening I play football."[115] German panzers and aircraft transformed the Kerch encirclement into a Soviet graveyard. Sergeant Ionescu's battery advanced behind the 4th Mountain Division. "The field of battle is a dreadful sight. Many burned tanks, people burned, dead horses, cars, destroyed carts, visions of apocalypse, terrible. The guns fired at a position today, night I slept in the field, the Russians also fired, enemy aircraft bombed, the field full of weapons."[116] Meanwhile, the Grodeck Motorized Brigade drove straight toward the port of Kerch to cut off Soviet escape. Its epic attack overran two defensive lines by 10 May, but then its luck ran out. Soviet counterattacks surrounded it; Colonel Radu Korne, commanding the Korne Detachment, was lightly wounded, and fuel and ammunition had to be parachuted by air. German aircraft accidentally mortally wounded Colonel Karl von Grodeck a few days later, so Korne directed the Grodeck Motorized Brigade's final advance with his arm in a sling.[117] Axis infantry and artillery trailed behind. Romanian troops often took revenge on Soviet prisoners of war for casualties taken during the advance. On 15 May, Sergeant Ionescu recorded, "For three days Russian prisoners pass. Today a partisan shot at a Romanian cavalryman. . . . [An officer] killed 11 Russians and a wounded [prisoner]. . . . A partisan Russian

FIGURE 7. "'Christ is risen!' cry the soldiers of the cross[,] embracing, and the Mongol hordes flee terrified of God's wrath," declared *Sentinela*'s editors on the front page of the newspaper's special Easter edition for April 1942. German triumphs that spring in Crimea and Ukraine, followed by a new summer offensive into southern Russia and the northern Caucasus, offered Romanian soldiers renewed hope in a final victory over Judeo-Bolshevism. From *Sentinela*, courtesy of Biblioteca Academiei Române.

officer was laughing when Mister First Lieutenant Constantinescu Andrei shot him. A few Russians prayed on [their] knees, crying, to be forgiven, they were not forgiven."[118] Axis troops on the hills overlooking Kerch watched the remnants of three Soviet armies escaping across the straits. The air suddenly emptied of German aircraft, but von Manstein's artillery began a slaughter lasting until 16 May. The German Eleventh Army captured 170,000 soldiers, 1,100 guns, and 250 tanks at a cost of only 7,588 casualties, including 988 Romanians.[119] German Luftflotte 4 had been called away from Crimea after a Soviet offensive in Ukraine disrupted the OKH's plans.

Four days earlier, the Stavka launched a two-pronged attack to encircle Kharkov. The first blow targeted the seam between the German Sixth and Seventeenth Armies, driving apart the German Koch Group and VI Corps and pushing up from the Izyum salient; but the second blow the next day, farther north against the seam between the German Sixth and Hungarian Second Armies, made little progress after knocking aside a Hungarian division, causing the Soviet commander to pause.[120] By then German Luftflotte 4 had arrived, so on 17 May, Marshal Bock counterattacked. The German First Panzer Army encircled the Izyum salient from the south, the German Seventeenth Army, with help from the VI Corps, held the Soviets armies in the bag, and then the German First Panzer and German Sixth Armies linked up on 22 May. The trapped Soviet armies tried to break out to the east under intense air attack. The VI Corps helped harry the enemy from the west until the end on 28 May. Marshal Antonescu had confiscated 85th and 93rd *Infanterie* Regiments' flags (symbols of regimental honor) in April for cowardice in 1st Infantry Division's retreat in February, but now he returned them for bravery in holding firm against Soviet attacks.[121] General Dragalina's troops assisted in mopping up Soviet resistance during June. The Axis captured 240,000 soldiers, 1,200 tanks, and 2,600 guns.[122] The OKW used some of the captured Soviet weapons in Ukraine and Crimea to partially reequip the Romanian Echelon I divisions for Case Blue.

The German Army's twin victories greatly boosted morale in the Romanian Army. After participating in the triumph at Kerch and hearing the radio trumpet victorious news from Izyum, Sergeant Ionescu excitedly jotted down, "Here they were hoping in a decisive victory [for] Christianity."[123] Soldiers in Echelon II divisions training in Romania and Transnistria were reassured of German invincibility and optimistic about the coming summer offensive. Around this time the Ministry of Defense introduced the Crusade against Communism medal that was awarded to soldiers who fought on the front or civilians who made an important contribution on the home front.[124] Army propaganda went into overdrive, with messages about Christian civilization and Soviet barbarity. The first issue of *Armata*, a magazine for officers, contained an article, "In the footsteps of the barbarians," with a two-page spread of photographs showing devastated Bălți, a Central Asian Soviet soldier, a ruined Russian Orthodox church in Transnistria, a cathedral in Smolensk turned into an atheist museum, women cleaning a reopened Romanian Orthodox church in Bessarabia, and a Romanian chaplain blessing the Soviet population in Transnistria after their "liberation."[125] Romanians' confidence in German victory was not as high as a year earlier, but it had recovered enough that the Antonescu regime initiated a new effort to purify Romania.

Marshal Antonescu approved plans to deport certain classes of Gypsies from Romania to Transnistria. Rumors about Gypsies being "colonized" in Transnistria began circulating among soldiers on the front after the fall of Odessa, the *conducător* began talking about it regularly in February, and the minister of internal affairs General Dumitru I. Popescu ordered a census of Gypsies in May.[126] The Antonescu regime soon decided it could not deport all Gypsies, especially because the Ministry of Defense needed Gypsies to serve as soldiers; but it targeted two groups of Gypsies deemed unproductive. On 1 June, General Vasiliu's gendarmes began the first of two waves of deportations, starting with nomadic Gypsies and then following with "criminal" Gypsies, that forcibly resettled twenty-five thousand people to "labor colonies" in Transnistria over the following four months.[127] Most Romanians supported the Antonescu regime's policy because they believed it was finally putting lazy or criminal Gypsies to work, but despite anti-Gypsy prejudice they did not condemn Gypsies as a people as they did Jews.

After the German Eleventh Army's victory in the Kerch peninsula, the Mountain Corps rounded up Romanian stragglers or deserters in the rear, conducted sweeps for partisans in the mountains, and organized searches for Jews and partisans in cities. The Mountain Corps hanged partisans as a warning to others but turned over Jews (and often the civilians who hid them) to Einsatzgruppe D, which now employed mobile gas vans to asphyxiate victims.[128] The General Staff warned soldiers not to let down their guard against Jews and partisans. General Șteflea reprimanded a battalion at Sevastopol for using a Jewish Soviet prisoner to tend its horses, claimed a shipload of female partisans trained in sabotage had landed at Kerch, and reported that two Jewish women from Chișinău posing as Soviet Moldavians had gotten jobs with army intelligence as translators in Transnistria.[129] Einsatzgruppe D decided to spare a few thousand Karaite Jews in Simferopol and Karasubazar because of Nazi racial theories that differentiated these ethnic Turks practicing Judaism from other Jews. Otherwise, SS troops soon murdered Crimea's remaining Jews, except for a few still in hiding and four to five thousand Jews behind enemy lines in Sevastopol.[130] While Einsatzgruppe D employed SS troops for the actual killing, it relied on German and Romanian soldiers to cordon off neighborhoods, conduct searches, and provide security.

Hitler demanded that General von Manstein seize Sevastopol to free Axis divisions for Case Blue but perhaps more importantly to further increase Axis faith in final victory.[131] On 2 June, the German Eleventh Army began a massive bombardment of the Soviet Independent Coastal Army's formidable defenses and 106,000 soldiers. In addition to more than 600 aircraft (German Luftflotte 4 had returned from Kharkov), von Manstein had 611 guns, including heavy siege howitzers and super-heavy guns, on a mere thirty-four kilometers of front. He possessed another important advantage: German and Romanian soldiers could taste victory. Departing from his usual practice, von Manstein had the 1st Mountain and 18th Infantry Divisions in the center of the Axis line. He had decided Sevastopol could only be taken by seizing the hills over Severnaya Bay in the north and the old Crimean War battlefield in the south, so the respective wings were assigned to a German corps reinforced with the 4th Mountain Division and another German corps incorporating several Romanian heavy artillery regiments.[132] This amalgamated force battered its way forward. Major Scârneci's troops rolled tires filled with explosives and grenades, nicknamed "firecrackers," onto Soviet positions.[133] Romanian infantry-artillery coordination was difficult owing to a shortage of radios, and sometimes infantry still attacked without artillery support, so soldiers infiltrated as far forward as possible to limit their exposure to enemy fire. A growing number of demoralized Soviet soldiers deserted, so Romanian troops used many prisoners for labor or as orderlies.[134] Sergeant Ionescu recorded all sorts of rumors, such as six hundred Romanian soldiers killed by jumping into a mined antitank trench; a Jewish woman captured firing a mortar alone after her Soviet comrades had fled; a group of Soviets surprised eating a meal in a tunnel and taken captive; an escaped Romanian soldier who said Soviet soldiers were shooting prisoners and that Soviet troops wanted to surrender but Stalin threatened to kill them.[135] Meanwhile, on the Kerch peninsula, the VII Corps helped destroy some small Soviet landings trying to divert Axis forces from Sevastopol and trained with captured Soviet weapons. Corporal Cârlan wrote, "While I was in [the] dormitory with Bucşe and Ciucureanu, Osiac fired with [a] Russian light machine gun and he was this close to shooting us."[136] Case Blue was fast approaching, but Sevastopol continued to hold out.

Meanwhile, the Antonescu regime weighed the fate of Romania's Jews. On 12 June, US bombers from North Africa attacked Romania's oil fields.

Mihail Sebastian noted, "The air-raid alert on Thursday to Friday night, and the rumors of bombing, frighten me less in themselves than because of the overheated, hysterical climate they might produce—as they did last year."[137] Around this time Gustav Richter, an SS representative in Bucharest, reported that Marshal Antonescu had agreed to allow Radu Lecca, who controlled the Jewish Central Office (a state-run institution responsible for implementing Jewish policy), to negotiate the deportation of Romania's remaining Jews to Poland.[138] The conditions for Jews differed greatly between Romania and Transnistria. Jews in Romania faced discrimination and were subject to conscription for labor, but they lived relatively normal lives, except for twenty-one thousand Jews in the Cernăuți ghetto. Jews in Transnistria endured harsh conditions in camps and ghettos, where death was commonplace. The Third Army remained obsessed with securing Odessa from Jews and partisans. Army intelligence believed twenty thousand Jewish men hid in the city because police were either "nonexistent," "thieves," or "Judaized," and camouflaged Jews in exchange for bribes. The Odessa Military Command ordered former Communist Party members who had not already done so to register with police, and 1,950 citizens presented themselves by 20 June. The command was aghast to discover that a third were working for the city government, so when a police commissar was caught employing a worker who was Jewish, it was seen as evidence that corrupt civil servants helped hide Jews and partisans.[139] Governor Alexianu had hired many former Soviet civil servants out of expediency to fill the ranks of the Governorate of Transnistria, and corruption was rampant, but at this moment in the war hunted Jews and partisans received little help from former communist comrades.[140] In Ukraine, on 22 June, the VI Corps joined the German Seventeenth Army's attack over the Donets River to seize better jumping-off points for the summer offensive. On 27 June, the Antonescu regime announced that Jewish men in Romania who avoided forced labor would be deported to Transnistria. If Case Blue succeeded in defeating the USSR, Nazi Germany could pressure Romania into surrendering its Jews.

Summer Offensive

Case Blue officially started on 28 June to much fanfare, even though it was much more modest than Operation Barbarossa. The OKH had only enough resources to attack with one of its three army groups. German Army Group South was expected to implement a series of intricately choreographed encirclements into southern Russia, destroying many Soviet armies in the process, and then turn south to seize oil fields and other economic resources of the Caucasus.[141] Echelon I divisions with the VI and Cavalry Corps joined the initial attacks, while those with the VII Corps prepared to follow. General Dumitrescu transferred the Third Army headquarters to Mariupol to coordinate Echelon II divisions arriving to support the follow-on attacks.[142] German liaison reports concluded that only the 6th, 7th, 13th, and 14th Infantry, plus the 2nd and 3rd Mountain Divisions, or fewer than half the Echelon II divisions, were capable of independent missions or heavy combat.[143] As German Army Group South broke through the Soviet front, the German Eleventh Army stormed Sevastopol.

General von Manstein's attacks progressed slowly, testing the Axis soldiers' endurance. After weeks of the same order to "push," Major Scârneci exploded in his diary at his superiors, "Lord, how stupid, unintentionally funny, wicked they are!"[144] Artillery and aircraft pounded the Soviet defenses mercilessly, making the front awash in flames. Sergeant Ionescu recorded, "From smoke the sun darkened. . . . Enemy aircraft bombed, bullets hiss in our area. Great fight in the air above the earth given by our boys. Something like in Revelation."[145] At midnight on 28–29 June, German troops reached Severnaya Bay and surprised Soviet defenders with an immediate assault by boat that successfully seized the port. On 30 June, the Stavka ordered an evacuation, opening the way to Sevastopol. As the Soviet defenses collapsed, von Manstein sent the 1st Mountain Division to pursue Soviet troops retreating into the Chersonese peninsula, moved the 18th Infantry Division to block the enemy from escaping into the mountains, and ordered the 4th Mountain Division to simply halt and make way for German divisions to occupy the city. When invited to toast victory, General Manoliu refused, huffily announcing he had not come to drink champagne outside Sevastopol, so the 4th Mountain Division was allowed to join the final attack on 1 July to fulfill Romanian honor. Soviet soldiers in camouflaged huts or catacombs resisted on the Chersonese peninsula. Major Scârneci believed commissars and fanatical communists, including "mad, wild women," prevented Soviet soldiers from surrendering. He found "distinctively kike-ish" propaganda cluttering the enemy shelters. "Willing-unwilling, we have to move on to harder measures. The work is not easy. By flames, with machine gun crossfire, grenades launched with cables, bottles with gasoline etc., we seek to intimidate them, to make them exit from catacombs. We also send them messages in the Russian language."[146] After a few days, Soviet troops began surrendering en masse. Many female Soviet soldiers and nurses were captured, so a separate prisoner of war camp was established for them.[147] Romanian soldiers often shot Jewish Soviet prisoners "trying to escape."[148] On 4 July, Sevastopol was officially declared captured. The final assault captured 60,000 Soviet troops in Sevastopol, plus 30,000 others in the Chersonese peninsula, but inflicted 35,500 Axis casualties, including 9,500 Romanians.[149] Einsatzgruppe D immediately butchered all Jews still in the city. Sevastopol's capture was a bloody affair.

The Mountain Corps finally received a respite. The Third Army distributed postcards not requiring postage, awarded medals, granted leave in rotation to 20 percent of each unit, and promised more financial aid to soldiers' families. Soldiers grumbled about spending much of their short leave on slow trains. "We Romanian soldiers are only good for Sevastopol, Kerch, Kharkov, but we don't have permission to use fast trains, even while for German soldiers special wagons are attached," a soldier was overheard to say.[150] More correspondence meant news from home about a hard spring, food shortages, and inflation. On 5 July, General Șteflea complained that some officers were making promises they could not keep, like soldiers' families would receive increased financial aid or divisions would be demobilized, and warned any morale boost was not worth soldiers' subsequent disillusion.[151] The Antonescu regime moved to alleviate soldiers' concerns about their families. On 8 July, Marshal Antonescu celebrated First Lieutenant Ioan Drăgănescu, killed outside Sevastopol eight months prior, and declared the state would care for his nine orphans. He also established military schools for orphans of soldiers and increased financial aid to soldiers' families to match inflation, offering soldiers a vision of a postwar military welfare state to motivate them.[152] A strange phenomenon of deserters trickling into Crimea asking to be assigned to frontline units began in February, increased in March, and peaked in July after it became common knowledge that the Mountain Corps would stay to help occupy Crimea and not join Case Blue.[153] A few were stragglers from the VI Corps at Izyum, but most of the several hundred deserters were from the 1st Fortification Division outside Odessa. This glorified construction unit was used to build defenses: first in Bessarabia after 1939, then in Moldavia after 1940, and finally in Transnistria after 1942. The 1st Fortification Division's officers neglected their men, leaving them in trenches on the coast as they themselves lodged in Odessa, and deserters reported cruelty and squalid conditions.[154] Some deserters claimed they had tried to volunteer for the front rather than spend the war sitting in the rear. Others were probably attracted by news of better food in Crimea. The Mountain Corps received "German rations" (which were in fact less than actual German rations), with greater quantity, higher quality, and more variety of food—so much so that a portion was kept back to create a reserve. Soldiers even got chocolate and candy meant to be used only as an emergency ration. General Avramescu reported his soldiers "got used to" these new rations very quickly.[155] The Mountain Corps accepted deserters' stories without question because it needed manpower.

Case Blue seemed a rousing success, and Romanian soldiers departed for the front in high spirits. On 6 July, the 2nd Mountain Division was the first Echelon II division to leave. Second Lieutenant Teodorescu recalled a celebratory atmosphere at the overcrowded train station in Deva, with people offering flowers and well-wishes: "All are faithful troops [with a] single desire: to vanquish!"[156] Case Blue had actually already failed. German Army Group South had conquered huge swaths of territory, but Soviet armies slipped out of encirclements, escaping to fight another day. Romanians were not aware of the failure, and Echelon II divisions left with high hopes, although at least one farewell was marred by soldiers firing off shots and panicking civilians.[157] Axis advances in southern Russia and North Africa increased confidence in final victory. Even anti-Nazi Alice Voinescu wrote, "I cannot stand the idea of a German peace . . . but the idea that the slaughter will continue to infinity is more terrible. I don't know what to desire, except for our and all Russia's neighbors' salvation."[158] The OKH improvised a new plan: German Army Group South would divide and try to seize two objectives at once. German Army Group A would break through at Rostov and turn south into the Caucasus; the Cavalry Corps and 2nd Mountain Division joined this attack. German Army Group B would strike east toward Stalingrad on the Volga River to protect the flank; the VI Corps supported this attack.[159] These diverging attacks could not both be supplied for long; nevertheless, the OKH felt there was no other option.

The Germans again drove forward. On 26 July, German Army Group A shattered the Soviet line on the Don River, and the Cavalry Corps entered the breach at Rostov. *Sentinela*'s front page declared, "The definitive victory of the soldiers of the Cross against paganism approaches with giant steps," and not so subtly another page in the same issue included a poem about Transylvania.[160] The next day, German Army Group B crossed the Don, where the VI Corps paused after marching twenty-five to thirty kilometers a day for over a month to keep pace with German panzers.[161] *Ecoul Crimeei* proclaimed, "The Situation of the Soviets is desperate."[162] Suddenly, the OKH decided the Caucasus was an operational dead end, switching the main effort to the Volga. The General Staff had to shift gears too, discarding detailed plans for Echelon II divisions to deploy in the Caucasus, and having to improvise a deployment to southern Russia on the fly. Antonescu was not pleased with the General Staff's slow response, complaining it was "stupid," "ridiculous," and worked "along a robotic system . . . with the rigidity of Old Man Scabbard."[163] On 7 August, General Șteflea penned an angry resignation to General Pantazi, arguing that his staff had done its best and requesting to be sent to command a division at the front. Pantazi smoothed Șteflea's ruffled feathers, and the latter went back to work.[164] The General Staff now became the MCG again and established a forward headquarters in Rostov, using some of the Third Army's staff left behind by General Dumitrescu, who had joined the Cavalry Corps to open the way for more Echelon I divisions into the Caucasus.[165]

Once the Cavalry Corps cleared the Azov Sea coast, Axis forces in Crimea could cross the Kerch Straits. Encountering only limited resistance from Soviet marines, who quickly evacuated, the 5th Cavalry Division snaked down the coast, seizing ports, while the 6th and 9th Cavalry Divisions (once more including the Korne Detachment) supported a German mechanized detachment's drive south to the Kuban River, where Soviet troops made a stand at Slavyanskaya, which fell on 11 August. Romanian soldiers took six hundred prisoners and executed fifty civilians after two cavalrymen were killed by snipers.[166] General Racovița then paused to regroup the Cavalry Corps, but General Dumitrescu thought he was taking too long and on 19 August sent General Ioan Arbore to direct the assault on Temryuk. But this time Soviet marines made a five-day stand. Racovița blamed Dumitrescu for making unrealistic demands and for sending Arbore. Dumitrescu in turn accused Racovița of giving the Soviets too much time to regroup.[167] Meanwhile, the 2nd Mountain Division joined the German First Panzer Army's thrust farther east, keeping up by using what Second Lieutenant Teodorescu called "our pedestrian engines," guarding the German panzers' flanks on the road to Maikop.[168] German Army Group A became increasingly spread out as it penetrated into the Caucasus.

German Army Group B had been stuck on the Don, but now refueled and supported by aircraft, it encircled two Soviet armies at Kalach, opening a path to the Volga. The German Fourth Panzer Army was temporarily halted by fierce Soviet counterattacks, and the VI Corps was even thrown back across the Aksay River, but on 18 August German panzers burst through at Tinguta, and Romanian infantry followed toward Stalingrad. The führer now dangled a prize before the *conducător*, offering to re-create Army Group Antonescu after the city's fall, which seemed imminent.[169] Hitler believed that Marshal Antonescu commanding in person at the front would improve Romanian soldiers' combat performance, and he likely knew commanding an army group would appeal to his Romanian counterpart, as it would be further proof that Romania contributed more to the German war effort than Hungary, adding weight to the argument that northern Transylvania should be returned. On 23 August, the German Sixth Army reached the Volga, encircling Stalingrad to the north, while the German Fourth Panzer Army approached from the south. Concurrently, in the Caucasus, on 27 August, the Cavalry Corps attacked across the Kuban, and four days later the Korne Detachment took Anapa off the march, opening a way for crossing the Kerch Straits. Nonetheless, the OKH faced insurmountable logistical problems supporting two offensives, because the farther German Army Group B advanced toward the Volga, the less fuel, ammunition, and supplies—not to mention soldiers, tanks, guns, and aircraft—German Army Group A received in the Caucasus.[170] Some German commanders even became desperate for Romanian troops to plug gaps in the line.

German Army Group A slowed to a crawl in the Caucasus as German Army Group B became stuck on the Volga. On 29 August, the German Fourth Panzer Army overran Stalingrad's southern suburbs, as the VI Corps took over its right flank on the Kalmyk Steppe.[171] Soviet resistance delayed the German Sixth Army's attack into Stalingrad's northern factory district. Railways and highways in Ukraine became crowded with Echelon II divisions heading to the Don to reinforce the German Army Group B. Meanwhile, on 2 September, Axis forces crossed from Kerch in Crimea, clearing the way with a small Romanian-German amphibious assault on a key island, to Taman in the Caucasus.[172] The same day, Colonel Carp (who had reportedly ordered his officers to "exterminate" Jews in Bessarabia the year before) and several other officers were killed in an ambush as the 7th *Roșori* Regiment advanced on Novorossiysk, so cavalrymen shot fifteen to thirty Soviet prisoners in revenge.[173] The German Seventeenth Army made one last attempt to force its way down the Black Sea coast. On 10 September, the 5th Cavalry Division helped storm Novorossiysk, taking the port, but Soviet forces clung to the rest of the city, blocking the way forward.[174] German troops also remained mired in Stalingrad. As the city's streets turned into a meat grinder, General Friedrich Paulus transferred German divisions from the German Sixth Army's left flank to reinforce shattered units, replacing them with Romanian divisions. On 12 September, the first Romanian troops took over part of the line on the Don. The following day, the German Sixth Army launched another assault into Stalingrad that quickly degenerated into nasty battles on bombed-out streets, offering perfect cover for the enemy.[175] By now the MCG doubted OKH assurances that Stalingrad would fall any day and began to prepare for a winter defense in southern Russia.

Autumn Stalemate

The German Sixth Army's failure to quickly take Stalingrad had immediate repercussions for Romania's holy war. On 16 September, General Șteflea ordered General Dumitrescu to transfer Third Army headquarters from the Caucasus to the Don to take over the Echelon II divisions. At the same time, Mihai Antonescu announced a temporary halt to deportations of Gypsies or Jews to Transnistria. Rumors of a third wave of deportations targeting all Gypsies had triggered some protests by the liberal elite. Liberal leader Constantin I. C. Brătianu wrote to Marshal Antonescu, "[Gypsies] are Orthodox . . . and play an important economic role in our country. . . . Why all this cruelty? What crime have they committed, these unfortunates? What advantage will result from this expulsion?"[176] Negotiations between Gustav Richter and Radu Lecca to send Jews to death camps in Poland had fizzled out by this point. International pressure from the papal nuncio and the Swiss embassy (which also passed along US protests), disapproval from King Mihai I and Queen Mother Helen, and opposition from some liberal intellectuals all contributed to the Antonescu regime's decision to pause deportations.[177] The lackluster news from the front was the final straw. Alice Voinescu, who had not yet heard that the deportations were suspended, despaired, "The recrudescence of antisemitism is a symptom of ever deeper barbarity, antichristianity. Now start the horrors with Gypsies too. Where will we arrive? When will we stop? More and more I feel that we are myopic!"[178] A temporary halt order could be reversed, however, meaning a German victory on the front could worsen the Holocaust in Romania.

German Army Group A tried to find a way around Soviet defenses at Novorossiysk in the Caucasus. But it had to do so without several German divisions, the VII Corps, and the 5th Cavalry Division, which had all been redirected to German Army Group B. Nevertheless, the German Seventeenth Army, including five Romanian (one Echelon II and four Echelon I) divisions tried to outflank the enemy by breaking through the Caucasus Mountains. Attacking into the forested foothills, hoping to break through to Gelendzhik, a port on the other side, the 3rd Mountain Division became overextended, and on 24–25 September Soviet counterattacks cut into its rear, causing the Romanians to retreat in disorder. Poor intelligence, bad terrain, and poorly trained reservists were to blame, but one report opined that Soviet soldiers were superior guerrilla fighters because of "the characteristic temperament of the [Russian] race."[179] Cavalryman General Racoviţa blamed the defeat on bad morale due to mountain troops' fixation on fighting Hungary instead of the USSR; he was berated for making these comments to German commanders. The Cavalry Corps proudly reported carrying the Romanian Orthodox cross into Moldavian villages discovered in the Caucasus, and the 7th *Roşiori* Regiment estimated that 60–70 percent of soldiers knew why they were still fighting so far from home.[180] Romanian soldiers still trusted in German victory over the Soviet menace.

The longer Stalingrad held out, however, the less confident Romanian soldiers felt about final victory. The VI Corps manned a thin line jutting sixty kilometers south of Stalingrad in front of a group of lakes before abruptly ending with nothing but empty steppe to its right flank. On 29 September, a Soviet attack drove back the Romanian defenders until a German counterattack stabilized the line behind the lakes.[181] The MCG now prepared to deploy Fourth Army headquarters from Romania to the Kalmyk Steppe to take command of the VI Corps (and the VII Corps once it arrived from the Caucasus). Hitler fantasized that Army Group Antonescu could defend a line along the Don and Volga after Stalingrad surrendered, so that German Army Group B could continue to Astrakhan on the Caspian Sea.[182] German Army Group B's supply staff officers soberly reported that logistics were stretched to the limit and advised pulling back from Stalingrad or face disaster, because the German Sixth Army, not to mention the Third and Fourth Armies, could not be supplied through the winter.[183] Hitler rejected the idea when the OKH suggested it, confident that the Stavka could not mount another major winter counteroffensive; but German and Romanian commanders were far less sanguine. As far away as Crimea, on 1 October, General Avramescu ordered extra vigilance because he worried about new Soviet landings.[184] The Mountain Corps believed the partisan threat was "nonexistent" in the peninsula due to earlier "radical measures" targeting Jews.[185] General Paulus hoped that fresh Romanian reinforcements would free up enough German troops to finally conquer Stalingrad.

Romanian soldiers still believed in the holy war and felt like crusaders as they marched through Ukraine. Whenever Romanian soldiers paused, Soviet villagers brought babies, children, and youths to be baptized by the chaplain. Soldiers acted as godfathers and provided small gifts of food or soap. Captain Dumitru Păsat, a company commander in the 991st Independent Infantry Battalion (one of four battalions formed from rehabilitation soldiers at Sărata), participated in ten baptisms on his way to the Don.[186] After weeks of empty steppe, First Lieutenant Gheorghe Tănăsescu with the 7th Artillery Regiment suddenly saw German aircraft, Romanian trucks loaded with wounded, and columns of Soviet prisoners of war. "It was the first contact with the front."[187] Romanian soldiers took over trenches from the German Sixth and Italian Eighth Armies along the Don. Soviet patrols exploited the Romanian soldiers' unfamiliarity with the new positions. During Tănăsescu's first night in the trenches, a team repairing a telephone line was jumped by the enemy, and two nights later soldiers laden with food for an observation post were ambushed.[188] Soviet bombardments caused Romanian troops to strengthen positions, but this soon became too difficult. Marin Ștefanescu recalled, "We couldn't [do much] with them, [as it was] winter, and we could not dig anything."[189] Romanian troops preferred German over Italian trenches because the former were better built.[190] On 10 October, Third Army headquarters in Morozowskaya officially took command of the I, II, V, and IV Corps, stretching west to east over 150 kilometers, with 143,000 soldiers.[191] Soviet bridgeheads over the Don at Serafimovich and Kletskaya represented serious threats, so General Dumitrescu requested aid from General Maximilian von Weichs, the commander of German Army Group B, to destroy them. Previous German attacks had failed to dislodge the Soviet defenders, and Stalingrad absorbed all available German resources, so von Weichs ordered Dumitrescu simply to dig in and hold on.[192] Army propaganda reassured troops entering the trenches that Judeo-Bolshevism's end was near. *Armata* prophesied, "Odessa fell in the autumn of 1941. *Stalingrad* will fall in the autumn of 1942."[193] Yet optimism faded as fall turned to winter and Stalingrad still resisted conquest.

Now the Third Army settled into trench warfare on the Don. Soviet patrols probed around the clock, and company-size attacks supported by tanks tried to capture small hills used for artillery observation. Shell shortages limited Romanian artillery to firing eight rounds per "stop" whenever infantry signaled distress; except during larger Soviet attacks, other fire had to be approved by battalion headquarters. A frustrated First Lieutenant Tănăsescu jotted, "I really like to look through [the] telescope and to see how the Russians enter, exit from [shelters], how couriers, cars and all else come and go. But I would like even more to fire with the gun into their heads."[194] The Third Army (and the VI Corps) had few antitank guns, so German Army Group B created schools near the front to train Romanian officers in leadership, antitank defense, and use of German mines.[195] Soldiers were promised promotion, leave, and a medal—even having sentences for desertion, theft, and other crimes of those sent to the front for rehabilitation expunged—for destroying a tank.[196] Romanian commanders ordered night patrols against Soviet concrete emplacements nicknamed "nails." In *Sentinela*, Private Neață takes a house turned into a bunker by crawling under barbed wire, going down the chimney, and popping out black from soot to capture the Soviets.[197] Reality was not so humorous. To the rear of Captain Păsat's sector was a cemetery with German and Italian dead at either end, "the middle was unoccupied, waiting for our Romanians."[198] His troops called it "Cernăianu's neighborhood," after their colonel who ordered repeated night patrols against the same enemy casemates regardless of losses. Soviet bombardments constantly targeted Romanian trenches. Petre Costea recalled that Soviet artillery was "the best" but Soviet aircraft were "crap."[199] Fighting on the Kalmyk Steppe was similar for the VI Corps but less intense.

German Army Group B assigned the Third Army and VI Corps rear areas to exploit because of its worsening supply crisis. Second Lieutenant Alexandru Teodorescu-Schei learned from a Cossack mayor in one of the villages he visited in the Don Bend that everything of value had already been evacuated by the Soviets or taken by the Germans, leaving nothing for the Romanians. He worried that requisitions and reprisals were driving villagers to become partisans. "Because of a murdered officer in Rostov, a whole street of men, women, and children were executed. An action of this type produces a reaction of hatred, creating in the rear a permanent festering source of revenge, not useful to an army of occupation."[200] Major Rășcănescu shared food, danced, and talked with locals when rotated off the line. "We are Romanians, not Germans," he emphasized to discourage partisan attacks.[201] Troops could be flogged for thieving from locals. Groups of soldiers often roamed villages in the rear, looking for food, and in one instance a Cossack policeman shot a Romanian rehabilitation soldier breaking into a house.[202] The supply situation was especially dire on the barren, sparsely populated Kalmyk Steppe. "The most acute lack however," recalled Captain Stan Gheorghe, "was exactly that element which counterbalances winter's weapons: fuel."[203] The absence of trees also meant there was little wood to construct shelters and shore up trenches. All these shortages weakened Romanian combat effectiveness.

Continued Soviet resistance at Stalingrad convinced the Antonescu regime that final victory might be years away, if ever. On 13 October, Mihai Antonescu announced that the temporary halt to deportations of Gypsies and Jews to Transnistria was now permanent.[204] A week later, the MCG established the Don Staff (dumping the name Army Group Antonescu) in Rostov to take over the Third, German Sixth, and Fourth Armies once Stalingrad surrendered, but the Romanian military attaché in Berlin informed the führer soon after that the *conducător* would not go to the front to command it—Marshal Antonescu was weak after falling seriously ill in July, but more importantly he wanted to distance himself from another failed German attempt to deliver final victory.[205] The MCG raised concerns with the OKH about a Soviet winter counteroffensive. On 22 October, Antonescu complained to Hitler that although Romanian divisions were inferior in manpower, firepower, and matériel to German divisions, General von Weichs demanded they defend wide swaths of front, especially on the Kalmyk Steppe.[206] VI Corps battalions were at 39–63 percent strength and manned a weak outpost line.[207] Third Army battalions were much stronger and held a more fortified line, but were being weakened. General Dumitrescu reported that battles that should have been more costly for Soviet attackers inflicted heavier losses on Romanian defenders because of inadequate trenches, poorly prepared artillery fire plans, inexperienced infantry, and insufficient "patriotic education." He believed soldiers were deserting, and threatened to punish officers who reported losses over 25 percent.[208] General Dăscălescu pointed out early reports were often wrong, and many missing were actually dead, evacuated, or mixed with other units.[209] Regardless, commanders were worried about their soldiers' motivation.

When it became clear that they were settling in for the winter, soldiers' morale dipped. The Third Army worried about soldiers' disheveled dress, sloppy salutes, and unsoldierly comportment.[210] The Mountain Corps reported that soldiers returning to the front from leave in Romania brought defeatism spread by "kikes, Polish refugees[,] and acolytes."[211] General Dumitrescu ordered officers to remain with enlisted men in the trenches, commanders to visit the front often, and troops to be reminded of the consequences of desertion. He reported that Echelon I divisions "appear[ed] much better" than Echelon II divisions, which demonstrated "apathy" or "lack of heart" during attacks.[212] The experienced veterans of Kharkov and Kerch on the Kalmyk Steppe were more cocksure than the less experienced recruits and veterans of Odessa on the Don. A IV Corps report complained soldiers did not know why they were fighting, infantry expected artillery to do most of the work, and some mortar teams did not fire, to avoid revealing their positions.[213] The MCG increased propaganda efforts. Chaplain Octavian Friciu visited troops on the Kalmyk Steppe to "give them nerve" with speeches to defeat "pagan fanaticism."[214] Petre Costea remembered, "[Morale] wasn't truly bad, they knew that they was [sic] fighting against . . . communism."[215] Despite commanders' concerns about soldiers' élan, there is little evidence to indicate morale was so bad that it significantly undermined soldiers' motivation.

The OKH and MCG did what they could to prepare for the Stavka's winter counteroffensive. One bright spot was the arrival of reinforcements from the Caucasus to the Kalmyk Steppe. On 31 October, Romanian infantry and cavalry unloaded at Kotelnikovo, where the Fourth Army headquarters had established itself. Constantin Mihalcea recalled that morale was good as the VII Corps rode into position to the VI Corps' right.[216] However, now the German Fourth Panzer Army had eighty-two thousand, or about twice as many, Romanian mouths to feed.[217] News from the Don was troubling. The MCG reported newly constructed Soviet bridges spanning the river and intercepted Soviet radio messages, confirmed by Soviet deserters and prisoners, that a major enemy attack was brewing. The OKH ordered German Luftflotte 4 and the (newly arrived) GAL to bomb the bridges and assembly areas north of the Don and transferred the German XXXXVIII Panzer Corps from the German Fourth Panzer Army to the Third Army because it identified no Soviet buildup on the Kalmyk Steppe.[218] The OKH mistakenly expected that the Stavka would target German Army Group Center that winter. Yet even had the OKH known exactly what the Stavka was planning, there were no more German (Romanian, Italian, or Hungarian) reserves to be had, nor the means to supply them if they existed, and no more time to prepare for the Soviet onslaught.

As German Army Group B tried to snuff out the last pockets of enemy resistance in Stalingrad, German Army Group A made one final effort in the Caucasus. On 2 November, the 2nd Mountain Division helped the German First Panzer Army take Nalchik, but four days later Soviet counterattacks forced it to halt short of the oil fields around Grozny. The German Seventeenth Army, with the Cavalry Corps plugging holes in its line, had settled in for trench warfare already. Corporal Cârlan admired the richness of the countryside as he laid phone lines near Novorossiysk, "But the women here—otherwise, like all in Russia—are very unkempt and lazy. . . . Drudge day, but a night free and one on guard, since we must keep our eyes peeled, because there are partisans here too."[219] German Army Group A had fallen far short of the OKH's unrealistic goals and now lay exposed.

The German Sixth Army had captured most of Stalingrad by this point, but only at great cost and by entrusting its flanks to Romanian forces. On 7 November, First Lieutenant Tănăsescu noted, "First day of winter in Russia. It snowed weakly. . . . Fired 18 hits with good effect on some troops that were moving in a ravine. All day we worked at finishing the stables. . . . Night, when I entered into [the] 'Palace,' it was like I was in heaven: warm and good."[220] The weather forced German and Romanian divisions to send many horses away to winter elsewhere, robbing them of mobility. The supply crisis deepened. German trains arrived less frequently to deliver supplies to the Third Army. The V Corps reported that soldiers only had boiled wheat or rye to eat, mail was infrequent, troops needed more winter gear, newspapers were few, radios were even fewer, and financial aid to soldiers' families was too little.[221] Dumitru Burciu remembered that supply NCOs desperate for ammunition for infantrymen steadily whittled down artillerymen's reserve of two hundred bullets to one hundred, then fifty, and finally five.[222] German trains simply stopped showing up for the VI and VII Corps. General Constantin Constantinescu-Claps, the Fourth Army commander, desperately begged General Şteflea to ship supplies from Rostov or even Romania.[223] General Dumitrescu became convinced that the Stavka would launch the winter counteroffensive on 8 November, anniversary of the October Revolution, but the date came and went without event. Instead, US and British forces landed in North Africa, causing a commotion in Romania. General Pantazi warned officers against "defeatist currents in the interior" that only wanted the "disintegration of national solidarity and army discipline."[224] Meanwhile, the Fourth Army reported that the VII Corps had few antitank ditches, no mines, insufficient trenches, and few concrete shelters.[225] Additionally, freezing lakes could soon support enemy troops. Axis aircraft bombed Soviet concentrations on the Don.[226] Soviet armies continued local attacks, forcing the Third Army to expend precious munitions. On 11 November, a Soviet attack beginning at noon required First Lieutenant Tănăsescu's entire artillery battalion to engage. "We fired constantly until night fell; in total 113 hits.... [Soviet assaults] were repulsed with great losses. Our infantry comported themselves very well.... For the first time, I heard around three bullets in a row whistling through the battery."[227] German Army Group B expected a strong Soviet attack against the Third Army but only now belatedly considered the possibility of another one against the German Fourth Panzer Army (by now a panzer army in name only), threatening the German Sixth Army with encirclement.[228]

Déjà Vu

Romanian soldiers might be forgiven for feeling they had been here before. For a second time they had contributed to mighty victories, advanced great distances, endured scorching heat and choking dust, suffered heavy losses, fought partisans, and executed Jewish communists, but they were once again in trenches confronting an implacable foe as winter neared. The Romanian Army had grown to 787,000 men, with 463,000 at the front (including 83,000 in Transnistria).[229] Even though gnawing doubts about final victory undermined morale, most Romanian soldiers remained committed to the holy war against Judeo-Bolshevism. Their ideological beliefs had, if anything, hardened after losing comrades, being attacked by partisans, and seeing the misery in which Soviet civilians lived. Furthermore, Romanian soldiers had continued to commit atrocities, against Jews of course, but also Soviet civilians, prisoners of war, and partisans, making them more complicit in Hitler's war of annihilation. Some still hoped the Red Army was too depleted to mount a winter counteroffensive, or Stalingrad's capture might cause a Soviet collapse. In any event, the Romanian Army was ready to go down fighting rather than simply give up, especially officers who were willing to enforce strict discipline if NCOs or enlisted men faltered.

Chapter 6

1942–1944: Holy War of Defense

As Geratimusz Morar's mountain company raced through the Yaila Mountains ahead of the pursuing enemy in April 1944, one of its trucks ran out of fuel, so he ordered a village mayor to provide carts and horses. Villagers claimed all the harnesses were worn out or missing. Morar threatened that if everything was not ready in thirty minutes, "Nothing will remain, y'all be shot."[1] Suitable harnesses suddenly appeared, and he and his men continued to Sevastopol to evacuate from Crimea. After the battle of Stalingrad, the Romanian Army fought for another year and a half alongside the German Army, helping to delay the Red Army's advance. By mid-1943, Romanian soldiers knew the Axis was losing the war, and morale steadily eroded. Poor morale, mounting casualties, and inferior equipment increasingly reduced Romanian divisions' combat effectiveness, prompting German commanders to amalgamate German and Romanian units to keep desperately needed soldiers in the fight. Romanian soldiers were increasingly motivated by fear: fear of death, fear of capture, fear of Soviet revenge, and fear of punishment by officers. Romanian soldiers could still lash out at times, but now they thought twice about killing Soviet civilians, prisoners of war, partisans, and even Jews, as their motivation to perpetrate atrocities waned. The proliferation of trench warfare helped sustain soldiers' motivation in the Caucasus and Crimea, and there were only a few isolated cases of mutiny on the front. Despite demoralization in Romania, there were no draft riots when the Antonescu regime ordered another general mobilization in early 1944 in response to the Red Army's approach, because Romanians saw no other option than to continue fighting, given their ideological belief in the danger of Judeo-Bolshevism. Following Stalingrad, Romania's holy war transformed into the defensive conflict that army propaganda had depicted since the USSR's initial occupation of northern Bukovina and Bessarabia.

Stalingrad

The Stavka's winter counteroffensive began with Operation Uranus, a double envelopment of the German Sixth Army that targeted the outnumbered, outgunned, and outclassed Romanian forces holding its flanks. On 19 November, at 5:30 a.m., an eighty-minute barrage began on the Don against the Third Army, blasting apart trenches and barbed wire, collapsing shelters with soldiers inside, and cutting communications. First Lieutenant Tănăsescu wrote, "Russian hits fell in all parts. . . . They also broke our telephone wire in many places and 1 1/2 hours we fired without guidance. . . . Since morning, there was a mist so one didn't see more than 150 m, which the Russians used to start the attack, especially to [the] left, where an intense bombardment of Katyusha [rocket artillery] lasted around 1/2 hour."[2] Tănăsescu was describing a Soviet tank army advancing out of the Serafimovich bridgehead, breaking through the II Corps, and creating a gaping hole near Bolshoy in the Third Army's center. Simultaneously, a Soviet army attacking from the Kletskaya bridgehead smashed through the IV Corps at Gromky on the Third Army's right flank.[3] Romanian artillery could not stop the enemy, concealed by fog, and by 9:30 a.m. Soviet tanks, with infantry leaping off, were among the Romanian guns. Artillerymen desperately tried to use their field pieces as antitank guns and fired over open sights trying to knock out tanks before retreating around noon because shells ran out; their ammunition dumps had been hit, and resupply trains were ambushed.[4] In between the Soviet breakthroughs, the V Corps repelled Soviet attacks. Tănăsescu's battery fired 281 shells. "Evening, when it quieted a little, I found that in our front [the Soviets] had great losses. To [the] left however, the situation is bad: our boys were forced to retreat. . . . Night we slept worried."[5] The German XXXXVIII Panzer Corps tried to ride to the rescue, first heading northeast toward Gromky, but then German Army Group B redirected it northwest to Bolshoy. By nightfall, after march and countermarch, the German 22nd Panzer and 1st Armored Divisions' motley collection of tanks had become separated and, low on fuel, came under attack from all directions. Soviet forces overran the 1st Armored Division's German liaison unit, wounding its officer and destroying its radio, hindering coordination with the German 22nd Panzer Division.[6] Soviet troops widened the breaches in the line and drove farther into the Third Army's rear through the night. sowing panic among Romanian support units.

With the German Sixth Army's left flank collapsing, the Stavka now ordered a second attack on its right flank on the Kalmyk Steppe. On 20 November, three Soviet armies slammed into the German Fourth Panzer Army after a forty-five-minute barrage beginning at 10 a.m. Second Lieutenant Virgil Dobrin recalled, "It was an apocalyptic sight. The response of our artillery was prompt, but feeble compared to the Soviet fire's massiveness. This had a powerful morale effect in the command post. And not without reason. The weak points of our defensive layout were well known."[7] A Soviet army steamrolled over the VI Corps. A horrified German officer watched: "The Romanians fought bravely, but against the waves of Soviet attack, they had no chance of resisting for long."[8] The front disintegrated, and a Soviet mechanized corps and a cavalry corps rushed forward into the gaps.[9] The Korne Detachment was the only mobile reserve in the area, and it was immediately overwhelmed. A German counterattack from Stalingrad saved the 20th Infantry Division from annihilation.[10] First Lieutenant Dr. Crișan Musețeanu arrived in Kotelnikovo that morning. "Around the houses in which were the offices of Fourth Army . . . was a bustle and an extraordinary agitation. Officers with cuckoos came and went, pallid and very worried."[11] Dazed soldiers short on ammunition surrendered in droves.[12] The Fourth Army reported, "[The VI Corps] no longer has infantry ammunition at all. . . . In Fourth Army's and Don Staff's warehouses in the zone one finds no infantry ammunition at all [even] with all our countless reports."[13] The Fourth Army had planned to take operational control of the VI and VII Corps from the German Fourth Panzer Army the next day, causing confusion over which headquarters was in charge of organizing the response to the Soviet attack.

While the Fourth Army retreated in disorder on the Kalmyk Steppe, the Third Army made a stand on the Don, even though it too was in serious trouble. The IV Corps was in full retreat from the Don. Second Lieutenant Dr. Mircea Cucu reported, "We received orders that every [man] should save himself however he could."[14] Held in reserve, the 15th Infantry Division now counterattacked into the Gromky breach. Meanwhile, the 7th Cavalry Division and the German XXXXVIII Panzer Corps counterattacked into the gaping hole at Bolshoy. Here the II Corps also withdrew in a rout, a German observer reported: "The attacked Romanian divisions are in full flight. . . . The Romanians' 'fright of the Russians' is tantamount to panic. No officer or unit obeys or is willing to obey."[15] In the middle, the V Corps was soon threatened with double envelopment. First Lieutenant Tănăsescu's sector near Bolshoy again came under attack. "We fired all ammunition and we remained only with around 10–12 projectiles for [an] intervention. All connections were broken with the observer and we could only speak with the regiment, which gave us orders to retreat."[16] Soviet forces threw back the 15th Infantry Division from Gromky. Second Lieutenant Nicolae Nicolau recalled an unequal battle: "Romanian soldiers, finishing incendiary bottles, sought in vain to set the tanks on fire with burning [bundles of] weeds."[17] Across the Gromky breach, the 1st Cavalry Division fled toward Stalingrad. Sergeant Lungu recalled, "As far as the eye could see, the plain was dotted with soldiers, wanderers, strays, and officers among them, of course without weapons. . . . [I ran] like a rabbit through the snow, not knowing in what direction."[18] The cold weakened soldiers forced from warm shelters. Major Răşcănescu's battalion moved to defend the 6th Infantry Division headquarters at Golovsky. "The snow was not great, circa 30–35 cm [approximately one foot], but it was frozen and it was very hard going, since we were continuously slipping. . . . I could not dig myself into the terrain. . . . Everyone was tired and beginning to freeze."[19] Soviet cavalry ranged throughout the Axis rear, capturing supply depots, hospitals, and support units to the Chir River.[20] Meanwhile, on the Kalmyk Steppe the VI Corps offered little resistance as Soviet forces rushed to cut off the German Sixth Army. Captain Constantin Lăţea's battalion commander was killed, and the regimental commander was replaced for being "in [a] state of shock."[21] Back on the Don, on 20–21 November, Generals Mazarini, Lascăr, and Ioan Sion, commanding the 5th, 6th, and 15th Infantry Divisions respectively, held a midnight war council to discuss a Soviet request that these divisions, plus remnants of the 13th and 14th Infantry Divisions, caught between Bolshoy and Gromky, surrender. Mazarini wanted to capitulate, but Lascăr and Sion voted to fight until ammunition ran out.[22] These Romanian forces still resisting on the Don became known as the Lascăr Group and were placed under the German XXXXVIII Panzer Corps.

German Army Group B ordered the Third Army to hold the Chir and the Fourth Army to defend where it stood. On 21 November, the MCG asked the OKH to order the Lascăr Group to break out to the I Corps (left virtually unscathed by the Soviet attack) to save something of the Third Army, but this request was denied, even though the 1st Armored (after briefly linking up with Lascăr Group) and the German 22nd Panzer Divisions were now in retreat.[23] The MCG declined to disobey the OKH. General Constantinescu-Claps questioned if German Army Group B or the MCG had final say, complained the stand-fast order was suicidal, and wanted to retreat toward Kotelnikovo. The MCG just repeated German Army Group B's orders to counterattack, fortify towns, and await resupply.[24] In reality no one controlled the Fourth Army's scattered soldiers on the Kalmyk Steppe, with some retreating toward Kotelnikovo while others headed for Stalingrad. Second Lieutenant Dobrin recalled, "The Germans looked at us with reservation, if not with hatred. . . . The day that followed, the psychic tension was increased by the news that was coming to us in connection with the imminent encirclement."[25] Hitler countenanced no retreat by the German Sixth Army, despite the rapidly advancing Soviet pincers closing in around Stalingrad.

Soviet forces completed a smaller encirclement of the Lascăr Group on 22 November. At dawn Romanian aircraft landed at Golovsky, unloading supplies and evacuating wounded, and then German planes dropped food, ammunition, and leaflets with promises of panzers coming to the rescue.[26] Fearing the worst, First Lieutenant Tănăsescu put on every piece of clothing possible to take with him into captivity. "Still, I nurtured hope, especially after the things heard on the radio, that the Germans will intervene as soon as possible." Instead, Soviet tanks with infantry riding on top appeared. His battery engaged, but another fled, making "such a racket that it gave the impression of the chariot races from the film 'Ben Hur'!"[27] Tănăsescu gave up trying to turn back panicked infantry with his pistol and joined the retreat to Golovsky.[28] Dumitru Burciu recalled the wounded's pitiful pleas, "'Hey comrade please shoot me, shoot me 'cause it's torturing me.'"[29] Another Soviet surrender request prompted another war council at 4 p.m. General Mazarini again wanted to surrender, but General Sion was dead set against it. General Lascăr argued honor would not allow them to disobey orders and surrender; however, it would allow them to disobey orders and break out.[30] Soviet assaults prevented a coordinated Romanian breakout. Captain Păsat, leading his surviving rehabilitation troops, described the massacre in the encirclement: "Flamethrowers, handled, like on a maneuver, by tankers never missed. When the flame finally reached [a fleeing soldier], you saw how he fell down and struggled engulfed in flames, until the tank crushed him with its heavy tracks . . . looking like a frog, a dog, or a cat that had been run over by a heavy car."[31] Lascăr and Mazarini were captured when Golovsky fell at 9 p.m. General Traian Stănescu took over the remaining forces.[32] Others broke out. Major Răşcănescu told his officers to tell their men, "I promise them that I'm getting them out of [the] encirclement and I will take [them] to their homes, children, parents etc., if they will listen to me and will execute my orders precisely, and those who don't want to are free to do what they want."[33] He marched at night, avoided villages, and evaded patrols. General Sion formed the 15th Infantry Division into a column over twelve kilometers long and after a harrowing night march linked up with the German 22nd Panzer Division, but with only thirty-six hundred soldiers and almost no heavy weapons.[34] Other small groups and individuals also escaped.

On 23 November, Soviet forces linked up on the Karpovka River, creating the Stalingrad pocket. Romanian and German soldiers competed to reach relative safety within the Stalingrad perimeter. Sergeant Lungu, his military police herding one hundred stragglers, engaged in a shootout with German guards at a bridge over the Don and saw cavalrymen cross the frozen river, with some plunging beneath the ice.[35] On the Chir, General Dumitrescu ordered *"the most severe measures for the suppression of the rout and panic in the rear of the front."*[36] The Soviet encirclement around the German Sixth Army remained porous, but the one around the Lascăr Group tightened. In some places demoralized and hungry Romanian soldiers surrendered, but in others they fought, even summarily executing captured Soviet tank crews—whom they despised—while letting captured Soviet infantry live. At 4 a.m. on 24 November, General Stănescu ordered half his forces on the Don to capitulate at dawn.[37] Tănăsescu wrote, "An endless column of men, horses, carts, guns and artillery material started from [the] village toward the Volga. After around 3 km, the first Russian soldiers appeared, very well equipped for winter . . . who began to rob us."[38] Meanwhile, near the Chir, General Sion tried to hold off a Soviet attack, even fighting on the front line himself, but his troops were exhausted, lacked ammunition, and were without heavy weapons, so he ordered a retreat at 11 a.m. before being cut down by shrapnel—the only Romanian division commander killed during the war.[39] Only eight hundred men of the 15th Infantry Division escaped with the German 22nd Panzer Division over the Chir, finally meeting back up with the 1st Armored Division. Stănescu surrendered the rest of the Lascăr Group later that day, as twenty-seven thousand men marched into captivity.[40] General Șteflea wrote to Dumitrescu, saying the defeat should not be exaggerated, that Soviet superiority in matériel was the cause, and no one was looking for scapegoats. "It must not be forgotten that the German power is so great that it cannot be defeated. So forward with unshaken faith in final victory." Dumitrescu scribbled in the margin of Șteflea's letter, "Very wise and correct words. This is also my Christian faith. Will be communicated to the troops."[41] On 25 November, there was still some isolated resistance on the Don. The next day, Major Rășcănescu's four hundred soldiers reached friendly lines after avoiding Soviet patrols, using Lipovan soldiers to deceive Soviet civilians, and marching quietly in darkness.[42] His was the last unit to escape the Don encirclement intact. Nearly 300,000 Axis troops, including 12,607 Romanian soldiers, were now trapped in the Stalingrad pocket.[43]

1942–1944: HOLY WAR OF DEFENSE

FIGURE 8. Romanian infantry and cavalry, like these, played an important role supporting German panzers during the relief attempt to save the German Sixth Army in the Stalingrad pocket in December 1942. The Romanian Army's lack of mechanized and motorized units in comparison to the German Army is illustrated by the stark contrast between the horse-drawn wagon and the assault gun. Bundesarchiv, Bild 101I-031-2437-29 / photo: Helmut Koch.

The Third and Fourth Armies had been decimated but continued to fight. The news that Marshal Erich von Manstein would command the newly formed German Army Group Don reenergized Axis troops, who expected him to perform some military magic to rescue the German Sixth Army. General Constantinescu-Claps marshaled the Fourth Army's thirty-nine thousand survivors into a screen, allowing the German 6th and 23rd Panzer Divisions to assemble at Kotelnikovo. General Dumitrescu whipped the Third Army's eighty-six thousand soldiers into a line on the Chir.[44] Finally, on 12 December, von Manstein launched Operation Winter Storm. German panzers supported by Romanian infantry reached the Aksay in a day, as the Popescu Cavalry Group (the 8th Cavalry Division reinforced with German units) protected the right flank. Passing cavalrymen shouted encouragingly to infantrymen, "Break the front!"[45] The breakthrough was an illusion, because German panzers were too few, Romanian troops lacked supplies, and Soviet resistance was too strong. On 18 December, von Manstein ordered a new attack after the German 17th Panzer Division arrived, but the day before, the Stavka had launched Operation Little Saturn against the Italian

Eighth Army on the Don, hoping to break through and cut off German Army Group A's retreat from the Caucasus.[46] The Italian Eighth Army's defeat exposed the Third Army. On 22 December, after the I Corps was encircled by Soviet forces, the Third Army withdrew to avoid total destruction.[47] The next day, von Manstein halted fifty-six kilometers from the Stalingrad pocket. On 26 December, Soviets forces counterattacked. Hoping to save what was left of the Fourth Army, Lieutenant Colonel Nicolae Dragomir, Constantinescu-Claps's chief of staff, instructed his commanders to make fake reports of being attacked and then retreat. The subterfuge leaked, and von Manstein ordered the Fourth Army to hold, but it made no difference.[48] Sergeant Emilian Ezechil remembered that Soviet tanks broke through, crushing guns and soldiers, who instinctually grouped together for protection, "leaving behind a red mass of blood and flesh steaming on the snow." Soviet troops took "lucky ones" prisoner, shooting the rest or stripping them naked: "And now go on foot to Bucharest!"[49] Constantin Mihalcea told his troops, "Boys! Don't anyone unstick from me, the one who unsticks from the battery, there they remain."[50] They avoided enemy columns, gathered stragglers, and followed a telegraph line to safety. The Third and Fourth Armies were finally pulled off the front respectively on 27 December and 3 January 1943.

Romanian soldiers' morale in the Caucasus plummeted when news of Stalingrad reached them. Rumors swirled: King Carol II was in Moscow, German troops abused Romanian soldiers, or Marshal Antonescu had been toppled.[51] On New Year's Day, King Mihai I praised "the righteous battle for the liberation of the invaded provinces," and Antonescu encouraged faith in "the destiny of our righteousness."[52] General Gheorghe Cialâk replaced General Racovița as the Cavalry Corps commander because the steady infantryman was better suited for the defensive fighting, and the hard-charging cavalryman was unenthusiastic about overseeing a retreat. Hitler wanted to leave behind Axis forces in the Caucasus as a "springboard" for a future counteroffensive but needed Antonescu's approval.[53] On 10–11 January, the two met to hammer out a deal. The *conducător* demanded Hungary contribute more soldiers, deliveries of German arms, and Nazi Germany to pay for oil and food from Romania with hard currency.[54] The führer promised Hungary would do its part, more German weapons, and gold and Swiss francs. While Nazi Germany was unable to force Hungary to field more divisions, Romania did receive some arms and payment in hard currency because its contribution to the Nazi war effort was so important. No other Axis leader wrung as many concessions out of Hitler as did Antonescu.[55] As the German First Panzer Army retreated to Rostov in Ukraine, it diverted the 2nd Mountain

Division and some German divisions to the German Seventeenth Army near Krasnodar in the Caucasus. Second Lieutenant Teodorescu remembered the greatest obstacle during the long march was "flooded terrain and crowded roads," and General Dumitrache recalled that while his men were crossing the Kuban, the enemy "does not show himself anywhere."[56] The Stavka was too preoccupied with reducing the Stalingrad pocket to harry German Army Group A's retreat.

Hitler ordered the encircled German Sixth Army to fight to the death, and Romanian soldiers caught in the Stalingrad pocket continued to resist out of conviction, hunger, and fear. After withdrawing from the Kalmyk Steppe, the 20th Infantry Division helped defend the southern perimeter, and the 1st Cavalry Division and the Voicu Detachment, both survivors from the Don, plugged holes in the western perimeter. General Paulus later praised these units: "In the circumstances, the fighting spirit and leadership displayed by the Romanian units in the Army under my command deserve special commendation. With the assistance of heavy weapons of the normal German type issued to them, and thanks to the determined leadership by their officers, these troops fought gallantly and showed great steadfastness in the face of all the hardships to which they were subjected."[57] General Tătăranu, now commanding the 20th Infantry Division, oversaw all Romanian soldiers in the Stalingrad pocket. He enforced strict discipline, authorizing Romanian and German gendarmes to summarily execute soldiers when necessary, to put every able-bodied soldier on the front line.[58] When Sergeant Lungu failed to gather twenty soldiers for the front for a German commander, "a Romanian mister major from command applied a couple canes to my back!"[59] A German air bridge failed to provide enough supplies to the pocket, so the 1st Cavalry Division's steeds were butchered. Sergeant Adam Peica remembered, "Soon the horse meat also ran out, consumed with economy so not to be forced to surrender ourselves to the Soviets, like what they asked us to do through megaphones."[60] Only soldiers who fought got rations. Between attacks soldiers moved as little as possible to conserve energy, and burned tires for warmth. Soldiers became covered in black soot, Captain Gheorghe recalled; "Only the eyes and the teeth broke that chromatic monotony."[61] On 13 January, Soviet armies annihilated the Hungarian Second Army on the Don, forcing German Army Group Don to retreat in haste. The same day, Tătăranu flew out of the Stalingrad pocket. When he met with Marshal Antonescu, General Pantazi, and General Șteflea, he claimed that Paulus had sent him to report on the situation and ask for transport aircraft. Antonescu accused him of dereliction of duty (arguing that the former deputy chief of staff knew that Romania had no transport aircraft to spare) and ordered him to return to Stalingrad to "rehabilitate" himself or face court-martial. However, on the way back, Tătăranu was interned in a hospital. Hitler later claimed he ordered Paulus to evacuate Tătăranu to save a valorous ally.[62] On 26 January, the 20th Infantry Division collapsed. Gheorghe recalled that he and other officers discussed suicide but did not follow through.[63] On 29 January, Soviet forces smashed the German Second Army on the Donets; at the same time, Paulus surrendered, after the shrunken Stalingrad pocket was cut in two. Finally, on 2 February, the German Sixth Army's last remnants capitulated, with ninety-one thousand Germans and three thousand Romanians surviving to enter captivity.

After the Red Army eviscerated the Axis armies, only the Romanian Army continued to fight alongside the German Army. During the Soviet winter counteroffensive, the Third and Fourth Armies suffered 109,000 casualties, the Italian Eighth Army 114,000, and the Hungarian Second Army 105,000.[64] The Third and Fourth Armies mustered 73,000 soldiers after leaving the line, but survivors straggled into Ukraine for months. The distance soldiers were found from the front determined if they were flogged as stragglers or court-martialed as deserters.[65] The OKH wanted to keep the Third and Fourth Armies near Rostov, but the MCG argued that most were support, not combat troops, demoralized, and not useful even for rear security. In a compromise solution, support troops went on to Transnistria, but combat troops stayed to guard the Azov Sea coast.[66] By spring, the Romanian Army still had six divisions on the front in the Caucasus, plus three divisions in the rear in Crimea or Ukraine, but the Hungarian Army only had two divisions in the rear, and the Italian Army withdrew all its divisions.[67] Despite the Axis armies' tremendous sacrifices, German leaders blamed their allies for the disaster at Stalingrad, contributing to the weakening of Nazi Germany's alliances with Romania, Hungary, and Italy.[68]

The German-Romanian alliance was never the same after Stalingrad. During the battle, General von Weichs claimed that Romanian troops did not fight, that Romanian officers were pro-British, and that Romanian commanders (except Generals Dumitrescu and Lascăr) disobeyed his orders; he wanted the 14th Infantry Division's staff court-martialed.[69] Firing back, Marshal Antonescu argued that the German XXXXVIII Panzer Corps abandoned the Third Army, that some German troops also panicked, and that German soldiers abused Romanian troops. Hitler ordered von Weichs to apologize and fired the German XXXXVIII Panzer Corps' commander. Marshal von Manstein promised to respect the Romanian Army's honor, but he also demanded that Lieutenant Colonel Dragomir be removed for his sneaky

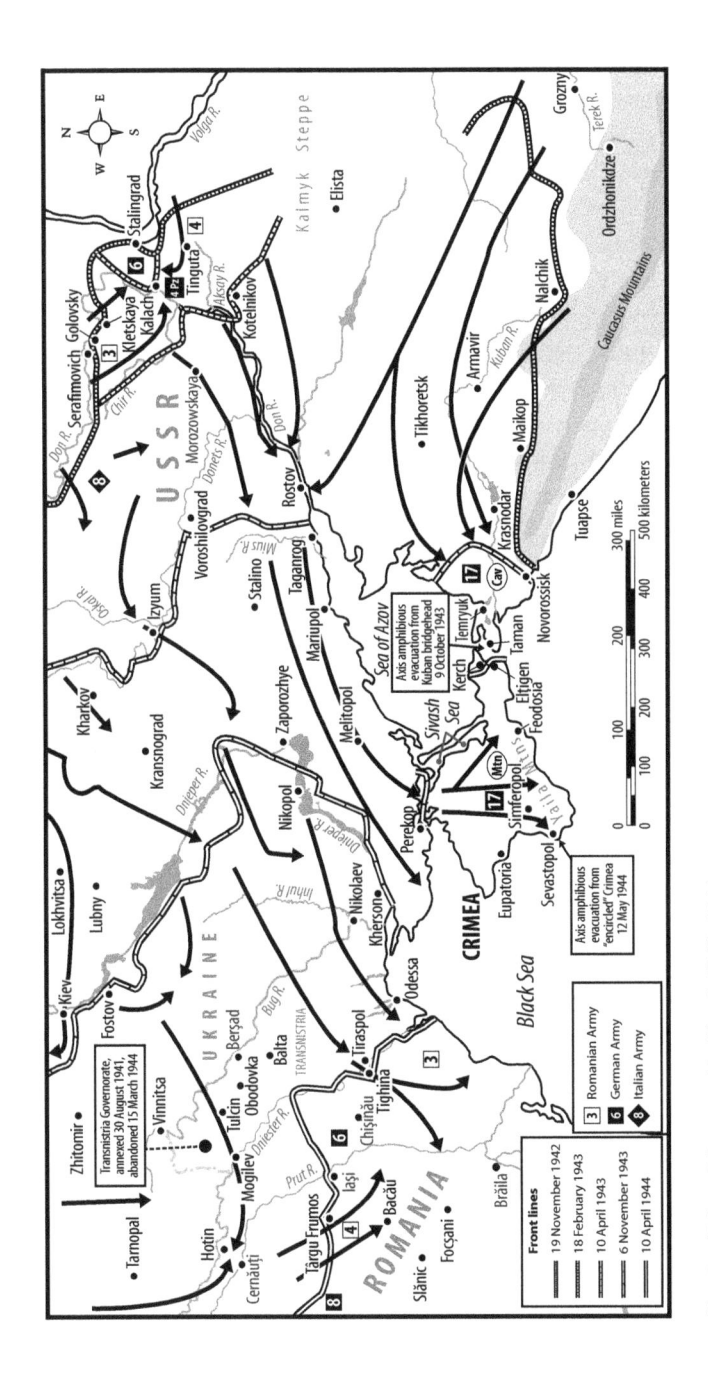

Map 4. Kuban, Crimea, and Iași front, 1943–1944

retreat orders.[70] General Constantinescu-Claps took responsibility and was fired instead. Additionally, following instructions from Antonescu, General Pantazi ordered every company, battery, or squadron to make a "corner of shame," with a list of deserters executed for cowardice, to mirror the "corner of honor," with a list of those killed in battle.[71] German soldiers continued to express their contempt for Romanian soldiers by kicking them off trains, throwing them out of shelters, and threatening them with weapons.[72] By now most Romanian soldiers understood their place in the German racial worldview; one Romanian soldier was overheard saying that after German victory, "We will be the Germans' slaves."[73] Yet most Romanians dreaded being the Soviets' victims even more. Alice Voinescu recorded, "The news that our boys are retreating in haste and in confusion toward Crimea and Rostov doesn't touch me with all the terror that it should press on me, it is yet an abstract pain, the time will yet come when I have to live it with whole being. I cannot conceive that the Russians are coming across Europe. Logically it's possible, [although] intuition refuses this monstrosity."[74] Romanian soldiers were willing to endure arrogant and sometimes abusive German comrades to hold back the Soviet enemy.

Kuban Bridgehead

Nazi Germany played on heightened anticommunist fears across Europe after Stalingrad to hold the Axis together.[75] The Antonescu regime tripled down on its holy war propaganda, focusing particularly on Soviet atrocities to remind soldiers of the consequences of defeat. An issue of *Armata* dedicated to the "fight against communism" had a cover of a death's head in a Bolshevik cap grinning above a burning city and bloody corpses with place names of Chișinău, Cernăuți, Odessa, Kharkov, Sevastopol, Smolensk, and Riga.[76] *Ecoul Crimeei* described "bestial Soviet revenge" against Soviet civilians in the Caucasus as Axis forces retreated.[77] Romanians made the connection that if the USSR was so vindictive against its own citizens, then it would treat its enemies worse. The possibility of Soviet victory was closely linked to Romanian fears of punishment for persecuting Jews. With the Axis alliance in disarray and the Soviet colossus seemingly unstoppable, Wilhelm Filderman wrote, "To those Romanians who tell me they are afraid that one day the Jews will seek revenge, as well as to those Jews who tell me that such revenge is desirable, I reply, 'no.'"[78] The Antonescu regime did not expect Stalin to be as forgiving as the leader of the Jewish community in Romania, and changed its policy toward Jews. Talks with the SS to deport Jews from Romania to Poland never resumed. The Jewish Central Office permitted a

Jewish aid committee to inspect ghettos and camps in Transnistria in January, with the goal of improving conditions for Jews.[79] Yet antisemitism among soldiers remained. After survivors from Stalingrad reached Transnistria in February, two drunk soldiers shot up the Balta ghetto, wounding a Jew and killing a Ukrainian, but commanders no longer ignored such indiscipline, and both men were arrested.[80] While the Antonescu regime stepped back from genocide, Jews in Romania continued to work in difficult conditions in labor battalions, and Jews in Transnistria in much grimmer conditions in ghetto factories or rural labor camps. Responding to German requests for labor, Governor Alexianu even sent thousands of Jews from Transnistria to Reichskommissariat Ukraine, where most were worked to death or murdered.[81] Ideology and complicity in the Holocaust kept Romanian soldiers motivated to fight for the Axis.

Yet as the Red Army grew in strength, the German Army had to increasingly prop up the Romanian Army. German Army Group A took over all Axis forces in Crimea and the Caucasus. The German Seventeenth Army created a two-hundred-kilometer-wide front extending to Krasnodar, manned by nine German and six Romanian divisions, that was dubbed the Kuban "bridgehead."[82] On 4 February, the Stavka attempted to outflank the Axis line at Novorossiysk with a land-sea operation, but German divisions halted the land assault, while the 10th Infantry Division, with German artillery support, wiped out the sea assault—except for a tiny Soviet beachhead. Meanwhile, the OKH placed Axis forces in Ukraine under German Army Group Don, renamed German Army Group South, and Marshal von Manstein orchestrated a crushing counterblow targeting overextended Soviet armies with German panzers from the Caucasus beginning on 21 February.[83] Romanian morale dropped as losses mounted in the Kuban bridgehead. On 23 February, a battalion in the 19th Infantry Division balked at returning to the line, so the German Seventeenth Army broke up the 10th Infantry, 19th Infantry, 3rd Mountain, and 6th Cavalry Divisions, plugging the best-performing Romanian battalions into understrength German divisions. The Cavalry Corps patrolled the southern coast with the other battalions and the 9th Cavalry Division. Finally, the 2nd Mountain Division, reinforced with German battalions, held the northern flank.[84] The MCG did not like this policy of amalgamation, but the OKH justified it, citing reports of poor Romanian morale.

While German Army Group South fought its way back to the Donets in Ukraine, the German Seventeenth Army retreated into the Taman peninsula in the Caucasus. Axis forces first attacked to throw Soviet pursuers off balance. On 3 March, General Dumitrache observed the 2nd Mountain

Division support a spoiling attack by German panzers: "The artillery's trajectories luminously write themselves in the dark sky, until dawn. . . . The village is conquered step by step, but the attack continues on terrain sodden by thaw and rain, that slows down armor's movement, which successfully encircles the little resistance that opposes."[85] As Axis troops pulled back in the north, the rest held firm in the south. Chaplain N. T. Cernea visited the 10th Motorized *Roșiori* Regiment's trenches outside Novorossiysk weekly to pass out little crosses, speak about why they were fighting, and hold meetings with replacements, encouraging them to fight "the enemy of faith and our Romanian Nation."[86] Romanian soldiers complained about insufficient leave, no mail, incompetent or abusive officers, worn-out equipment, bad rations, and abuse from German soldiers. News from home did not improve morale, as family members wrote of corrupt village officials, shortages of all kinds, and paltry financial aid.[87] More soldiers deserted or went absent without leave, some finding ways to cross from the Kuban bridgehead into Crimea. On 8 March, two hundred Romanian "strays" detained for disorderly behavior were marched through Feodosia looking downtrodden and were photographed by German troops, who mockingly exclaimed, "And these fight for our Greater Reich!"[88] After shepherding survivors from Stalingrad back to Romania and Transnistria, the MCG again reverted to the General Staff.

On 10 March, the Third Army again became responsible for soldiers east of the Dniester, and began rounding up stragglers in Ukraine. The General Staff and the Fourth Army established gendarme "dams" on either side of the Bug to intercept stragglers; reports indicated that two to three thousand deserters hid in Moldavian villages across the border in Reichskommissariat Ukraine.[89] The General Staff instructed that soldiers caught "without justification" in the rear would not return to Romania but instead "be intensively retrained also with iron discipline" at Training Center No. 3 in Tiraspol in Transnistria.[90] Gendarmes found 2,172 stragglers in villages around Rostov, Mariupol, Melitopol, Zaporozhye, and Dnepropetrovsk in March. Marshal Antonescu reaffirmed that deserters should be sent to the front for rehabilitation after two months (or four months for second-time deserters) at Sărata or Tiraspol; however, he ordered "recidivists" to have the letter *D* (for detained) tattooed on their hands so they could be shot if they deserted again. The Third Army complained that "weak repressive measures" resulted in scores deserting from Tiraspol Training Center in months to come. Whereas German deserters were tried quickly and shot, Romanian deserters took months to be sentenced and then were sent for rehabilitation to the front, where they could desert once more, and so reacted with "indifference" to threats of court-martial.[91] General Dumitrescu never received authorization from General Pantazi to summarily execute deserters.

The General Staff tried to improve morale among some 110,000 soldiers still on the front, most in the Kuban bridgehead.[92] At the end of March, it rotated the depleted 2nd Mountain Division out of the Kuban bridgehead, replacing it with the well-rested 4th Mountain Division from Crimea. General Avramescu anxiously reported that many newly arrived soldiers wore Soviet uniforms (even officers lacked braid, proper caps, and belts), sold food or equipment, got drunk, and thieved. When asked to explain, "I come from [the] front" was their catch-all excuse.[93] Chaplain Ion Popescu held conferences in Feodosia for Lent, promising soldiers if they "will not swear, steal, desert, or self-mutilate . . . [they] will keep a more genuine and more beautiful fast than that of food."[94] The General Staff issued a pamphlet for soldiers going on leave, reminding them of communism's crimes, instructing that they talk to their families only about victories, sacrifice, bravery, and enemy losses. It concluded, "Either we vanquish in [the] East, or we disappear as [a] State from the map of the world!"[95] On 23 March, Chaplain Grigorie Enăchescu lectured to soldiers in Crimea on communism, claiming it grew out of Freemasonry and Judaism, and expounded on how it would obliterate nation, religion, and family. "Conclusion: *Communism is kike-ish and facilitates the coming of the kike ideal.*"[96] An article in *Soldatul* several days later bluntly declared in bold letters, "The Bolsheviks will never forgive any people."[97] The stabilization of the front and the coming of spring temporarily raised morale as Romanian soldiers hoped for another German summer offensive to somehow restore the situation.

German Army Group South held a strong position along the Mius and Donets Rivers up to the Kursk salient by 23 March in Ukraine, and the German Seventeenth Army occupied the so-called Blue Line on 6 April in the Taman peninsula. The Blue Line consisted of six successive positions along a front of eighty kilometers that offered Axis soldiers protection from Soviet firepower. The trenches also enabled officers and NCOs to keep tighter control over enlisted men. The sudden improvement of the situation eased soldiers' fears of immediate defeat. In *Sentinela*'s comic strip, Private Neață is told that his recent promotion to corporal was a mistake, so he attempts to hang himself, but the rope breaks, causing him to exclaim, "A good sign! The one above doesn't want me to upset Marița or let the [Soviet] bumpkins escape."[98] Soldiers got the message that they had escaped destruction and needed to keep fighting, just like Neață.

Soviet forces launched sustained attacks against the Kuban bridgehead from 14 April to 11 May and 20 May to 6 June. Corporal Cârlan estimated

Soviet progress by the sound of artillery and air bombardments. "All night I couldn't sleep from fleas and from the noise produced by bombs thrown by enemy airplanes and by a.[nti] a.[ircraft] guns that continuously fired at Russian airplanes."[99] Recently deployed to Mariupol, aircraft from the I Air Corps flew across the Azov Sea to provide support for the "rabbits," as infantrymen were nicknamed by airmen, in their warren-like trenches.[100] Now the 1st Mountain Division swapped places with the 3rd Mountain Division, and Romanian soldiers temporarily made up 40 percent of Axis troops in the Kuban bridgehead.[101] Major Scârneci landed in Taman with his mountain battalion from Crimea. On 22 June, the second anniversary of Operation Barbarossa, he unhappily wrote, "[Marshal Antonescu,] we long ago fulfilled your command, we've even gone the extra mile. We crossed many waters, slower, faster, and deeper: the Dniester, the Bug, the Dnieper, the greater and lesser Inhul. We even crossed over seas . . . where we will shed blood and where again we will bury our dead, the budding hope of the nation. Don't you believe that we have long ago fulfilled the command? Don't you consider it is enough?"[102] Meanwhile, the Antonescu regime ordered prefects to hold "national-patriotic demonstrations" in Romania. General Pantazi blamed poor morale of soldiers training in Moldavia on officers for not prioritizing moral education, and on the local "Jewish element" for spreading defeatist rumors.[103] In the Kuban bridgehead, Scârneci was unimpressed with the German soldiers his men were replacing because they emerged from shelters with alcohol and girlfriends: "The famous German discipline unravels. Debauchery begins to take its place."[104] Romanian soldiers' remaining faith in final victory ebbed the longer a German summer offensive failed to materialize.

Operation Citadel was supposed to reassure Nazi Germany's allies, especially Romania, that the German Army was still capable of defeating the Red Army. The OKH only had enough forces to plan a local attack to pinch off the Kursk salient. Hitler finally ordered the attack on 5 July after months of hemming and hawing. The battle of Kursk was, as one historian put it, "a complete and utter misfire."[105] German panzers failed to break Soviet defenses. Anglo-American landings in Sicily on 10 July convinced Hitler to suspend the floundering attack three days later. Major Scârneci took perverse pleasure in Italy's predicament because of its role in the Second Vienna Award: "Italian brothers, it seems to me, your goose is cooked."[106] German propaganda inflated Soviet losses at Kursk. In the Kuban bridgehead, Corporal Cârlan thought the clash at Kursk was a "satisfactory result for the Germans," but in Bucharest, Mihail Sebastian scoffed at the "fantastic figures."[107] The Stavka first organized a counterattack at Kursk and then launched attacks along the entire eastern front, seizing the strategic initiative from the OKH.[108] The Stavka assigned just enough Soviet forces to the Kuban bridgehead to keep up the pressure on German Army Group A.

Romanian soldiers' morale in this strategic backwater was mixed. The German Seventeenth Army held firm against a Soviet attack from 16 to 22 July, but Soviet patrols and local attacks steadily ground down Axis forces. The 19th Infantry Division reported replacements "melting" away, and officers argued that the unit should be replaced.[109] Companies or squadrons formed completely of rehabilitation soldiers from Sărata Training Center proved unreliable, so they were broken up and dispersed as squads or troops.[110] Commanders blamed units' poor morale on rehabilitation soldiers.[111] The OKH finally delivered fifty battle-worn Czech-made tanks to the General Staff, but in Crimea and on the condition they be used in the Kuban bridgehead.[112] The US bomber raid on the Ploiești oil refineries on 1 August made little impression on frontline troops. Romanian troops increasingly resented German soldiers. On 3 August, after Soviet forces seized a foothold across a river in a German battalion's sector, requiring Romanian reinforcement, Corporal Cârlan noted, "The battle's result: the Russians were annihilated until the last of [the] Romanians."[113] Yet most soldiers still believed they were fighting for Greater Romania. On 4 August, sixty-six years since the siege of Plevna, and twenty-four years since the occupation of Budapest, Major Scârneci declared, "Our dream here is to reintegrate our beloved fatherland, and we will do it."[114] Chaplains ministered to wounded; blessed soldiers, weapons, and shelters; and baptized and married civilians. Chaplain Nicolae Petrache built shelters for wounded, designed a cemetery, and oversaw the renovation of a church at the urging of soldiers.[115] Soldiers had time for some relaxation, saving up alcohol for benders or attending soccer matches. Soldiers often overstayed leave in Crimea, but gendarmes just hustled them onto a boat rather than sending them to court-martial.[116] Another Soviet attack occurred from 7 to 12 August, but the Axis defenses held. Axis casualties since occupying the Blue Line were a relatively light 51,795 German and 9,668 Romanian soldiers.[117] Only when Soviet attacks broke through German Army Group South in Ukraine, with Kharkov falling on 22 August, did Hitler finally order the Kuban bridgehead abandoned.

General Erwin Jaenecke initiated a phased evacuation of the German Seventeenth Army, which Soviet attacks tried to disrupt. Corporal Cârlan recorded, "During almost every night and morning until around 9 guns roar, 'Katyusha' is heard singing sinisterly, machine guns bark, Romanian 'Stukas' cross every day toward the Russians, from whence they all always return back."[118] On 3 September, Italy capitulated when Anglo-American forces landed on the peninsula. Mihail Sebastian wrote in Bucharest, "Italy has surrendered! I was at the Athénée Palace. . . . In the lobby I watched the news travel like an electric current from person to person."[119] Soldiers in the Kuban bridgehead barely registered the news as they started leapfrogging backward four days later. On 8 September, after Major Scârneci turned over a sector, he recorded, "During the night, the Russians tried an incursion. . . . They were quickly laid low. . . . Toward dawn, the Russians attacked stronger, with about a company, in the Germans' sector. . . . In some places they succeeded to penetrate to the trenches. Reserves, artillery and mortars promptly intervened and the Russians turned tail."[120] On 10 September, the Stavka tried to cut off the Axis retreat, recapturing Novorossiysk six days later, and on 22 September the Soviets landed a force in the rear, but the 19th Infantry Division threw it back into the sea.[121] The narrow straits and heavy air cover eased evacuation. Cârlan noted, "Not one enemy plane bothered us in the time that we crossed the sea. While we went on the sea, a violinist from the artillery played [for] us a little, making us remember beautiful days once lived."[122] Gendarmes reported that some soldiers arriving in Crimea did "not understand the action of retreating from the Kuban, where they had impenetrable positions."[123] By 9 October, 177,355 German soldiers, 50,139 Romanian soldiers, 25,139 Russian auxiliaries, 27,457 Soviet civilians, and 72,899 horses—plus heavy equipment—had escaped, with only 5,000 German and 600 Romanian losses.[124] The German Seventeenth Army was immediately threatened with being cut off again, however.

"Encircled" Crimea

Confusion reigned in Crimea. While German Army Group South retreated from eastern Ukraine, the OKH ordered German Army Group A, now including the reconstituted German Sixth Army, to hold a front from Zaporozhye on the Dnieper to Melitopol to the Azov Sea to protect Crimea.[125] The German Sixth Army's twelve German divisions were bolstered by the 24th Infantry Division (cobbled together from survivors from Stalingrad and two rehabilitation battalions from Sărata), and the 4th Mountain Division, rushed north from Crimea after evacuating the Kuban bridgehead. The German Seventeenth Army prepared to evacuate Crimea. General Jaenecke was not an inspiring leader and did little to prepare a defense.[126] He might have lacked confidence because he now had only two German and seven Romanian divisions—all understrength. The German Seventeenth Army deemed the 10th Infantry, 19th Infantry, 3rd Mountain, and 6th Cavalry Divisions capable of frontline combat (if reinforced with German "corset stays") but considered the 1st Mountain, 2nd Mountain, and 9th Cavalry Divisions suitable for rear security duties only.[127] On 6 October, General Hugo Schwab replaced General Avramescu (trading places as the commanders of the Mountain and III Corps), who did not want the unenviable task of defending the doomed peninsula. Schwab had commanded the 9th Infantry Division at Odessa and on the Don before heading the III Corps in Transnistria. Major Scârneci fumed that an "arrogant, lazy, and, above all, stupid Saxon" now commanded the Mountain Corps.[128] Schwab and General Cialâk set to work sorting out the mess of Romanian divisions in Crimea.

Romanian soldiers feared a "second Stalingrad" in Crimea. Corporal Cârlan recorded, "When we left from the Kuban front no one asked themselves: where are we going? Everyone was thinking about escape, but now everyone asked themselves: *where?*"[129] Lieutenant Colonel Victor Isăceanu arrived to take command of the 13th *Călărași* Regiment, finding it "in [a] state of moral ruin," and set to work getting troops "back in hand." He restored discipline, but soldiers "were marching without footgear, almost barefoot, in summer blouses, full of lice! The officers, who had lost their baggage in the battles in Kuban, were in the same state."[130] Deserters and stragglers wandered Crimea. On 12 October, General Pantazi instructed each corps to establish a regiment to "reeducate" first-time deserters for two months before sending them back to their units, while only soldiers guilty of "serious" desertion should be sent for court-martial.[131] A group of forty mountain troops pretending to be on leave took a train to Tighina before splitting up to sneak across the Dniester. The Third Army increased gendarme patrols in Kherson, a stop between Crimea and Romania, because of drunken soldiers and deserters.[132] Soldiers began listening more to Radio Moscow: "Romanian soldiers! Your fate in Crimea is sealed, do not believe the Germans. They lie to you. . . . Desert while you have the chance. Surrender!" Major Scârneci scoffed, "I wonder to whom? The Tatars in Crimea?"[133] A handful of Romanian soldiers joined partisans in the mountains. On 27 October, Major Scârneci left Crimea after being reassigned to Brașov. His mountain battalion, now mostly replacements and rehabilitation soldiers, was probably not very inspired by his parting speech. "Ask for all means of fire. Don't defend and cross over [to] the enemy only with the power of chests and bayonet. Spare to the maximum soldiers' blood, which is so noble, so precious. The enemy is cunning and steadfast. He possesses many means of fire that he does not spare."[134] On 29 October, Soviet attacks defeated the German Sixth Army, driving it back to the Dnieper. Sergeant Ionescu evacuated from Kherson and spent the rest of his war transporting supplies for the Third Army while reading "good books," particularly the New Testament.[135] During the battle, the

4th Mountain and 24th Infantry Divisions both suffered two-thirds casualties, including a large number of deserters (many of whom were rehabilitation soldiers), and were combined into the 4th/24th Infantry Division.[136] Soviet armies now threatened to burst into Crimea and capture the German Seventeenth Army.

General Jaenecke organized a slapdash defense. A hodgepodge German-Slovak force blocked the Perekop isthmus, and the Bălan Group (three mountain battalions with artillery, antitank guns, and tanks) rushed to the Sivash Sea. General Schwab authorized company commanders to flog and even shoot soldiers for indiscipline, but only "after a good thinking-over and only in *the moment* of the occurrence of the infractions."[137] On 1 November, Soviet forces launched land and sea attacks. Soviet troops encountered resistance at Perekop but found the Sivash Sea undefended until the Bălan Group arrived, delaying them until German reinforcements could come up. Concurrently, Soviet troops landed at Eltigen, and several days later even more disembarked near Kerch. After turning over the Eltigen beachhead to the 6th Cavalry Division, German troops raced north toward Kerch. By 6 November, Axis forces had contained the Sivash Sea bridgehead.[138] The Kerch beachhead remained dangerous. Corporal Cârlan recorded, "About the front one hears that we were closed [in] by the Russians at Perekop, where hard fighting is going on. Many are afraid that we'll fall prisoner, if we don't die."[139] Some men deserted to join groups of soldiers-turned-bandits in hills around Simferopol.[140] A few searched out the partisans. A private who escaped partisan captivity said they treated Romanian soldiers well, but anyone who tried to leave was shot, and only a few became trusted comrades.[141] Although the German Seventeenth Army managed to parry enemy attacks, it was cut off from the rest of German Army Group A.

The Mountain and Cavalry Corps experienced manpower and morale crises. On 24 November, General Schwab reported that his units had taken "pretty big" losses and demanded that replacements and soldiers on leave to be sent by air without delay.[142] To raise morale, he declared, "It is required that *the familial aid for those found on the front in CRIMEA* and for those found in country, to not be the same, *but at least 2 times greater for the first.*"[143] After committing the reliable Romanian divisions, the German Seventeenth Army was forced to amalgamate unreliable Romanian units into German divisions. Lieutenant Colonel Isăceanu's 13th *Călărași* Regiment was sent to Perekop, where "the morale of all was disastrous." His cavalrymen (foot-bound after losing their horses) lacked stomach for a fight. In the first Soviet attack, one squadron broke under artillery bombardment and "fled without opening fire." Isăceanu remembered, "German officers, hearing that I had soldiers unchanged for 2 1/2 years, remained astonished."[144] German Army Group A wanted to evacuate the German Seventeenth Army, but Hitler would have none of it and managed to convince Marshal Antonescu to support his decision. On 28 November, he informed Antonescu that Crimea would be defended "by all means" and promised supplies, German reinforcements, and restoration of a land corridor.[145] By now Romania was beginning to resemble a reluctant ally of Nazi Germany.

Hitler's obsession with holding on to Crimea was not irrational. The OKH estimated that the German Seventeenth Army was tying down three Soviet armies, plus air and naval assets, and denying the Stavka a base for Soviet air or amphibious attacks against Romania and Bulgaria.[146] Crimea was relatively easily supplied by sea. Two more weak German divisions soon arrived, but no overland connection was ever restored. On 4 December, the 6th Cavalry and 3rd Mountain Divisions, backed by German assault guns, artillery, and aircraft, launched an attack on the Eltigen bridgehead and destroyed it in three days, capturing 2,300 prisoners. On 11 December, Romanian troops trapped and captured another 1,500 Soviet troops who had broken out during the fighting.[147] Thereafter, 125,000 German troops (many of whom were airmen or seamen providing support) and 65,000 Romanian soldiers dug in for winter.[148] One German infantry division, plus the 6th Cavalry and 3rd Mountain Divisions, held the Kerch perimeter; two German infantry divisions blocked Perekop; the 10th and 19th Infantry Divisions hemmed in the enemy Sivash Sea beachhead; the 9th Cavalry Division patrolled the western coast; and the 1st and 2nd Mountain Divisions guarded the southern mountains and coast. Amalgamation meant that Romanian divisions were reinforced by German battalions, and vice versa. The German Seventeenth Army could not have held on to Crimea without the Cavalry and Mountain Corps.

The immediate crisis having passed, Romanian commanders focused on trying to revive morale. General Schwab requested that General Dumitrescu again grant leave, in time for Christmas, and suggested soldiers who had been on the front for twenty-four months or more be rotated home once a replacement arrived.[149] This well-intentioned plan backfired. Soldiers who had the requisite number of months became mutinous when they were not sent home immediately because of a shortage of replacements.[150] The General Staff instructed each regiment's second in command to focus on propaganda and formed seven-man teams comprising an officer, three "propaganda missionaries" (peacetime teachers who were also veterans), and three musicians to raise spirits.[151] In later weeks, *Ecoul Crimeei* declared, "Only Germany can save humanity from Bolshevism," while *Sentinela* proclaimed,

"Victory or Death."[152] Army propaganda did not improve morale very much, as soldiers awaited the next overwhelming enemy attack.

Soviet advances elsewhere on the front led the Antonescu regime to reverse policy toward Romanian Jews in Transnistria. While German Army Group A maintained a bridgehead at Nikopol over the lower Dnieper, German Army Group South had been thrown back across the river almost everywhere else.[153] German Army Group A assigned the Third Army to protect its rear and the Black Sea coast, with the II Corps in Transnistria and the III Corps (the 4th/24th Infantry Division, a German division, and a Slovak division) between the Bug and Dnieper.[154] General Dumitrescu reported signs of low morale: poor appearance, lackadaisical salutes, drunkenness, fights, and folk songs with new subversive lyrics.[155] The Governorate of Transnistria steadily adopted a more humane attitude when dealing with Jews. A Jewish survivor recalled, "No one was abusive, not the officers, not the soldiers, not the military prosecutors, not the pharmacists, not the agricultural engineers. The ['kikes'] had now become 'the Jewish gentlemen.'"[156] Under pressure from diplomats, the royal family, and Jewish leaders, Marshal Antonescu promised to repatriate 54,000 surviving Romanian Jews (leaving Soviet Jews behind) from Transnistria. Between 20 and 25 December, General Vasiliu's gendarmes escorted 11,370 Jews (over half from the Dorohoi region) and hundreds of young orphans back over the Dniester.[157] The Holocaust in Romania grew nearer its end with every Red Army victory.

The approach of Soviet armies caused a surge of partisan activity in German Army Group A's rear, especially in Crimea. The Third Army reported "intense activity" by partisans in the peninsula's southern mountains. The SSI reported Soviet civilians eagerly awaited liberation from "German slavery," and groups of ten to twenty, and sometimes up to five or six hundred partisans, organized more than one hundred attacks just around Simferopol after the peninsula was cut off. "The reprisals carried out by the German authorities and in part also those by the Romanian [authorities] accentuated even more the appetite for revenge of the locals, who are only waiting for the opportune moment."[158] The German Seventeenth Army prioritized keeping roads to Sevastopol clear of partisans in anticipation of having to withdraw. General Jaenecke ordered General Schwab to clear the mountains of an estimated seven to eight thousand partisans.[159] The Mountain Corps used both its divisions to sweep the area between 29 December and 9 January 1944, resulting in 1,934 dead, 121 wounded, and 2,763 captured partisans, for 44 dead and 197 wounded Romanians.[160] Although many partisans escaped, their logistical base was destroyed. Then the 1st and 2nd Mountain Divisions, independent of each other, conducted four smaller antipartisan operations from 16 to 30 January, resulting in 172 dead and 498 captured partisans, plus hundreds of burned huts, for 26 dead and 89 wounded Romanians. These antipartisan sweeps were less successful because partisans were alerted, terrain was difficult, and coordination was poor.[161] Schwab asked for more troops, but all Jaenecke could offer was some aircraft.[162] Nonetheless, the Mountain Corps scattered the partisan movement in the southern mountains. Captain Ioan Tobă—a cavalryman who fought at Odessa before being assigned to a mounted mountain unit—became a famous antipartisan fighter. *Ecoul Crimeei* reported he proudly carried a Soviet flyer saying he was "possessed of a devil" and offering a reward to kill him for butchering partisans. Tobă styled himself as "Hetman," a traditional Cossack title for military leaders, and his soldiers marched singing, "Long live the squadron / Which gave so many heroes / Long live the 'Hetman' too / The proudest among us."[163] Not all soldiers in Crimea were demoralized; there were still diehards willing to fight and commit atrocities.

The repatriation of Romanian Jews from Transnistria was short-lived. On 5 January, Soviet armies easily broke through German Army Group South, nearly destroying a German panzer corps at Kirovograd, and then again on 24 January, trapping two German corps at Korsun and culminating in disaster for Axis forces.[164] Soviet attacks battered German Army Group A's bridgehead on the Dnieper. Thus, on 27 January, Marshal Antonescu stopped repatriating Romanian Jews from Transnistria and instead began evacuating Romanians and Soviet Moldavians. "Welcoming Jews would provoke a lot of resentment," he believed.[165] Romanians had seized Jewish property or otherwise benefited when Jews had been deported from Bukovina and Bessarabia, so few would be happy to see them return. The Antonescu regime did not want to alienate the public by seemingly treating Jews well.

The Stavka maintained pressure against Crimea while Soviet forces advanced in Ukraine. On the Sivash Sea, Corporal Cârlan recorded, "About 12 Russian art.[illery] begins to bombard terribly. One awaits an attack on their part. Our artillery responds with little delay, but with such power, that the Russians are forced to stop the bombardment. . . . For the first time in my life I understood how great is the spiritual pain of a man who feels that he will separate himself from life and from those dear to him."[166] Lieutenant Colonel Iscăceanu's 13th *Călărași* Regiment at Perekop was subjected not only to barrages but also megaphones broadcasting Romanian songs intermixed with calls to surrender.[167] Soviet propaganda claimed Romanian prisoners were treated better than German prisoners, while Romanian counterpropaganda said they would be shot or worked to death.[168] Food, supplies, and ammunition were delivered by sea from Odessa. Soldiers made the most of the glut of supplies dumped in Crimea; some became quite good at faking documents to avoid inquisitive gendarmes or to obtain rations from German canteens.[169] So long as Axis troops held Transnistria, Hitler would not allow Crimea to be evacuated.

Transnistria, and the region between the Bug and Dnieper, also experienced an uptick in partisan activity. Romanian occupation in Transnistria was relatively light compared to German occupation in Reichskommissariat Ukraine, so few locals became partisans until Soviet forces approached, at which point Romanian authorities began evacuating everything that was not nailed down, and German police started deporting locals to work in Germany.[170] Transnistria lacked mountains, forests, or swamps, and Odessa was filled with Romanian and German police, so partisans hid in wooded regions to the north. Where previously only a handful of Soviet diehards had operated, now groups of thirty, fifty, or a hundred partisans organized attacks on railroads, bridges, communications, warehouses, town halls, and gendarme posts.[171] The Third Army took firm action in Transnistria and between the Bug and Dnieper by posting warnings of "grave sanctions" for supporting partisans, detaining former Soviet officers or NCOs (local Ukrainians previously paroled from prisoner of war camps to go home and work their farms to produce food for the Axis war effort), seizing hostages, and maintaining order through raids, checks, expedited trials, and public executions.[172] Nevertheless, Romanian civilian authorities lost control of the northern counties, not just to partisans but also to marauding German soldiers or their Cossack auxiliaries who threatened Romanian gendarmes guarding stores of food and other supplies.[173] On 1 February, General Gheorghe Potopeanu replaced Governor Alexianu, disbanded the Governorate of Transnistria, and formed the Military Administration of the Territory between the Dniester and Bug Rivers. Partisan attacks continued to increase as German Army Group A retreated.

The Antonescu regime began mobilizing its last manpower reserves for Romania's final defense. In Ukraine, on 8 February, Soviet forces destroyed the Nikopol bridgehead, and soon German Army Group A retreated back over the Dnieper, prompting Marshal Paul von Kleist, General Jaenecke, and Marshal Antonescu to beg Hitler to evacuate Crimea—but he steadfastly refused.[174] In Romania, that same day, the General Staff called up nineteen-year-olds and ordered fifteen-to-eighteen-year-olds in Moldavia, Bukovina, and Bessarabia to register, "to know the number of youths suitable for military service."[175] In Crimea, the German Seventeenth Army constructed fallback positions. On 11 February, General Cialâk reported that the NCOs and enlisted men's morale had fallen, especially in the 13th *Călărași* and 3rd *Roșiori* Regiments, but officers' morale was steady. He blamed "lack of homogeneity" (meaning 2,567 rehabilitation soldiers), slow rotation of soldiers with twenty-four months or more on the front, and barren terrain on the Sivash Sea coast. Cialâk reported taking "radical measures" against deserters in the Cavalry Corps and urged sending more replacements, separating rehabilitation soldiers from other troops, and increasing financial aid to soldiers' families.[176] The demoralized soldiers of the 13th *Călărași* Regiment were put to work digging defenses for German troops in the sticky clay on the Sivash Sea and even cleaning up German soldiers' trash in the trenches, "a degrading situation that revolted the soldiers."[177] Letters from home asked why soldiers were not returning home, reported families and farms in crisis, and complained that plenty of other men at home had never fought on the front or only at Odessa.[178] German Army Group A managed to reestablish a line on the Inhul River by 29 February, but it did not stay there long.

The German Army's disintegration signaled the beginning of the end of Romania's holy war. On 4 March, the Stavka launched a spring offensive. Soviet forces broke through German Army Group South near Uman, with designs to liberate the rest of Ukraine. Wilhelm Filderman implored Marshal Antonescu to let Romanian Jews join the flood of refugees fleeing the approaching front, but on 7 March, General Vasiliu allowed only 1,846 orphans under age fifteen to be repatriated.[179] The next day, in preparation to evacuate Crimea, the 1st Mountain Division began a four-day operation sweeping the highway to Sevastopol of partisans, capturing 275 prisoners while incurring 17 casualties.[180] On 14 March, Antonescu finally relented and authorized a general repatriation of Romanian Jews from Transnistria. The following day, German Army Group A assumed control of Transnistria, and the General Staff began remobilizing the Fourth Army, initially consisting of just the IV Corps and an ad hoc armored group, to defend Moldavia and Bessarabia.[181] Despite having a year to prepare, the Romanian Army was unready to defend the homeland.

Iași Front

After the manpower and matériel losses at Stalingrad, and with its most experienced and best-equipped soldiers in Crimea, the General Staff only had poorly trained and badly equipped troops in Romania. On 18 March, Soviet forces crossed the Dniester at Mogilev into northern Bessarabia before the Fourth Army arrived. Marshal Antonescu and General Ștelea wrote to Hitler and General Kurt Zeitzler, the new chief of the OKH, the next day begging for help. Antonescu complained he had not been kept abreast of events and warned of serious consequences if Bessarabia fell. Șteflea admitted that General Racovița, now commanding the Fourth Army, lacked the means to halt the Soviets.[182] If ever there was a time for Romania to abandon Nazi Germany, this was it, but the Antonescu regime did not seriously consider it. The Horthy regime in Hungary did. Hitler ordered Hungary occupied on 19 March, much to the delight of Antonescu, who used a 23–24 March meeting between the dictators to rail against Hungarian treachery and ask for northern Transylvania's return.[183] In Crimea, Corporal Cârlan noted, "Evening I listen to [the] radio that the Russians have crossed the Dniester in the Bălți region and that the Romanian and German troops resist with vigor."[184] In reality, German troops retreated in confusion, and Romanian soldiers mobilized slowly. Soviet armies crossed the Prut into northern Moldavia on 26 March from the east, and two days later, after another breakthrough, at Tarnopol, Soviet troops crossed the Dniester into northern Bukovina from the north, linking up around Hotin. Cernăuți fell without a fight. Hitler and Antonescu scrambled to improvise a defense.

The OKH devised a unique command structure in Romania. General Ferdinand Schörner, now commanding German Army Group A, created two new subordinate formations: German Army Group Wöhler by amalgamating the German Eighth and Fourth Armies in Moldavia and Army Group Dumitrescu by uniting the German Sixth and Third Armies in Bessarabia and Transnistria. This gave Marshal Antonescu an army group ostensibly under Romanian command that he had demanded without giving a Romanian commander overall control of Axis forces in Romania.[185] The German Eighth Army chaotically fled into Bukovina; German soldiers even murdered a few Jews recently repatriated from Transnistria before hurrying south. Emil Dorian noted, "The information brought by countless refugees from the north of Moldavia, if it is to be trusted, indicates utter havoc. The German soldiers are selling their military wear, begging for bread, and deserting."[186] The German Sixth Army tried to hold on to southern Transnistria, bending back to protect Odessa, until it was practically trapped against the seashore.[187] The Third Army withdrew into southern Bessarabia. Stragglers were not court-martialed, but General Dumitrescu clarified this was "only an act of generosity and of parental understanding and in no way a sign of tolerance."[188] On 30 March, he reported that German troops pillaged southern Transnistria, locals regretted the end of Romanian occupation, partisans again were hiding in Odessa's catacombs, and that German and Romanian soldiers were apathetic. An officer overheard *basarabeni* discuss desertion, since "in the year 1940 they proceeded the same and nothing bad happened."[189] On 3 April, General Racovița exhorted the Fourth Army as it marched to reinforce the German Eighth Army, "No one should abandon the post of battle that he was bestowed and it is better to let him die on [the] spot than to let [the] enemy advance. . . . Take heart soldiers! Will you possibly be less than our ancestors? Will you possibly be less than your parents who made Greater Romania? Will you permit the wicked enemy to defile further our villages and cities, our wives and children, our churches and observances?"[190] The next day a new threat to soldiers' families and homes suddenly appeared in the skies over Romania. The US Fifteenth Air Force began a bombing campaign with a raid targeting Bucharest's rail yards, which were filled with refugees fleeing the front, killing 2,942 people, wounding 2,126 others, and damaging hundreds of buildings.[191] On 5 April, German Army Group A was renamed German Army Group South Ukraine.

German Army Group South Ukraine appeared on the brink of collapse, but some factors, especially Romanian soldiers' willingness to sacrifice their lives for Greater Romania, enabled it to stabilize the front. The Stavka calculated that if Soviet forces seized Iași and Chișinău, the Antonescu regime would collapse, so it relentlessly drove its armies forward toward these tantalizingly close objectives.[192] However, exhausted Soviet armies slowed because of overstretched supply lines and muddy roads caused by bad weather.[193] Conversely, Axis forces fell back on a virtually intact railway network run by the so-called "Second Army" of Romanian Railways. Furthermore, Romanians still supported the Antonescu regime and its alliance with Nazi Germany, so there was no partisan movement to sabotage trains or attack convoys. Additionally, hilly terrain in Moldavia and Bessarabia favored the defenders.[194] Finally, fresh divisions of Romanian soldiers were thrown into the fight. These men may not have been enthusiastic about Romania's holy war, but they were determined to protect their nation and religion from the expected ravages of Judeo-Bolshevism.

The Stavka now launched an attack against Crimea as well. Soviet assaults pinned the German division at Perekop on 8 April, but the main attack came against the 10th and 19th Infantry Divisions on the Sivash Sea the following day and quickly penetrated.[195] Corporal Cârlan's 38th *Infanterie* Regiment was chased by Soviet soldiers shouting, "Where are you running to, huh, motherfuckers, 'cause we will put our hands on you before Sevastopol!" and "We will get to Constanța before you!" A comrade urged him to throw away his equipment. "I can't, they'll shoot me if I arrive without the [radio] set to our boys."[196] The German Seventeenth Army began a pell-mell, every-man-for-himself race to Sevastopol. Two German troops stopped the truck Cârlan had jumped into and shot the driver before being subdued by other Romanian soldiers.[197] On 10 April, Odessa fell as the German Sixth Army finally retreated from southern Transnistria. The German Eighth and Fourth Armies slowed Soviet attacks in Moldavia, but only at great cost, and some Romanian units broke and ran. General Racovița wildly claimed that 80 percent of *basarabeni* had deserted and ordered *basarabeni* reassigned from combat to support units. "[*Basarabeni*] can be left, however, [who are] the elements of trust who are also determined to fight." A later report showed that only 10 percent of *basarabeni* went missing.[198] On 12 April, Hitler finally authorized General Jaenecke to begin evacuations in Crimea—but only support troops, as he expected the German Seventeenth Army to hold Sevastopol. That same day, General Schwab ordered the Mountain Corps to man the old Soviet defenses north of Severnaya Bay. Again, that day, Soviet troops won a bridgehead over the Dniester at Tighina, at the junction of the German Sixth and Third Armies, threatening to advance into southern Bessarabia. The next day, Marshal Antonescu authorized commanders to summarily execute soldiers for desertion, cowardice, looting, self-mutilation, insubordination, or striking a superior.[199] Romanian commanders did not actually order many Romanian soldiers shot, but General Schörner was ruthless toward German soldiers, insisting on a firing squad or a noose for indiscipline.[200] Strict discipline, desperate Romanian counterattacks, and deft German panzer maneuvering finally blunted Soviet spearheads thrusting toward Iași and Chișinău.

German Army Group South Ukraine stabilized the front by 17 April. The line followed the Carpathian foothills in northern Moldavia, jutted east across central Moldavia north of Iași, continued over the Prut into central Bessarabia north of Chișinău, and turned south along the Dniester in southern Bessarabia. Having shortened the front, General Schörner could provide German divisions to bolster hard-pressed Romanian corps. Marshal Antonescu was adamant that "Romanian Divisions should not be splintered; [however,] the mixing of German Divisions with Romanian ones on the front, is very desired."[201] German divisions were assigned to Romanian corps and vice versa; this was amalgamation on a grand scale. Also, fresh Romanian units continued to arrive. Second Lieutenant Gheorghe Netejoru recalled that when the first battalion in his regiment left for the Iași front, the colonel gave a speech to the entire unit assembled in neat ranks: "He bids us that, 'victorious, after the end of the war, we'll meet in the same formation [*componență*].' In this moment, on the faces of soldiers one reads sadness. . . . I cannot forget these brave heroes who sacrificed their lives for the forging of an ideal: Greater Romania."[202] When his battalion reached the front, it found a live-and-let-live atmosphere: "Less than a hundred meters away in front of a casemate was a spring from which our boys as well as our enemies took water."[203] This would soon change. German troops and supplies arrived through Hungary, further strengthening German Army Group South Ukraine. Constantin Mancaș, only sixteen years old, had been evacuated from Iași to Târgu Jiu and "worked over there to load wagons, unload materials" while training on weekends.[204] Axis resistance continued to stiffen on the Iași front.

The German Seventeenth Army had even managed to establish a defense around Sevastopol in Crimea. The Mountain Corps fought off Soviet tanks probing in the north as the Axis line extended south, with units arriving by sea or by road.[205] Partisans did not impede Axis soldiers on mountain roads in large part due to the Mountain Corps' previous antipartisan sweeps. Soon, 81,700 German and 46,700 Romanian soldiers gathered within the Sevastopol perimeter.[206] Corporal Cârlan (and his radio) joined Romanian soldiers on the Chersonese peninsula, sheltering from Soviet aircraft in the same catacombs once used by Soviet troops, desperately awaiting evacuation. After seeing no vessel, "We went back to the first point of embarkation very overwrought (steaming) at the Germans, with weapons loaded ready to shoot at them." But they left without violence. At the embarkation point Cârlan saw "a veritable cemetery of destroyed vehicles and carts."[207] Soviet aircraft and submarines threatened ships during the daylong voyage. Cârlan's ship carried one thousand people, including Tatars who wept as they left their native country. After an uncomfortable night, "around 1130 a black streak appeared on the horizon. It was the Romanian seashore. . . . Since on the deck of the ship were many people, at the cry of one who was standing alongside me:—Land, Romania is visible!—all rushed to see Romanian land, which we desired so much and where loved ones waited for us so long."[208] When they landed at Constanța an air raid reminded them that Romania was no longer a safe haven from the war.

The front and the home front had become one and the same. US and British aircraft tried to throttle Axis logistics by bombing railroad centers, causing many Romanians to seek shelter in the countryside, although Jews were not permitted to leave the cities. "Still," Emil Dorian opined, "even if Jews were allowed into rural areas, it would be inadmissible to let them leave Bucharest: how could civil defense function without them? Most of the physicians, demolition crews, office heads, engineers, stretcher bearers are Jewish."[209] Stories spread of Soviet soldiers committing crimes, including mass rape, in occupied territory. On 21 April, General Racovița encouraged civilians to evacuate an area six kilometers behind the front, stressing the need to remove girls ten or older.[210] Marshal Antonescu saw soldiers stealing from civilians during an inspection of the Iași front, so General Racovița reminded commanders even "the smallest transgressions" could be punished by death.

A spate of executions, including two company commanders, followed, to emphasize the need for greater discipline in Romania than previously in the occupied USSR.[211] Antonescu blamed the General Staff for the Romanian Army's defeat outside Stalingrad and its current state of unpreparedness; furthermore, he often made agreements with General Schörner about strategy and operations without involving General Șteflea. On 23 April, Șteflea composed an indignant missive. He demanded these accusations stop and that he be consulted before major decisions. "I no longer have the moral authority and neither the possibility to continue leading the Great General Staff and in consequence I ask to be replaced."[212] Antonescu ignored Șteflea's resignation. Meanwhile, the Fourth Army counterattacked in Moldavia. The commander of the 6th Infantry Division ordered soldiers judged to be deserters in previous fighting be rehabilitated for joining a costly counterattack, but Antonescu confiscated the 18th and 90th Mountain Groups' colors for "reprehensible conduct" in another clash.[213] The German Sixth and Third Armies penned in the Soviets' Tiraspol bridgehead in Bessarabia. On 25 April, the 10th *Vânători* Regiment endured a three-hour bombardment in shelters, emerging to blast apart an enemy attack.[214] Meanwhile, US air raids revived old accusations of Jewish treachery. Emil Dorian recorded, "There are still people, even in the centrally located, elegant shelters, who believe that the American air raids are made with the help of Romanian Jews, and who loudly accuse the Jews of rejoicing when the city is bombed!"[215] Fear of Soviet vengeance and strict discipline deterred soldiers and civilians from organizing pogroms this time.

The Stavka continued efforts to dislodge German Army Group South Ukraine from Romania and Crimea. Hitler suspended evacuation from Crimea on 27 April after he discovered that General Jaenecke had evacuated combat along with support troops, and fired him. Nevertheless, twenty-eight thousand German and twenty-one thousand Romanian soldiers, plus twenty-three thousand Slovak troops, Russian auxiliaries, Soviet prisoners, and Soviet civilians, had already been evacuated.[216] On 2 May, Soviet attacks in Moldavia attempted to break through the Fourth Army. The General Staff committed every available soldier—including the so-called 101st, 102nd, 103rd, and 104th Mountain Commands and the 110th Infantry Brigade (all consisting of three battalions composed of training or support troops from the depots of the mountain and infantry divisions decimated in Crimea)—and German Army Group South Ukraine plugged breakthroughs with German panzers.[217] Axis troops halted the enemy after six days; however, Mircea Ionescu-Quintus remembered soldiers nicknamed it the battle of "shame" [*rușinoasă*]—a play on the name of the village of Ruginoasa near Târgu

Frumos where the fiercest fighting took place—because they needed to be rescued by their allies.[218] Soviet forces had better luck in Crimea. On 5 May, a Soviet attack pinned down Sevastopol's northern perimeter, held by the 1st and 2nd Mountain Divisions, followed by a stronger attack against the southern perimeter on 7 May, forcing Axis forces to withdraw.[219] Two days later Hitler finally approved general evacuation, saving another 29,000 German and 15,000 Romanian soldiers, plus 4,000 Russian auxiliaries, by sea before 13 May. However, 7,000 German and 4,000 Romanian troops drowned after transports were sunk, and 53,500 German and 22,000 Romanian soldiers were left behind, killed or captured.[220] The Stavka decided against more attacks in Romania following the reconquest of Crimea.

German Army Group South Ukraine set to work tidying up the front and securing the rear in Romania, which included demanding the General Staff keep tight control over Jews. The German Sixth Army attacked the long, narrow Tașlîc bridgehead jutting thirty kilometers across the Dniester toward Chișinău, eliminating it after a week of fighting on 15 May.[221] Desperate for manpower, the General Staff emptied Chișinău's prisons, sending inmates to the Third Army for rehabilitation. General Dumitrescu liberally employed the lash; 491 soldiers were flogged that month, most for desertion, compared to 75 the month prior.[222] General Schörner complained that refugees, including minorities, were returning to the evacuation zone and betraying Axis positions to the enemy.[223] During the evacuation of Transnistria, officials managed to repatriate 10,744 Romanian Jews, and more found their way across the Dniester on their own.[224] Also, Jews had evacuated from Moldavia. Consequently, on May 16, the General Staff ordered Jewish refugees to register in whatever city they were now in, or return to the city where they had been registered, if it had not been overrun.[225] Marshal Antonescu made it clear to German commanders that Jews were not to be massacred in Romania. The German Sixth Army eliminated several other smaller Soviet bridgeheads over the Dniester, but it could not squeeze out the last one at Tiraspol. The Fourth Army conducted a spoiling attack at Iași.[226] On 30 May, flanked by Romanian infantry divisions, German panzer divisions spearheaded the attack and in two days took a bite out of the Soviet line with light losses. Then German panzer divisions shifted west, to repeat the feat on 2 June, but it took four days of bloody fighting because now alerted Soviet troops offered tenacious resistance. Soviet counterattacks were aided by US air raids against Iași to disrupt Axis movement and communication. The two German attacks created a tiny bulge and collected fifteen hundred prisoners but failed to reconquer the hills overlooking Iași used to direct Soviet artillery fire.[227] German and Romanian soldiers now entrenched and awaited the next Soviet offensive.

Romanian soldiers did not lack food, mail, or leave, but the enemy's obvious superiority depressed morale. Iași and Chișinău were threatened by Soviet armies, and no city was safe from US air raids; the General Staff had already announced that any soldier whose family was affected by bombing would receive fifteen to twenty days of leave.[228] The General Staff organized a propaganda blitz to try to raise morale. An article in *Soldatul*, "What Soviet liberation means," refuted communist ideology, arguing that communism meant oppression, unpaid labor, and exploitation of workers. "Such things, capitalism did not do anytime or anywhere."[229] Officers held moral education meetings, especially with new recruits, to remind troops that they fought to resist Soviet aggression, restore Greater Romania, preserve Christian civilization, and protect their families. Chaplains and propaganda missionaries preached faith in holy war and final victory; soldiers preferred to play sports in their free time.[230] While soldiers still believed in Romania's holy war against Judeo-Bolshevism, they did not believe in Nazi Germany's final victory, especially with news of defeats on other fronts. On 6 June, Alice Voinescu excitedly wrote, "Yesterday the Americans entered Rome! Today they landed in Normandy, creating a second front . . . realizing, finally, the promised liberating invasion. I cannot imagine what is going on over there, I only have the feeling that it's the beginning of the finale of this war."[231] After hearing US bombers drone toward another city and reports of US fighter-bombers roaming the skies attacking cars, carts, and people on highways and byways around Bucharest, Mihail Sebastian quipped, "It's strange that they have time for raids on Romania when they are so busy in Italy and France."[232] Anglo-American progress raised hopes among Romanians that somehow or another US and British soldiers might land in the Balkans and reach Romania before Soviet troops broke through on the Iași front. Until then the Romanian Army needed the German Army's help to hold back the Red Army.

The Iași front remained quiet, but aggressive Soviet patrolling bled strength and weakened morale. Second Lieutenant Netejoru recalled that both sides sent "specially prepared soldiers" to raid enemy trenches and take "hostages" to gather intelligence.[233] The Fourth and Third Armies together suffered on average thirty-six hundred casualties a month from patrols, artillery and air bombardments, local attacks, and desertions.[234] Faith in victory was at an unequaled low. On 6 July, Colonel Mitica Panaite, an artillery instructor in Focșani, scribbled, "We remained few, few indeed who still believe in the good ending! [As] for me my optimism has not waned, but probably you need to be German to still be able to believe."[235] Desertion

1942–1944: HOLY WAR OF DEFENSE

FIGURE 9. Despite catastrophic losses in men and equipment at Stalingrad and further loses of soldiers and matériel in Crimea, the Romanian Army managed to mobilize enough poorly trained and badly equipped soldiers to defend Romania with the help of the German Army. Trench warfare on the Iași front inflicted thousands of casualties a month, including this wounded soldier being borne by comrades to the rear in May 1944. The growing casualty lists, the transfer of German panzers out of Romania, and Soviet superiority sapped Romanian morale. Bundesarchiv, Bild 101I-024-3533-24 / photo: Wolff.

increased. Deserters tended to be from regions it was assumed would be annexed by the USSR or that were currently occupied by Soviet troops; the 14th Infantry Division reported its deserters over the previous month were 128 *basarabeni*, 12 *bucovineni*, 57 troops from occupied Moldavia, and 57 others. Many formed bandit groups to wait out the war, hiding in forests around Chișinău with support from villagers.[236] A few deserted to the enemy. The 4th Mountain Division (formerly the 4th/24th Infantry Division) reported that fourteen *basarabeni* had deserted in the previous month because "Russian propaganda megaphones had promised [that they could] return to their families."[237] Most Romanian soldiers remained committed to defending their homeland from the Soviet menace, but they knew that even with their German ally at their side, the enemy was stronger.

German commanders were not impressed by Romanian soldiers, especially officers, at this time. One German liaison officer recalled, "These officers seemed none too anxious to get near the fighting. When I mentioned to the Rumanian officers that their staffs were much too far removed from the front, they responded that there was 'sufficient telephone wire' available."[238] On 25 July, General Johannes Friessner arrived in Slănic to take over German Army Group South Ukraine (General Schörner took Friessner's old position as German Army Group North commander after Hitler decided to swap the two), and he was stunned to find the Iași front being denuded of German panzer divisions.[239] The OKH needed these precious forces to save German Army Group Center from destruction after the Stavka launched a summer offensive in Byelorussia a month previously. Compounding the direness of the situation, Friessner noted, was that "enthusiasm for the war had dropped below zero" in Romania and Hungary. "With the Soviet danger now getting closer and closer to their own borders, one might have thought that a firm will to resist had now arisen—far from it! Hungary, in particular, persisted in its passive stance." He held Marshal Antonescu in great esteem, however, crediting him alone for compelling Romania's general mobilization in the face of opposition from his cabinet and the king.[240] German commanders hardly ever interacted with Romanian soldiers, who they assumed lacked motivation, so they based the Romanian Army's unexpectedly good performance on the *conducător*'s supposedly unique ability to exert his will upon his soldiers—an explanation more in line with German commanders' Nazi worldview than reality. Antonescu could not have organized the defense of Romania without the support of his ministers, the officer corps, and the public united by common ideology.

Nonetheless, Romanian soldiers' morale plumbed new lows as German panzer divisions packed up and left. On 31 July, General Racovița went on leave, leaving General Avramescu as acting commander of the Fourth Army, and delayed coming back—effectively abandoning his post. The next day, the V Corps reported that troops "do not hesitate to show . . . their desire to conclude the peace as quickly as possible." Yet it insisted their morale was still sound: "Our battle is regarded confidently, figuring that, without the barrier of the Army, the Country would be the prey of bolshevism."[241] On 2 August, General Korne, now commander of the 1st Armored Division, reported, "This passing of unending motorized columns caused to give birth in the souls of all a vague fear that we will be abandoned by our allies." His soldiers worried about their families, mocked euphemisms for defeat (like "after hard battles," "retreat following a plan established previously," and "shortening of the front") used in propaganda, and spread rumors—including about an "A-C Plebiscite" to vote for Marshal Antonescu or King Carol II and the presence of British military police in Soviet-occupied Romania, making it safe to desert. Korne requested that soldiers and civilians be told the German panzer divisions' departure benefited them because then Nazi Germany could win battles elsewhere to protect Romania.[242] Once there had been nine German panzer or panzer grenadier divisions; now there were only three, plus the 1st Armored Division.[243] The OKH believed the Stavka lacked enough forces for offensives in Byelorussia and Romania at the same time and argued that German Army Group South Ukraine would not be attacked.

Marshal Antonescu was not so confident. The General Staff constructed three fallback positions in case of a Soviet offensive: the Dacia, Trajan, and Decebal Lines. Lastly, the Focşani-Nămoloasa-Brăila (FNB) Line blocked the way into the Wallachian plain. On 5 August, during what was to be their final meeting, Antonescu suggested Hitler abandon southern Bessarabia and most of Moldavia and withdraw to a line along the Carpathians, the FNB Line, and the Danube that could be held by Romanian divisions alone to free more German divisions to defend Poland, but the führer reasoned this was a scheme by the *conducător* to abandon the Axis.[244] The debate with Hitler was acrimonious, but Antonescu concluded by swearing to fight to the end. By now the Romanian Army mustered 1,077,000 soldiers.[245] German Army Group South Ukraine had over 380,000 German and 420,000 Romanian troops on the front, but the Soviet armies arrayed against it had slightly more soldiers and many more tanks, artillery, trucks, and aircraft.[246] The Soviet Black Sea Fleet prepared an amphibious landing on the Romanian coast.[247] Before ordering the offensive, the Stavka asked the Anglo-Americans to stop bombing Romania, and the final US air raid occurred on 19 August. During forty-two daylight and twenty-three nighttime raids, US and British bombers had destroyed 157 locomotives, 619 passenger cars, 3,010 freight cars, 1,525 tanker cars, and 10 other vehicles, thus hampering the movement of Axis troops and supplies to the front and reducing oil deliveries to Nazi Germany to a trickle. The Allied raids also caused civilian casualties of 7,600 dead and 7,600 wounded, and wrecked 46,523 homes.[248] Despite alarming reports from frontline commanders in Romania, neither the OKH nor German Army Group South Ukraine predicted a Soviet offensive.[249]

Understrength, badly equipped, poorly trained, and demoralized Romanian soldiers were unable to offer much resistance when the Stavka finally unleashed its offensive against Romania. On 20 August, after Soviet forces launched local attacks along the whole front the day before, Soviet armies advanced, following two massive morning barrages lasting an hour and a half. The main blow hit the Fourth Army between Târgu Frumos and Iași and quickly broke through the VI and IV Corps.[250] Emerging from a shelter, Second Lieutenant Boris Alexianu looked down into the Jijia Valley near Iași: "T-34 tanks and enemy infantry, literally 'flooded' the valley in front of our position. . . . We imposed calm, patience on ourselves and exactly executed the order. The torrent continued approaching. At the appearance of the signal[,] the deafening pitter-patter is unleashed from all our weapons; and the 'Bofors' [antiaircraft guns] fire at tanks and also at people; the torrent keeps thinning, many [of the enemy] fall, some advance in leaps, we continue to reap widely."[251] After the German unit next to Alexianu's position retreated, his squadron was encircled, forcing it to break out. The second attack, from the Tiraspol bridgehead, hit the seam between the German Sixth and Third Armies, driving west toward the Prut. The German Sixth Army, now commanded by General Maximilian Fretter-Pico, was threatened with double envelopment. General Friessner reacted slowly, hindered by a communications breakdown, but he believed the holes in the Iași front could be plugged and that the situation on the Dniester was not serious.[252] By evening Soviet troops had entered Iași.

The OKH ordered German Army Group South Ukraine to counterattack, but it took some convincing to get the General Staff to agree. Marshal Antonescu, General Ștefleaa, and General Avramescu met with General Otto Wöhler at his headquarters in Bacău. The Romanians wanted to retreat to the FNB Line, but the German demanded a stand on the Trajan Line. Antonescu finally agreed with Wöhler.[253] On 21 August, counterattacks by the Fourth Army all failed, and the Soviets overran the Trajan Line. The German Sixth Army proved unable to cut off the Soviet spearhead from the Tiraspol bridgehead, and the Third Army suffered grievous losses on the Dniester.[254] Hitler allowed General Fretter-Pico to order a retreat, but the German Sixth Army was already half encircled, and soon traffic jams delayed panicked German infantry trying to outrun Soviet tanks.[255] The next day, while Cetatea Albă fell to a Soviet amphibious attack, Antonescu met General Friessner at Slănic. The *conducător* convinced the general that reaching the FNB Line before Soviet forces got there was more important than trying to rescue the German Sixth Army, and obtained permission to order the Fourth and Third Armies to retreat.[256] After Antonescu returned to Bucharest, Avramescu resigned in protest when the German LVII Corps refused to withdraw with the Fourth Army according to the prearranged timetable, so Ștefleaa took command. The chances of the Fourth Army reaching the FNB Line and the Third Army escaping to the Danube to establish a defense strong enough to halt the enemy, however, were slim to none.

"Second Stalingrad"

Despite the catastrophe outside Stalingrad, the Romanian Army had continued to make an important contribution to the German war effort on the eastern front by fighting in the Kuban bridgehead and Crimea. Romanian soldiers' motivation remained sound, even if morale grew poor. Ideology remained just as important during the long retreat from Russia and the Caucasus as it had been during the previous advances. The Romanian Army increasingly leaned on propaganda and strict discipline to maintain motivation, but poor morale and especially shortages of heavy weapons undermined its combat effectiveness. Amalgamation of Romanian and German units enabled the Romanian Army to continue fighting alongside the German Army against the Red Army to stave off defeat. There was a direct connection between the fighting on the front and the Antonescu regime's treatment of Jews in Romania and Transnistria, which became less harsh. Yet demoralized soldiers could still lash out at Soviet civilians, prisoners of war, and partisans. Finally, the Stavka engineered a replay of Stalingrad in Romania, breaking through the Fourth and Third Armies to encircle the German Sixth Army in central Bessarabia, eviscerating the Romanian Army for a second time in less than two years.

Chapter 7

Propaganda and Discipline

The Antonescu regime worried about soldiers' motivation, so the General Staff increased propaganda efforts and enforced strict discipline. Because of Romanians' ideological beliefs, most soldiers accepted army propaganda messages about holy war, defending European civilization, German-Romanian comradeship, and the threat of Judeo-Bolshevism. However, soldiers were increasingly less convinced by army propaganda's promises of final victory, especially in the aftermath of Stalingrad. The Romanian Army maintained strict discipline through various means, the most notorious being corporal punishment, but also including penal, capital, and financial sanctions. The General Staff transformed an old practice, the rehabilitation of officers through bravery in combat, into an extensive new system, including NCOs and enlisted men, that provided the Romanian Army desperately needed manpower. Yet commanders administered discipline selectively, harshly punishing cowardice or indiscipline on the front while ignoring war crimes in the rear, particularly if committed against Jews or partisans—which most saw as one and the same. The Romanian Army's propaganda efforts and strict discipline reinforced its solders' motivation in the holy war against Judeo-Bolshevism.

Propaganda

During the interwar period, Romania focused limited resources on propaganda to defend claims to Bessarabia and Transylvania.[1] Despite calls by the SSI to create a propaganda ministry, propaganda remained a sub-secretariat of the Ministry of Foreign Affairs. Interwar governments increasingly used censorship to shape public opinion. The short-lived Goga-Cuza government claimed a quarter of journalists were Jews, and it shuttered left-wing presses.[2] When King Carol II declared his royal dictatorship, he shut down party presses, leaving only state-sanctioned news. On 3 October 1939, Carol II created a propaganda ministry, but on 20 September 1940 General Antonescu disbanded it. Antonescu continued censorship under his military dictatorship, so criticism of his regime occurred surreptitiously, by circulating letters by hand.[3] On 30 April 1941, Vice–Prime Minister Mihai Antonescu reestablished the Ministry of National Propaganda, modeling it on Joseph Goebbels's Ministry of Popular Enlightenment and Propaganda in Nazi Germany, so that "all journals attack at the same time the same problem."[4] Alexandru Marcu, an intellectual with contacts in Fascist Italy, was minister of propaganda, but Mihai Antonescu constantly involved himself trying to improve organization, raise standards, and increase funding for propaganda.[5] The General Staff's Propaganda Service coordinated with the Ministry of Propaganda. Initially, the Propaganda Service was subordinated to Section II Intelligence, but on 1 December 1941 it became independent. The now renamed Propaganda Section was divided into seven offices: education, propaganda, and counterpropaganda in the ranks; press and censorship; education, propaganda, and counterpropaganda through photography, cinema, and megaphones; studies and assessments; collaboration with allies' propaganda services; propaganda and counterpropaganda targeting the enemy; and propaganda and counterpropaganda targeting workers in militarized factories.[6] At the Propaganda Section's largest incarnation, in mid-1942, it had 161 office staff and field personnel.[7] Propagandists included two- or three-man photo/journalist teams, film crews, mobile cinemas, loudspeakers, theater groups, and the Army Choir.[8] The Propaganda Section's resources were limited, so it relied on German commanders to help with extra materials, content, and funding, especially in Crimea, where German and Romanian propagandists worked closely together.[9] Despite its small size, the Propaganda Section worked tirelessly and greatly influenced soldiers on the front through various mediums.

Radio offered the possibility of reaching every soldier, but the Romanian Army suffered from a lack of radio receivers. In May 1941, it only had 116 radio receivers. Consequently, on 7 June 1941, the General Staff equipped units down to the battalion level, using nine hundred radios confiscated from Jews.[10] Most were not battery powered, so were not useful in the field once the war started. Soldiers compensated by using combat radio transmitters to tune in to broadcasts, but there was a shortage of those too. The Third Army repeatedly asked for battery-powered radios, so in December 1941 the Propaganda Section purchased radios wherever possible, arguing they were "necessary [for] the maintaining of the morale of the soldiers, among whom are observed manifestations of longing for family and home."[11] Propaganda flooded the airwaves: *The Soldier's Hour, The German-Romanian Hour, The Italian-Romanian Hour, The Casualties' Hour,* and *Radio Mail.* Music stations followed.[12] Radios had difficulty picking up signals from Romania in the USSR, so beginning in February 1942, the German Eleventh Army began Romanian-language broadcasts from Simferopol in Crimea, with daily news and twice-weekly variety shows continuing for over two years.[13] Radios remained in short supply, but there was always something to listen to if soldiers had one.

Film was a powerful propaganda tool. Romania had few cinemas, and soldiers were often in remote locations, so the General Staff created mobile cinemas to project films outdoors. These were used after the withdrawal from northern Bukovina and Bessarabia in 1940 to help raise morale.[14] The mobile cinemas were constantly on the road in 1941, first in eastern Romania, showing films to 10,830 soldiers, 9,300 civilians, and 13,422 wounded, and then in Transnistria, where another 52,000 soldiers and 22,600 civilians watched films.[15] The Propaganda Section cranked out newsreels celebrating victories as quickly as possible: "Soldiers Cross the Prut," "The Liberation of Bukovina," "The Liberation of Bessarabia," and "Romanian Troops across the Dniester: Penetrating the Stalin Line." A long documentary *Our Holy War* covered the campaign in depth.[16] The Propaganda Section also provided entertainment, including Romanian and German movies like *The Merry Women, The Bears' Paradise, Pat and Pataschon,* and *Truxa.*[17] Mobile cinemas did not cross the Bug. In German-occupied cities cinemas screened motion pictures in German and Romanian, so Romanian soldiers watched a lot of German newsreels and films.[18] Soldiers consumed a steady diet of light comedies but also propaganda while on the front.

Spectacle entertained and propagandized. Initially, the Propaganda Service used existing performance groups; for example, in July 1941 the six-member Struggle and Light theater troupe was exempted from military service to organize entertainment "for the workers in militarized factories and also for the wounded soldiers in hospitals."[19] In June 1942 the Propaganda Section created theater teams to entertain soldiers in Transnistria and Crimea. This was so successful that in October 1942 it recruited "mixed" theater groups of twenty-two men and eleven women for forty-five-day tours to entertain troops across Ukraine and southern Russia.[20] The sixty-strong Army Choir joined them. By the end of January 1943, the four groups had put on 145 shows, mostly in Transnistria and Crimea, but also in southern Russia and even the Caucasus.[21] The shows consisted of patriotic hymns, folk songs, ballroom dances, folk dances, poems, recitations, plays, jokes, and acrobatics. Spectacles brought a bit of Romania to soldiers far from home to remind them why they were fighting.

Newspapers were the most common form of propaganda. *Sentinela* was issued weekly to soldiers from December 1939 until September 1944. *Soldatul* was handed out thrice weekly to troops from June 1941 to August 1944. *Armata* was available for purchase by officers twice monthly between May 1942 and April 1944. Finally, *Ecoul Crimeei* was distributed weekly to soldiers in Crimea from March 1942 to March 1944. The supply of newspapers on the front was chronically short because of distance, bad roads, and insufficient transport. Already in July 1941, the Third Army complained it had received only eight hundred copies of *Sentinela* and *Soldatul* when it needed at least fourteen thousand. When roads turned to mud in autumn and ice in winter, deliveries broke down; even aircraft could not transport newspapers in bad weather. In February 1942, the 10th Infantry Division commander in Crimea offered to pay to ship five hundred copies of *Sentinela* for his officers.[22] The improvement of logistics in the spring meant more newspapers arrived. Additionally, *Ecoul Crimeei* started printing in Simferopol. The German Eleventh Army provided a captured Soviet printing press, and the Mountain Corps supplied the editors and newsprint paper.[23] Although newspaper supplies never again dipped as low as in the winter of 1942, copies could be difficult to find on the front. In March 1943, the Propaganda Section printed 117,500 copies of *Sentinela*, only half for the front; 49,600 copies of *Soldatul*, only half for the front; 12,000 copies of *Armata*, a third for the front; and 4,000 copies of *Ecoul Crimeei*, all for the front.[24] A third of soldiers were illiterate, lessening the demand for newspapers, while the two-thirds who were literate passed around copies and read aloud to those who could not read.

The most popular army propaganda was probably the comic strip *The Misadventures of Private Neață*, in *Sentinela*. The General Staff employed Neagu Rădulescu, an interwar writer, playwright, and caricaturist, to produce cartoons for the newspaper's "Cheerful Page." At first Rădulescu drew vignettes about a peacetime army: an army doctor inspecting a recruit with a bent back and flat feet; a regular officer trying to discern the skills of a clueless reserve officer; a private caught canoodling with a female cook by an officer; and a sergeant asking a Gypsy recruit, "Who stole my bread, hey Gypsy?" "Respectfully mister sergeant, what serial number did it have?"[25] Then Rădulescu created a four-panel comic strip focused on Private Neață, which would run from January 1940 to September 1944. Consequently, Neață navigated the changing political landscape under King Carol II, the National Legionary State, the Antonescu regime, and King Mihai I. The cheerful peasant soldier's hijinks became hugely popular with soldiers and civilians alike—two volumes of Neață's misadventures were published in 1942 and 1943, selling twenty thousand copies—and inspired copycats, including a children's book and a short-lived comic strip called *The Life of Private Stan*, printed in *Soldatul*.[26] Rădulescu's comic strip offers an interesting perspective on military culture and propaganda themes during Romania's holy war.

Initially the comic strip focused on the humorous trivialities of army life, but increasingly it delivered propaganda messages. Punch lines were at Neață's expense and mocked his clumsiness, bad luck, and stupidity. After being told by a taxi driver what it would cost to drive him and an officer's luggage into town, Neață asks how much it would be to take just the bags.[27] After an officer commands his soldiers to tell a colonel inspecting the unit that they were from Wallachia because that was where the colonel was from, Neață does so, but when he is then asked from which village, he proceeds to name his hometown in Moldavia.[28] After the territorial losses of 1940, the comic strip focused on the need to restore Greater Romania. Neață's wife Marițica bids him adieu in January 1941: "Dear Neață because your holiday leave has ended and you are returning to the barracks, look, here is a sprig of basil. Put it under your pillow for Epiphany and you will dream of what you desire for the New Year." He dreams of "Greater Romania! From the Dniester to the Tisza!"[29] In another strip, an officer finds him weeping next to a broken wagon wheel and asks, "What is with you Neață, why are you crying, is a tooth hurting you, or have you got too many chores?" He responds he was sad because it reminded him of Greater Romania: "Like her, it is missing a few spokes . . . Bukovina, Transylvania, and Bessarabia." He promises to hold on to the damaged wheel until he helps "to put the spokes of the country back in place."[30] Such saccharine patriotism was common throughout the comic strip.

Neață underwent a transformation after the war started. While still buffoonish at times, he was also cunning. In contrast, Rădulescu depicted Red Army soldiers as cowardly, demoralized, dirty, and drunk—sometimes racialized with Asian features. Notably, Jews never appear. Neață outsmarts Soviet "bumpkins" through a mixture of peasant cleverness and bravery. A couple of tropes repeated in the comic strip: Neață having to figure his way out of a sticky situation after being surprised unarmed; Neață finding a way to surprise Soviet soldiers to capture them; Neață visiting home; Neață interacting with German and Italian allies, etc. In one comic strip, Neață masquerades as a woman parading through the streets in Stalingrad to lure sex-starved Soviet soldiers into captivity.[31] Another issue has Neață meet his German counterpart Fritz, with whom he shares food and cigarettes before they go off together to fight Bolsheviks.[32] He also meets Giovanii, an Italian private, and even teaches him and Fritz a Romanian folk dance (unsurprisingly, a Hungarian private never appears).[33] Rădulescu presented an idealized and desensitized vision of the front. Killing, mutilation, and death are almost always out of sight. Neață regularly received leave to visit home. German-Romanian comradeship was respectful. Nevertheless, Romanian soldiers enjoyed the escape from the reality of the front with which they were all too familiar.

The propaganda in the comic strip became more blatant with time, particularly when it came to the war's progress. Rădulescu always depicted the war as going well. On 22 June 1943, the second anniversary of Operation

FIGURE 10. In this episode from *The Misadventures of Private Neața* from November 1942, Neața decides to dress as a woman to prowl the streets of Stalingrad. He uses recently acquired feminine wiles to lure sex-starved Red Army troops: "How handsome you are, cutie pie; such very uncommon soldiers. Come with me!" They follow until he removes his wig and pulls a pistol. "OK, buddy, and now, since I have brought you into our lines, hands up for I am corporal Neața" From *Sentinela*, courtesy of Biblioteca Academiei Române.

Barbarossa, the comic strip showed Neață first challenging a giant Soviet soldier, then booting him over the Dniester in 1941, followed by rounding up surrendering Soviet troops in 1942, and finally standing atop the Soviet goliath in 1943.[34] This narrative must have invited derision from soldiers. On 1 December 1943, Neață meets up with Horia, a soldier from Transylvania, to celebrate twenty-five years since the creation of Greater Romania, and says to him, "I swear to you that I won't give up until justice is done for us and our land!"[35] Neață was shown wounded for the first time in May 1944. After perching his helmet atop a mass of bandages on his head, he refuses two weeks' leave and marches to the front, saying, "I may be missing Marițica but first above all I must clean the country's ground of enemies."[36] When Rădulescu introduced the comic strip, Neață was funny and relevant, but once the war turned against the Axis he became pedantic and divorced from reality.

The Propaganda Section reinforced the ideological beliefs underlying soldiers' motivation to fight and commit atrocities. Officers were most exposed to propaganda, since they were most literate and most likely to receive newspapers or have access to a radio, but NCOs and enlisted men were not bereft of army propaganda. Officers spread propaganda through personal conversations, moral education, and speeches. Chaplains helped disseminate propaganda, too. Bishop Ciopron had expanded the number of chaplains from 30 in 1937 to 108 in 1943, so every regiment had one.[37] They passed out newspapers, prayer books, or crosses and integrated propaganda into sermons. Finally, the Propaganda Section began recruiting propaganda missionaries, who were sent to the front to raise morale. Not everyone was swayed by the holy war rhetoric, but most Romanians felt that the war was justified. Mircea Ionescu-Quintus remembered, "The truth is it was not a Christian war against the unbelievers. No. I never felt that I was . . . a crusader. . . . I felt that I was part of some Romanian troops that did their duty first to liberate a part of occupied county and then to go just as we had committed, together with German allies, until where it was no longer possible. . . [and then] we were thinking to escape to return home."[38] Propaganda could not boost spirits by convincing troops that they should believe in final victory following Stalingrad; however, it helped maintain hate and fear of Judeo-Bolshevism to motivate soldiers to keep fighting in a losing cause.

Discipline

German and Soviet observers looked down on Romanian officers as being physically abusive; however, the Romanian Army's strict discipline needs to be put into context. The Red Army's code of military justice included imprisonment, time in a labor camp, and execution with confiscation of property. After the war started, the Stavka established blocking detachments to police stragglers and ordered cowardice, self-mutilation, desertion, and even failed attacks to be punished by execution, resulting in tens of thousands of soldiers being shot. The Stavka later established penal battalions to offer soldiers a chance to redeem themselves rather than be executed.[39] The Nazis altered the German Army's code of military justice so that cowardice, self-mutilation, and desertion were equated to treason. Between thirteen and fifteen thousand soldiers were executed, according to the OKH's official numbers, although the total was probably higher.[40] Comparatively, the Romanian Army's code of military justice included imprisonment, rehabilitation for officers, and execution. After the invasion of the USSR, the General Staff reintroduced flogging, expanded rehabilitation to all ranks, and periodically authorized blocking detachments and executions for cowardice, self-mutilation, and desertion. Yet the total number of executions was probably only in the hundreds. In the context of the time, the Romanian Army's discipline was strict, but not as deadly as in the German Army or Red Army.

Corporal Punishment

Officers had been beating, slapping, and kicking NCOs and enlisted men from the very first days of the invasion. On 21 July 1941, the minister of defense General Iacobici complained that despite corporal punishment having been "totally banned," it remained common, citing a case where a captain broke a private's jaw, requiring hospitalization. He warned that officers guilty of such physical abuse would be sanctioned.[41] Indeed, some were, but most abusive officers went unreported and thus unpunished. NCOs and enlisted men feared retaliation, so they usually composed anonymous denunciations when they reported abusive officers. These accusations often also included claims of corruption and claims that the officer had a Jewish mistress. Army praetors usually believed the word of officers over NCOs or enlisted men. The epidemic of looting in northern Bukovina and Bessarabia caused a spike in reports against officers. On 24 July 1941, Iacobici claimed that most of these denunciations were "calumnious" and became angry that officers did not do more to clear their good name.[42] The Third Army blamed enlisted men "influenced by bad elements" for writing a letter in March 1942 to the Council of Ministers denouncing some officers in the 10th Infantry Division.[43] To avoid leaving scars or broken bones—evidence that army praetors could not ignore—officers tended to slap subordinates. On 7 July 1942,

Sergeant Ionescu overloaded with machine guns and other equipment horse-drawn caissons and field kitchens meant only for transporting artillery shells and rations, which was against regulations because it overtaxed and wore out horses, and thereby attracted a superior's ire. "Today I was hit with 4–5 slaps by Captain Dobrinoiu from Battalion I, who is the horse doctor."[44] On 28 September 1942, Ionescu summed up the Romanian Army's strict discipline: "During the march I was insulted by [a] superior and I was listened to by [an] inferior[;] this conforms to military rank and indiscipline, [because if] orders [are] not executed exactly by soldiers, [and] without insults [being effective, then that] is cause for hitting."[45] While soldiers generally accepted a few slaps and kicks now and then as part of army life, any officer who became too abusive put his life in jeopardy. The Mountain Corps reported in June 1943 that in Crimea when an officer slapped an enlisted man, a group of nearby soldiers muttered, "Why does Mr. First Lieutenant not come to fight on the front, rather than hit innocent people here. Many officers who were used to hitting, were shot by their own troops."[46] Physical abuse was more common in the rear than on the front. Marin Ștefanescu recalled that frontline life encouraged solidarity between officers and enlisted men: "They didn't keep hitting. . . . Officers' attitude changed toward soldiers on the front. 'Cause they also slept in trenches with us."[47] Old habits died hard, however.

V. Aurel Ciornei called the reintroduction of flogging after the invasion of the USSR "Antonescu's mistake," but commanders in the field actually initiated the process.[48] There is little evidence of flogging until the Third Army crossed the Dniester. During the reconquest of northern Bukovina and Bessarabia, commanders tolerated an extraordinary level of indiscipline while soldiers and gendarmes carried out orders to "cleanse the terrain" of Jews, but once in Ukraine they turned to flogging to restore discipline. Some officers decided that the normal practice of using a belt was not sufficient for some infractions. On 8 August 1941, three men from Major Scârneci's mountain battalion's scout company raped a Ukrainian girl. "They were harshly sanctioned—25 shovels to the back each in front of the whole battalion. Mother and little girl began to cry and asked me to forgive them, but I didn't give heed, the villains received their complete punishment."[49] General Dumitrescu was an old-fashioned disciplinarian for whom flogging was the preferred punishment not only for rape, looting, and desertion but also brawling, drunkenness, improper dress, and poor comportment.[50] General Antonescu supported bringing back the practice, but General Iacobici worried it would be abused. On 14 August 1941, Article 135 of *The Regulation on the Interior Service for Troops of All Arms* authorized the use of corporal punishment, but Article 140b required floggings to be ordered by the regimental or battalion commander, supervised by a doctor, administered by a belt on the back, and restricted to a maximum of twenty-five lashes. Iacobici emphasized that flogging required a "long procedure" and was only for "lack of respect and grave mistakes."[51] General Pantazi continued trying to prevent flogging from being abused after he became minister of defense. On 15 April 1942, frustrated with the glacial pace of the Third Army Praetoral Service's processing of stragglers and deserters, Dumitrescu ordered that soldiers caught absent without leave should be summarily flogged and sent to the nearest combat unit.[52] Pantazi countermanded this order but required courts-martial judging cases of desertion to last no more than three days. On 24 May 1942, the Third Army's chief of staff General Arbore testily declared, "They will follow the path of Justice—with rapid procedure."[53] Commanders used flogging on a regular basis through the end of the war. Sergeant Ezechil recalled that when the 2nd *Călărași* Regiment arrived on the Kalmyk Steppe in November 1942, a soldier received twenty-five lashes after stealing three chickens. "The villagers, shaking their heads, said the sergeant could have eaten all the chickens in the village and still would not have merited this shame."[54] Romanian troops were accustomed to the sight. Dumitru Burciu, who witnessed a flogging as a private, declared, "I don't condemn Antonescu for those twenty-five hits. This punishment limited incorrect behavior."[55] Commanders meted out fewer lashes for other lesser infractions. In December 1943, two corporals guarding a prison in Tiraspol received fifteen lashes "for inappropriate dress and failure to supervise the prisoners that they were escorting."[56] Commanders leaned most heavily on flogging to maintain discipline in the rear.

Penal Punishment

Imprisonment was a common consequence for indiscipline. Soldiers received "arrest" or "severe arrest," confinement to quarters or imprisonment with reduced rations respectively, for a few days to a few weeks, depending on the offense. More serious crimes could be punished with months, years, or even a life sentence of incarceration and hard labor. There are plenty of cases of soldiers receiving long prison sentences for protecting Jews. After the fall of Odessa, Sergeant Nicolae Tănase started a relationship with Vera Sepel, bringing food, clothing, and fuel to her in the Slobodka ghetto. In January 1942, he tried to help her escape deportation by getting her on a train to Moldavia, but they were caught by a railroad employee. Tănase was sentenced to three years for falsifying documents for a Jew and another five years for trying to remove a Jew from a ghetto.

Sepel received five years.[57] Thieves, looters, and smugglers often received long prison sentences. In February 1943, Private Mihai Lubescu, who had deserted a year earlier, pretended to be a sergeant gathering up stragglers after the defeat at Stalingrad. He presented fake orders to German officers to obtain rations for fictitious Romanian soldiers, sometimes enlisting stragglers for greater credibility. An Italian war correspondent recalled, "Wherever he showed up he was received as a benefactor. . . . Every door was opened to him and hardly anyone objected to his demands."[58] A suspicious Cossack policeman uncovered the subterfuge, but a search found only Lubescu's pretty Ukrainian girlfriend before sending him to a Third Army court-martial in Mariupol for impersonating an NCO. Deserters also received long prison sentences, but many never served the time because they were needed on the front.

Rehabilitation

The General Staff expanded a preexisting policy of rehabilitation that allowed soldiers, particularly deserters, to be punished without the army losing desperately needed manpower. Article 415 of the Code of Military Justice stipulated that an officer sentenced to one month to twelve years of "correctional incarceration" in time of war could be stripped of his rank, have his prison sentence suspended, and be sent to fight as an ordinary private until he redeemed himself through acts of bravery. Once rehabilitated, he would be restored to his former rank. At the outset, rehabilitation was voluntary and often did not strictly adhere to Article 415. The first petitions for rehabilitation arrived from prisons in Romania that were bursting at the seams with over nine thousand Legionaries.[59] Iron Guardists wrote General Antonescu declaring their patriotism, hatred of bolshevism, and loyalty to his regime, and asked to be sent to the front.[60] Some of these Legionary petitions had hundreds of signatures. On 26 June 1941, the Ministry of Defense ordered that released Legionaries who were reserve officers should remain privates for five years because they were unsuitable for command owing to "moral incapacity." The need for officers was so great that many commanders ignored the order, and some even assigned Iron Guardists to command or staff positions, much to the displeasure of the Ministry of Defense.[61] Officers accused of cowardice or incompetence, usually following a disorderly retreat, often petitioned for a chance to restore their honor (and pensions) even before sentencing. On 1 September 1941, two lieutenants of the 5th *Grăniceri* Regiment awaiting a court-martial in Chișinău on charges of cowardice asked to be sent to the front. Antonescu approved the requests, not even stripping the men of their rank, but warned that any further examples of weakness would result in their being shot in front of their soldiers.[62]

Prisons crowded with deserters, looters, and other malefactors, and the Romanian Army's need for manpower, prompted the Ministry of Defense to expand and systematize rehabilitation. On 2 March 1942, the Ministry of Defense promulgated General Order No. 240 applying Article 415 to NCOs and enlisted men. After court-martial, their sentences would be suspended, and they would be assigned to a frontline infantry or cavalry regiment. Once an army or corps commander praised the soldier for bravery in a daily order, he became eligible for rehabilitation by decree; if he was killed before the process was complete, the soldier's family could request a postmortem rehabilitation.[63] Soldiers detained east of the Dniester were escorted to the nearest Third Army (or Mountain Corps) court-martial. Groups of rehabilitation soldiers were usually greeted by the regimental colonel, and the regimental chaplain may have made a speech, like the one given by Chaplain Nicolae Petrache about the "sublime gesture of parental indulgence of the Marshal *Conducător*, who wants their reformation [*îndreptarea*], and the duty they have to distinguish themselves through acts of arms, which will wash [away] mistakes made."[64] Some rehabilitation soldiers preferred prison to the front. On 29 May 1942, Sergeant Ionescu recorded a rumor that a deserter serving ten to twelve years who volunteered for rehabilitation had "returned to prison to carry out the punishment, he doesn't want to fight."[65] Other rehabilitation soldiers fought committedly, particularly demoted officers. Major Scârneci credited a rehabilitation soldier, a former officer and Legionary, and two others with slowing a Soviet counterattack at Sevastopol in June 1942 with grenades, bayonets, fists, and even teeth to allow comrades to escape.[66] Most rehabilitation soldiers were less motivated. Sergeant Ezechil recalled a rehabilitation soldier in his platoon. An officer had slapped the former law student during training, and in turn the man punched the officer, so he was court-martialed and sent to Crimea. After fighting at Kerch, this individual deserted, because he felt he should have been rehabilitated for bravery. He lived with a Russian family in the peninsula until he was caught and returned to his unit on the Kalmyk Steppe.[67] Commanders on the front dispersed rehabilitation soldiers among units as individual replacements.

The General Staff also created entire units of rehabilitation soldiers. In April 1942, the General Staff decided to establish a special training center for imprisoned soldiers, political prisoners, and even common criminals held in prisons west of the Dniester. The General Staff selected a site in southern Bessarabia. The first choice was the partly deserted town of Arciz (most ethnic Germans left in 1940 when they were resettled to Poland by the Nazis, and most Jews evacuated with the Soviets or were shot by the Romanians in 1941), but worries about recently released convicts easily deserting by train meant that the more isolated, and similarly emptied, town of Sărata was chosen.[68] On 8 May 1942, General Alexandru Poenaru took command of Sărata Training Center No. 5. Officers and NCOs without convictions were chosen to retrain and later command the rehabilitation soldiers. The first wave of convicted soldiers, political prisoners, and criminals soon arrived, with more to follow.

Sărata Training Center had a glum atmosphere. General Poenaru reported that most training officers and NCOs were unhappy about their assignment, political prisoners were uncomfortable being lumped together with criminals, and criminals "do not seem dedicated to giving up bad habits."[69] Each rehabilitation soldier was released from prison on his own recognizance and received ten days' leave before having to report to Sărata. Poenaru defended this practice to the General Staff, arguing that seeing their families would improve rehabilitation soldiers' morale, and those prone to desert could easily do so from Sărata anyway.[70] Soldiers' desertion or going absent without leave was a constant issue at Training Center No. 5. Captain Păsat, training a company of rehabilitation soldiers, recalled, "Weekly, 2–3 of those who had deserted were brought back to me, and, again weekly, another 2–3 left, almost as if they were on a rotation."[71] Yet 97 percent of men released from prison reported to Sărata, 87 percent remained after two months of training, and 80 percent arrived on the front.[72] Poenaru organized the 991st, 992nd, 993rd, and 994th Independent Infantry Battalions sequentially in June, July, August, and September. Rehabilitation soldiers at Sărata were mostly guilty of desertion. Of 1,009 men in the 992nd Independent Infantry Battalion, there were 486 deserters, 123 thieves, 88 Legionaries, and the remainder were guilty of striking officers, beating enlisted men, forging papers, manslaughter, rape, or other charges.[73] Poenaru believed that 80 percent of rehabilitation soldiers could be counted on, but Păsat thought 70 percent of these men were "brutes, without law, without God."[74] Whatever their character, the Romanian Army needed these men as replacements on the front.

These rehabilitation battalions were unruly in the rear, but when flanked by regular units, and put in the situation of kill or be killed, they fought fiercely. The most reliable rehabilitation soldiers were Legionaries, as they were the most ideologically motivated. After three months of retraining, the 991st, 992nd, and 993rd Independent Infantry Battalions left for the Don in September, October, and November—the 994th left for the Caucasus in December. After departing, each one became "independent" of Sărata Training Center

No. 5, hence their designation. They arrived in time to be mauled in the battle of Stalingrad. The 991st was encircled with the Lascăr Group, and the 992nd was badly handled on the Chir. Iron Guardists later claimed that rehabilitation battalions were really "suicide battalions" designed to kill them because of their political beliefs, but regular battalions had similar losses.[75] Both the 991st and 992nd Independent Infantry Battalions were disbanded, while the 993rd became part of the 24th Infantry Division guarding the Azov Sea coast. The General Staff denied Sărata Training Center's request to rehabilitate all survivors from the Don and Chir battles.[76] Subordinated to a German mountain division, the 994th Independent Infantry Battalion fought bravely in the Caucasus (over one hundred of its men received an Iron Cross) but was undisciplined in the rear. General Simion Coman, the new commandant at Sărata Training Center, reported that 30 percent of troops in rehabilitation battalions at the front were "very good," 35 percent exhibited "many oscillations," and 20 to 30 percent "comported themselves *animalistically*, without thought of rehabilitation, without discipline, and only running after loot."[77] Desertions rose as the officers and NCOs who had retrained the rehabilitation soldiers were killed or wounded. Rehabilitation battalions' satisfactory performance meant they continued to be used.

The General Staff expanded the Sărata Training Center's mission. General Coman provided replacements for the 993rd and 994th Independent Infantry Battalions and formed the 995th, which also joined the 24th Infantry Division. Additionally, Training Center No. 5 began forming labor battalions that worked in Romania and Transnistria. Sărata started having difficulty finding even semi-reliable manpower as prisons were emptied, however. The Târgu Jiu internment camp sent more Iron Guardists, including even "notorious Legionaries," to Sărata, but these were among the last. Prisons began sending minorities. By October 1943, Sărata Training Center had organized the 1001st through 1017th Labor Battalions, each with around 500 soldiers, totaling 8,189 troops, including: 1,338 ethnic Hungarians, 1,634 ethnic Russians, and 961 Jews (assigned to the segregated 1016th and 1017th Jewish Labor Battalions).[78] There was not enough room in Sărata for all these men, and subsidiary training centers were created in nearby villages. Rehabilitation battalions' increasingly poor performance in combat resulted in their dissolution. Primary groups formed while retraining at Sărata Training Center were gone, replacements were the dregs of prisons, and survivors from Stalingrad did not want to be encircled, so morale was extremely low. Therefore, the 993rd and 995th Independent Infantry Battalions disintegrated when the 24th Infantry Division was attacked at Mariupol. Both rehabilitation battalions were disbanded in November 1943, with surviving rehabilitation soldiers dispersed into the ad hoc 111th and 112th *Infanterie* Regiments assigned to the 4th/24th Infantry Division.[79] Only the 994th Independent Infantry Battalion, now reassigned to the 19th Infantry Division in Crimea, continued to fight.

Following Stalingrad, the Third Army processed an influx of stragglers and deserters, many of whom became rehabilitation soldiers. The Third Army established the Tiraspol Training Center No. 3 in Transnistria, so soldiers sentenced for desertion and other crimes east of the Dniester could be retrained before being sent back to the front. Some units created separate rehabilitation companies or platoons with all these replacements. Commanders were not happy about the growing number of rehabilitation soldiers on the front. On 14 June 1943, an SSI report recorded a soldier saying that sending Legionaries for rehabilitation had turned "the field of honor" into "the field of exile."[80] Commanders of elite mountain or cavalry units were especially unhappy. On 24 August 1943, Major Scârneci complained that his mountain battalion had been filled with cavalrymen, gendarmes, *grăniceri*, even sailors, and now rehabilitation soldiers. "[If] it is said that the front line is the 'Altar of the Fatherland,'" he quipped, "what kind of altar, with such angels as these?"[81] Lieutenant Colonel Isăceanu recalled that when he greeted rehabilitation soldiers sent to the 13th *Călăraşi* Regiment in Crimea, "the only question that I put to them was . . . for how many years they had been condemned. It embarrassed me to also ask them about the motive of the act for which they had been condemned."[82] Soldiers in mountain and cavalry units had strong esprit de corps, and many had fought together for two years or more, so tight-knit veterans looked on replacements, especially rehabilitation soldiers, with skepticism. When two rehabilitation NCOs immediately deserted, Scârneci scribbled, "I suspect that they were prisoners in the USSR. From there, after they took a course in espionage, they were dropped by plane on our front. The sergeant spoke good Russian. [The platoon] fired after them with all weapons [when they ran to the enemy]."[83] Other soldiers kept a wary eye on distrusted rehabilitation soldiers.

Rehabilitation declined as the front reached Romania. On 1 April 1944, the Third Army still had 3,899 rehabilitation soldiers.[84] After the fall of Crimea, the 994th Independent Infantry Battalion was finally disbanded. Meanwhile, Tiraspol Training Center No. 3 and Sărata Training Center No. 5 evacuated by barge up the Danube to Tirol on the Serbian border. The Tirol Training Center formed the 996th and 997th Independent Infantry Battalions in June, but lacking equipment, they did not see combat on the Iaşi front. Some rehabilitation soldiers in labor battalions requested to be sent to the front so that they would have a chance to be rehabilitated, since those stuck constructing roads or working farming fields in Romania or Transnistria could

Table 3. Sărata Training Center No. 5, 1942–1944

SOLDIERS SENT TO SĂRATA	
Returned to prison or judged unfit for rehabilitation	2,356
Sent to the front for rehabilitation	7,770
Sent to labor battalions east of the Dniester in the operational zone	7,053
Sent to labor battalions west of the Dniester in Romania	1,812
Organized and prepared to immediately leave for the front	1,956
Remaining at the training center	2,135
Total	23,082
SOLDIERS SENT TO THE FRONT FROM SĂRATA	
Proposed for rehabilitation and returned to their original units	1,544
Special rehabilitation based on the Code of Military Justice	38
Renounced rehabilitation and completed sentences after returning from the front	87
Remaining on the front	1,822
Killed on the front	775
Missing on the front	3,269
Recovered at the training center and situation being clarified	235
Total	7,700

Source: AMNR, Fond Centru de Instrucție Nr. 5 Sărata, dosar 40, f. 100.

not demonstrate the bravery necessary to be cited to begin the process.[85] Between May 1942 and June 1944, 23,082 soldiers passed through Sărata Training Center No. 5, including 7,770 sent to the front in rehabilitation battalions (see table 3). Over 11,000 rehabilitation soldiers served with the Third Army as individuals or in separate rehabilitation units. Rehabilitation was remarkably successful in providing the Romanian Army desperately needed manpower for the eastern front.

Capital Punishment

Threatening to shoot soldiers became a cliché in the Romanian Army. Commanders initially shied away from threatening capital punishment in northern Bukovina and Bessarabia. Meanwhile, the MCG maintained strict discipline in Moldavia. On 3 July 1941, General Antonescu personally instructed that a second lieutenant in the *Grăniceri* Division accused of searching Jewish businesses in Galați for weapons as a pretext to thieve should "be immediately executed if his guilt was established."[86] Commanders on the front did not go so far, despite the atrocities their soldiers committed against Jews. On 12 July, General Dumitrescu ordered soldiers caught looting or illegally requisitioning food to be punished "severely."[87] It took another month before

CHAPTER 7

General Ciupercă went further and threatened to execute soldiers for [...] in the rear. Contrarily, commanders issued more sanguinary threats [...]ing breakdown of discipline on the front. On 20 July, after reports that some troops fled at first contact with the enemy while taking the Stalin Line, Dumitrescu ordered officers to shoot soldiers who panicked others and to set up machine guns "to fire without mercy" on fleeing soldiers.[88] It is unlikely many commanders carried out this order, since machine guns were needed on the front lines, not toward the rear.

German demands for stricter Romanian discipline in the rear and desperate fighting on the front prompted Romanian commanders to threaten capital punishment more frequently. On 20 August, the *conducător* argued that Soviet civilians should see Romanian soldiers "as liberators from the Bolshevik yoke, and not as barbarians who came to rob them, mock them, and to kill them," and ordered soldiers committing atrocities *"to be executed on the spot without mercy."*[89] The next day, General Dumitrecu reported that General von Schobert had told Marshal Antonescu that the German Eleventh Army shot soldiers for theft, illegal requisitioning, and rape. Therefore, he ordered that Third Army soldiers caught in the act of theft or rape "will be punished with death," that their officers who permitted such crimes will be sent to court-martial "for complicity with the guilty," and that Third Army gendarmes should "execute a very severe supervision" over frontline troops. Dumitrescu emphasized that ethnic German soldiers were to be treated with kid gloves, however.[90] Also on 20 August, General Ioanițiu claimed that some units at Odessa "hesitated to attack or attacked without élan," even retreating after Soviet counterattacks, so he ordered machine gun squads to be organized into blocking detachments to fire on fleeing troops.[91] Again it is unclear if this order was carried out, and if it was, these ad hoc blocking detachments were not made permanent. General Ciupercă, and later General Tătăranu (who ran operations at Odessa while General Iacobici split his time between the MCG and the Fourth Army), complained that courts-martial were too "indulgent," because between July and September only 11 death sentences were given in 336 trials, despite the *conducător*'s order to "apply the maximum penalty."[92] The Fourth Army demanded more death sentences, including for civilians caught with arms, but army magistrates were uncooperative.[93] A few dozen soldiers were executed outside Odessa, mostly for self-mutilation.

The threat of capital punishment was invoked in times of crisis, and a few soldiers were executed, to ensure it carried weight. Following the creation of the Kuban bridgehead, General Dumitrescu temporarily gave commanders of divisions or ad hoc groups authority to approve summary executions, since they were cut off from the nearest court-martial in Mariupol.[94] On 8

February 1943, the General Staff ordered officers to inform enlisted men that all but one of twelve deserters from Stalingrad arrested near Kiev had been sentenced to death.[95] On 13 April 1944, as Soviet forces threatened Romania, Marshal Antonescu issued Order No. 10.523 allowing commanders to execute soldiers without a court-martial for desertion, cowardice, looting, self-mutilation, rebellion, insubordination, or striking an officer. Army magistrates pushed back. Soon General Racovița, commanding the Fourth Army, clarified that only commanders of regiments or detachments "operating isolated" could order executions, and even then had to first obtain approval from the division commander.[96] On 20 August, Second Lieutenant Ion Lăzărescu recalled that a major ordered him to machine-gun soldiers retreating during the second Iași-Chișinău offensive, but he refused. The major shouted into the phone, "You want to give me advice? I fought at the Don! . . . Take the measures!"[97] Lăzărescu did not comply. On 22 August, General Șteflea, the acting Fourth Army commander, wrote an order that soldiers retreating without permission should be shot, but his chief of staff Lieutenant Colonel Dragomir refused to countersign it.[98] While it was easy to threaten soldiers with capital punishment, it was difficult to actually have the order carried out.

The number of summary executions is unknown, as they left no paper trail, but official records indicate relatively few soldiers were shot, and only men guilty of self-mutilation regularly received death sentences.[99] Many offenders had their sentences commuted or were sent to the front for rehabilitation. The Antonescu regime was not particularly bloodthirsty toward its citizens—except for Jews. The *Siguranță* (literally Safety), the secret police responsible for suppressing dissent, did not use violence on the same scale as the Gestapo or the NKVD. The Antonescu regime imprisoned 10,617 people for political crimes during the war: 4,830 to one-to-fifteen years; 5,185 to fifteen-to-twenty-five years; 277 to life of hard labor; 313 to death (all but 72 commuted); and 22 killed in interrogation—plus 5,463 people interned for other reasons.[100] Likewise, commanders did not execute many thousands of soldiers. Probably five hundred to one thousand soldiers were shot by firing squad after court-martial, summarily, or by blocking detachments during the campaign in the Soviet Union.

Financial Punishment

The stick of financial punishment cannot be examined without first addressing the carrot of financial incentive. The chance to win a medal motivated soldiers, especially honor-obsessed regular officers. Second Lieutenant Crișan recalled, "Most of the active officers were eager to go right away into combat . . . looking for promotions, military awards and decorations, and

FIGURE 11. Although executions at the front, such as these snapshots, probably taken in August 1943, of what seems to be a group of soldiers shot for desertion, were relatively rare, the Romanian Army shot enough soldiers to ensure that capital punishment remained a tool for maintaining strict discipline in the ranks even after the war turned against the Axis. Courtesy Arhivele Militare Naționale Române.

even a lot of good-sized rich farmland, when they received high valor decoration."[101] The Order of Mihai the Brave, awarded only to officers, came with twenty-five acres. Yet enlisted men also appreciated medals, which often came with leave. On 2 September 1941, Major Scârneci passed out Military Virtue, Manliness and Faith, and Queen Marie medals under moonlight, safe

FIGURE 11. (Continued)

from enemy aircraft. "The Gypsy Marşavela also receives a decoration. He is very haughty. Tomorrow, of course he will pilfer more fowls. He even asked for leave so his gypsy woman can see him, with [his] decoration."[102] Military Virtue, awarded to NCOs and enlisted men, came with ten to fifteen acres in northern Bukovina or Bessarabia; rehabilitation soldiers greatly prized Military Virtue, since winning it could erase their sentence. German commanders also doled out medals to Romanian soldiers on a regular basis. Romanian commanders picked up the German practice of giving leave and cash prizes to soldiers for brave acts. On 27 April 1944, in response to German inquiries, Marshal Antonescu promised 10,000 lei for each tank or aircraft destroyed.[103] Yet, as a historian argued in regard to Soviet cash prizes, "It is hard to imagine men taking undue risks simply for a wad of [money]."[104] However, it is easy to imagine soldiers taking risks for their family's financial well-being.

The General Staff cut off pensions and financial aid to families as financial punishment. Both regular officers and *reangajat* NCOs looked forward to a pension, but being sentenced for an infraction disqualified them from receiving it. Rehabilitation offered the only way to restore good standing. Sergeant Major Ioan Meița was thrown out of the army for "incapacity" in September 1941 and sentenced to two months in prison for "calumnious denunciation" of his captain. He wrote a letter in August 1942, after being assigned to a transmission battalion for rehabilitation, begging that wire repairs he made under fire count as frontline combat so that he could qualify to be rehabilitated and would "not remain expelled from the Army and without a pension . . . as well as to be able to care for my family."[105] In September 1939, the state began giving financial aid to families of soldiers who were called up. In June 1941, it increased financial aid to families of soldiers mobilized for the front. The General Staff suspended financial aid to families and even confiscated family property to punish soldiers court-martialed for infractions.[106] In August 1942, Private Ioan Bortică was sentenced to a year's incarceration for beating a civilian, and he volunteered for rehabilitation, but he was also assigned to a support unit. In June 1943, he wrote a petition saying his wife had been living with her parents in poverty in Cernăuți and asked to be transferred to a frontline unit "to have the possibility, even with the sacrifice of [my] life, to be able to pull out of squalor. . . [my wife]."[107] Soldiers knew they could be rehabilitated even after death; thus risking their life could still help their family.

Some soldiers found ways to profit from the holy war. The Romanian Army had a problem similar to that of the German Army, as the state wanted to seize Jewish property, but soldiers were first on the spot.[108] When soldiers shot Jews, they used the chance to enrich themselves by seizing valuables. Peasants often bribed gendarmes to shoot Jews being deported to Transnistria, in order to strip them of their clothing and valuables.[109] Soldiers could easily transport loot back across the Prut at first. Romanian soldiers continued to loot across the Dniester, but Romanian officers, Romanian gendarmes, and German gendarmes finally reined them in. Einsatzgruppe D laid claim to Jewish wealth in Reichskommissariat Ukraine, but the Governorate of Transnistria grabbed Jewish loot in Transnistria, while the Central Office of Romanianization expropriated Jewish homes and businesses in Romania. Officers complained they were missing out on a bonanza while they were risking their lives on the front.[110] On 11 July 1942, General Pantazi declared 25 percent of expropriated Jewish property was reserved for "our heroes on the front."[111] Soldiers in Crimea found little left to loot. Moreover, the General Staff restricted how much Romanian troops could mail, while the OKH allowed German soldiers to send large packages for free.[112] On 28 May 1942, Sergeant Ionescu complained that NCOs and enlisted men were limited to three postcards a month, while officers sent trainloads of loot home.[113] Soldiers occupying Transnistria had a chance to make quick cash through smuggling and black-market activity. Odessa experienced an economic boom, facilitated by corruption as the city became a center of illicit trade.[114] Tensions developed between frontline and rear-area troops. An SSI informant in 1943 reported a soldier suggesting that "all officers and the rest of the personnel staffing field hospitals, guide centers, and 'Red Cross' canteens ought to be shot, because they busy themselves only with [black-market] business and dirty things on the backs of soldiers and wounded."[115] Greed was an important motivation for many soldiers, especially when it came to murdering Jews.

Morale

Historians have been remarkably cavalier in concluding that Romanian soldiers' morale was weak, that it rapidly collapsed east of the Dniester, and was easily swayed by Soviet counterpropaganda.[116] The myth that Romanian soldiers suffered from chronically poor morale after crossing the Dniester is based on biased German sources and apologist Romanian accounts that discount ideology as a major motivating factor for Romanian soldiers. Additionally, many historians exaggerate the effect that the battle of Odessa had on the Romanian Army's morale and claim this "pyrrhic victory" convinced most Romanians that "they had already paid their blood dues to the Axis in full."[117] These arguments disregard Romanian soldiers' ability to see beyond one battle or to understand that German final victory was necessary for Romania's holy war to be successful. Furthermore, such claims ignore the Propaganda Section's morale-boosting efforts that constantly reminded soldiers why they were fighting deep in enemy territory. The Romanian officer corps remained committed to the end of the campaign against the USSR and maintained strict discipline to keep their soldiers in line even when morale was low. The previous narrative chapters have shown how the Romanian Army used propaganda and discipline to motivate soldiers. They also showed how the Romanian Army's morale fluctuated over time. When the invasion of the USSR started, Romanian soldiers' morale was extremely high. The Fourth Army's morale became depressed during the battle of Odessa, but the city's fall and the Fourth Army's subsequent demobilization buoyed spirits and gave soldiers a chance to recover. The Third Army's morale remained high as it participated in victorious German encirclements, but it dipped during the winter crisis beginning in December 1941. The Romanian Army's morale had recovered by the spring. By July 1942, Echelon I divisions had developed a cocksure attitude that they were the toughest troops. Echelon II divisions departed for the front in good spirits, confident in victory. In November 1942, as the first snow appeared and Stalingrad held out, morale dipped on the front. Of course, the defeat at Stalingrad caused morale to plummet, but it had recovered by March 1943. Only when no new German summer offensive occurred, compounded by Nazi Germany's defeat at Kursk in July and August 1943 and Italy's armistice with the Allies in September 1943, did faith in final victory finally dissipate. Despite halting the Red Army in northeastern Romania in March 1944 with the German Army's help, the Romanian Army now faced an enemy whose military superiority was obvious. The consequences for morale were inevitable.

CHAPTER 8

Women and Minorities

During the Second World War, the Romanian Red Cross recruited tens of thousands of female volunteers, and the Romanian Army drafted tens of thousands of ethnic, religious, and racial minorities; however, both women and minorities are overlooked in Romanian military histories. Women and minorities provided the Romanian Army indispensable womanpower and manpower on the front and at home, so women's and minorities' motivation must be examined. The ideologies that motivated men to report for duty as soldiers motivated women to volunteer as nurses or medical assistants. Female voluntarism provides strong evidence of popular support for Romania's holy war. Although ethnic minorities were not attracted to Romanian nationalism, religious and racial minorities were often staunch patriots. Religion, antisemitism, and anticommunism transcended ethnic, religious, and racial boundaries. Nevertheless, the General Staff distrusted minorities and relegated most of them to military service in labor detachments. The Antonescu regime restricted Jews from military service, but it increasingly depended on Jewish labor service in military workshops and on military-related projects. Ethnic Germans and Gypsies fought in the Romanian Army on the front in the greatest numbers; however, SS recruitment of ethnic Germans and the Antonescu regime's deportation of certain Gypsy groups undermined these soldiers' motivation and morale.

Women

Gender and class strictly circumscribed how women could support Romania's holy war. At a Legionary rally on 28 September 1940, General Antonescu informed Iron Guardist women, "At home [men] must find goodwill, warmth, and order. You must make this happen. . . . Then shall we ask you to fulfill three great tasks: raising children, social welfare, and defending our borders."[1] On 9 April 1941, to centralize social welfare efforts he established the Consiliu de Patronaj al Operelor Sociale, or the Patronage Council of Social Works, and made his wife, Maria Antonescu, its president. The Patronage Council adopted a Blue Cross as its symbol. It competed with the Romanian Red Cross, established in 1876, whose honorary president was Queen Mother Helen. During the First World War, Queen Marie had filled this role, and she was celebrated as the "mother of the wounded," donning a nurse's habit and tending to soldiers and civilians in need. Between 1916 and 1919, tens of thousands of women followed her example, joining the Red Cross to work in civilian or military hospitals and operate canteens.[2] This set the stage for a lopsided competition between Queen Mother Helen and Maria Antonescu over who would be the Marie of the Second World War—although neither one attained the same status of female sainthood. The Red Cross attracted many more female volunteers than the Blue Cross, owing to its greater prestige. On 14 May 1941, the Decree-Law for the Organization of National Labor allowed unemployed citizens, including women, to be drafted for labor service.[3] The Antonescu regime feared alienating large landholding or middle-class families by requiring their daughters to work, and it needed peasant women to labor in the fields, so it only ever drafted a few working-class women for labor service. Nevertheless, the state encouraged boyar and middle-class women to volunteer to serve with either the Red Cross or the Patronage Council.

Nurses

Female volunteers gravitated toward the Red Cross because of its established reputation and association with the Romanian Army. Anticipating the need for medical personnel, the Red Cross offered free courses in nursing in Bucharest and other cities, although few attended before June 1941.[4] Nursing was still equal parts charitable work performed by untrained volunteers and medical treatment by skilled professionals; in fact, nurses were either *surori de caritate*, "sisters of charity," or *auxiliare sanitare*, "female sanitary auxiliaries."[5] Women rushed to volunteer at first. The War Sisters of

Charity Association, numbering eight hundred veterans of the First World War, immediately offered their services for the front when the holy war was declared. The General Staff demurred. These women were undeterred and began raising funds and collecting materials for the war effort.[6] The Romanian Army's Sanitary Service rushed to create hospitals with Red Cross help. Emil Dorian supervised the conversion of an agricultural school into a hospital in Găiești. The town's older ladies and young women set up beds, collected supplies, and scrubbed surfaces. Dorian noted wryly, "They made their appearance dressed in the proper Red Cross uniform, expressing their regret that there were no wounded."[7] There was soon no shortage. In Bucharest, Alice Voinescu volunteered to change bandages. Conversing with wounded soldiers, she found herself attached to "these simple, but very intelligent and good people," but she was horrified by their repeated use of "kike" in conversations "that encapsulates the worst in them."[8] Most Red Cross volunteers remained in Romania, but some followed the front. Maria Moruzi-Brăescu toured Bessarabia inspecting medical facilities and suggested the MCG allow the Red Cross to establish hospitals and canteens.[9] The Romanian Army preferred matronly nurses for the front. The Red Cross agreed nurses must be morally irreproachable but wanted young, single women who could cope mentally and physically with the demands. On 23 August 1941, working in a hospital in Bălți packed with wounded from Odessa, Elise George reported, "We each have a pavilion where we try to do all that [is] humanely possible to comfort so much misery that it is terrible. For [the] moment, we are holding up well, but I do not believe that [my fellow nurse] Dina will be able to support more of this hell. . . . *No one* should be sent here who doesn't have an iron will and a strong work ethic and [an] exceptional physique."[10] Female volunteers who could not handle the front could leave at any time.

Red Cross personnel also crossed the Dniester. The traditional Romanian Army, unlike many other armies during the conflict, did not enlist women as female auxiliaries so they served only as Red Cross nurses in field hospitals without army uniforms, rank, or pay. (The progressive Romanian Air Force formed the 108th Light Transport Squadron, the famed *Escadrilă albă*, or White Squadron, with female pilots trained to fly air ambulances, and they received air force uniforms, rank, and pay.) Soldiers thought a woman in uniform was unnatural; in *The Misadventures of Private Neață*, female Soviet soldiers were drawn as fat, ugly trolls who were easily captured.[11] In addition to army doctors and sanitary auxiliaries, field hospitals had a chief nurse, a nurse section supervisor, and a nurse for every twenty soldiers (field hospitals usually had three hundred beds).[12] On 10 October 1941, after inspecting Field Hospital No. 22 in Selz near Odessa, General Iacobici praised its doctors for turning a church and two crumbling schools into a model hospital with six hundred beds (often treating a thousand soldiers), bathroom, kitchen, heaters, and even electricity. He highlighted the efforts of sisters of charity under Georgeta Ghica and Maria Moruzi-Brăescu, who washed windows when not tending wounded.[13] Most Red Cross volunteers departed with the Fourth Army back to Romania in November 1941. Some stayed in Transnistria under the Third Army. Two Red Cross nurses, including one whose husband was an officer occupying the city, established a canteen in Odessa that in January 1942 served daily six hundred to a thousand cups of tea or coffee, two hundred portions of soup, and one hundred loaves of bread. They proudly nourished "our frozen soldiers" who "had not tasted anything hot [in] 5–6 days."[14] The General Staff was forced to rely on more female volunteers on the front when the war did not quickly end.

Initially, few Red Cross personnel crossed the Bug, but the number expanded following the spring 1942 remobilization. On 17 February, at a Patronage Council meeting attended by Queen Mother Helen, Vice–Prime Minister Mihai Antonescu promised that if women did their part in the holy war, it would "open the gates to the new Romanian women of tomorrow."[15] Many women again offered to serve. The Red Cross also hired Soviet women to help in hospitals. The Third Army believed they might spread defeatism, spy, or even poison troops. General Dumitrescu instructed the Red Cross not to hire more local women and requested lists of those already employed.[16] On 27 June, the General Instructions on Jewish Forced Labor included allowing territorial corps in Romania to conscript Jewish women between eighteen and forty to work as seamstresses or washerwoman; several thousand Jewish women eventually worked for the military.[17] By now the Sanitary Service, Red Cross, and Blue Cross had established an extensive network of canteens: military canteens in Bucharest, Brașov, Predeal, Sinaia, Ploești, Buzău, Mărășești, Tecuci, Galați, Brăila, Bârlad, Roman, Iași, Ungheni, Falciu, Cernăuți, Chișinău, Românești, Cetatea Albă, and Tiraspol; Red Cross canteens in Birzula, Rozdilna, Njecajanoje, Golta, Odessa, Nikolaev, and Lemberg (Lvov); and Blue Cross canteens in Giurgiu, Timișoara, and Tighina.[18] Additionally, Red Cross personnel helped in field hospitals in Crimea. On 7–8 July 1942, Maria Antonescu visited one German and two Romanian field hospitals on the peninsula.[19] Red Cross collections abounded to provide soldiers food, gifts, and medicine. On 12 July, proceeds from a soccer match in Simferopol were donated to the Red Cross.[20] One malcontent dressed as a lieutenant made a small bundle pretending to collect for the Red Cross on trains in Romania before being arrested.[21]

Nurses' enthusiasm for the holy war waned after Stalingrad, but the army asked more of them. On 3 April 1943, the General Staff argued that the Red Cross needed "exemplary" discipline and introduced stricter regulations about transfers between hospitals or canteens. From then on assignments would be posted each month so that nurses could no longer decide to go home (or to another hospital or canteen they liked better) whenever it suited them.[22] After officers set up a canteen for poor and orphaned high school students in Prahova County, General Pantazi ordered depot commanders to do the same across Romania with support from the Blue Cross. He upbraided officers' wives and daughters for not volunteering enough with the Blue Cross: "Officers' wives must work on the internal front to be equal to the sacrifice of the country's soldiers who are fighting on [the] front."[23] The Red Cross issued another call for female volunteers to train at an infirmary school in Sinaia.[24] By now, Red Cross canteens had also been established in Kherson, Dzhankoy, Simferopol, Kerch, and Taman, where sisters of charity provided a hot meal and a kind word to soldiers.[25]

While army propaganda stressed nurses' virtue, jokes and rumors abounded about their being useless socialites or immoral whores.[26] Nurses generally associated with officers because both groups came from the same social milieu, and officers had freedom to visit Red Cross canteens. Major Scârneci and his officers developed a friendship with two "very cute and friendly" nurses at a Red Cross station in Feodosia. They often visited one another, even participating in local Islamic ceremonies. "Together with them, we marry pair after pair of Tatars. We are *Kum* (godfather) and *Kuma* (godmother). It will be more difficult at the baptism of the newborns, as we have to assist in the circumcision and that we do not like."[27] Such relationships fueled rumors of illicit affairs. On 4 August, the Third Army complained that officers and NCOs did not show "a proper attitude" toward nurses: using disrespectful language, spreading salacious rumors, and trying to persuade nurses to join them at meals but calling those who did whores. "[Sisters of charity] made the sacrifice of leaving their families to serve the army far from the country . . . day and night, without taking notice of fatigue. . . . For this [reason] not only should the R.[ed] C.[ross] female personnel not be subjected to offenses and insults, but they will be given all due respect required by decorum."[28] Soldiers turned to illicit brothels in Transnistria or German army brothels in Ukraine or Crimea (in Simferopol alone there were six "houses of tolerance").[29] Some local prostitutes found day jobs in military or Red Cross canteens, reinforcing soldiers' association of sisters of charity with sex workers. As the Romanian Army retreated in 1943, Red Cross personnel were evacuated. Ultimately, 2,754 sisters of charity and 2,430 female sanitary auxiliaries served east of the Dniester.[30]

Female volunteers continued to play an important role when the front reached Romania. Army propaganda printed lists of volunteers, usually around a hundred men and a dozen women, to try to demonstrate continued support for Romania's holy war. On 23 March 1944, *Soldatul* claimed, "Along with men, women also give an impressive number of volunteers for war. . . . The deed of the new volunteers who asked to leave for [the] front proves once more the spirit of sacrifice with which our people is animated."[31] Chaplain Gheorghe Bejgu compared Romanian women to the myrrh bearers, the women present at the crucifixion of Christ, and exhorted them not to lose faith in the holy war.[32] The Red Cross helped treat soldiers on the Iași front, while the Blue Cross provided care for invalids, orphans, widows, and soldiers' families to the rear. The Patronage Council never managed to dethrone the Red Cross as the preferred organization for female volunteers.

Entertainers

A few dozen women worked as entertainers on the front. The Propaganda Section hired singers, dancers, and actresses for the "mixed" theater groups traveling through Ukraine, Crimea, and southern Russia between September 1942 and January 1943. Female entertainers' motivation went beyond money. While they signed on for forty-five days, most stayed twice that, and some took no holiday leave. For example, Any Lupașcu remained on the front for over one hundred days before falling ill and returning home.[33] The theater groups put on hundreds of shows for groups of one thousand soldiers or more, plus Soviet civilians. A program from autumn 1942 illustrates a typical spectacle: group entrance; Royal Hymn (performed by an orchestra); Prayer for Romania (recited by an NCO); "At the well with a bucket" (female singer); Neață at Concentration (comic sketch); "Donia" and "Ciocârlia" (pan flute solo); "Who will take me?" (couplet by a female singer); "The Japanese" (juggling and acrobatics by a husband-wife duo); "Hey pal who stands watch?" (duet); Tyrol Ballet (male and female dancers); peasant joke sketches; magic tricks; imitations; "It was Fate! to me" (comedy couplet); comedic acrobatics; "You cannot hit us" (comedic couplet); "Badea told me"; Romanian dances; "Agrici left to hunt"; "Am I right? I am!"; parade by the theater group; patriotic recitation; closing words; and final choir.[34] Female performers helped boost homesick soldiers' morale on the front.

Corporal Constanța Moisescu

During a visit to Crimea in May 1943, a certain mountain soldier caught the eye of a war correspondent. "I saw how feminine tresses flowed from underneath the mountain beret almost down to the shoulders. The delicate soldier in front of me was a woman."[35] A female soldier was not unprecedented. During the First World War, Ecaterina Teodoroiu first volunteered as a nurse in 1916, but after her hometown of Târgu Jiu was overrun and her brother killed, she fought as a soldier until she was killed in 1917. She was widely celebrated afterward as a singular example of female sacrifice.[36] Constanța Moisescu was from a town near Brașov called Bușteni. She sent a petition to Marshal Antonescu asking to be sent to the front as a soldier in July 1942, after which she was selected for an audience with the *conducător* in Predeal, where "I explained to him that I had no other reason except for love of country. Neither sentimental delusion, nor desire for fame. I wanted to follow the same life as our soldiers, to live with them the same heights, and to face death together with them." He approved. After basic training, Private Moisescu requested to join the "green devils" (reportedly a Soviet nickname for Romanian mountain troops) and trained at the Mountain Corps depot until being sent to Crimea in November 1942. "Here I served just like a soldier: sentry duty, marches, shooting, fears of combat. I get no special treatment any different from my comrades. This winter I remained on the front line for 23 days without being relieved."[37] Because of her stalwart service she was soon promoted to corporal. *Soldatul* stated that women should support the war effort by taking their men's place at the plow and giving succor as nurses, but also pointed out that Romania now had "its heroine" for this new war against a greater enemy: "Her soul sought to defeat the weakness of body and bending the law of nature took up arms together with men."[38] Therefore, there was no need for other women to get any ideas about serving in combat. Unfortunately, Corporal Moisescu's fate is unknown. One thing is for sure: she did not become a national icon like Second Lieutenant Teodoroiu.

Minorities

The General Staff was suspicious of minorities, but it needed their manpower. The most distrusted of course were Jews. The General Staff directed policy regarding Jewish forced labor in Romania. Ironically, ethnic Germans also caused the General Staff much concern because of rising pro-Nazism among the group before joining the Axis; and even afterward, ethnic Germans raised trouble because the führer pressured the *conducător* into granting semiautonomy to local ethnic Germans and allowing the Waffen-SS to recruit from among the group in southern Transylvania. Nonetheless, ethnic Germans served in the Romanian Army in greater numbers at the front than any other minority except for perhaps Gypsies. The General Staff perceived ethnic minorities as unreliable and relegated them to labor or training roles in Romania, but a handful still served on the front. The General Staff considered religious minorities to be subversive, particularly neo-Protestant sects and Eastern Orthodox heretics or schismatics; however, it did not persecute them, so long as they fulfilled their military duty without protest. Despite brave service on the front lines, Gypsies were unable to escape racial discrimination in the Romanian Army, and many were even expelled from its ranks for being of the wrong class of Gypsy.

Jews

The Romanian Army did not welcome Jews into its ranks after general mobilization. On 9 January 1940, after he reported as a private, Mihail Sebastian visited a friend in the regimental adjutant's office, who told him the next call-up would only be Jews. "I don't understand why.... I suppose it's okay in time of war. You can form special units of Jews and send them to be mowed down at the front. But what sense does it make now?"[39] The General Staff prohibited segregated Jewish units, but some commanders organized them surreptitiously. In border regions, territorial corps often assigned Jews and other minorities to labor battalions to build fortifications. After its territorial losses, Romania lost half its Jewish population. The myth of Jewish betrayal during the withdrawal from northern Bukovina and Bessarabia and King Carol II's attempt to join the Axis resulted in moves to expel Jews from the Romanian Army. On 8 August, a royal decree changing the status of Jews included banning Jews who received citizenship after 1918 from being officers and implying Jews would have to perform labor service instead of military service. A week later, the General Staff ordered all Jews, except medical officers or NCOs in the Sanitary Service and enlisted men in labor detachments, demobilized.[40]

The Antonescu regime finished purging Jews from the military. On 4 December, the *conducător* signed the Law on the Military Status of Jews that excluded Jews from military service, obligating Jews to pay military taxes and requiring them to provide *muncă de folos obștesc*, or "work in [the] community interest."[41] Many commanders complained they still needed Jewish officers and NCOs with professional training. On 27 January 1941, General Antonescu allowed commanders to retain Jewish doctors, pharmacists, veterinarians, engineers, and architects until Christian replacements arrived. Jews received pay and remained in uniform but had no rank and wore Star of David insignia.[42] On 24 March, the General Staff declared the Romanian Army free of Jews. Because reserve officers could not be mobilized for more than thirty days in peacetime, however, the Sanitary Service experienced a severe shortage of doctors.[43] Consequently, on 28 May, the General Staff allowed Jewish doctors to be remobilized.[44] On 21 June, Emil Dorian recorded, "Today I was ordered by cable to report for military duty. . . . The rumors and alarm in the [capital] seemed to indicate that we will go to war any day now. . . . My dear ones are dismayed and terrified by what can happen today to a mobilized Jew."[45] The Ministry of Internal Affairs also had a few thousand Jews working in internment and labor camps by this time.

Once the holy war began, the Ministry of Defense again rid the army of Jews, but then took control of Jewish labor. After being detached to Găiești to establish a hospital, Emil Dorian's superior avoided telling people he was Jewish (he did not wear a Star of David insignia), but after two weeks he was outed when the General Staff ordered Jewish doctors again demobilized. Now it was wartime, and reserve officers could be mobilized indefinitely, providing the Sanitary Service with Christian replacements. "The high society of Găiești learned that it had harbored 'a beast, a traitor, a commando, etc., etc.,'" Dorian noted. "On the train, Jewish doctors from all over, on their way home, the war behind them."[46] While military service had ended, labor service now began. The Antonescu regime issued a new law on 14 July. Jewish men from eighteen to fifty could be drafted as individuals, in small groups, or as large detachments for 60 to 120 days (depending on the age group) each year.[47] Labor detachments were either "interior" (local, with the individual providing his own meals and returning home each night) or "exterior" (elsewhere, with the army providing food and shelter). Jews were exempted for illness, infirmity, or other reasons. On 2 August, the MCG ordered those eligible Jewish men called up. The Ministry of Internal Affairs initially had responsibility for mobilizing Jews, but within days incompetence and corruption had thrown the entire process into chaos. Recruiting centers were negligent in screening Jews, businesses tried to hold on to skilled Jewish workers, and wealthy Jews paid bribes for exemptions. Thereafter, the Ministry of Defense took the lead. On 8 August, the MCG issued new regulations to clarify the recruitment and assignment of Jews, create an "order of urgency" for Jewish labor detachments, and outline the responsibilities for recruiting centers, territorial corps, and the MCG in mobilizing and administering Jewish laborers.[48] The military, in coordination with civilians, assigned most Jewish labor detachments to work on railways, roads, or farms. The hard work was exhausting and sometimes dangerous. On 15 October, Dorian noted a "young man returned from forced labor, his hand hemorrhaging, whom Gentile doctors refused to treat—worse, they even undid his bandage, only to send him away, wound exposed, spurting blood."[49] By 3 November, of 84,042 Jewish men registered for labor, 47,345 were working, 11,933 were available, 9,365 were exempted, and 15,399 were unclear.[50] Marshal Antonescu was not pleased with these results. He believed too many Jews had been exempted because of corruption and too many skilled Jewish professionals had been assigned to unskilled heavy labor because of incompetence. The MCG blamed Jewish labor detachments' low productivity on work-shy Jews, the Ministry of Internal Affairs' early bungling, and commanders' lax discipline.[51] The General Staff believed it could rationalize and expand the system of Jewish work in the community interest.

The General Staff's effort to increase Jewish labor detachments' productivity failed even before it began. As the General Staff drafted new plans, it ordered eligible Jewish men to shovel snow on streets and railways, useful but also humiliating work. In Bucharest, a lady from an old boyar family refused to have her sidewalk cleared. "This kind of work is done by servants, not by intellectuals."[52] However, most Romanians believed Jews had it too good. On 19 February, the General Staff reported that soldiers visiting from the front became demoralized when they saw "insolent" and "defiant" Jews safe from the front in Romania.[53] The General Staff demanded a review of Jews exempted during the first labor drive, to identify those who had bribed officials to avoid work in the community interest—as indeed some Jews had—so that the second labor drive would be more successful. Radu Lecca persuaded Marshal Antonescu to appoint him to head the review process, which started on 4 March, and which he turned into a corrupt system of Jews paying kickbacks to lawyers and "honoraria" to review commissions in exchange for exemptions.[54] By the time the review commissions finished, they had exempted 38,123 Jews out of 87,591, leaving just 39,212 eligible for labor.[55] This forced the General Staff to scale down its plans.

The General Staff introduced new organization and stricter discipline to try to squeeze as much productivity as possible out of Jewish laborers. On 27 June 1942, the General Staff introduced *muncă obligatorie*, or "compulsory work," specifically for Jews. It wanted Jews from twenty to forty to serve in exterior labor detachments, younger or older Jews to serve in interior labor detachments, and Jewish craftsmen of any age to serve in army workshops. The General Staff wanted bigger and better-administered Jewish labor detachments, with five hundred Jews and three reserve officers, three reserve NCOs, one Jewish administration officer or NCO, one Jewish doctor, ten reserve enlisted men, and two supply enlisted men. It stressed that Jews should receive sufficient pay, shelter, and food, and even financial aid for their families.[56] The General Staff also authorized stricter discipline, including flogging Jews for even minor offenses and deporting Jews, along with their families, to Transnistria for evading or deserting compulsory work.[57] Jewish labor detachments continued to experience shortages of all kinds despite the General Staff's instructions. Jewish families with the means sent money, food, and clothing. On 16 July, a lieutenant was caught transporting around thirty kilograms of clothing, food, medicine, and letters from a Jewish couple in Botoşani, with whom he had stayed, for their son with a Jewish labor detachment near Hotin. He confessed to "being touched by the sufferings of a mother" but denied accusations of "un-patriotism."[58] The General Staff dispatched ninety-three Jewish doctors in uniform to provide medical care for divisions in Transnistria, reportedly upsetting soldiers who initially saluted the Jews, thinking they were officers.[59] Jewish doctors, the 3rd Security Division reported, "enter unhindered and alone" into ghettos and camps to observe conditions, share information, and take messages back to Romania.[60] The General Staff had already created teams of twenty Jewish craftsmen, supervised by an NCO, in army workshops in Transnistria.[61] On 16 September, Mihai Antonescu suspended deportations of Jews and Gypsies to Transnistria. Only 306 (plus 249 family members) out of 12,086 "delinquent" Jews had been deported by this point.[62] General Şteflea tried in vain to persuade Marshal Antonescu to remove Radu Lecca and void the exemptions he had approved for Jews. Lecca had pocketed bribes, but he also funneled enormous amounts of money from the Jewish Central Office (responsible for collecting the exemption taxes paid by Jews who were granted an exemption) to members of the Antonescu regime who protected him.[63] The General Staff's changes and emphasis on strict discipline did not make Jewish labor detachments markedly more productive.

The General Staff succeeded in maximizing the number of Jews performing compulsory labor in the third labor drive, but it continued to experience supply troubles, poor leadership, and limited motivation. Some reserve officers and NCOs commanding Jewish labor detachments were corrupt and abusive, beating Jews, stealing packages, extorting money, or selling supplies. On 10 January 1943, Dorian noted, "Jews in a labor camp near Cotroceni [a Bucharest suburb], many intellectuals among them, were beaten up yesterday by the soldiers in the regiment because of 'insufficient output'—in the colonel's view and following his order."[64] Yet such behavior by officers was not uncommon in regular labor detachments with Romanians and other minorities. The General Staff considered permanent compulsory work, seizure of property, and execution as punishments to replace the threat of deportation to Transnistria, but it never implemented these options.[65] That spring, the General Staff demanded the assignment to external labor detachments of all but the most indispensable Jews between twenty and forty years of age, the annulment of exemptions for Jews working for public institutions or holding academic degrees, the conscription of Jewish women, and better policing of Jews who tried evading compulsory labor. By 30 June, 50,246 Jews out of 102,139 were working.[66] Radu Lecca continued to siphon off funds from the Jewish Central Office; Maria Antonescu's Patronage Council received billions of lei in particular.[67] The General Staff prioritized the construction of fortifications, including the FNB Line, assigning many Jewish labor detachments to engineering and fortification projects.[68]

The fourth labor drive was disrupted by Soviet forces overrunning northeastern Romania. The General Staff had started registering and mobilizing Jews for compulsory labor in February 1944, much earlier in the year than before, and even created new Jewish labor detachments using Jews who had recently been repatriated from Transnistria.[69] After Axis forces halted the enemy, the General Staff threw Jewish laborers into constructing fortifications in Moldavia and Bessarabia. Additionally, Jews were used in civil defense battalions in cities to respond to the damage done by US and British bombers. The Jewish Central Office continued collecting exemption taxes. On 23 August, 31,463 Jews were working in external and interior Jewish labor detachments.[70] Despite the Antonescu regime's early efforts to rid the Romanian Army of Jews, it increasingly relied on Jewish compulsory labor as the holy war dragged on.

Ethnic Germans

Many ethnic Germans, especially Saxons and Swabians in Transylvania, resented living under Romanian rule. Sigmund Landau bristled at being a "tolerated foreigner" in his homeland, with people shouting "Speak Romanian!" at him and scuffles breaking out between Romanian and ethnic German students.[71] The development of a pro-Nazi movement exacerbated tensions between ethnic Germans and Romanians. On 26 October 1939, a report indicated that many regular officers treated ethnic German reserve officers like suspects, but others "behaved themselves irreproachably . . . showing them even sympathy."[72] Following the loss of territory in 1940, Romania's ethnic German population declined from 745,000 to 542,000, concentrated in southern Transylvania. The Antonescu regime tamped down Romanian hostility toward ethnic Germans after the Second Vienna Award. Three days prior to Romania joining the Axis, on 20 November 1940, Nazi Germany extracted an important concession from General Antonescu: the formation of the German Ethnic Group in Romania, which granted ethnic Germans greater autonomy and increased Nazi influence over them. Thus, ethnic Germans would have a choice between serving in the Romanian Army or the Waffen-SS.

The Antonescu regime tried to limit SS recruitment, but ethnic Germans voted with their feet. The Nazis immediately organized the 1,000-Mann-Aktion to recruit volunteers for the Waffen-SS over the winter.[73] Although the Romanian Army granted ethnic German soldiers privileges now denied other minorities (reading German newspapers, writing letters in German, and speaking German), many ethnic Germans preferred to serve in the German Army, where food, uniforms, and pay were better, and officers did not physically abuse soldiers.[74] Sigmund Landau fawned over German troops recently arrived in Brașov. "These lads, when compared to our nose-picking, spitting, foul-smelling Romanian troopers, were incredibly well-disciplined when on duty, jolly and friendly when off duty. Their uniforms were smart and always spotless and, to the delight of our tradesmen, they were absolutely rolled in money."[75] Thousands of ethnic Germans volunteered for the Waffen-SS, joined the German Ethnic Group, or found employment with a German unit. In January 1941, Landau became a translator for a German Luftwaffe antiaircraft unit in Ploiești. Once the war started, he accompanied the German Eleventh Army to Tighina, Nikolaev, Kherson, and Simferopol, but in December he was forced to return to Romania because Marshal Antonescu had protested to Hitler that the German Army was assisting ethnic Germans to evade the draft in Romania. "I was sick with apprehension," was Landau's reaction. "I shall never submit to the Romanians!"[76] He and a friend did what hundreds of other young ethnic Germans did: sneaked across the border into Hungarian-occupied northern Transylvania (in their case) or German-occupied Serbia to join the Waffen-SS. However, not all ethnic Germans were so reluctant to serve in the Romanian Army.

Other ethnic Germans answered draft notices. Vasilache Mătușa remembered his unit had many Saxons, whom he called "the Germans' Gypsies" because German troops often treated them condescendingly.[77] Some ethnic German troops decided to desert after reporting for duty. Petre Mortun served in an antiaircraft battery with Romanians, Germans, Hungarians, Ukrainians, and Russians, "all the languages that we needed," he joked.

However, Saxons started to desert during training, and more followed suit when on the front close to German units.[78] Most ethnic German deserters were NCOs or enlisted men. Ethnic German officers, including Generals Schwab and Carol Schmidt, did not desert. General Artur Phelps got permission from General Antonescu to resign from the Romanian Army in 1940, going on to command a Waffen-SS division in 1941 and then a corps in 1944. The Antonescu regime revoked the citizenship of ethnic Germans who evaded the draft or deserted. Despite some desertions, almost five thousand ethnic German soldiers were serving in Echelon I divisions in May 1942 (see table 4). This number probably doubled once Echelon II divisions mobilized for Case Blue. Although they were few in comparison to the total strength of the Romanian Army, ethnic Germans had an outsize importance because of the number of former Austro-Hungarian officers, technically skilled NCOs, and translators.

At first, the German Ethnic Group was a way to avoid military service, but it became the surest way to end up on the front. The German Ethnic Group established paramilitary youth and adult groups, enrolling 31,000 youths and 36,640 men respectively, and ethnic Germans in the Romanian Army resented them. On 23 June 1942, a report recorded Saxon soldiers complaining, "We are militiamen with familial obligations and we fulfill [our] service with pleasure on [the] front, but why do Saxon youths go about by automobile on the streets of Brașov and receive large salaries from the Saxon Ethnic Group? Eligible Saxon youths should come to the front and show their patriotism and love for Germany here!"[79] As the OKW became increasingly desperate for manpower, however, the SS snapped up Saxons. On 13 April 1943, Marshal Antonescu was required to sign an agreement allowing the SS to recruit even more heavily in Romania, and a month later he also agreed not to strip ethnic Germans who left Romania of their citizenship. He managed to obtain an

Table 4. Minorities in the Third Army, May 1942

MINORITY GROUP	OFFICERS	NCOS/ENLISTED
Germans	679	4,080
Hungarians	8	386
Yugoslavs	35	99
Slovaks	14	58
Bulgarians	3	27
Russians	0	6
Ukrainians	0	2
Other	16	87

Source: AMNR, Fond Armata 3–a, dosar 1118, f. 1.

assurance that ethnic German officers, NCOs, or specialists (artillerymen, mortarmen, telephone/telegraph operators, air crew, and sailors) already in the Romanian Army could not be recruited into the SS.[80] Officially, ethnic Germans were supposed to volunteer, but reports indicate that Saxons came under intense pressure from the SS and their local cronies. Some Saxons approached the 2nd Mountain Division depot commander, asking that their sons be drafted by the Romanian Army to avoid "volunteering" for the SS. Brașov police reported during the SS-directed enrollment on 17–18 April, "Only a relatively small number of Saxons received the recruitment operations with enthusiasm. The rest with indifference, and a good portion among them are anxious."[81] Nearly sixty thousand ethnic Germans eventually joined the SS. Although most served in the Waffen-SS, many ended up in SS Death's Head units that administered concentration and extermination camps, including Auschwitz. Another fifteen thousand ethnic Germans served in the German Army or worked for the Todt Organization. Finally, forty thousand ethnic Germans served in the Romanian Army.[82]

Ethnic Hungarians

Ethnic Hungarians, 1,425,507 people or 7.9 percent of the population, represented the largest minority in Greater Romania, so the Romanian Army mistrusted them the most—after Jews. Many Reform (Calvinist) priests, most of whom were ethnic Hungarians, were antiwar and backed Carol II's policy of armed neutrality after September 1939, believing that this would keep Romania out of the wider conflict and protect Transylvania's ethnic Hungarians, contributing to low rates of draft evasion by ethnic Hungarians following general mobilization.[83] The Carlist regime needed minority backing, particularly from ethnic Hungarians, to deter Soviet and Nazi threats, so the General Staff accommodated minority soldiers, allowing them to write letters, read newspapers, and watch entertainment in Hungarian, German, Yiddish, Russian, and Ukrainian. Nonetheless, the Romanian Army heavily censored all such materials, sure they were full of anti-Romanian sentiments. Army intelligence became convinced that ethnic Hungarian reserve officers spied for the Hungarian Army.[84] On 20 June 1940, the duty officer at the Fourth Army headquarters warned against putting an ethnic Hungarian sentry outside. "If one takes into account that the chauffeurs [of the staff cars] are of the same origin, we can expect a surprise in a [time of] need."[85] After the Second Vienna Award, only 363,206 ethnic Hungarians remained in southern Transylvania. The Antonescu regime took a harder line against minorities in the ranks, so the Romanian Army banned foreign-language newspapers, required letters to be written in Romanian, and placed minority soldiers under increased surveillance. Anti-Hungarian sentiments in the Romanian Army were kept in check, however.

Fear of a tit-for-tat response kept the Antonescu regime's treatment of ethnic Hungarians from becoming too harsh during the war. On 24 June 1941, General Ioanițiu ordered officers to discipline ethnic Hungarian soldiers caught committing infractions with "much tact" because he worried how ethnic Romanians in the Hungarian Army would be treated in response. He argued there were more Romanians in northern Transylvania than Hungarians in southern Transylvania, so "the consequences will all be in our disfavor."[86] Ethnic Hungarians began evading the draft in greater numbers following the invasion of the USSR, and enough crossed the border that the Hungarian Army created a security battalion in Cluj consisting of many deserters from southern Transylvania.[87] Yet most ethnic Hungarians did not go to such extreme lengths. Petre Mortun had a good opinion of ethnic Hungarians in his unit on the front. "I got along better with the Hungarian [soldiers] than the Romanian . . . the Romanian were more stubborn. [The Hungarian] was more obedient, he spoke slower, but was more obedient."[88] Ethnic Hungarians were often assigned to support units on the front as cooks, carriage drivers, and artillery loaders. The Romanian Army found it difficult to balance its need for trained soldiers with its suspicion of ethnic Hungarians, however, leading to counterproductive policies.

During remobilization for Case Blue, the Ministry of Defense requested lists of ethnic Hungarian NCOs who had been trained in the Austro-Hungarian or Romanian Armies, in order to best employ them on the front, at army schools, or in labor detachments.[89] There were only four hundred ethnic Hungarians in Echelon I divisions in May 1942 (see table 4), but hundreds more went east with Echelon II divisions. Army intelligence believed Hungarian agents advised ethnic Hungarian soldiers to desert after reaching the front to deprive the Romanian Army of both a soldier and his equipment.[90] On 21 September, the General Staff ordered "severe measures that all the soldiers of ethnic Hungarian origin to be closely supervised the whole period of transportation and not be allowed to make contact with the Hungarian soldiers and railway personal, not under any circumstance."[91] The next day Marshal Antonescu suspended leave for all ethnic Hungarian soldiers, even in Romania, because of reports of a few ethnic Hungarian deserters on the front. Approximately seven hundred ethnic Hungarian soldiers served at military schools, plus twenty thousand in labor detachments (see table 5). On 11 December, the General Staff passed along a request from the artillery officer school asking the ban on leave be lifted because most ethnic Hungarians

Table 5. Situation of labor detachments, December 1943

CATEGORY	UNITS	EFFECTIVES	DATE CREATED	LOCATION	MINORITY
Agriculture	30	15,930	Apr.–Jul. '43*	Territorial Corps	Mixed
Forestry	58	43,502	Oct. '41	Forest districts	Mixed
Factory	5	1,950	Apr.–Jul. '42	Transylvania	
Petroleum	4	810	Aug. '43	Prahova Valley	
Road	13	25,412	Apr. '42	Transn., Romania	Mixed
Railroad	28	57,337	Apr. '42	Transyl., Mold.	42,320 Minorities
Train station	6	1,200	Apr. '42	Transnistria	
Special	5	1,500	May '43	Military schools	700 Hungarians
Sărata	17	14,516	May/Sept. '43	Transn., Romania	Mixed
Fortification	10	3,722	Aug./Dec. '43	Dobruja, Transyl.	
Total	176	165,930			
Railroad	4	1,056	Apr. '42	Territorial Corps	Jews
Road	8	6,000	Apr. '42	Bessarabia	Jews
Engineer	5	6,709	Apr. '43	Moldavia	Jews
Civilian	32	8,414	Sept. '42	Various cities	Jews
Sărata	2	1,994		FNB Line	Jews
Total	49	24,197			
General total	225	190,127			

*These agricultural labor detachments were demobilized during the winter.

Source: ANIC, Fond Preşedinţia Consiliului de Miniştri: Cabinetul Militar, dosar 35/1944, f. 7.

"proved themselves however to be good soldiers" and could easily desert anyway, so the ban needlessly alienated them.[92] Despite the Antonescu regime's fears of Hungarian subversion, most ethnic Hungarians did what was asked of them for Romania's holy war.

Slavic Minorities

Greater Romania also had a substantial Slavic population. Slavic minorities predominated in Bukovina, Bessarabia, and Dobruja, and included 595,000 ethnic Ukrainians, 409,000 ethnic Russians, and 366,000 ethnic Bulgarians.[93] Romania lost most Slavic minorities after the Soviet occupation of northern Bukovina and Bessarabia and the Bulgarian occupation of southern Dobruja. The Romanian-Bulgarian population exchange in Dobruja presented the challenge of what to do with ethnic Bulgarians who remained after the border revision. In September 1940, the General Staff ordered ethnic Bulgarian officers to turn in uniforms and return home to be resettled. The following month, the Ministry of Defense clarified that ethnic Bulgarian officers whose families had lived in northern Dobruja since before the Russo-Turkish War of 1877–1878 "will be considered as Romanians, because some were raised in Romanian schools," and could retain their positions in the Romanian Army.[94] The General Staff relegated most of the remaining Slavic soldiers to labor detachments; however, some still served in regular units in support roles.

While the Romanian Army primarily saw Jews as the communist fifth-column threat, it also targeted Slavic minorities during Operation Barbarossa. Lipovans (Russian Orthodox Old Believers) in particular were accused of insulting the army in 1940 and being Soviet agents in 1941. The absurdity that these religious nonconformists supported the USSR simply because they were ethnic Russians was lost on Romanian commanders. The MCG ordered a halt to all crossings of the Danube and its branches, the impounding of private vessels in the Danube delta, police to reinforce soldiers securing the region, and the removal of Lipovan men from the delta in Dobruja to internment camps in Wallachia. On 6 July, 165 Lipovans arrived from Tulcea in Călărași, the same day as one of the two Iași "death trains."[95] On 14 July, as Army Group Antonescu advanced, the XI Corps reported lakes in southern Bessarabia were crowded with Lipovan fishermen, who might have been recruited as Soviet agents, left behind to signal enemy aircraft and report friendly troop movements. General Ghineraru, then commander of the 1st Fortification Brigade, proposed restricting Lipovans from fishing.[96] Meanwhile, in northern Bukovina and northern Bessarabia, Ukrainian nationalists, encouraged by German commanders, began forming militias, raising the Ukrainian flag over towns and villages. Romanian soldiers and Ukrainian militiamen clashed in places. Mihai Antonescu advocated deporting ethnic Ukrainians—along with Jews—across the Dniester, but his efforts came to naught.[97] Instead, the MCG ordered gendarmes and *grăniceri* to advance and block the return of Slavic minorities who had fled across the Dniester. Additionally, on 24 July, eight thousand Poles and six thousand Ukrainians, resettled in Bessarabia by Soviet authorities during the occupation, were expelled over the Dniester.[98] Locals serving in the Red Army deserted as it retreated. On 10 August, the Fourth Army reported that an ethnic Bulgarian officer who had previously served in the Romanian Army appeared in Ismail, claiming that while he had been forced to join the ranks of the Red Army, he had contributed little and deserted as soon as possible.[99] Romania again had a large population of ethnic Ukrainians, ethnic Russians, and ethnic Bulgarians after the Romanian Army reconquered northern Bukovina and Bessarabia; however, the Red Army had taken most military-age men with it when it retreated.

The occupation of Transnistria added more ethnic Ukrainians, ethnic Russians, and ethnic Bulgarians. Of 82,057 Soviet prisoners of war held in Romania, the General Staff paroled 13,682 who were from northern Bukovina, Bessarabia, and Transnistria.[100] The Antonescu regime calculated these men would contribute more by working their farms at home, and Soviet citizens returning to Transnistria were none too anxious to join the partisan movement, as in 1942 the USSR still seemed near defeat (although this changed by 1944). The Governorate of Transnistria effectively ran the province for the General Staff, mobilizing the population for agricultural and industrial labor for Romania's war effort, so the General Staff did not conscript for labor detachments from Transnistria. In Romania most ethnic Ukrainians, ethnic Russians, and ethnic Bulgarians were assigned to labor battalions alongside Romanians. The General Staff drafted a report about creating segregated Ukrainian units, but the scheme was never adopted.[101] Just two ethnic Ukrainians, six ethnic Russians, and thirty ethnic Bulgarians served with the Third Army east of the Dniester in May 1942 (see table 4), compared to tens of thousands who worked in labor detachments in Romania in December 1943 (see table 5). There is no indication that Slavic minorities avoided the draft or deserted in any great numbers; it probably helped that most were assigned to labor service in Romania rather than to combat units on the front.

Religious Minorities

There were small but growing neo-Protestant and Romanian Orthodox sects in Greater Romania. Around one hundred thousand citizens were religious minorities of varied ethnic backgrounds, concentrated in Transylvania and Bessarabia. The General Staff was suspicious of Christian religious sects because many did not recognize state authority and preached pacifism.[102] In contrast, 150,000 Muslims, mostly ethnic Turks concentrated in Dobruja, had no compunction about serving the state or fighting. After 1939, neo-Protestants, heretical or schismatic Orthodox believers, and Muslims entered the Romanian Army in greater numbers than ever before. On 20 June 1940, the Military Bishopric called Adventist proselytizing "unspeakably dangerous."[103] "Adventist" was a catch-all term denoting any neo-Protestant sect, because this group caused the most trouble for the Romanian Army. The General Staff ordered chaplains to confront neo-Protestant soldiers "showing them their waywardness [rătăcirea]."[104] Baptist, Adventist, Jehovah's Witness, and heretical or schismatic Orthodox soldiers were followed, and surveilled at worship services. In stark contrast, the General Staff backed Bishop Ciopron's request to recruit four Muslim imams as chaplains, to cater to

Muslim soldiers.[105] Romania lost most of its Muslim population along with southern Dobruja in 1940. Additionally, only about twenty-five thousand Baptists and fifteen thousand Adventists remained after the loss of northern Transylvania and Bessarabia.[106] Nevertheless, the Antonescu regime made life difficult for religious minorities remaining in Romania.

Most Romanian members of religious minorities found ways to accommodate themselves with the Antonescu regime, but several groups did not. Just three days after seizing power, on 9 September 1940, General Antonescu outlawed neo-Protestant and heretical or schismatic Romanian Orthodox sects, including Adventists, Baptists, Evangelists, Jehovah's Witnesses, Pentecostals, Inochentiști, and Stiliști (Romanian Orthodox Old Calendar believers). When the Romanian Army drafted religious minorities, it had the most problems with Adventist and Inochentiști conscientious objectors. Adventists usually donned uniforms without much protest; difficulties began when they were asked to hold a rifle or swear the army oath. The Romanian Army made no concessions. On 5 April 1941, the General Staff went out of its way to order that every soldier, no matter his religion, had to attend the mass oath-taking being broadcast by radio of the first contingent of soldiers swearing allegiance to Antonescu as *conducător*.[107] When Romania's holy war began in June 1941, most neo-Protestants supported the cause. Second Lieutenant Crișan, a Baptist, believed Bessarabia was part of Greater Romania, and he later admitted, "I, like any other Rumanian, was apprehensive of any foreign-language-speaking fellow."[108] Neo-Protestants also believed that Judeo-Bolshevism was a threat to Christian civilization. Most neo-Protestants were willing to fight, but convinced Adventists tried to obtain noncombat assignments as drivers, cooks, or orderlies. On 18 July, the Third Army reported, "In the cases when they do not succeed in getting a position that shields them from having to shoot, they desert."[109] Inochentiști, followers of a charismatic and millennialist Romanian Orthodox sect, also refused to recognize the state's authority or bear arms. The Antonescu regime dealt harshly with these groups that refused to fight.

Adventists and Inochentiști continued to be a thorn in the side of the Romanian Army as the holy war continued. Some imprisoned for conscientious objection owing to religious convictions accepted the offer for rehabilitation and were sent to Training Center No. 5 in Sărata after May 1942. Captain Păsat assigned an Adventist to his company staff. "We keep this soldier only to watch and eavesdrop on the discussions and eventually on the plans [of the other soldiers] to rob the population."[110] In August, the Antonescu regime deported two thousand Inochentiști to Transnistria as punishment for "a general revolt" against military service.[111] On 28 December, Marshal

Antonescu reissued his ban on neo-Protestant and heretical or schismatic Orthodox sects, but few abandoned their faith. On 2 June 1943, Private Corneliu Florescu, part of the ground crew of the 3rd Bomber Fleet, despite discussions with a captain and a chaplain signed a declaration proclaiming, "I am penetrated by my Adventist teachings, I do not accept any of the other religions that are legal in the Romanian State.... This is my final decision; I remain Adventist, I do not accept the [Romanian Orthodox] cross, I do not bow, and I do not accept giving the oath on the flag because I do not accept these forms as valid."[112] Harsh prison sentences convinced a few believers to renounce their faith, at least officially. On 18 November, Chaplain Pantelimon Birău crowed that forty-four "religious sectarians" condemned to one to twenty-five years hard labor in Cernăuți had reconverted in exchange for pardons.[113] All religious minorities faced discrimination, but only those that refused to fight faced persecution.

Yet even neo-Protestants who initially supported the crusade against communism came to question the righteousness of Romania's cause. After fighting at Odessa, Second Lieutenant Crișan was demobilized and reassigned to a depot battalion in Timișoara. A weak leg from an infection as a youth meant he first trained replacements and then managed a militarized factory rather than go back to the front. "The balls and parties were many and social events filled out leisure time. We lived one day at the time.... Some of my Baptist friends, more modest in their social status, and people from the countryside discussed among themselves and once in a while would ask me, 'Is this the world's end? We live like the people of Sodom and Gomorrah!'"[114] Religious minorities looked to a miracle to save Romania from an approaching Judeo-Bolshevik apocalypse.

Gypsies

Gypsies were the most assimilated of any minority but faced intense racial prejudice. The reprehensible legacy of five centuries of Gypsy slavery from 1385 to 1856 meant Gypsies were impoverished and marginalized in Romania.[115] Gypsies' status had improved somewhat by the interwar period, as a growing number left boyar estates to the city to become workers or join the middle class. Nomadic Gypsies sustained a free, if hardscrabble, life on the margins of society by moving from place to place in caravans. Gypsies were spread across Greater Romania, but most resided in Wallachia, spoke Romanian, were Romanian Orthodox, and often even self-identified as Romanian. Romanians valued Gypsies as musicians and craftsmen, but also slandered them as layabouts and thieves. Eugenicists went even further, claiming Gypsies were racially inferior to Romanians and blaming high rates of intermarriage between Romanians and Gypsies, especially in Transylvania, for weakening the race.[116] A census counted 208,700 Gypsies in Romania after the territorial losses of 1940, but it is likely there were more, because many did not identify as Gypsies, either because of assimilation or fear of stigmatization.[117]

Most Gypsies patriotically supported the holy war for the same reasons as their fellow citizens, but most Romanians had trouble understanding this. Romanians believed Gypsies were cowards. Officers often chose Gypsies as their orderlies, especially if they were musically gifted, reinforcing stereotypes that Gypsies wanted to avoid combat. While non-nomadic, or so-called sedentary, Gypsies were easily conscripted, draft boards found it difficult to track down nomadic Gypsies, contributing to the belief that Gypsies were draft dodgers. On 5 December 1941, Major Scârneci sat down with Private Toba, another officer's orderly, whom he described as "a black and ugly Gypsy," to talk about his life at home. "He is also fighting here in Crimea before fortress Sevastopol. But for what? For his poverty? I take a postcard and following his words—as he is illiterate—I write to his family at home and I regret to the bottom of my soul that I cannot do more for him. . . . The country does not think of him, nay there's talk to . . . colonize them in Transnistria."[118] Gypsies fought bravely and won medals that they wore proudly. Petre Costea recalled, "They were the same as us . . . they listened to our orders."[119] Yet Romanians remained convinced Gypsies were cowards. Mircea Ionescu-Quintus conceded "Gypsies . . . did not flee" in battle but argued that "they were more fearful" than Romanians.[120] This comment might reflect the effect discrimination had on Gypsy soldiers' morale, particularly after nomadic and "criminal" Gypsies were deported to Transnistria.

The deportation of Gypsies in Romania was not supposed to affect Gypsy soldiers at the front, but it often did. On 1 May 1942, the Ministry of Internal Affairs started planning to deport nomadic Gypsies and soon added "criminal" Gypsies, including vagabonds, the unemployed, and refugees. The Ministry of Defense made no protest about deporting 9,188 nomadic Gypsies as it assumed that they already did nothing for the war effort; however, it did intervene to reduce the target number of sedentary Gypsies to be deported from 31,438 to 12,497. On 1 June, gendarmes began rounding up nomadic Gypsies. It took weeks for caravans to trundle east, but the nomadic Gypsies made the trek with little loss of life, and some even believed promises of receiving land in Transnistria.[121] Any illusions were dashed at the Dniester, where gendarmes stole valuables, Romanian National Bank agents forced Gypsies to exchange lei for nearly worthless occupation currency, and

Governorate of Transnistria agents seized animals and carts.[122] The roundup and transportation of "criminal" Gypsies did not go so smoothly. These deportations were carried out by train, and scores died, including children, due to incompetence and indifference. On 4 August, the 3rd Security Division reported there were soldiers among these Gypsies, some of whom had been demobilized after fighting at Odessa or on leave from the front. "All were evacuated casually, without being sorted, but sent in a big pile. These [men] are claiming the rights earned through law and military service."[123] On 2 September, General Vasiliu pushed gendarmes to deport as many Gypsies as possible, regardless of criteria. Two weeks later, Mihai Antonescu temporarily halted deportations after 11,474 nomadic and 13,245 sedentary Gypsies had been sent to Transnistria.[124] On 30 September, the Ministry of Defense complained the Ministry of Internal Affairs had deported sedentary Gypsies who were supposed to be exempt, including veterans of the First World War, landholders, soldiers' families, and even "Gypsies dressed in military gear."[125] The Romanian Army did little to rectify the situation. On 3 October, the General Staff explained recent events, clarified that nomadic Gypsies still mobilized should be sent to Transnistria, claimed no sedentary Gypsy soldiers' families were deported by mistake, and ordered other Gypsy soldiers to remain with their units. The General Staff argued that if any Gypsy soldiers' families had been deported, it was because they had asked to accompany family members. Commanders were to compile lists of Gypsy soldiers who claimed their families had been mistakenly deported.[126] A week later, the Ministry of Defense reported it had intervened to permanently halt deportations, citing the late season and the Ministry of Internal Affairs' undisciplined gendarmes. It instructed the General Staff "to correct these mistakes" by giving Gypsy soldiers travel papers so they could track down their families and either settle with them in Transnistria or get them repatriated to Romania.[127] On 13 October, Mihai Antonescu permanently suspended deportations to Transnistria. The Mountain Corps reported that Gypsy soldiers whose families had been deported were angry, "especially those that comported themselves well on [the] front."[128] Patriotic service had proved a flimsy shield against racism.

Gypsy soldiers at the Sărata Training Center were demoralized too. Courts-martial sentenced Gypsies at a higher rate than Romanians, so a large proportion of rehabilitation soldiers sent to Sărata for retraining were Gypsies. General Poenaru blamed the high number of desertions from Sărata on Gypsy soldiers and criminals. He claimed, "The majority of [deserters] are Gypsies or have a repulsive physical feature that initially inspires pity. . . . Pickpockets and career deserters are the worst soldiers."[129] Poenaru read out the General Staff's report on the deportation of Gypsies to the assembled rehabilitation soldiers, but he added that nomadic and "criminal" Gypsies at the Sărata Training Center would not be deported to Transnistria. Instead, they would still be sent to the front.[130] This "agitated" Gypsy soldiers, who said they could not understand why they had to fight to protect their families from communism when their families had just been deported to Transnistria. Colonel Iancu Ghenescu, second in command at Sărata, asked the Gypsy soldiers if they would rather go back to prison. They responded, "We'd rather die." He quipped, "The yearning of the Gypsy for liberty is well known."[131] Many of these demoralized men deserted on the way to or at the front.

Gypsy soldiers had little success in rescuing their families. On 18 December, the Ministry of Defense informed Corporal Gheorghe Bălteanu that his family was in good health except for his wife Giga, who "asked on her own" to be deported because her parents and siblings had been seized by gendarmes, and she could not abandon them to their fate. He was offered no recourse to repatriate his wife.[132] Rumors spread of more deportations, depressing Gypsy soldiers' morale. On 14 January 1943, the General Staff told the Third Army to allay eight Gypsy soldiers' fears since "their families were not deported to Transnistria but are remaining at their domiciles."[133] The conditions in labor colonies were terrible, with many Gypsies dying from starvation, disease, and exposure in the winter; Gypsy survivors called Transnistria the "Valley of Wailing."[134] Gypsy soldiers continued to petition to have their families repatriated. On 12 March, the General Staff acknowledged that Gypsy soldiers' wives were in labor colonies in Transnistria, but it claimed these women had hidden their identity to accompany family members being deported or in hopes of obtaining land; moreover, it argued many were really "concubines," not wives. Many Gypsy marriages had not been legalized by the state (due to a tradition of child marriage), so they were not technically exempt from deportation as Gypsy soldiers' legal spouses. Moreover, the Ministry of Internal Affairs claimed the threat of typhus prevented the repatriation of Gypsy soldiers' families from Transnistria. The General Staff ordered Gypsy soldiers appearing in Transnistria be told their families would be repatriated whenever possible and to return immediately to duty or risk joining them in a labor colony.[135] Some Romanian officers tried to help Gypsy enlisted men. Private Gheorghe Zăilă finally received leave after two years on the front, only to discover that his wife, three children, mother, and sister had been deported. His pioneer battalion was refitting in Transnistria after surviving Stalingrad, so he was able to track down his family, but found only one child and his sister alive. On 24 August, Zăila's major wrote a petition on his behalf. "Our unit is readying to abandon Transnistria to go in Country, I ask you to deign to accelerate the forms for repatriation, so that his family can go together with the Battalion, taking into account the pecuniary situation and merit of this soldier."[136] The reply is unknown, but if the petition was granted, it would have been one of only a pitiful few.

The Antonescu regime delayed repatriation of Gypsies from Transnistria for as long as possible. On 13 January 1944, the General Staff ordered commanders to stop authorizing Gypsy soldiers to fetch families from Transnistria because only the General Inspectorate of Gendarmes had that power.[137] The Ministry of Internal Affairs conducted a hurried and confused evacuation of labor colonies in Transnistria, complicated by Soviet forces overrunning the territory, so by May 1944 fewer than six thousand Gypsies had been repatriated to Romania.[138] Others may have found their own way home.

Gypsy soldiers were probably the most motivated minority in the Romanian Army, despite the discrimination they faced—at least until the Antonescu regime deported nomadic and "criminal" Gypsies, undermining Gypsy soldiers' morale. As First Lieutenant Ezechil later wrote in homage, "[Gypsies] paid heavily their tribute of blood in the two world wars, just for the simple fact that they were Romanian citizens."[139] The Romanian Army did little to reward these men for their patriotic service.

Overlooked

The experiences of women and minorities offer new and important perspectives of the Romanian Army. Red Cross nurses provided valuable womanpower for hospitals and canteens, female entertainers reminded soldiers that they were not forgotten on the front, and Jewish women were conscripted as labor for the military in Romania. For all of the General Staff's exaggerated concerns, minority soldiers generally served dutifully. After being expelled from the ranks, Jews became a vital source of skilled and unskilled labor for the Romanian Army. Ethnic Germans made an important contribution to frontline operations. Ethnic Hungarian, Ukrainian, Russian, and Bulgarian soldiers working in labor detachments at home freed Romanian soldiers for the front. Religious minorities proved willing to fight, with the notable exceptions of Adventists and Inochentiști. Gypsies suffered a tragic fate because, despite fighting bravely in battle, they were accused of cowardice, and many lost loved ones deported to Transnistria. The Romanian Army could not have fought for as long as it did without the contribution of women and minorities.

Epilogue

With the Iași front in disarray, Marshal Antonescu flew back to Bucharest and planned to create a national redoubt in southern Transylvania. He was convinced by National Peasant and Liberal leaders, his wife, and Mihai Antonescu that he had to meet with the king the next day, 23 August. Mihai Antonescu arrived punctually at 3 p.m., greeted by King Mihai I and General Sănătescu, chief of the military household, but Marshal Antonescu was late. After the *conducător*'s report, the king asked if it was not time for an armistice. Antonescu said he would only seek an armistice if the Germans approved and, even then, accept one only on the conditions the Anglo-Americans promised the Soviets would not occupy Romania and delay border changes until after a peace conference. The king and Sănătescu pushed Antonescu to resign. He refused, arguing that Axis forces could hold the FNB Line or retreat into the Carpathian Mountains. The king stood up, "If that's how things are, then there's nothing more for us to do." On this signal, a captain and three NCOs entered and arrested the *conducător* and the vice-premier. Antonescu yelled "Tomorrow you will all be executed!"[1] Then the royal conspiracy swiftly decapitated the Antonescu regime by summoning and arresting the minister of defense, the minister of internal affairs, the chief of the gendarmerie, and the prefect of Bucharest. Only the chief of the SSI smelled a rat, and he alerted the German Military Mission. General Iosif Teodorescu, commanding the Capital Military

Command, was persuaded to lock down Bucharest. At 10:30 p.m., in a radio broadcast, King Mihai proclaimed the "only way to save the country from total catastrophe" was to abandon Nazi Germany. He declared a government of national unity and announced an armistice with the Soviet Union.[2]

The German-Romanian military divorce was initially cordial. General Heinz Guderian later claimed, "Rumanians deserted in large numbers to the enemy and turned their guns against the allies of yesterday."[3] This face-saving mischaracterization obscures a more complex reality. The officer corps was taken completely unawares by the royal coup, although General Racovița later claimed he knew of the conspiracy, to explain his prolonged absence from his command.[4] Commanders accepted Mihai I's action because the king was technically head of the military, and they were disillusioned with the German Army. General Dumitrescu informed General Friessner, "I cannot take another attitude than that which H. M. the King and the new government took."[5] Romanian resistance to Soviet forces disintegrated as units decided between continued resistance, capitulation, or escape as news of the armistice reached them. On 24 August, Second Lieutenant Ion Suța's battalion broke out of a Soviet encirclement. "The German captain, the battalion's commander, communicated to me in a very sober tone, but respectfully, 'Comrade, Romania betrayed and from 23 August fights against us,' and that, if I desire to go with them, I can go in their column that already had formed. We remained stupefied, myself and all the Romanian soldiers and officers grouped under my command. I could not understand why my superior commanders abandoned us."[6] Suța's unit went its own way but was soon captured. Soviet troops ambushed General Schwab and his driver as the VII Corps retreated. He committed suicide to avoid capture, one of the few Romanian officers to do so, probably because he feared terrible treatment in Soviet captivity as an ethnic German.[7] At Focșani, Colonel Panaite saw German and Romanian troops pass by for days. He was content to allow German soldiers "afraid even of their own shadow" pass unmolested, even after news that the German Luftwaffe had bombed Bucharest.[8] German air raids left seven dead, twenty-two wounded, and one hundred damaged buildings, a pinprick compared to previous US and British bombing, but the new government used these "terror attacks" to try to whip up public anger against the new foe.[9] Now that Nazi Germany had openly attacked Romania, on 25 August, the Ministry of Internal Affairs ordered soldiers and gendarmes to intern German soldiers.[10] Panaite started disarming German troops, but he did not detain any of them until Soviet patrols arrived in Focșani four days later. This gentlemanly truce on the front did not extend to the rear.

German forces were the first to attack their erstwhile Romanian ally. Instead of accepting Mihai I's offer to provide German forces safe passage to retreat, Hitler had ordered the German Military Mission to attack and to rescue Marshal Antonescu.[11] Yet of the thirty-five thousand German soldiers near Bucharest and Ploiești, just two to three thousand were combat troops, so Romanian troops easily blocked the German effort to seize the capital.[12] Romanian units then moved to intern German soldiers, airmen, and sailors from Constanța to Brașov.[13] Corporal Cârlan had been called up to help defend the FNB Line, but by the time he reported to his regiment in Brăila, it was guarding German captives instead. "Many among our soldiers looked on with sadness at these prisoners with whom until yesterday we were comrades in arms and now we treat them as enemies. There were however Romanian soldiers that during the night robbed them of wedding rings, watches, pens etc."[14] Meanwhile, Soviet armies continued to advance, to finish encircling the German Sixth Army. The Third Army tried fighting its way out over the Danube, but Soviet marines landed by sea and trapped the 9th Infantry Division near Sărata.[15] The Fourth Army kept ahead of Soviet forces only by leaving behind many soldiers and much equipment to be captured. Most of the German Eighth Army reached the Carpathians, but one German corps was encircled on the Prut on 29 August. The next day, the first Soviet units (including the Tudor Vladimirescu Division recruited from Romanian prisoners of war) paraded through Bucharest. Sergeant Ezechil's unit outside Bucharest was told, "[Soviet troops] will not forget about the conflict [we] had with them. They will try to provoke us to make a scene."[16] Mihail Sebastian noted Romanian civilians' mixed reaction to Soviet soldiers: "People in the street are still bewildered. Great explosions of enthusiasm, but also a certain reserve. Many passersby look askance at 'the applauding [kikes].'"[17] No one was exactly sure what the future held, because no armistice had yet been signed between Romania and the Soviet Union.

Soviet soldiers mimed the role of liberators, but Romanian troops saw them as occupiers. Colonel Panaite was forced to join celebratory meals with a Soviet general in Focșani. "Again good food and wine and good humor for him; as for us it is our sad, very sad heart." On 4 September, he scribbled, "I like the optimism [of] Lt. Col. Batoiu (He believes the Russians will be destroyed by [the] British)."[18] By now, some Romanian units had joined the Soviet attack into northern Transylvania. Major Rășănescu, now serving with the 3rd Motorized *Vânători* Regiment, had been caught and, "following threats even with pistols," disarmed, but the 1st Armored Division convinced the Soviet captors that it would be of greater use fighting the German enemy than being sent into captivity.[19] The German Sixth Army's resistance collapsed the next day. Nearly 200,000 German soldiers of German Army Group South Ukraine never left Romania.[20] The Third and Fourth Armies lost 8,305 killed, 24,989 wounded, and 153,884 missing before the signing of an armistice on 12 September.[21] Romania's holy war was over, but now it was forced to join the USSR's antifascist crusade.

Armistice

Romania had delayed negotiating an armistice for as long as possible, in part because the Antonescu regime feared that if it tried, Nazi Germany would occupy the country and replace the government with a Legionary puppet regime, but primarily because most Romanians abhorred the idea of the USSR seizing control of their homeland. In January 1943, the *conducător* had mentioned to the führer the idea of a compromise peace with the US and Britain, so that Nazi Germany could destroy the Soviet Union.[22] Hitler had dismissed the notion. In September 1943, after Allied landings in Sicily, the Antonescu regime had reached out on its own to US and British representatives. Marshal Antonescu instructed a diplomat assigned to Switzerland to inform Allied representatives that he had joined the Axis only to liberate northern Bukovina and Bessarabia (and strengthen claims on northern Transylvania), had been forced to advance to the Don, had not persecuted Jews, could not evacuate the Kuban bridgehead because his generals would be shot, and blocked Hitler from installing a Legionary puppet regime.[23] The Antonescu regime was already sowing the seeds of the myth that Romania was a reluctant ally of Nazi Germany. Mihai Antonescu and even Iuliu Maniu became obsessed with convincing the Anglo-Americans to land in the Balkans and preempt the Soviets from occupying Romania.[24] Politicians were not the only ones to hope the US would counterbalance the USSR in Romania. Second Lieutenant Crișan remembered, "[We] sensed that the war would soon come to an end and that the Americans would not allow Russia to take over Rumania. Why not? No one could say for sure why not."[25] American and British agents refused to deal with the Antonescu regime's diplomats in Turkey or Maniu's representatives in Egypt. Only when Soviet armies seemed poised to overrun Axis defenses in March 1944 did Romania finally contact the USSR, but negotiations in Sweden went nowhere.[26] If the king had not acted, Antonescu probably would not have agreed to an armistice.

Mihai I had been a willing figurehead until Stalingrad. In 1941, he visited the front at Țiganca and Odessa, promoted the *conducător* to marshal, received the Order of Mihai the Brave from Marshal Antonescu at the victory parade in Bucharest, and met with Hitler. To their credit, the king and Queen Mother Helen prevented some Romanian Jews from being deported to Transnistria and privately protested mass reprisals against Soviet Jews in Odessa. In 1942, Mihai visited the front in Crimea; however, he also opposed deporting Jews to Poland.[27] In February 1943, he invited members of the outlawed Liberal and National Peasant Parties to a royal hunting trip, which signaled his growing opposition to the Antonescu regime.[28] In March 1943, Antonescu chose General Sănătescu as chief of the military household. The *conducător* trusted him to keep the king informed about military events, as he now demanded, but isolated from political intrigues. Sănătescu commanded the Fourth Army headquarters between 11 February 1943 and 24 January 1944, so he had access to up-to-date information. At first, he mediated between Antonescu and Mihai I, but he soon put the king in contact with purged Carlist officers who saw the young monarch as a way back into power. Meanwhile, in 1943 and 1944, the king publicly expressed hopes for peace but also still backed the holy war.

Mihai launched his coup after a year of planning, and finally did what no one else was willing to do: make a deal with Stalin. The primary royal conspirators were General Sănătescu; General Gheorghe Mihail, former chief of staff; General Aurel Aldea, former minister of army endowment; and Colonel Dumitru Dămăceanu, chief of staff of the Capital Military Command.[29] In June 1944, outlawed parties, including the Romanian Communist Party, created the clandestine National Democratic Bloc to give the palace coup a democratic veneer.[30] The king did not trust the Romanian Army and had seen how quickly the German Army had occupied Italy and Hungary after those countries tried to leave the Axis. Therefore, he waited until the Red Army had broken through at the front to launch his coup. The provisions of the Soviet-Romanian armistice were appropriately harsh for an enemy that had joined the German invasion from the first day (Hungary and Finland both waited for Soviet attacks before declaring war), carried out atrocities across the USSR, and occupied Transnistria. After seeing Soviet newsreels, Mihail Sebastian wrote, "These Russian soldiers who walk the streets of Bucharest, with their childlike smile and their friendly churlishness, are real angels. How do they find the strength not to set everything on fire, not to kill and plunder, not to reduce to ashes this city that houses the mothers, wives, sisters, and lovers of those who killed, burned, and laid waste to their country?"[31] The armistice's twenty articles demanded, among other things, free movement for the Red Army, the turnover of Soviet prisoners of war, payment of Soviet occupation costs, reparations worth $300 million, punishment of war criminals, and dissolution of groups "of a Fascist type."[32] However, topping the list at Article 1, the Romanian Army had to field twelve divisions to help the Red Army fight the German Army.

Antifascist Crusade

Romania's alliance with the USSR against Nazi Germany proved unpopular. The new General Staff confronted significant challenges after the disaster on the Iași front: many soldiers who had escaped capture simply went home; vital equipment was lost; and Nazism, which it was now required to fight against, was not seen as a threat. Prime Minister General Sănătescu could not call on anticommunism or antisemitism, but he used nationalism and religion to motivate soldiers to fight to salvage something of Greater Romania. Article 19 of the armistice promised the return of "Transylvania or of the greater part of it" to Romania; however, Article 4 confirmed the loss of northern Bukovina and Bessarabia. Consequently, those *bucovineni* and *basarabeni* still in the Romanian Army had little incentive to keep fighting. The Third Army reported that *basarabeni* were asking to be demobilized or at least given leave to find their families and decide whether to resettle in Romania or remain in the Soviet Union.[33] In *Sentinela*'s third-to-last issue, Private Neață celebrates the king's proclamation and joins Soviet-Romanian troops attacking a Hungarian soldier in northern Transylvania. "Forward, comrades, for us the sun has risen!"[34] Soldiers were less enthusiastic in real life. Colonel Panaite spent 14 September reading the armistice's articles, each "one heavier than the other." Two days later in Bucharest, his battalion swore an oath to King Mihai. "The idiot from [headquarters] struggled to explain the oath and the allying with the U.S.S.R."[35] Soldiers were conditioned to follow orders whether they understood why they were still fighting or not.

A German-Hungarian offensive solidified support for the king and the armistice. The Third and Fourth Armies' remnants helped the Soviet Second Ukrainian Front (the equivalent of an army group) force the Transylvanian frontier. Sergeant Ezechil recalled bloody frontal attacks uphill against well-prepared defenses. "Many times, it occurred that our artillery fire did not synchronize itself with the advance of the troops. Because of this, projectiles fell many times on our own troops."[36] The General Staff remobilized the First Army to parry Axis thrusts on the western border. The Tirol Training Center sent the 988th, 989th, 990th, 998th, and 999th Independent Infantry Battalions into battle.[37] Second Lieutenant Crișan fled his post in Arad, evading Axis patrols until meeting Soviet forces. "Soon they were coming s from every direction, it seemed. It was the most amazing thing seen. An ocean of people marching!"[38] Soviet forces concentrated he First Army's screen and, beginning on 18 September, drove Axis forces back. Concurrently, Soviet-Romanian forces reached the Mureș River in northern Transylvania, and mountain troops stormed Târgu Mureș on 28 September. Some artillerymen scrawled "To the Tisa!" on guns as hopes rose that Romania might at least obtain its "natural" border in the west, if not the east.

Romanian holy war propaganda was replaced by Soviet antifascist crusade propaganda. Article 15 demanded an end to "hostile" propaganda, and Article 16 granted censorship powers to the Allied (Soviet) Control Commission. *Ecoul Crimeei* and *Armata* had already stopped printing, and now *Soldatul* and *Sentinela* followed suit. Soviet propaganda focused on crushing fascism and liberating workers, but these goals did not resonate with Romanian soldiers—except the Tudor Vladimirescu Division. The promise of adequate rations convinced ninety-eight hundred Romanian prisoners to "volunteer" to fight for the Red Army in October 1943.[39] Stalin had relaxed Soviet antireligious policy a month earlier, so Russian Orthodox priests blessed the Tudor Vladimirescu Division's colors when its soldiers swore an oath to Soviet-Romanian friendship.[40] Yet for most Romanian soldiers, Soviet propaganda was unpersuasive, especially with news of Soviet crimes in Romania. Second Lieutenant Teodorescu received letters from home reporting, "Three Russians, around 11 o'clock at night threatened with pistols and obligated us to open the door to them. They entered and circulated all over, continuously threatening with pistols. . . . They were wandering after [things] to steal."[41] Soviet soldiers in Romania looted, raped, and murdered to a degree German troops had never approached, undermining Romanian soldiers' morale at the front.

Discipline remained strict, but corporal punishment was again banned. On 28 September, General Racovița, now minister of defense, abrogated flogging regulations, declaring that "beating was always considered as a degrading punishment," and then, on 13 October, ordered, "I completely ban this brutal manner of punishing."[42] Although floggings ceased, unsanctioned beatings and slaps did not. Rehabilitation continued. The Tirol Training Center had sent five thousand soldiers to the front, but heavy losses resulted in all but the 999th Independent Infantry Battalion being disbanded.[43] Tirol had only thirteen hundred men left, mostly ethnic Hungarians in labor battalions, because it had released Jews and Slavic minorities.[44] General Sănătescu ended compulsory labor for Jews. The General Staff disbanded Jewish labor battalions, but it feared that Jews and other minorities might flood into the officer and NCO corps. The new chief of staff, General Mihail, suggested capping minority cadets in reserve officer and reserve NCO schools to 25 percent of each class.[45] Old prejudices did not disappear just because Romania had switched sides.

The Fourth Army helped break through Hungarian defenses in Transylvania, and Soviet-Romanian forces occupied Cluj on the way to the Tisa. The First Army followed Soviet troops across the Tisa to the southwest. On 20 October, an Axis counterattack with German panzers enveloped the Mindszent bridgehead, capturing the 4th Infantry Division, and five days later another Axis counterattack drove a panicked 2nd Infantry Division back over the river. Soviet-Romanian forces recovered and attacked toward Budapest. On 25 October, the Fourth Army helped finish liberating northern Transylvania.[46] It was not turned over to Romanian civilian rule but kept under Soviet military administration as leverage over the government in Bucharest.[47] Discipline kept soldiers fighting, even if they doubted the wisdom of continuing the antifascist crusade across the Tisa.

General Sănătescu attempted to use the armistice to Romania's advantage. He had fielded twenty-four divisions, hoping Romania might be recognized as a member of the Allies and secure better terms at the postwar peace treaty. The Stavka wanted to limit Romanian claims to being an important ally, create more combat-effective Romanian divisions, and remove any challenge to Soviet occupation in Romania. On 26 October, the Allied (Soviet) Control Commission halved the Romanian Army and disbanded the Third Army, along with the Cavalry, Mountain, Mechanized, I, III, and V Corps.[48] General Sănătescu protested that twelve divisions was a minimum, not a maximum, contribution according to the armistice. General Rodion Malinovsky, the Soviet Second Ukrainian Front commander, allowed two additional divisions to be sent to the front and the Guard Division to remain mobilized in Bucharest. Malinovsky also instructed the Romanian Communist Party to arm a "Patriotic Guard" and establish the National Democratic Front, excluding the Liberal and National Peasant Parties, on Stalin's orders. Many in Mihai I's clique felt betrayed by the Anglo-Americans, whom they expected to offer protection from Sovietization.[49] The General Staff compiled reports on Soviet atrocities, hoping to win Anglo-American support. Soviet crimes consisted mostly of theft—the scale of rape and murder never came close to what occurred later in Hungary and Germany.[50] The Allied (Soviet) Control Commission began seizing goods, materials, industrial infrastructure, and other items as reparations. Unlike Romanians' grumblings about the Germans acting like occupiers, the Soviets were true occupiers.

Romanian soldiers endured a difficult winter. On 1 November, the Fourth Army reached the Tisa. The First Army lost operational control of its forces, and the VII Corps was plugged into a Soviet army that fought into Budapest's eastern suburbs on 7 November. Artillerymen now plaintively chalked "We crossed the Tisa" on their guns as 210,006 Romanian soldiers fought in Hungary.[51] On 23 November, the Fourth Army started a monthlong effort to push into Slovakia, even as Soviet confiscation of Romanian trains exacerbated supply shortages. On 5 December, the Romanian Communist Party forced General Sănătescu to resign. He switched positions with chief of staff General Nicolae Rădescu.[52] The Antonescu regime had imprisoned Rădescu at Târgu Jiu for a year for outspoken anti-German comments, so he could not be accused of being a fascist. Rădescu raised the Romanian Army's frontline strength to 248,430 soldiers.[53] A month earlier, the 2nd Mountain Division had been demobilized, but now it was remobilized. Second Lieutenant Teodorescu recalled they departed for the front in worse spirits and conditions than for Operation Barbarossa, Case Blue, or reconquering northern Transylvania. "Our 'mastery' had changed. It no longer mattered to them that in two days was Christmas Eve, which for some families could also have been the last in which they would have been together. Presence on the front was not pressing. Then, in full winter, for our new 'mastery,' it probably no longer mattered the conditions in which the fighters were traveling."[54] Fighting in Slovakia was bloody. Romanian troops attacked uphill against dug-in German soldiers, and when they crested a ridge they faced a new line of defenses on the next height. The Fourth Army made slow progress in the mountains. Starting on New Year's, the VII Corps participated in a Soviet assault on Budapest. On 16 January 1945, two kilometers from the Danube, the Soviet Second Ukrainian Front pulled the VII Corps off the line and sent it to Slovakia, so Romanian troops would not share in the victory when the city fell a few weeks later.[55] On 8 February, the General Staff reported morale in the Fourth Army was "near zero," and some soldiers fatalistically exposed themselves to enemy fire, saying, "Let it end already, however it will be, dead or crippled. The country forgot us. Only we have the duty to die for it."[56] The Tirol Training Center (rechristened on 14 February the Tirol Camp for Reeducation of Condemned Soldiers) kept sending rehabilitation soldiers to the front, including a few Legionaries.[57] Romanian soldiers' motivation was probably at its lowest point of the whole war.

Some Romanian soldiers captured by the German Army agreed to fight the Red Army. German recruiters approached hundreds of Romanian officers and NCOs who had been in Nazi Germany for training when Romania abandoned the Axis. Captain "Hetman" Tobă jumped at the chance to fight. Many Romanian soldiers captured in Hungary, including the 4th Infantry Division commander General Chirnoagă, also agreed. A few Romanian soldiers even deserted to join the German enemy, like Captain Ilie Sturdza. He was a translator for the Fourth Army, commanded by his father-in-law General Avramescu, and deserted with some Iron Guardists to join a Romanian "government in exile," in which his father, Prince Mihail Sturdza, was minister of foreign affairs. Nazi Germany established this puppet regime under Horia Sima in Vienna.[58] Chirnoagă became minister of defense. The "National Army" grew to six thousand Romanian soldiers used for labor. The Waffen-SS decided to recruit a combat division from Romanian prisoners, eventually organizing three grenadier regiments, but only one saw battle (and it was destroyed defending Pomerania).[59] These Romanian turncoats and diehard fascists were a reminder, if any was required, to Soviet commanders that the Romanian Army had been their most determined enemy after the German Army.

The NKVD went so far as to arrest, and possibly execute, a Romanian general. Article 14 of the armistice required Romania to apprehend and prosecute war criminals. Marshal Antonescu and the others arrested during the royal coup were delivered to the NKVD and flown to Moscow. More arrests followed, including Generals Șteflea, Trestioreanu, Korne, and Cialâk, but they were imprisoned in Bucharest. On 12 February 1945, the People's Tribunal in Bucharest had General Macici, then commanding the First Army, arrested; he was replaced by General Vasile Anastasiu. The Soviet Second Ukrainian Front had been shuffling command of the Fourth Army between Generals Avramescu and Dăscălescu.[60] On 2 March, during his second stint commanding the Fourth Army, Avramescu and his chief of staff General Dragomir were arrested by the NKVD. Because his son-in-law had deserted to the Legionary government in Vienna, and he had his wife and daughter with him on the front, the NKVD became convinced Avramescu was sabotaging the Fourth Army's attacks and was planning to desert. They arrested his family the following day. His daughter committed suicide, but his wife survived eleven years in Siberia. The official Soviet report says a German aircraft killed Avramescu on 3 March, but a Soviet bullet seems more likely.[61] His disappearance was shrouded in mystery at the time, frightening the already demoralized officer corps.

With Nazi Germany's defeat in sight, Stalin moved to install a pro-communist Romanian government. On 6 March, Petru Groza, leader of the socialist Ploughman's Front that had allied with the Romanian Communist

Party, became prime minister. General Sănătescu remained chief of staff; however, an increasingly pro-communist General Vasiliu-Rășcanu became minister of defense. On 13 March, General Malinovsky transferred control of northern Transylvania to Groza, to bolster his popularity.[62] On 19 March, Groza passed a law allowing officers or NCOs to be retired "if they surpass army staff needs." Quickly 70 generals, 1,878 officers, 4,081 NCOs, and 1,139 specialists were purged.[63] Additionally, Malinovsky moved the Tudor Vladimirescu Division from Slovakia to Bucharest. The following month, the Red Army organized the Horia, Cloșca, and Crișan Division (named after Romanians who led a peasant uprising in Transylvania in 1784) from Romanian prisoners of war, commanded by General Lascăr, which was also assigned to the capital. The First and Fourth Armies' combat effectiveness precipitously declined, as they could not replace equipment or soldiers lost in battles in Slovakia. Corporal Cârlan became a telephone operator because all radios had broken down, and then he became a rifleman, owing to the desperate need for replacements. On 18 April, after a German counterattack was repulsed, his colonel told him, "Look, Cârlan, for the way how you've done your duty until now, the country gifts you a wristwatch. Wear it with luck!"[64] The Soviet Second Ukrainian Front sent the 2nd Tank Regiment over the Danube into Austria and then the Czech Protectorate.[65] The First and Fourth Armies, down to 172,081 men, finally crossed the Czech border around 1 May.[66] At 4 a.m. on 9 May, as his column neared Brno, Cârlan saw antiaircraft fire, spotlights, and rockets. Then shouts of "Krieg Kaput!" informed him the war was over. "I cannot describe the joy that I felt when I found out this news. My heart beat so hard, that I held my hand on my chest from fear, as if, to not break me. But the tears!"[67] His unit had no time to celebrate, because it had orders to help round up Russian auxiliaries who had been fighting for the German Army hiding in the mountains. Finally, on 12 May, the First and Fourth Armies halted one hundred kilometers from Prague. Romania's part in the antifascist crusade had ended.

Aftermath

Romania's butcher's bill on the eastern front was high. The Romanian Army suffered 71,585 dead, 243,622 wounded or sick, and 309,533 missing (including over 120,000 captured by the Soviets after the royal coup but before the signing of the armistice) during the holy war between 22 June 1941 and 23 August 1944.[68] The Red Army recorded taking 187,367 Romanian prisoners of war, and 132,000 were repatriated by 1956—for a mortality rate of

29 percent during captivity.[69] The remaining 120,000 missing were unidentified dead. The Antonescu regime was responsible for th of 300,000 Romanian and Soviet Jews in Bukovina, Bessarabia, an nistria. (The Horthy regime sent another 132,000 Romanian Jews from northern Transylvania to their deaths at Auschwitz.) Romanian soldiers also helped round up and murder tens of thousands of Soviet Jews east of the Bug, particularly in Crimea. Only 50,000 of 125,000 to 145,000 Romanian Jews deported to Transnistria in 1941 returned in 1944.[70] The number of Soviet Jews who survived in Transnistria was probably comparable. Of 25,000 Gypsies deported by the Antonescu regime in 1942, historians estimate half died by 1944.[71] The Romanian Army lost another 21,035 killed, 90,344 wounded or sick, and 58,443 missing during the antifascist crusade between 24 August 1944 and 9 May 1945.[72] By the end of the Second World War, only 300,000 Jews, or less than half the prewar Jewish population of Greater Romania, had survived.[73]

People's Tribunals in Bucharest and Cluj offered token justice to Jewish victims. While 2,700 cases were identified, only half were prosecuted. Moreover, just 187 people were sentenced by the People's Tribunal in Bucharest, which focused on war crimes by Romanians, compared to 481 people by the People's Tribunal in Cluj, which dealt with war crimes by Hungarians.[74] The People's Tribunal in Bucharest tried soldiers, gendarmes, prefects, and civilians in May, June, and July 1945, including General Topor, for directing military police to help "cleanse the terrain" in northern Bukovina and Bessarabia; General Calotescu, for crimes as governor of Bessarabia; General Trestioreanu, for the Odessa massacre; General Macici, also for the Odessa massacre; and Lieutenant Colonel Isopescu, for mass executions in Golta County in Transnistria. Most received long prison sentences; the king commuted Macici's death sentence. Some officers were arrested but released for lack of evidence, like Generals Iacobici, Dumitrescu, and Dăscălescu, although all had ordered reprisals targeting Jews, partisans, and civilians. In April 1946, Antonescu and twenty-three other high-ranking members of his regime and the Legionary movement were put on trial. The prosecutors blamed the *conducător* for the war and highlighted crimes against Jews, Gypsies, and religious sects. However, the trial backfired. Most Romanians saw Antonescu's defense as dignified and honorable. Iuliu Maniu even testified on his behalf at the trial. On 17 May, the court ruled that thirteen of the accused (including six Legionary leaders in absentia) should be executed. King Mihai tried to commute all the death sentences to life in prison, but he succeeded only with General Pantazi and two others.[75] On 1 June, a firing squad shot Marshal Antonescu, Mihai Antonescu, General Vasiliu, and

Gheorghe Alexianu. The *conducător* immediately became an anticommunist martyr.[76] This concluded the People's Tribunals' work.

Communist courts punished more war criminals over the years. On 30 December 1947, Prime Minister Groza forced the king to abdicate and go into exile before declaring the Romanian Socialist Republic. The Romanian Communist Party took power soon afterward. Between 1948 and 1956 new war crimes trials imprisoned generals like Racovița, Ciupercă, Constantinescu-Claps, and Korne. Constantinescu-Claps managed to have his sentence of fifteen years' hard labor, for ordering a group of partisans hanged, reduced owing to testimony of Jews from Bacău who credited him with protecting Jews in Moldavia from being persecuted when the front came again to Romania in 1944.[77] Others, like General Iacobici, were rearrested and reimprisoned, and later died in prison. A few died before being tried, like General Dumitrescu, or escaped punishment, like General Dăscălescu, who lived in a peasant hut in the countryside for the rest of his life. While the Romanian Communist Party used war crimes trials for political purposes, these men were guilty. In fact, more soldiers should have been held responsible for the multitude of war crimes committed by the Romanian Army on the eastern front.

Romania's Holy War

Romania's holy war fit comfortably within Nazi Germany's European crusade against Bolshevism. Nationalism, religion, antisemitism, and anticommunism formed the basis of the close collaboration between the Romanian Army and the German Army on the battlefield against the Red Army. Additionally, ideology explains why Romanian soldiers, and gendarmes, were more than willing to follow orders to "cleanse the terrain" in northern Bukovina and Bessarabia and cooperate with SS troops to implement the Final Solution in the Soviet Union. The Soviet occupation of northern Bukovina and Bessarabia was much more traumatic to Romania than the subsequent Hungarian occupation of northern Transylvania or the Bulgarian occupation of southern Dobruja. This galvanized Romanians to support the Antonescu regime and its decision to join the Axis. Romanian soldiers were highly motivated to fight and commit atrocities when the invasion of the USSR commenced. Romanian soldiers remained motivated after liberating northern Bukovina and Bessarabia and crossing into Ukraine, because army propaganda reminded them why they were fighting, and officers used strict discipline to maintain unit cohesion as primary groups were destroyed in battles. Although poor training, lack of heavy weapons, and shortages of equipment limited the combat effectiveness of the Romanian Army, it was the German Army's most valued ally on the eastern front and made a vital contribution to its campaigns in Ukraine, Crimea, the Caucasus, and southern Russia. Romanian troops committed atrocities against Soviet prisoners of war, partisans, and civilians throughout the fighting. The Romanian Army's morale varied between units and fluctuated over time, influencing its motivation, but it remained sound until after the Soviet victory at Stalingrad and the German defeat at Kursk. Only then did poor morale begin to significantly undermine motivation. The amalgamation of Romanian and German units enabled Axis forces to defend the Kuban bridgehead and the Crimea peninsula. The Romanian Army made one final effort to defend Romania from the Red Army, but the German Army had become too weak to prop up its ally, and the whole house of cards soon collapsed. Romania joined the USSR's antifascist crusade under duress, and morale dipped ever lower as the Romanian Army advanced into northern Transylvania, Hungary, and Slovakia. After the Second World War, the script was flipped, creating the myth of Romania as a reluctant member of the Axis and an enthusiastic convert to the Allies that has endured for nearly eight decades. Hopefully, this book finally dispels that fable.

NOTES

Introduction

1. Teodor Halic and Iuliu Dobrin, interview with the author, Bucharest, 2009.
2. Marin Ştefanescu, interview with the author, Târgu Mureş, 2012.
3. Horst Boog et al., *Germany and the Second World War*, vol. 4, *The Attack on the Soviet Union*, trans. Dean S. McMurry, Ewald Osers, and Louise Willmot (Oxford: Clarendon, 1996), 408.
4. Geoffrey P. Megargee, *War of Annihilation: Combat and Genocide on the Eastern Front, 1941* (Plymouth, UK: Rowman & Littlefield, 2006), xi, 5–7, 33–39.
5. ACNSAS, Fond Documentar, dosar 8178, f. 11.
6. Matatias Carp, *Holocaust in Rumania: Facts and Documents on the Annihilation of Rumania's Jews—1940–1944*, trans. Seán Murphy (Budapest: Primor, 1994).
7. Gavin Bowd, *Memoria războiului, 1941–1945* (Bucharest: Editura Pro Historia, 2006), 30.
8. Alexandru Cretzianu, *Relapse into Bondage: Political Memories of a Romanian Diplomat* (Iaşi: Center for Romanian Studies, 1998); Raul Bossy, *Recollections of a Romanian Diplomat, 1918–1969: Diaries and Memoirs of Raoul V. Bossy*, ed. and trans. G. H. Bossy and M.-A. Bossy (Stanford, CA: Hoover Institution, 2003).
9. Heinz Guderian, *Panzer Leader*, trans. Constantin Fitzgibbon (Cambridge, MA: Da Capo, 1996), 367; Erich von Manstein, *Lost Victories*, ed. and trans. Anthony G. Powell (St. Paul, MN: Zenith, 2004), 206–8; Johannes Friessner, *Verratene Schlachten: Die Tragödie der deutschen Wehrmacht in Rumänien und Ungarn* (Hamburg: Holsten-Verlag, 1956), 44–50.
10. Platon Chirnoagă, *Istoria politică şi militară a răsboiului României contra Rusiei sovietice, 22 iunie 1941–23 august 1944*, 2nd ed. (Madrid: Editura Carpatii, 1986), 131–34.
11. Michel Sturdza, *The Suicide of Europe: Memoirs of Prince Michel Sturdza, Former Foreign Minister of Rumania* (Belmont, MA: Western Islands, 1968), xxv–xxvi.
12. Bowd, *Memoria războiului*, 67.
13. Aurel Kareţki and Maria Covaci, *Zile însângerate la Iaşi (28–30 iunie 1941)* (Bucharest: Editura Politică, 1978).
14. Jean Ancel, ed., *Documents concerning the Fate of Romanian Jewry during the Holocaust* (New York: Beate Klarsfeld Foundation, 1986).
15. Maria Bucur, *Heroes and Victims: Remembering War in Twentieth-Century Romania* (Bloomington: Indiana University Press, 2009), 232–37.
16. Mark Axworthy, Cornell Scafes, and Christian Craciunoiu, *Third Axis, Fourth Ally: Romanian Armed Forces in the European War, 1941–1945* (St. Petersburg, FL: Hailer, 1995), 10, 355.

17. Alex Mihai Stoenescu, *Armata, mareșalul și evreii* (Bucharest: Editura RAO, 2010).

18. Minority Rights Information System, *Final Report of the International Commission on the Holocaust in Romania*, 306, http://miris.eurac.edu/mugs2/do/blob.pdf?type=pdf&serial=1117716572750.

19. Vladimir Solonari, *Purifying the Nation: Population Exchange and Ethnic Cleansing in Nazi-Allied Romania* (Washington, DC: Woodrow Wilson Center, 2010), 171–77.

20. Diana Dumitru, *The State, Antisemitism, and Collaboration in the Holocaust: The Borderlands of Romania and the Soviet Union* (New York: Cambridge University Press, 2016), 4.

21. Jean Ancel, *The History of the Holocaust in Romania* (Lincoln: University of Nebraska Press, 2011), 152–53, 179–83, 217, 229.

22. Alesandru Duțu, *Armata română în război, 1941–1945* (Bucharest: Editura Enciclopedică, 2016), 110, 131.

23. Karl-Heinz Frieser et al., *Germany and the Second World War*, vol. 8, *The Eastern Front 1943–1944: The War in the East and on the Neighbouring Fronts*, trans. Barry Smerin and Barbara Wilson (Oxford: Clarendon, 2007), 232.

24. John A. Lynn, *Bayonets of the Republic: Motivation and Tactics in the Army of Revolutionary France, 1791–1794* (Boulder, CO: Westview, 1996), 35.

25. Ibid., 23–25.
26. Ibid., 30.
27. Ibid., 26.
28. Ibid., 26–30.
29. Ibid., 36.
30. Ibid., 36–37.
31. Ibid., 35–36.

32. David A. Bell, *The First Total War: Napoleon's Europe and the Birth of Warfare as We Know It* (New York: Houghton Mifflin, 2007), 5, 7–8.

33. Isabel V. Hull, *Absolute Destruction: Military Culture and the Practices of War in Imperial Germany* (Ithaca, NY: Cornell University Press, 2005), 100.

34. Alexander Watson, *Enduring the Great War: Combat, Morale and the Collapse in the German and British Armies, 1914–1918* (Cambridge: Cambridge University Press, 2008), 140.

35. ANIC, Fond Ministerul de Război: Cabinetul Ministrului, dosar 137 vol. 1, f. 182, 342; ANIC, Fond Ministerul de Război: Inspectoratul General al Armatei, dosar 75, f. 85–90, 155–61.

36. ANIC, Fond Ministerul de Război: Cabinetul Ministrului, dosar 256, f. 85–89.

37. Gary Sheffield, *Command and Morale: The British Army on the Western Front, 1914–1918* (South Yorkshire, UK: Praetorian, 2014), 154.

38. Ibid., 158.

39. Vasile Scârneci, *Viața și moartea în linia întâi: Jurnal și însemnări de război, 1916–1920, 1941–1943* (Bucharest: Editura Militară, 2013).

40. Evsevie M. Ionescu, *Însemnări din război: Jurnalul unui sergent (1941–1944)* (Bucharest: Editura Militară, 2005).

41. Ștefan Cârlan, *Păstrați-mi amintirile! Jurnal de război (1942–1945)* (Bucharest: Editura Militară, 2007).

42. Constantin Pantazi, *Cu mareșalul până la moarte: Memorii* (Bucharest: Editura Publiferom, 1999); Ion Grosu, *Memoriile unui ofițer de informații* (Bucharest: Editura Militară, 2009).

43. Gheorghe Rășcănescu, *Erou la Cotul Donului: Însemări din război, 1941–1944* (Bucharest: Editura Militară, 2017); Dumitru Păsat, *Memoriile căpitanului Dumitru Păsat, 1941–1945* (Bucharest: Humanitas, 2015).

44. George F. Wieland, *Bessarabian Knight: A Peasant Caught between the Red Star and the Swastika: Immanuel Weiss's True Story* (Lincoln, NE: American Historical Society of Germans from Russia, 1991); Sigmund Heinz Landau, *Goodbye, Transylvania: A Romanian Waffen-SS Soldier in WWII* (Mechanicsburg, PA: Stackpole Books, 1985); George Crisan, *An Amazing Life: Escape from Romania* (New York: Vantage, 1990).

45. Emilian Ezechil, *La porțile infernului: 1941–1945* (Bucharest: Tritonic, 2008); Dumitru Teodorescu, *Mândria vânătorului de munte* (Baia Mare: Editura Marist, 2013); Gheorghe Netejoru, *Și eu am luptat în est: Spovedania unui fost prizonier de război* (Bucharest: Editura Militară, 2010).

46. Quoted in Pavel Moraru, *Armata lui Stalin văzută de români* (Bucharest: Editura Militară, 2006), 36, 39.

47. Quoted in Boog et al., *Germany and the Second World War*, 4:407.

48. Boog et al., *Germany and the Second World War*, vol. 6, *The Global War: Widening of the Conflict into a World War and the Shift of the Initiative 1941–1943*, trans. Ewald Osers et al. (Oxford: Clarendon, 2001), 110.

49. Grant Harward, "First among Un-equals: Challenging German Stereotypes of the Romanian Army during the Second World War," *Journal of Slavic Military Studies* 24, no. 3 (July 2011): 439–80.

50. Richard L. DiNardo, *Germany and the Axis Powers: From Coalition to Collapse* (Lawrence: University Press of Kansas, 2005), 105, 120, 146.

51. Ibid., 148–49.

52. Ibid., 131–32.

53. Antony Beevor, *Stalingrad, the Fateful Siege: 1942–1943* (New York: Penguin Books, 1998), 83.

54. Holly Case, *Between States: The Transylvanian Question and the European Idea during World War II* (Stanford, CA: Stanford University Press, 2009), 185, 95.

55. Ibid., 79–82.

56. For criticism see Ion Popa, *The Romanian Orthodox Church and the Holocaust* (Bloomington: Indiana University Press, 2017); for celebration see Gheorghe Nicolescu, Gheorghe Dobrescu, and Andrei Nicolescu, eds., *Preoți în tranșee: 1941–1945* (Bucharest: Fundația General Ștefan Gușă, 1999).

57. Compare Axworthy, Scafes, and Craciunoiu, *Third Axis, Fourth Ally*, 140–44, with Ancel, *History of the Holocaust in Romania*, 8–20.

58. Very similar to the role it played in Nazi Germany's war of annihilation; see Yitzhak Arad, *The Holocaust in the Soviet Union* (Lincoln: University of Nebraska Press, 2009), 67, 71.

59. Cornel Scafeș et al., *Armata română, 1941–1945* (Bucharest: Editura R.A.I., 1996), 14–16, and Duțu, *Armata română în război*, 7.

60. Axworthy, Scafes, and Craciunoiu, *Third Axis, Fourth Ally*, 61.

61. Mark Axworthy, "Peasant Scapegoat to Industrial Slaughter: The Romanian Soldier at the Siege of Odessa," in *Time to Kill: The Soldier's Experience of War in the West, 1939–1945*, ed. Paul Addison and Angus Calder (London: Pimlico, 1997), 231.

62. Ancel, *History of the Holocaust in Romania*, 62–65.

63. Mioara Anton, *Propagandă și război, 1941–1944* (Bucharest: Tritonic, 2007), 184–238.

64. Ibid., 116.

65. Axworthy, "Peasant Scapegoat to Industrial Slaughter," 229.

66. Omer Bartov, *Hitler's Army: Soldiers, Nazis, and War in the Third Reich* (Oxford: Oxford University Press, 1992), 60–61.

67. Allan Millett and Williamson Murray, eds., *Military Effectiveness*, 2nd ed., vol. 1, *The First World War* (Cambridge: Cambridge University Press, 2010), 2–3.

68. Götz Aly, *Hitler's Beneficiaries: Plunder, Racial War, and the Nazi Welfare State* (New York: Holt Paperback, 2006), 152–55, 224–43.

69. Lynn, *Bayonets of the Republic*, 38–39.

70. Axworthy, Scafes, and Craciunoiu, *Third Axis, Fourth Ally*, 27–40.

71. Anton, *Propagandă și război*, 188.

1. Ideology of Holy War

1. Nicholas M. Nagy-Talavera, *The Green Shirts and the Others* (Iași: Center for Romanian Studies, 2001), 344–45.

2. Robert O. Paxton, *The Anatomy of Fascism* (New York: Knopf, 2004), 42–43.

3. Similar to dynamics among German soldiers; see Christopher Browning, *Ordinary Men: Reserve Police Battalion 101 and the Final Solution in Poland* (New York: Harper Perennial, 1998), 184–85.

4. Bartov, *Hitler's Army*, 34.

5. Maria Bucur, *Eugenics and Modernization in Interwar Romania* (Pittsburgh: University of Pittsburgh Press, 2002), 2–4; Solonari, *Purifying the Nation*, 62.

6. Alexander Dallin, *Odessa, 1941–1944: A Case Study of Soviet Territory under Foreign Rule* (Iași: Center for Romanian Studies, 1998), 255–56, 263–64.

7. Ioan Scurtu, ed., *Pe marginea prăpastiei: 21–23 ianuarie 1941*, vol. 1 (Bucharest: Editura Scripia, 1992), 130.

8. Dennis Deletant, *Hitler's Forgotten Ally: Ion Antonescu and His Regime, Romania 1940–1944* (New York: Palgrave Macmillan, 2006), 79, 86.

9. Keith Hitchins, *The Romanians, 1774–1866* (Oxford: Clarendon, 1996), 27, 163–67.

10. Radu R. Florescu, *The Struggle against Russia in the Romanian Principalities, 1821–1854* (Iași: Center for Romanian Studies, 1997), 99–117; Hitchins, *Romanians*, 199–214.

11. Hitchins, *Romanians*, 185–97.

12. Ibid., 231–49.

13. Ibid., 293–94.

14. Benedict Anderson, *Imagined Communities: Reflections on the Origin and Spread of Nationalism*, rev. ed. (London: Verso, 2006), 36–38, 43–46.

15. Keith Hitchins, *Rumania, 1866–1947* (Oxford: Clarendon, 1994), 9.

NOTES TO PAGES 20-25

16. Hitchins, *Romanians*, 304–16; Hitchins, *Rumania*, 11–14.

17. Alex Drace-Francis, *The Making of Modern Romanian Culture: Literacy and the Development of National Identity* (London: Tauris Academic Studies, 2006), 166.

18. Constantin Bărbulescu, *România medicilor: Medici, țărani și igienă rurală în România de la 1860 la 1910* (Bucharest: Humanitas, 2015), 256.

19. Hitchins, *Rumania*, 171.

20. Bărbulescu, *România medicilor*, 334.

21. Hitchins, *Rumania*, 167–69; Henry L. Roberts, *Rumania: Political Problems of an Agrarian State* (New Haven, CT: Yale University Press, 1951), 3–4.

22. The number of dead remains contested, officially two thousand to twenty-five hundred, but possibly as much as eleven thousand; see Petre Otu, *Mareșalul Alexandru Averescu: Militarul, omul politic, legenda* (Bucharest: Editura Militară, 2009), 59.

23. Hitchins, *Rumania*, 179–80.

24. Ioan Scurtu, *Istoria românilor în timpul celor patru regi*, vol. 2, *Ferdinand I* (Bucharest: Editura Enciclopedică, 2011), 39.

25. Hitchins, *Rumania*, 222–23.

26. Irina Livezeanu, *Cultural Politics in Greater Romania: Regionalism, Nation Building, and Ethnic Struggle, 1918–1930* (Ithaca, NY: Cornell University Press, 1995), 51–56, 93–97.

27. Charles King, *The Moldovans: Romania, Russia, and the Politics of Culture* (Stanford, CA: Hoover Institution, 1999), 28–35.

28. Livezeanu, *Cultural Politics in Greater Romania*, 10, 12.

29. Ștefan Cristian Ionescu, *Jewish Resistance to "Romanianization," 1940–44* (New York: Palgrave Macmillan, 2015), 8–11.

30. Colonel C. Cepleanu, "Educațiunea națională (Conferința ținută ofițerilor din regimental 'Mihai Viteazul Nr. 6' în ziua de 16 Februarie 1927)," *România militară* 59, no. 9 (September 1927): 25.

31. Dimitrie Gusti, ed., *Enciclopedia României*, vol. 1 (Bucharest: Imprimeria Națională, 1938), 144.

32. Charles Upson Clark, *Greater Romania* (New York: Dodd, Mead, 1922), folded map insert.

33. Dennis Deletant, *Romania under Communist Rule* (Iași: Center for Romanian Studies, 1999), 12.

34. Hitchins, *Romanians*, 36.

35. Drace-Francis, *Making of Modern Romanian Culture*, 54–55.

36. Lucian N. Leustean, *Orthodoxy and the Cold War: Religion and Political Power in Romania, 1947–65* (New York: Palgrave Macmillan, 2009), 13.

37. Hitchins, *Romanians*, 313–14.

38. Lucian N. Leustean, "'For the Glory of Romanians': Orthodoxy and Nationalism in Greater Romania, 1918–1945," *Journal of Nationalism and Ethnicity* 35, no. 4 (August 2007): 718.

39. Ibid., 720.

40. Ibid., 723–24.

41. Gusti, *Enciclopedia României*, 1:422.

42. Livezeanu, *Cultural Politics in Greater Romania*, 135.

43. Leustean, "'For the Glory of Romanians,'" 727–28.

44. Roland Clark, "Nationalism, Ethnotheology, and Mysticism in Interwar Romania," *Carl Beck Papers*, no. 2002 (September 2009): 17.
45. Roland Clark, *Holy Legionary Youth: Fascist Activism in Interwar Romania* (Ithaca, NY: Cornell University Press, 2015), 122, 128–30.
46. Quoted in Ilie Manole, ed., *Armata și biserica* (Bucharest: Colecția "Revista de Istorie Militară" 1996), 172–73. Emphasis in original.
47. Marian Moșneagu, Petrișor Florea, and Dan Prisăcaru, coords., *Armata română și cultele* (Brăila: Editura Istros, 2014), 139.
48. Locot. Gh. Popovici, "Pericolul 'adventist' în armata," *România militară* 56, no. 9 (September 1924): 82.
49. Quoted in Manole, *Armata și biserica*, 181.
50. Alesandru Duțu, Florica Dobre, and Leonida Loghin, *Armata română în al doilea război mondial, 1941–1945: Dicționar enciclopedic* (Bucharest: Editura Enciclopedică, 1999), 89.
51. Ancel, *History of the Holocaust in Romania*, 44–49; Popa, *Romanian Orthodox Church and the Holocaust*, 31.
52. Andrei Oișteanu, *Inventing the Jew: Antisemitic Stereotypes in Romanian and Other Central-East European Cultures* (Lincoln: University of Nebraska Press, 2009), 315–19, 228–34.
53. For an overview of the history of blood libel see Helmut Walser Smith, *The Butcher's Tale: Murder and Anti-Semitism in a German Town* (New York: W. W. Norton, 2002), 91–133.
54. Oișteanu, *Inventing the Jew*, 408, 410.
55. Carol Iancu, *Evreii din România: De la excludere la emancipare* (Bucharest: Hasefer, 2009), 46.
56. Oișteanu, *Inventing the Jew*, 411.
57. Debórah Dwork and Robert Jan van Pelt, *Holocaust: A History* (New York: W. W. Norton, 2002), 24.
58. Oișteanu, *Inventing the Jew*, 11.
59. Carole Fink, *Defending the Rights of Others: The Great Powers, the Jews, and International Minority Protection, 1878–1938* (Cambridge: Cambridge University Press, 2004), 5.
60. Quoted in Bărbulescu, *România medicilor*, 233.
61. Iancu, *Evreii din România*, 232–33.
62. Ibid., 239.
63. Ibid., 148.
64. Ibid., 285.
65. Paul Hanebrink, *A Specter Haunting Europe: The Myth of Judeo-Bolshevism* (Cambridge, MA: Belknap Press of Harvard University Press, 2018), 53–54.
66. Ancel, *History of the Holocaust in Romania*, 84.
67. Ezra Mendelsohn, *The Jews of East Central Europe between the World Wars* (Bloomington: Indiana University Press, 1983), 173.
68. Iancu, *Evreii din România*, 150; Livezeanu, *Cultural Politics in Greater Romania*, 10.
69. Livezeanu, *Cultural Politics in Greater Romania*, 243.
70. Clark, *Holy Legionary Youth*, 28–31, 57–58.
71. Quoted in Horia Bozdoghină, *Antisemitismul lui A. C. Cuza în politica românească* (Bucharest: Curtea Veche, 2012), 95.

72. Ibid., 107, 134–35.
73. Dumitru, *State, Antisemitism, and Collaboration in the Holocaust*, 77.
74. Bozdoghină, *Antisemitismul lui A. C. Cuza în politica românească*, 173.
75. Ibid., 166–70.
76. Lucian Nastasă-Kovacs, ed., *Pogromul itinerant sau decembrie antisemit: Oradea, 1927* (Bucharest: Curtea Veche, 2014), 74–76.
77. Dumitru, *State, Antisemitism, and Collaboration in the Holocaust*, 84.
78. Michael Stivelman, *The Death March* (Rio de Janeiro: Editora Nova Frontiera, 1997), 76.
79. Pavel Moraru, *La hotarul românesc al Europei: Din istoria siguranței generale în Basarabia, 1918–1940* (Bucharest: Institutul Național Pentru Studiul Totalitarismului, 2008), 163–67; Dumitru, *State, Antisemitism, and Collaboration in the Holocaust*, 91.
80. Quoted in Paul A. Shapiro, "Faith, Murder, Resurrection: The Iron Guard and the Romanian Orthodox Church," in *Antisemitism, Christian Ambivalence, and the Holocaust*, ed. Kevin P. Spicer (Bloomington: Indiana University Press, 2007), 150.
81. Glenn E. Torrey, *The Romanian Battlefront in World War I* (Lawrence: University Press of Kansas, 2011), 268–70.
82. Ibid., 275–78.
83. Quoted in Marin C. Stănescu, *Armata română și unirea Basarabiei și Bucovinei cu România, 1917–1919* (Constanța: Ex Ponto, 1999), 231.
84. Quoted in Petre Otu, *Mareșalul Constantin Prezan: Vocația datoriei* (Bucharest: Editura Militară, 2008), 279.
85. Torrey, *Romanian Battlefront in World War I*, 323–24; Laura Engelstein, *Russia in Flames: War, Revolution, Civil War, 1914–1921* (New York: Oxford University Press, 2018), 454–58.
86. Gheorghe Mărdărescu, *Campania pentru desrobirea Ardealului și ocuparea Budapestei (1919)* (Baia Mare: Editura Marist, 2009), 180–81.
87. Moraru, *La hotarul românesc al Europei*, 75.
88. Dumitru, *State, Antisemitism, and Collaboration in the Holocaust*, 95.
89. Alexandru-Murad Mironov, "And Quiet Flows the Dniester: Life and Death on the Romanian-Soviet Border, 1918–1940," *Arhivele Totalitarismului* 19, no. 3 (2011): 39.
90. Timothy Snyder, *Bloodlands: Europe between Hitler and Stalin* (New York: Basic Books, 2010), 53.
91. Quoted in Moraru, *La hotarul românesc al Europei*, 106.
92. Donald Hall, *Romanian Furrow* (London: Bene Factum, 2007), 164.
93. Quoted in Moraru, *La hotarul românesc al Europei*, 108–9.
94. Deletant, *Romania under Communist Rule*, 11.
95. Ibid., 12–14.
96. Hanebrink, *Specter Haunting Europe*, 14, 28–31.
97. Ibid., 31–37.
98. Dumitru, *State, Antisemitism, and Collaboration in the Holocaust*, 78.
99. Some Romanian historians still do too; see Moraru, *La hotarul românesc al Europei*, 154.
100. Mironov, "Quiet Flows the Dniester," 34.
101. Deletant, *Romania under Communist Rule*, 15.
102. Mărdărescu, *Campania pentru desrobirea Ardealului și ocuparea Budapestei*, 221.

103. AMNR, Fond Armata 4-a, dosar 27, f. 10.
104. Paxton, *Anatomy of Fascism*, 16.
105. Clark, *Holy Legionary Youth*, 1.
106. Ibid., 64–65.
107. Corneliu Zelea Codreanu, *For My Legionaries* (York, SC: Liberty Bell, 1990), 221.
108. Ibid., 7, 9–11.
109. Quoted in Rebecca Haynes, *Romanian Policy towards Germany, 1936–1940* (New York: St. Martin's, 2000), 33.
110. Roland Clark, "Fascists and Soldiers: Ambivalent Loyalties and Genocidal Violence in Wartime Romania," *Holocaust and Genocide Studies* 31, no. 3 (Winter 2017): 411–12.

2. Army Culture, Interwar Politics, and Neutrality

1. John Manolescu, *Permitted to Land: An Autobiography* (London: Staples, 1950), 5.
2. Ibid., 8.
3. Radu Florescu, *General Ioan Emanoil Florescu: Organizer of the Romanian Army* (Boulder, CO: East European Monographs, 2007), 7.
4. Dan V. Pleshoyano, *Nicolae Pleșoianu and the National Regeneration Movement in Wallachia*, trans. Kathe Lieber (Boulder, CO: East European Monographs, 1991), 6.
5. Florescu, *General Ioan Emanoil Florescu*, 25, 52.
6. Gh. Al. Savu, ed., *The Army and the Romanian Society* (Bucharest: Military Publishing House, 1980), 229.
7. Florescu, *General Ioan Emanoil Florescu*, 41.
8. Dumitru-Dan Crîșmaru, *Elita militară românească în timpul lui Carol I (1866–1914)* (Bucharest: Editura Militară, 2017), 192.
9. Torrey, *Romanian Battlefront in World War I*, 170.
10. Ionuț Isaia Jeican, Florin Botiș, and Dan Gheban, "*Typhus Exanthematicus* in Romania during the Second World War (1940–1945): Reflected by Romanian Medical Journals of the Time," *Clujul Medical* 88, no. 1 (2015): 83.
11. Horia Vladimir Șerbănescu, "Caricatura militară în presa umoristică românească de la unire până la războiul cel mare," *Studii și cercetări de istoria artei, Artă plastică* 47, no. 3 (2013): 28–31.
12. Crîșmaru, *Elita militară românească în timpul lui Carol I*, 92–94.
13. Ibid., 18; Gusti, *Enciclopedia României*, 1:682.
14. Crîșmaru, *Elita militară românească în timpul lui Carol I*, 26–28.
15. Nicolae Dăscălescu, *General Nicolae Dăscălescu: Sacrificiu, glorie și supliciu* (Bucharest: Editura Militară, 2014), 53.
16. Maior Emanoil Leoveanu, "Pericolul ce ne amenință," *România militară* 56, no. 5 (May 1924): 70–71.
17. Victor Luca, Mihai V. Zodian, and Cătălin Radu, eds., *Războiul ofițerilor de rezervă (1941–1944, fragmente)* (Bucharest: Socitatea Scriitorilor Militari, 2003), 57.
18. Ion Grosu, *Memoriile unui ofițer de informații* (Bucharest: Editura Militară, 2009), 74.
19. Livezeanu, *Cultural Politics in Greater Romania*, 213.
20. David B. Ralston, *The Army of the Republic: The Place of the Military in the Political Evolution of France, 1871–1914* (Cambridge, MA: MIT Press, 1967), 1–5, 9–25.

21. Deletant, *Hitler's Forgotten Ally*, 38.
22. Manolescu, *Permitted to Land*, 8.
23. Dăscălescu, *General Nicolae Dăscălescu*, 20; Luca, *Războiul ofițerilor de rezervă*, 34.
24. Crîșmaru, *Elita militară românească în timpul lui Carol I*, 82–83.
25. AMNR, Fond Corpul Grănicerilor, dosar 2751, f. 1199.
26. Dăscălescu, *General Nicolae Dăscălescu*, 57.
27. Gheorghe Athanasescu, *Jurnal, 1926–1940* (Bucharest: Editura Vremea, 2018), 39.
28. Maior Ionescu-Sinaias, "Problema socială, morală și materială a corpului ofițeresc," *România militară* 56, no. 10 (October 1924): 77–78.
29. Pantazi, *Cu mareșalul până la moarte*, 3.
30. Axworthy, Scafes, and Craciunoiu, *Third Axis, Fourth Ally*, 63.
31. Scafeș et al., *Armata română*, 99.
32. AMNR, Fond Corpul Grănicerilor, dosar 2529, f. 68–78.
33. Teodorescu, *Mândria vânătorului de munte*, 12.
34. Alexander Statiev, "The Ugly Duckling of the Armed Forces: Romanian Armor, 1919–1941," *Journal of Slavic Military Studies* 12, no. 2 (1999): 220–21, 225.
35. Luca, *Războiul ofițerilor de rezervă*, 40.
36. Călin Hentea, *Brief Romanian Military History*, trans. Cristina Bordianu (Lanham, MD: Scarecrow, 2007), 102.
37. Mihai Chiper, *Pe câmpul de onoare: O istorie a duelui la români* (Bucharest: Humanitas, 2016), 90–92, 96, 98.
38. Pantazi, *Cu mareșalul până la moarte*, 3–4.
39. Chiper, *Pe câmpul de onoare*, 252–53.
40. Moșneagu, Florea, and Prisăcaru, *Armata română și cultele*, 116.
41. Roger Reese, *Red Commanders: A Social History of the Soviet Army Officer Corps, 1918–1991* (Lawrence: University Press of Kansas, 2005), 2–3.
42. Crîșmaru, *Elita militară românească în timpul lui Carol I*, 64.
43. Quoted ibid., 53.
44. Otu, *Mareșalul Constantin Prezan*, 43.
45. Torrey, *Romanian Battlefront in World War I*, 180–83.
46. Athanasescu, *Jurnal*, 90–91.
47. Luca, *Războiul ofițerilor de rezervă*, 29–30.
48. Ibid., 35, 53.
49. Ibid., 38, 40.
50. Ibid., 31.
51. Robert A. Doughty, *Pyrrhic Victory: French Strategy and Operations in the Great War* (Cambridge, MA: Belknap Press of Harvard University Press, 2005), 25–27.
52. Torrey, *Romanian Battlefront in World War I*, 17.
53. Doughty, *Pyrrhic Victory*, 503.
54. Alexander Statiev, "When an Army Becomes 'Merely a Burden': Romanian Defense Policy and Strategy (1918–1941)," *Journal of Slavic Military Studies* 13, no. 2 (2000): 70–72; Axworthy, Scafes, and Craciunoiu, *Third Axis, Fourth Ally*, 40; DiNardo, *Germany and the Axis Powers*, 100.
55. "Răsboi de poziție, sau răsboi de mișcare?," *România militară* 53, no. 2 (February 1921): 136–37.
56. Crîșmaru, *Elita militară românească în timpul lui Carol I*, 11, 75–80.

57. Torrey, *Romanian Battlefront in World War I*, 15.
58. Otu, *Mareșalul Constantin Prezan*, 27.
59. Athanasescu, *Jurnal*, 39.
60. Iancu, *Evreii din România*, 200.
61. Ibid., 201.
62. Deborah S. Cornelius, *Hungary in World War II: Caught in the Cauldron* (New York: Fordham University Press, 2011), 42–43.
63. Quoted in Glenn E. Torrey, ed., *Romania and World War I* (Iași: Center for Romanian Studies, 1999), 368.
64. Grant Harward, "Purifying the Ranks: Ethnic and Minority Policy in the Romanian Armed Forces during the Second World War," *Studies in Ethnicity and Nationalism* 13, no. 2 (October 2013): 167–69.
65. Reese, *Red Commanders*, 19–20.
66. Marcel-Dumitru Ciucă, Aurelian Teodorescu, and Bogdan Florin Popovici, eds., *Steonogramele ședințelor consiliului de miniștri guvernarea Ion Antonescu*, vol. 8 (Bucharest: Arhivele Naționale ale României, 1997), 381–82.
67. Quoted in Solonari, *Purifying the Nation*, 119–20.
68. League of Nations, *Armaments Year-Book*, Seventh Year (Geneva: League of Nations, 1931), 765.
69. Manolescu, *Permitted to Land*, 17.
70. Rebecca A. Emrich, *In Search of the Lost Ones: The German Soldiers of Transylvania in the Second World War and Their Stories* (Vancouver: For Love of Books, 2011), 5.
71. League of Nations, *Armaments Year-Book*, Seventh Year, 767.
72. Luca, *Războiul ofițerilor de rezervă*, 57.
73. Roger R. Reese, *Stalin's Reluctant Soldiers: A Social History of the Red Army, 1925–1941* (Lawrence: University Press of Kansas, 1996), 120–21.
74. Anton Bacalbașa, *Moș teacă—Din viața militară* (Iași: Editura Junimea, 1989), 65.
75. Grosu, *Memorii unui ofițer de informații*, 74.
76. Wieland, *Bessarabian Knight*, 17–18.
77. Quoted in Beevor, *Stalingrad*, 184.
78. Hitchins, *Romanians*, 175; Hitchins, *Rumania*, 336.
79. Bacalbașa, *Moș teacă—Din viața militară*, 121.
80. Hentea, *Brief Romanian Military History*, 111.
81. Wieland, *Bessarabian Knight*, 18.
82. Căpitan Radu Dinulescu, "Chestiuni de organizare și gospodărie în corpurile de trupă," *România militară* 60, no. 3 (March 1928): 36.
83. Hentea, *Brief Romanian Military History*, 87, 114.
84. Larry L. Watts, *Romanian Cassandra: Ion Antonescu and the Struggle for Reform, 1916–1941* (Boulder, CO: East European Monographs, 1993), 50.
85. Mihail Sebastian, *Journal, 1935–1944: The Fascist Years*, trans. Patrick Camiller (Chicago: Ivan R. Dee, 2000), 18.
86. Manolescu, *Permitted to Land*, 9.
87. Quoted in Emrich, *In Search of the Lost Ones*, 5.
88. Bacalbașa, *Moș teacă—Din viața militară*, 123.
89. Ibid., 80.

90. Dennis E. Showalter, "Army and Society in Imperial Germany: The Pains of Modernization," *Journal of Contemporary History* 18, no. 4 (Fall 1983): 600–601.

91. Marcel Fontaine, *Jurnal de război: Misiune în România, noiembrie 1916–aprilie 1918*, trans. Micaela Ghițescu (Bucharest: Humanitas, 2016), 75–76.

92. Căpitan Emil Vasiliu, "Prerogătiva pedepselor disciplinare," *România militară* 77, no. 3 (March 1939): 73.

93. Halic and Dobrin interview.

94. Watts, *Romanian Cassandra*, 49.

95. General C. Dragu, "Reducerea serviciului militar activ. Aplicarea principiilor democratice (Urmare și sfârșit)," *România militară* 57, no. 3 (March 1925): 21.

96. Bacalbașa, *Moș teacă—Din viața militară*, 60.

97. Șerban Popa, "Să ne iubim țara, regele și neamul," *Cuvinte către ostași*, no. 2 (Bucharest, 1940).

98. Medic General de divizie dr. I. Antoniu și medic Lt.-Colonel dr. I. Bălănescu, "Rolul armatei in educația sanitară a poporului," *România militară* 53, no. 3 (April 1921): 429–32.

99. Medicul Lt.-Colonel Bălănescu, "Privire generală asupra igienei militare (Urmare)," *România militară* 50, no. 4 (April 1923): 387.

100. Ibid., 386.

101. Axworthy, Scafes, and Craciunoiu, *Third Axis, Fourth Ally*, 60.

102. Ralston, *Army of the Republic*, 3.

103. Hitchins, *Rumania*, 383.

104. Colonel Pascal, "Note asupra înființarei unei industrii militare în România," *România militară* 53, no. 9–10 (September–October 1921): 895–96.

105. Hitchins, *Rumania*, 365.

106. Grosu, *Memoriile unui ofițer de informații*, 149.

107. General Negrei, "Despre nevoile ofițerilor și modul cum ar putea fi ușurate," *România militară* 55, no. 11 (November 1923): 1031.

108. Ibid., 1034–38.

109. League of Nations, *Armaments Year-Book*, Fourth Year, 746.

110. Watts, *Romanian Cassandra*, 46.

111. Martin Thomas, "To Arm an Ally: French Arms Sales to Romania, 1926–1940," *Journal of Strategic Studies* 19, no. 2 (1996): 244–45.

112. Paul D. Quinlan, *The Playboy King: Carol II of Romania* (Westport, CT: Greenwood, 1995), 39–46, 65–77.

113. Hitchins, *Rumania*, 412.

114. Athanasescu, *Jurnal*, 42, 52.

115. Maior N. Diaconescu, "Technica revoluționară a bolșevismului," *România militară* 60, no. 7–8 (July–August 1928): 131.

116. A.B.C., "Nevoia introducerii pregătirii preregimentare la noi," *România militară* 66, no. 10 (October 1929): 43.

117. Ibid., 44–46.

118. General Virgil Economu, "Pregătirea preregimentară (Urmare)," *România militară* 67, no. 1 (January 1930): 3.

119. Grosu, *Memoriile unui ofițer de informații*, 152.

120. Scurtu, *Istoria românilor în timpul celor patru regi*, vol. 3, *Carol II*, 64–65.

121. Hitchins, *Rumania*, 415.
122. Oțu, *Mareșalul Constantin Prezan*, 344; Watts, *Romanian Cassandra*, 47.
123. Chirnoagă, *Istoria politică și militară a răsboiului României contra Rusiei sovietice*, 132.
124. Reese, *Stalin's Reluctant Soldiers*, 3–4.
125. Deletant, *Hitler's Forgotten Ally*, 41; Camelia Ilie, "Processing the Political Image of a King: An Overview of the Interwar and Communist Discourse about Carol II of Romania," *Revista de științe politice* 47 (2015), 207–8.
126. Journalists continue to repeat these stories spread by the king's enemies and later by communist historians; see Misha Glenny, *The Balkans: Nationalism, War, and the Great Powers, 1804–1999* (New York: Penguin, 1999), 443; and Robert D. Kaplan, *Balkan Ghosts: A Journey through History*, new ed. (New York: Picador, 2005), 85–86. Some have tried to rehabilitate Carol II; see Ilie, "Processing the Political Image of a King," 212–13.
127. Athanasescu, *Jurnal*, 75.
128. Quoted in Quinlan, *Playboy King*, 124.
129. Scurtu, *Istoria românilor în timpul celor patru regi*, vol. 3, *Carol II*, 148; Bogdan Bucur, "Budgetary Austerity Measures Taken by Romania during the Great Recession of 1929–1933 and Reflected in the Specialized Press of the Time," *Revista română de jurnalism și comunicare* 6, no. 3 (2011): 35.
130. Christophe Midan, *Carol al II-lea și teroarea istoriei, 1930–1940*, trans. Daniela Codruța Midan (Bucharest: Editura Militară, 2008), 12–13.
131. Watts, *Romanian Cassandra*, 61.
132. Ibid., 63.
133. Athanasescu, *Jurnal*, 85.
134. Scurtu, *România în timpul celor patru regi*, vol. 3, *Carol II*, 150–51.
135. Clark, *Holy Legionary Youth*, 103–6.
136. Pantazi, *Cu mareșalul până la moarte*, 1, 5.
137. Ibid., 13.
138. A. L. Easterman, *King Carol, Hitler and Lupescu* (London: Victor Gollancz, 1942), 15.
139. Grosu, *Memoriile unui ofițer de informații*, 170.
140. Oișteanu, *Inventing the Jew*, 59–61.
141. Antonescu was severely ill from around July 1942 to February 1943. Detractors say Antonescu was suffering from syphilis; see Ancel, *History of the Holocaust in Romania*, 473, 482, 489, 660n9. Defenders say he was fighting malaria; see Pantazi, *Cu mareșalul până la moarte*, 218, 222–23, 234. Before mass production of penicillin inducing malarial fever was a treatment for syphilis; see M. Karamanou et al., "Julius Wagner-Jauregg (1857–1940): Introducing Fever Therapy in the Treatment of Neurosyphilis," *Psychiatriki* 24, no. 3 (July–September 2013): 208–12. Therefore, Antonescu was probably being treated for syphilis with malaria.
142. Deletant, *Hitler's Forgotten Ally*, 38.
143. Quoted ibid., 70.
144. Quoted ibid., 68.
145. Pantazi, *Cu mareșal până la moarte*, 66.
146. Quinlan, *Playboy King*, 150–51.

147. Athanasescu, *Jurnal*, 113.
148. Deletant, *Hitler's Forgotten Ally*, 39.
149. Watts, *Romanian Cassandra*, 2, 17, 45.
150. Axworthy, Scafes, and Craciunoiu, *Third Axis, Fourth Ally*, 27–28.
151. Thomas, "To Arm an Ally," 235, 247.
152. Paul N. Hehn, *A Low Dishonest Decade: The Great Powers, Eastern Europe, and the Economic Origins of World War II, 1930–1941* (New York: Continuum, 2002), 263–65; Axworthy, Scafes, and Craciunoiu, *Third Axis, Fourth Ally*, 29.
153. Thomas, "To Arm an Ally," 252; Bernád, *Rumanian Aces of World War 2*, 8–9.
154. Midan, *Carol al II-lea și teroarea istoriei*, 54.
155. Dan Prisăcaru, *În avanpostul luptei pentru supraviețuire: Apărarea națională României și frontul secret în vâltoarea anilor 1938–1940* (Bucharest: Editura Militară, 2014), 41.
156. Haynes, *Romanian Policy towards Germany*, 2, 75, 170,
157. Maior Alex I. Țenescu, "Câteva considerațiuni asupra războiului și în special asupra războiului viitor," *România militară* 74, no. 3 (March 1937): 39.
158. Prisăcaru, *În avanpostul luptei pentru supraviețuire*, 76.
159. Armin Heinen, *Legiunea "arhanghelul Mihail": Mișcare socială și organizație politică*, trans. Cornelia and Delia Eșianu (Bucharest: Humanitas, 2006), 254–56.
160. Clark, *Holy Legionary Youth*, 37–38; Scurtu, *Pe marginea prăpastiei*, 1:20.
161. Heinen, *Legiunea "arhanghelul Mihail,"* 385.
162. Quoted in Watts, *Romanian Cassandra*, 144.
163. Dana Beldiman, *Armata și mișcarea legionară, 1927–1947* (Bucharest: Institutul Național Pentru Studiul Totalitarismului, 2002), 33.
164. Ibid., 29.
165. Hitchins, *Rumania*, 419.
166. Nagy-Talavera, *Green Shirts and the Others*, 410.
167. Rebecca Ann Haynes, "Reluctant Allies? Iuliu Maniu and Corneliu Zelea Codreanu against King Carol II of Romania," *Slavonic and East European Review* 85, no. 1 (January 2007): 132–34.
168. Rebecca Haynes, "Germany and the Establishment of the Romanian National Legionary State, September 1940," *Slavonic and East European Review* 77, no. 4 (October 1999): 705.
169. Quoted in Solonari, *Purifying the Nation*, 120.
170. Hitchins, *Rumania*, 423.
171. Deletant, *Hitler's Forgotten Ally*, 44.
172. Ancel, *History of the Holocaust in Romania*, 46.
173. Popa, *Romanian Orthodox Church and the Holocaust*, 20.
174. Midan, *Carol al II-lea și teroarea istoriei*, 106.
175. Heinen, *Legiunea "arhanghelul Mihail,"* 350–51.
176. Pantazi, *Cu mareșalul până la moarte*, 72; Solonari, *Purifying the Nation*, 121.
177. Manolescu, *Permitted to Land*, 26.
178. Ibid., 27–30.
179. General V. Economu, "Războiul care vine," *România militară* 77, no. 2 (February 1939): 3.
180. Midan, *Carol al II-lea și teroarea istoriei*, 131–32.

181. Teodorescu, *Mândria vânătorului de munte*, 21.
182. Haynes, *Romanian Policy towards Germany*, 123–24.
183. Quoted in Andreas Hillgruber, *Hitler, regele Carol și mareșalul Antonescu: Relațiile germane-române (1938–1944)*, 2nd ed. trans. Maria Alexe (Bucharest: Humanitas, 2007), 138–39.
184. Clare Hollingworth, *There's a German Just behind Me* (London: Right Book Club, 1943), 33.
185. Chirnoagă, *Istoria politică și militară a răsboiului României contra Rusiei sovietice*, 91.
186. Prisăcaru, *În avanpostul luptei pentru supraviețuire*, 226–30.
187. Cretzianu, *Relapse into Bondage*, 154.
188. Editorii, "Războiul din Finlanda," *Sentinela*, 15 January 1940, 6.
189. Chris Bellamy, *Absolute War: Soviet Russia in the Second World War* (New York: Vintage Books, 2008), 90; Karel C. Berkhoff, *Motherland in Danger: Soviet Propaganda during World War II* (Cambridge, MA: Harvard University Press, 2012), 194.
190. AMNR, Fond Corpul de Munte, dosar 53, f. 408; AMNR, Fond Comandamentul Militar al Capitalei, dosar 810, f. 238.
191. AMNR, Fond Armata 4-a, dosar 33, f. 2–4.
192. Midan, *Carol al II-lea și teroarea istoriei*, 194.
193. Vasile Bărboi et al., eds., *Armata română în vâltoarea războiului* (Bucharest: Editura "Vasile Cârlova," 2002), 30.
194. Mihai Pelin, *Săptămîna patimilor (23–28 iunie 1940): Cedarea Basarabiei și a nordului Bucovinei* (Bucharest: Compania, 2008), 55.
195. Prisăcaru, *În avanpostul luptei pentru supraviețuire*, 233.
196. Axworthy, Scafes, and Craciunoiu, *Third Axis, Fourth Ally*, 40; Scafeș et al., *Armata română*, 107, 122–24, 130, 152.
197. Ovidiu Marius Miron, *Jandarmeria română în perioada interbelică, 1919–1941: Mit și realitate* (Lugoj: Editura Dacia Europa Nova, 2003), 35, 46.
198. Hollingworth, *There's a German Just behind Me*, 37.
199. AMNR, Fond Armata 4-a, dosar 277, f. 214–19.
200. Sebastian, *Journal*, 265–66.
201. AMNR, Fond Armata 4-a, dosar 270, f. 36–37.
202. Crisan, *Amazing Life*, 115–16.

3. 1940–1941: From Neutral to Axis

1. Regele Carol II, "Cuvântarea M.S. Regelui la Chișinău," *Sentinela*, 15 January 1940, 1.
2. Axworthy, Scafes, and Craciunoiu, *Third Axis, Fourth Ally*, 14.
3. Teodorescu, *Mândria vânătorului de munte*, 28.
4. Quoted in Dinu C. Giurescu, *Romania in the Second World War (1939–1945)*, trans. Eugenia Elena Popescu (New York: Columbia University Press, 2000), 21.
5. Cretzianu, *Relapse into Bondage*, 178.
6. Quoted in Pelin, *Săptămîna patimilor*, 40–42.
7. Prisăcaru, *În avanpostul luptei pentru supraviețuire*, 356; Bellamy, *Absolute War*, 90.

8. Quoted in Midan, *Carol al II-lea și teroarea istoriei*, 266.
9. Prisăcaru, *În avanpostul luptei pentru supraviețuire*, 358; Cretzianu, *Relapse into Bondage*, 180.
10. Bărboi et al., *Armata română în vâltoarea războiului*, 31.
11. AMNR, Fond Armata 4-a, dosar 381, f. 289.
12. Midan, *Carol al II-lea și teroarea istoriei*, 270–71.
13. Quoted in Pelin, *Săptămîna patimilor*, 106.
14. AMNR, Fond Secția II-Informații, dosar 982, f. 116.
15. Wieland, *Bessarabian Knight*, 20.
16. Constantin Mihalcea, interview with the author, Brăila, 2012.
17. Giurescu, *Romania in the Second World War*, 24.
18. Quoted in Bărboi et al., *Armata română în vâltoarea războiului*, 32.
19. AMNR, Fond Corpul de Cavalerie, dosar 124, f. 255.
20. Pelin, *Săptămîna patimilor*, 197.
21. Mihalcea interview.
22. Florica Dobre, Vasilica Manea, and Lenuța Nicolescu, eds., *Anul 1940: Armata română de la ultimatum la dictat, Documente*, vol. 1 (Bucharest: Editura Europa Nova, 2000), 94.
23. USHMM, RG-25.003M, reel 382, frames 118–19.
24. Bărboi et al., *Armata română în vâltoarea războiului*, 31.
25. AMNR, Fond Corpul de Cavalerie, dosar 124, f. 257.
26. Ibid., dosar 87, f. 66–67.
27. Midan, *Carol al II-lea și teroarea istoriei*, 276.
28. Quoted ibid., 277.
29. Pelin, *Săptămîna patimilor*, 219.
30. Marjorie Knittel, *The Last Bridge: Her Own True Story, Elvera Ziebart Reuer* (Aberdeen, SD: Midstates Printing, 1984), 52.
31. Ibid., 53.
32. Ibid., 56.
33. Cretzianu, *Relapse into Bondage*, 184–85.
34. Pelin, *Săptămîna patimilor*, 198.
35. AMNR, Fond Armata 4-a, dosar 272, f. 120.
36. Quoted in Pelin, *Săptămîna patimilor*, 121.
37. Wieland, *Bessarabian Knight*, 22–25.
38. Quoted in Midan, *Carol al II-lea și teroarea istoriei*, 277.
39. Dobre, Manea, and Nicolescu, *Anul 1940*, 1:156–60.
40. Quoted in Pelin, *Săptămîna patimilor*, 131.
41. Solonari, *Purifying the Nation*, 161.
42. Dobre, Manea, and Nicolescu, *Anul 1940*, 1:63–64.
43. Don Levin, *The Lesser of Two Evils: Eastern European Jewry under Soviet Rule, 1939–1941*, trans. Naftali Greenwood (Philadelphia: Jewish Publication Society, 1995), 38.
44. Quoted in Midan, *Carol al II-lea și teroarea istoriei*, 280.
45. AMNR, Fond Armata 4-a, dosar 209, f. 7–11.
46. Ibid., f. 4–7.
47. Quoted in Solonari, *Purifying the Nation*, 163.
48. AMNR, Fond Armata 3-a, dosar 135, f. 2, 7.

49. AMNR, Fond Armata 4-a, dosar 309, f. 103.
50. Bărboi et al., *Armata română în vâltoarea războiului*, 33.
51. AMNR, Fond Corpul de Cavalerie, dosar 87, f. 87–91.
52. John Doyle Klier, *Russians, Jews, and the Pogroms of 1881–1882* (Cambridge: Cambridge University Press, 2011), xiii, 18–25.
53. Quoted in Bărboi et al., *Armata română în vâltoarea războiului*, 34.
54. Ancel, *History of the Holocaust in Romania*, 72–73.
55. AMNR, Fond Secția II-Informații, dosar 941, f. 15.
56. Ibid., f. 49, 57; ACNSAS, Fond Documentar, dosar 4087, f. 64.
57. ACNSAS, Fond Documentar, dosar 4087, f. 41.
58. Ibid., f. 134.
59. Ibid., f. 180.
60. AMNR, Fond Armata 4-a, dosar 381, f. 299; AMNR, Fond Secția II-Informații, dosar 941, 16, 26, 56.
61. AMNR, Fond Secția II-Informații, dosar 941, f. 13.
62. J. Alexandru et al., eds., *Martiriul evreilor din România, 1940–1944: Documente și mărturii* (Bucharest: Editura Hasefer, 1991), 36; Ancel, *History of the Holocaust in Romania*, 75.
63. Carp, *Holocaust in Rumania*, 239. Rumors about LANC supporters applying "blue stamps" to homes, and even of pogroms that did not occur, were common among Jews in eastern Romania during the interwar years; see Dumitru, *State, Antisemitism, and Collaboration in the Holocaust*, 88–89.
64. Carp, *Holocaust in Rumania*, 240.
65. Alexandru, *Martiriul evreilor din România*, 37.
66. Ibid., 38.
67. Ibid., 39.
68. AMNR, Fond Secția II-Informații, dosar 941, f. 126; AMNR, Fond Corpul de Cavalerie, dosar 90, f. 25.
69. Radu Ioanid, *The Holocaust in Romania: The Destruction of Jews and Gypsies under the Antonescu Regime, 1940–1944* (Chicago: Ivan R. Dee, 2000), 42.
70. Alexandru, *Martiriul evreilor din România*, 34.
71. Carp, *Holocaust in Rumania*, 243; AMNR, Fond Secția II-Informații, dosar 941, f. 128.
72. Quoted in Ancel, *History of the Holocaust in Romania*, 76.
73. AMNR, Fond Secția II-Informații, dosar 941, 466.
74. Carp, *Holocaust in Rumania*, 238–39.
75. Dobre, Manea, and Nicolescu, *Anul 1940*, 1:99.
76. AMNR, Fond Secția II-Informații, dosar 941, f. 167.
77. Quoted in Giurescu, *Romania in the Second World War*, 205.
78. Quoted in Midan, *Carol al II-lea și teroarea istoriei*, 281.
79. Dobre, Manea, and Nicolescu, *Anul 1940*, 1:169–70.
80. Quoted in Halik Kochanski, *The Eagle Unbowed: Poland and the Poles in the Second World War* (Cambridge, MA: Harvard University Press, 2012), 77.
81. AMNR, Fond Secția II-Informații, dosar 941, f. 469.
82. AMNR, Fond Armata 4-a, dosar 206, f. 1–2; AMNR, Fond Corpul de Cavalerie, dosar 87, f. 164.
83. AMNR, Fond Armata 4-a, dosar 381, f. 253; ibid., dosar 341, f. 27.

84. AMNR, Fond Corpul de Munte, dosar 24, f. 119.
85. Ibid., dosar 53, f. 170.
86. Ibid., f. 39, 124.
87. Alexandru, *Martiriul evreilor din România*, 36.
88. Carp, *Holocaust in Rumania*, 242.
89. Dobre, Manea, and Nicolescu, *Anul 1940*, 1:178, 189.
90. Quoted in Minority Rights Information System, *Final Report of the International Commission on the Holocaust in Romania*, 61, http://miris.eurac.edu/mugs2/do/blob.pdf?type=pdf&serial=1117716572750.
91. Scafeș et al., *Armata română*, 14; Midan, *Carol al II-lea și teroarea istoriei*, 284.
92. Dobre, Manea, and Nicolescu, *Anul 1940*, 1:vi.
93. Easterman, *King Carol, Hitler and Lupescu*, 215.
94. Quoted in Bărboi et al., *Armata română în vâltoarea Războiului*, 34.
95. "Editorial pe prima pagină," *Sentinela*, 7 July 1940, 1.
96. Neagu Rădulescu, "Pățaniile soldatului Neață," *Sentinela*, 14 July 1940, 7.
97. AMNR, Fond Corpul de Cavalerie, dosar 88, f. 109–12.
98. Clark, *Holy Legionary Youth*, 222.
99. Quoted in Giurescu, *Romania in the Second World War*, 32.
100. Solonari, *Purifying the Nation*, 121–22.
101. Deletant, *Hitler's Forgotten Ally*, 47.
102. Ioanid, *Holocaust in Romania*, 19–23.
103. Case, *Between States*, 1–2, 31–33.
104. Giurescu, *Romania in the Second World War*, 51.
105. Quoted in Midan, *Carol al II-lea și teroarea istoriei*, 295.
106. Quinlan, *Playboy King*, 214; Haynes, "Germany and the Establishment of the Romanian National Legionary State," 711, 708–10.
107. Beldiman, *Armata și mișcarea legionară*, 85; Haynes, "Germany and the Establishment of the Romanian National Legionary State," 719–20.
108. Quinlan, *Playboy King*, 215.
109. Haynes, "Germany and the Establishment of the Romanian National Legionary State," 713–14, 717.
110. Ibid., 718.
111. Quinlan, *Playboy King*, 216; R. G. Waldeck, *Athene Palace: Hitler's "New Order" Comes to Romania* (Chicago: University of Chicago Press, 2013), 173–80.
112. Dobre, Manea, and Nicolescu, *Anul 1940*, 2:284–85, 158.
113. Ibid., 2:124.
114. USHMM, RG-25.003M, reel 382, frames 539–40.
115. Ioan T. Lungu, *De la Stalingrad la Gherla: Roman document* (Timișoara: Editura de Vest, 1993), 10.
116. Quoted in Bărboi et al., *Armata română în vâltoarea războiului*, 36.
117. Plt. Mj. Adm. C. Vâlceanu, "Pământ cere dușmanul," *Sentinela*, 8 September 1940, 5.
118. Case, *Between States*, 115.
119. Ibid., 98–99, 102–3.
120. Quoted in Deletant, *Hitler's Forgotten Ally*, 52.
121. Pantazi, *Cu mareșalul până la moarte*, x–xiii, 78.

122. Ibid., 85.
123. Haynes, "Germany and the Establishment of the Romanian National Legionary State," 721–22.
124. Clark, Holy Legionary Youth, 222.
125. Solonari, Purifying the Nation, 95–114.
126. Axworthy, Scafes, and Craciunoiu, Third Axis, Fourth Ally, 40.
127. Ion Antonescu, "Cuvânt către ostași," Sentinela, 8 September 1940, 3.
128. Ion Antonescu, "Primele infăptuiri ale conducătorului Statului," Sentinela, 15 September 1940, 6.
129. "Conducătorul Statului Român General Ion Antonescu," Arma Cuvântului, no. 4–5 (August–September 1940): 4.
130. "Pe prima pagina," Sentinela, 15 September 1940, 1; Nelu Constantinescu, "Duhul și disciplina legionară," Sentinela, 29 September 1940, 5.
131. Pantazi, Cu mareșalul până la moarte, 87.
132. Halic and Dobrin interview.
133. Hollingworth, There's a German Just behind Me, 180.
134. Waldeck, Athene Palace, 239; AMNR, Fond Armata 4-a, dosar 403, f. 51.
135. Easterman, King Carol, Hitler and Lupescu, 217.
136. Hollingworth, There's a German Just behind Me, 40.
137. A common tactic of fascist regimes; see Paxton, Anatomy of Fascism, 119–28.
138. Quoted in Giurescu, Romania in the Second World War, 61.
139. Ionescu, Jewish Resistance to "Romanianization," 5.
140. Clark, Holy Legionary Youth, 224–25.
141. Ibid., 228–29.
142. "Soldatul german," Sentinela, 1 December 1940, 3.
143. Boog et al., Germany and the Second World War, 4:399.
144. Ibid., 4:401.
145. Axworthy, Scafes, and Craciunoiu, Third Axis, Fourth Ally, 41; DiNardo, Germany and the Axis Powers, 98.
146. "Darul de Crăciun pentru ostași," Sentinela, 5 January 1941, 1.
147. Pantazi, Cu mareșalul până la moarte, 111–12.
148. Deletant, Hitler's Forgotten Ally, 64.
149. Solonari, Purifying the Nation, 134.
150. Clark, Holy Legionary Youth, 230–32.
151. Cretzianu, Relapse into Bondage, 229.
152. Heinen, Legiunea "arhanghelul Mihail," 422–23.
153. Solonari, Purifying the Nation, 135.
154. Giurescu, Romania in the Second World War, 74–75.
155. "Soldatul român asigură unirea și lineștea țării," Sentinela, 26 January 1941, 1.
156. Gheorghe Băgulescu, "Chemarea bravilor veterani," Sentinela, 26 January 1941, 3.
157. Clark, Holy Legionary Youth, 232–33.
158. Rădulescu, "Pațaniile soldatului Neață," Sentinela, 2 February 1941, 7.
159. USHMM, RG-25.003M, Fond Ministerul de Război: Cabinet, dosar 293, c. 121A–122A.
160. Deletant, Hitler's Forgotten Ally, 69, 81–82.
161. Nicolae Staicu, interview with the author, Constanța, 2012.

162. AMNR, Fond Armata 4-a, dosar 403, f. 222; Ciucă, *Stenogramele ședințelor consiliului de miniștri guvernarea Ion Antonescu*, 3:490.
163. AMNR, Fond Armata 4-a, dosar 403, f. 26; ibid., dosar 573, f. 49.
164. DiNardo, *Germany and the Axis Powers*, 100.
165. Scurtu, *Pe marginea prăpastiei*, 2:64.
166. Giurescu, *Romania in the Second World War*, 94; Pantazi, *Cu mareșalul până la moarte*, 127.
167. Aly, *Hitler's Beneficiaries*, 94–97, 103–5.
168. DiNardo, *Germany and the Axis Powers*, 101.
169. Quoted in Boog et al., *Germany and the Second World War*, 4:404.
170. AMNR, Fond Armata 3-a, dosar 305, f. 157.
171. ANIC, Fond Ministerul de Război: Cabinetul Ministrului, dosar 56 bis, f. 13.
172. Chirnoagă, *Istoria politică și militară a răsboiului României contra Rusiei sovietice*, 167.
173. AMNR, Fond Armata 3-a, dosar 370, f. 92–96.
174. AMNR, Fond Corpul de Munte, dosar 374, f. 11, 18; AMNR, Fond Corpul de Cavalerie, dosar 228, f. 240.
175. AMNR, Fond Armata 3-a, dosar 305, 99.
176. Boog et al., *Germany and the Second World War*, 4:405.
177. AMNR, Fond Corpul de Munte, dosar 118, 69; Ciucă, *Stenogramele ședințelor consiliului de miniștri guvernarea Ion Antonescu*, 3:554.
178. Vasile Arimia et al., eds., *Antonescu-Hitler: Corespondență și întilniri inedite (1940–1944)*, vol. 1 (Bucharest: Cozia, 1991), 95, 103–4.
179. For the Commissar Order see Christopher Browning, *The Origins of the Final Solution: The Evolution of the Nazi Jewish Policy, September 1939–March 1942* (Lincoln: University of Nebraska Press, 2004), 424–28. What was said off the record can be pieced together; see Gerhard Weinberg, "Hitler and the Beginning of the Holocaust," in *Lessons and Legacies*, vol. 10, *Back to the Sources: Reexamining Perpetrators, Victims, and Bystanders*, ed. Sara R. Horowitz (Evanston, IL: Northwestern University Press, 2012), 6, 11n4, 11n5.
180. AMNR, Fond Armata 3-a, dosar 411, f. 17, 16.

4. 1941: Holy War and Holocaust

1. Deletant, *Hitler's Forgotten Ally*, 82–83.
2. Mihai Antonescu, "Războiul sfânt a început," *Soldatul*, 28 June 1941, 1.
3. Alice Voinescu, *Jurnal*, vol. 1 (Bucharest: Polirom, 2013), 302.
4. Watson, *Enduring the Great War*, 141.
5. Edward B. Westermann, *Hitler's Police Battalions: Enforcing Racial War in the East* (Leavenworth: University Press of Kansas, 2005), 18–19.
6. Similar to what the German Army did in Belgium in the First World War; see John Horne and Alan Kramer, *German Atrocities: A History of Denial* (New Haven, CT: Yale University Press, 2001), 113–18.
7. Waitman Wade Beorn, *The Wehrmacht and the Holocaust in Belarus* (Cambridge, MA: Harvard University Press, 2014), 7.
8. AMNR, Fond Armata 4-a, dosar 629, f. 208. Emphasis (underlining) in original.

9. Quoted in Solonari, *Purifying the Nation*, 151.
10. AMNR, Fond Armata 3-a, dosar 624, f. 17–20.
11. Arimia et al., *Antonescu-Hitler*, 1:107–9.
12. AMNR, Fond Armata 4-a, dosar 875, f. 95.
13. AMNR, Fond Armata 3-a, dosar 426, f. 67, 66.
14. Jean Ancel, *Prelude to Mass Murder: The Pogrom in Iași, Romania, June 29, 1941 and Thereafter*, trans. Fern Seckbach (Jerusalem: Yad Vashem, 2013), 30.
15. Mark Axworthy, *The Romanian Army of World War II* (Oxford: Osprey, 1991), 4.
16. ACNSAS, Fond Documentar, dosar 8178, f. 76.
17. "Camarzi în lupta," *Sentinela*, 22 June 1941, 1.
18. Toma Vladescu, "Visul nostru care se împlenește," *Sentinela*, 22 June 1941, 7.
19. For Romanian strength see Scafeș et al., *Armata română*, 18; for German and Soviet strength see Bellamy, *Absolute War*, 181; for Axis airpower see DiNardo, *Germany and the Axis Powers*, 111.
20. Bellamy, *Absolute War*, 177.
21. Alexandru Armă, *București sub bombardamente (1941–1944)* (Bucharest: Editura Militară, 2015), 17; AMNR, Fond Armata 3-a, dosar 314, f. 458.
22. Ancel, *Prelude to Mass Murder*, 83, 75–76.
23. AMNR, Armata 4-a, dosar 781, f. 76, 78; AMNR, Comandamentul Militar al Capitalei, dosar 269, f. 26, 118, 120, 121; Armă, *București sub bombardmente*, 24.
24. AMNR, Fond Corpul Cavalerie, dosar 292, f. 413–14.
25. Dénes Bernád, *Rumania Aces of World War 2* (Oxford: Osprey, 2003), 15–16.
26. Duțu, *Armata română în război*, 26–28.
27. Ancel, *Prelude to Mass Murder*, 490–505.
28. Ioanid, *Holocaust in Romania*, 95.
29. USHMM, RG-25.003M, reel 2, frames 25, 76, 95–96.
30. AMNR, Fond Armata 4-a, dosar 748, f. 105; AMNR, Fond Armata 3-a, dosar 51, f. 320.
31. Henry Eaton, *The Origins and Onset of the Romanian Holocaust* (Detroit: Wayne State University Press, 2013), 75.
32. Ioanid, *Holocaust in Romania*, 68.
33. Carp, *Holocaust in Rumania*, 142.
34. One historian's attempt to create a rational organization chart from this hodgepodge of groups leading back to General Antonescu fails to convince the author that there was method to the madness; see Ancel, *Prelude to Mass Murder*, 70–71.
35. Ioanid, *Holocaust in Romania*, 69.
36. AMNR, Fond Armata 4-a, dosar 272, f. 55.
37. Ancel, *Prelude to Mass Murder*, 30–34, 522.
38. I. Dumitru, "Acum un an," *Soldatul*, 28 June 1941, 1.
39. Quoted in Ancel, *Prelude to Mass Murder*, 90–91.
40. Quoted in Carp, *Holocaust in Rumania*, 186.
41. Ibid., 148.
42. USHMM, RG-25.004M, reel 35, frame 312.
43. Ibid., reel 45, frame 80.
44. Ancel, *Prelude to Mass Murder*, 26.

45. USHMM, RG-25.004M, reel 13, frame 886.
46. Ancel, *Prelude to Mass Murder*, 143–44.
47. Carp, *Holocaust in Rumania*, 151.
48. USHMM, RG-25.004M, reel 35, frame 314.
49. Carp, *Holocaust in Rumania*, 152; Ancel, *Prelude to Mass Murder*, 167.
50. Ioanid, *Holocaust in Romania*, 72.
51. Quoted in Ancel, *Prelude to Mass Murder*, 146; quoted in Ioanid, *Holocaust in Romania*, 75.
52. Ancel, *Prelude to Mass Murder*, 172.
53. Accounts differ between two hundred or two thousand "free" slips; see ibid., 170–71.
54. Carp, *Holocaust in Rumania*, 154; Ancel, *Prelude to Mass Murder*, 185.
55. USHMM, RG-25.004M, reel 35, frames 359–60.
56. Ibid., reel 13, frame 887.
57. USHMM, RG-25.004M, reel 13, frame 889.
58. Ancel, *Prelude to Mass Murder*, 241–43, 257; Ioanid, *Holocaust in Romania*, 79.
59. Ancel, *Prelude to Mass Murder*, 141–42; USHMM, RG-25.004M, reel 35, frames 346, 357–58.
60. Ioanid, *Holocaust in Romania*, 83–84.
61. Quoted in Ancel, *Prelude to Mass Murder*, 261.
62. USHMM, RG-25.004M, reel 65, frame 445.
63. Ibid., reel 8, frame 228.
64. Ioanid, *Holocaust in Romania*, 86.
65. Ancel, *Prelude to Mass Murder*, 545.
66. AMNR, Fond Armata 3-a, dosar 481, f. 14.
67. AMNR, Fond Armata 4-a, dosar 781, f. 17.
68. USHMM, RG-25.004M, reel 14, frame 716.
69. Ibid., reel 35, frame 305.
70. AMNR, Fond Armata 3-a, dosar 481, f. 24–25.
71. Ibid., dosar 325, f. 12.
72. AMNR, Fond Armata 4-a, dosar 781, f. 34.
73. USHMM, RG-25.004M, reel 25, frames 806–7.
74. DiNardo, *Germany and the Axis Powers*, 113–14.
75. "Oştile creştine pătrund adânc în ţara iadului," *Soldatul*, 1 July 1941, 1.
76. AMNR, Fond Armata 3-a, dosar 325, f. 4.
77. Quoted in Solonari, *Purifying the Nation*, 153.
78. Grigorescu Mircea, "Jidovii, unelte ale bolşevismului," *Soldatul*, 3 July 1941, 1.
79. Quoted in Bărboi et al., *Armata română în vâltoarea războiului*, 66.
80. USHMM, RG-25.004M, reel 9, frames 1069–71.
81. ACNSAS, Fond Informativ, dosar 6347, f. 57, 266–67.
82. AMNR Fond Corpul de Munte, dosar 468, f. 30–31; ibid., dosar 108, f. 114.
83. Ibid., dosar 638, f. 53.
84. AMNR, Fond Armata 3-a, dosar 325, f. 27–28.
85. Dumitru Nimigeanu, *Însemnările unui ţăran deportat din Bucovina* (Bucharest: Editura Vestala, 2015), 41–56, 29–31.
86. Dumitru, *State, Antisemitism, and Collaboration in the Holocaust*, 149.

87. Ibid., 153–56; Solonari, *Purifying the Nation*, 178–79, 196.
88. Ioanid, *Holocaust in Romania*, 96–97.
89. AMNR, Fond Corpul de Munte, dosar 638, f. 59.
90. Scârneci, *Viața și moartea în linia întâi*, 113.
91. Yitzhak Arad, Shmuel Krakowski, and Shmuel Spector, eds., *The Einsatzgruppen Reports: Selections from the Dispatches of the Nazi Death Squads' Campaign against the Jews, July 1941–January 1943* (New York: Holocaust Library, 1989), 19.
92. Florian Bichir, ed., *Cruciada diviziei de cremene cu tricolorul în Caucaz: Viața și memoriile generalului Ioan Dumitrache, cavaler al "crucii de fier"* (Bucharest: Editura Militară, 2018), 44–46.
93. Like German panzer and motorized divisions; see Ben Shepherd, *Hitler's Soldiers: The German Army in the Third Reich* (New Haven, CT: Yale University Press, 2016), 84.
94. ACNSAS, Fond Documentar, dosar 8178, f. 27, 29–30.
95. ACNSAS, Fond Informativ, dosar 203760, f. 8–9; ACNSAS, Fond Documentar, dosar 8178, f. 28.
96. Stivelman, *Death March*, 108.
97. Quoted in Bărboi et al., *Armata română în vâltoarea războiului*, 65.
98. USHMM, RG-25.003M, reel 1, frames 496, 518, 520, 587.
99. Ancel, *Prelude to Mass Murder*, 506, 511.
100. AMNR, Fond Armata 3-a, dosar 624, f. 34–35; AMNR, Armata 4-a, dosar 646, f. 142–45; dosar 661, f. 206.
101. David Stahel, *Kiev 1941: Hitler's Battle for Supremacy in the East* (Cambridge: Cambridge University Press, 2012), 270.
102. Solonari, *Purifying the Nation*, 175.
103. Ancel, *Prelude to Mass Murder*, 224.
104. Browning, *Origins of the Final Solution*, 225, 228.
105. Arad, Krakowski, and Spector, *Einsatzgruppen Reports*, 19, 57, 105.
106. Paul A. Shapiro, *The Kishinev Ghetto, 1941–1942: A Documentary History of the Holocaust in Romania's Contested Borderlands* (Tuscaloosa: University of Alabama Press, 2015), 9–10.
107. AMNR, Fond Armata 4-a, dosar 781, f. 92–95.
108. Dăscălescu, *General Nicolae Dăscălescu*, 78–79.
109. AMNR, Fond Armata 4-a, dosar 784, f. 7–9.
110. Dăscălescu, *General Nicolae Dăscălescu*, 77.
111. Arad, Krakowski, and Spector, *Einsatzgruppen Reports*, 34–35; Ancel, *Prelude to Mass Murder*, 514.
112. Ioanid, *Holocaust in Romania*, 172.
113. AMNR, Fond Armata 3-a, dosar 411, f. 102.
114. Shapiro, *Kishinev Ghetto*, 18.
115. AMNR, Fond Armata 4-a, dosar 867, f. 361–62.
116. Ioanid, *Holocaust in Romania*, 31–34.
117. USHMM, RG-25.004M, reel 44, frames 641–42.
118. AMNR, Fond Armata 3-a, dosar 426, f. 51.
119. Ottmar Trașcă, ed., *"Chestiunea evreiască" în documente militare române, 1941–1944* (Iași: Institutul European, 2010), 176.

120. AMNR, Fond Corpul de Cavalerie, dosar 287, f. 7–9.
121. AMNR, Fond Armata 3-a, dosar 411, f. 43; ibid., dosar 325, f. 59.
122. Ibid., dosar 497, f. 226; ibid., dosar 498, f. 18.
123. DiNardo, *Germany and the Axis Powers*, 114.
124. Axworthy, Scafes, and Craciunoiu, *Third Axis, Fourth Ally*, 47–49; Bărboi et al., *Armata română în vâltoarea războiului*, 80–81; Duțu, *Armata română în război*, 71–73.
125. Anton, *Propagandă și război*, 200–201.
126. Bellamy, *Absolute War*, 144, 176.
127. Quoted in Charles Messenger, *The Last Prussian: A Biography of Field Marshal Gerd von Rundstedt, 1875–1953* (London: Brassey's, 1991), 149.
128. Scârneci, *Viața și moartea în linia întâi*, 115.
129. Ibid., 116.
130. AMNR, Fond Corpul de Munte, dosar 108, f. 143.
131. ACNSAS, Fond Personal, dosar 10617, vol. 3, f. 175.
132. Quoted in Solonari, *Purifying the Nation*, 201.
133. Lungu, *De la Stalingrad la Gherla*, 11.
134. Solonari, *Purifying the Nation*, 175–76.
135. Arad, Krakowski, and Spector, *Einsatzgruppen Reports*, 107–8; Shapiro, *Kishinev Ghetto*, 26, 28–30.
136. USHMM, RG-25.003M, reel 121, frames 393–97.
137. AMNR, Fond Armata 4-a, dosar 843, f. 311–12, 858.
138. AMNR, Fond Armata 3-a, dosar 421, f. 14.
139. AMNR, Fond Armata 4-a, dosar 645, f. 148, 152, 155–59.
140. Bartu Buzea, interview with the author, Brăila, 2012.
141. Duțu, *Armata română în război*, 65.
142. Trașcă, *"Chestiunea evreiască" în documente militare române*, 187, 189.
143. Solonari, *Purifying the Nation*, 182.
144. Dumitru, *State, Antisemitism, and the Holocaust*, 182–86.
145. Scârneci, *Viața și moartea în linia întâi*, 119–21.
146. Ibid., 122–23.
147. ACNSAS, Fond Personal, dosar 10617, vol. 3, 84, 87, 175.
148. Bichir, *Cruciada diviziei de cremene*, 51.
149. Arimia et al., *Antonescu-Hitler*, 1:118.
150. AMNR, Fond Armata 4-a, dosar 766, f. 85.
151. Ibid., dosar 793, f. 258, 338, 432.
152. Buzea interview.
153. Browning, *Origins of the Final Solution*, 253–67.
154. USHMM, RG-25.004M, reel 95, frames 23–24, 47–48.
155. Ibid., reel 26, frames 22–25, 67, 89–90.
156. Ibid., reel 25, frames 1172–73; reel 95, frames 17–18.
157. Ioanid, *Holocaust in Romania*, 119.
158. AMNR, Fond Armata 4-a, dosar 781, f. 137, 134.
159. Axworthy, Scafes, and Craciunoiu, *Third Axis, Fourth Ally*, 49.
160. Ioanid, *Holocaust in Romania*, 120–21.
161. Quoted in Deletant, *Hitler's Forgotten Ally*, 151.

162. AMNR, Fond Armata 4-a, 844, f. 776; USHMM, RG-25.004M, reel 17, frame 339.
163. Simon Geissbühler, *Iulie însângerat: România și holocaustul din vara lui 1941*, trans. Ioana Rostoș (Bucharest: Curtea Veche, 2015), 156–60.
164. Ionescu, *Însemnări din război*, 31–32.
165. AMNR, Fond Corpul de Munte, dosar 244, f. 16.
166. Scârneci, *Viața și moartea în linia întâi*, 125–26.
167. Ibid., 127.
168. AMNR, Fond Armata 3-a, dosar 453, f. 5.
169. Axworthy, Scafes, and Craciunoiu, *Third Axis, Fourth Ally*, 50.
170. Quoted in Boog et al., *Germany and the Second World War*, 4:597.
171. Duțu, *Armata română în război*, 84.
172. Lungu, *De la Stalingrad la Gherla*, 13.
173. Quoted in Bărboi et al., *Armata română în vâltoarea războiului*, 100.
174. USHMM, RG-25.003M, reel 18, 29–30, 182.
175. David Stahel, *Operation Barbarossa and Germany's Defeat in the East* (Cambridge: Cambridge University Press, 2009), 335–36, 388, 393–96.
176. Arimia et al., *Antonescu-Hitler*, 1:121–22.
177. Scârneci, *Viața și moartea în linia întâi*, 132.
178. USHMM, RG-25.003M, reel 18, frames 187–88, 183–84.
179. DiNardo, *Germany and the Axis Powers*, 118.
180. Axworthy, Scafes, and Craciunoiu, *Third Axis, Fourth Ally*, 51.
181. AMNR, Fond Armata 4-a, dosar 772, f. 403; ibid., dosar 672, f. 1; ibid., dosar 658, f. 146; ibid., dosar 629, f. 247; ibid., dosar 784, f. 23.
182. Ibid., dosar 721, f. 171.
183. Vladimir Solonari, *A Satellite Empire: Romanian Rule in Southwestern Ukraine, 1941–1944* (Ithaca, NY: Cornell University Press, 2019), 21–22.
184. AMNR, Fond Armata 3-a, dosar 481, f. 120–26.
185. Bărboi et al., *Armata română în vâltoarea războiului*, 92.
186. AMNR, Fond Armata 4-a, dosar 793, f. 971.
187. Duțu, *Armata română în război*, 100. Moreover, 10 to 15 percent of shells reportedly did not explode; see Fond Armata 4-a, dosar 845, f. 362.
188. AMNR, Fond Armata 4-a, dosar 843, f. 412–14.
189. Axworthy, Scafes, and Craciunoiu, *Third Axis, Fourth Ally*, 51–52.
190. Ioanid, *Holocaust in Romania*, 143.
191. AMNR, Fond Armata 4-a, dosar 793, f. 537; SIA, Fond Inspectoratul Clerului Militar, F.II.4.1575, dosar 286, c.159–60.
192. Axworthy, Scafes, and Craciunoiu, *Third Axis, Fourth Ally*, 52.
193. BMMN, Fond Manuscrise, MSS 656, f. 30–31.
194. AMNR, Fond Armata 4-a, dosar 766, f. 728.
195. Duțu, *Armata română în război*, 94.
196. Axworthy, Scafes, and Craciunoiu, *Third Axis, Fourth Ally*, 53.
197. AMNR, Armata 4-a, dosar 772, f. 251.
198. AMNR, Fond Corpul de Munte, dosar 118, f. 253.
199. Pantazi, *Cu mareșalul până la moarte*, 134–35, 140.
200. Boog et al., *Germany and the Second World War*, 4:606.

201. Constantin Iancu, *Să te împaci cu . . . tine*, ed. Alexandru Birou (Constanța: Editura "Neliniști metafizice," 2009), 36.
202. Constantin Salcia, "Bolşevicii continuă să ucida prizonierii," *Soldatul*, 20 September 1941, 2; Axworthy, "Peasant Scapegoat to Industrial Slaughter," 230; Scârneci, *Viața și moartea în linea întâi*, 118.
203. Duțu, *Armata română în război*, 96.
204. Wilfried E. Ott, "De ce rezistă bolşevicii?," *Soldatul*, 30 September 1941, 2.
205. Bichir, *Cruciada diviziei de cremene*, 59.
206. AMNR, Fond Corpul de Munte, dosar 481, f. 2–5.
207. Scârneci, *Viața și moartea în linia întâi*, 165.
208. Bichir, *Cruciada diviziei de cremene*, 60.
209. Ibid., 61–62; Duțu, *Armata română în război*, 124–25; Robert M. Citino, *Death of the Wehrmacht: The German Campaigns of 1942* (Lawrence: University Press of Kansas, 2007), 57–58.
210. DiNardo, *Germany and the Axis Powers*, 116.
211. Boog et al., *Germany and the Second World War*, 4:612, n285.
212. AMNR, Fond Armata 4-a, dosar 772, f. 451; ibid., dosar 773, f. 189.
213. Răşcănescu, *Erou la Cotul Donului*, 99; AMNR, Fond Armata 4-a, dosar 1416, f. 235.
214. Răşcănescu, *Erou la Cotul Donului*, 98.
215. S. Mehendinți, "De ce ne batem?," *Sentinela*, 5 October 1941, 5.
216. AMNR, Fond Secția II-Informații, dosar 992, f. 45–46.
217. DiNardo, *Germany and the Axis Powers*, 119.
218. Răşcănescu, *Erou la Cotul Donului*, 106.
219. Ibid., 107–10.
220. Duțu, *Armata română în război*, 100.
221. AMNR, Fond Armata 4-a, dosar 870, f. 541–42.
222. Ibid., dosar 860, f. 412.
223. Dallin, *Odessa*, 70–72.
224. AMNR, Fond Armata 4-a, dosar 860, f. 540.
225. Rădulescu, "Pățaniile soldatului Neață," *Sentinela*, 19 October 1941, 7.
226. Răşcănescu, *Erou la Cotul Donului*, 116–17.
227. Quoted in Ancel, *History of the Holocaust in Romania*, 354.
228. Ioanid, *Holocaust in Romania*, 143–44.
229. Ibid., 130; USHMM, RG-25.004M reel 14, frames 584–86.
230. Solonari, *Purifying the Nation*, 208.
231. Ioanid, *Holocaust in Romania*, 177.
232. AMNR, Fond Armata 4-a, dosar 870, f. 510–15.
233. Duțu, *Armata română în război*, 110.
234. AMNR, Fond Armata 4-a, dosar 870, f. 609.
235. USHMM, RG-25.004M, reel 14, frames 577–81.
236. Quoted in Ioanid, *Holocaust in Romania*, 179.
237. USHMM, RG-25.004M, reel 31, frame 51.
238. Ibid., reel 30, frames 549–51.
239. Quoted in Ioanid, *Holocaust in Romania*, 180.
240. Arad, Krakowski, and Spector, *Einsatzgruppen Reports*, 209.

241. Ioanid, *Holocaust in Romania*, 182.
242. Dumitru, *State, Antisemitism, and Collaboration in the Holocaust*, 210.
243. Quoted in Ancel, *History of the Holocaust in Romania*, 359.
244. Ibid., 369; Ioanid, *Holocaust in Romania*, 208.

5. 1941–1942: Doubling Down on Holy War

1. Ionescu, *Însemnări din război*, 47–48.
2. AMNR, Fond Armata 4-a, dosar 866, f. 348; ANIC, Fond Preşedinţia Consiliului de Ministri: Cabinetul Militar, dosar 2–1940, f. 1.
3. ANIC, Fond Preşedinţia Consiliului de Ministri: Cabinetul Militar, dosar 2–1940, f. 5, 8; Duţu, *Armata română în război*, 125.
4. David Stahel, *Operation Typhoon: Hitler's March on Moscow, October 1941* (Cambridge: Cambridge University Press, 2013), 4.
5. Manstein, *Lost Victories*, 206–8.
6. The first lists suspiciously consisted mainly of headquarters troops and officers and NCOs of combat units, so the whole project was started over to make sure enlisted men who had won medals got the land grants; see AMNR, Fond Armata 3-a, dosar 281, f. 25, 31, 111; Ionescu, *Însemnări din război*, 34.
7. AMNR, Fond Armata 4-a, dosar 866, f. 487.
8. Sebastian, *Journal*, 432.
9. AMNR, Fond Armata 4-a, dosar 870, f. 71.
10. Emil Dorian, *The Quality of Witness: A Romanian Diary, 1937–1944*, ed. Marguerite Dorian, trans. Mara Soceanu Vamos (Philadelphia: Jewish Publication Society of America, 1982), 173.
11. Stahel, *Operation Barbarossa*, 159–60, 199.
12. Bellamy, *Absolute War*, 268.
13. Halic and Dobrin interview.
14. Citino, *Death of the Wehrmacht*, 59–61.
15. AMNR, Fond Corpul de Munte, dosar 118, f. 368.
16. AMNR, Fond Armata 3-a, dosar 283, f. 93–95.
17. Scârneci, *Viaţa şi moartea din linia întâi*, 187.
18. Giurescu, *Romania in the Second World War*, 94.
19. AMNR, Fond Armata 3-a, dosar 313, f. 71.
20. AMNR, Fond Corpul de Munte, dosar 118, f. 378.
21. Duţu, *Armata română în război*, 131.
22. AMNR, Fond Corpul de Munte, dosar 118, f. 413.
23. Scârneci, *Viaţa şi moartea din linia întâi*, 194.
24. Rădulescu, "Păţaniile soldatului Neaţă," *Sentinela*, 5 October 1941, 7.
25. Ionescu, *Însemnări din război*, 39.
26. Arad, Krakowski, and Spector, *Einsatzgruppen Reports*, 63, 73, 111, 166.
27. ANIC, Fond Preşedinţia Consiliului de Ministri: Cabinetul Militar, dosar 31/1941, f. 22–92.
28. Arad, *Holocaust in the Soviet Union*, 202.
29. Kiril Feferman, *The Holocaust in the Crimea and the North Caucasus* (Jerusalem: Yad Vashem, 2016), 157.

30. Ibid., 123, 133, 146.
31. Bellamy, *Absolute War*, 458.
32. Scârneci, *Viața și moartea din linia întâi*, 227–29.
33. Citino, *Death of the Wehrmacht*, 63–64; Axworthy, Scafes, and Craciunoiu, *Third Axis, Fourth Ally*, 67.
34. Sebastian, *Journal*, 454.
35. AMNR, Fond Armata 3-a, dosar 369, f. 351, 412.
36. Crisan, *Amazing Life*, 135.
37. AMNR, Fond Armata 3-a, dosar 624, f. 95.
38. Jean Ancel, *Transnistria*, vol. 1 (Bucharest: Editura Atlas, 1998), 52–53.
39. Eric C. Steinhart, *The Holocaust and the Germanization of the Ukraine* (New York: Cambridge University Press, 2015), 40–41, 75–77, 80.
40. Ibid., 117–20.
41. AMNR, Fond Armata 3-a, dosar 731, f. 7, 17, 32–33, 44, 69.
42. Steinhart, *Holocaust and the Germanization of the Ukraine*, 120–26.
43. Ibid., 128.
44. Ioanid, *Holocaust in Romania*, 185.
45. Quoted in Deletant, *Hitler's Forgotten Ally*, 176.
46. AMNR, Fond Armata 3-a, dosar 452, f. 2.
47. Citino, *Death of the Wehrmacht*, 65.
48. AMNR, Fond Armata 3-a, dosar 452, f. 8–11.
49. Feferman, *Holocaust in the Crimea and the North Caucasus*, 158.
50. Ionescu, *Însemnări din război*, 48.
51. AMNR, Fond Armata 3-a, dosar 511, f. 6.
52. AMNR, Fond Corpul de Munte, dosar 499, f. 162.
53. Ibid., f. 165–66.
54. Duțu, *Armata română în război*, 142.
55. USHMM, RG-25.003M, reel 18, frames 709–10, 713.
56. Steinhard, *Holocaust and the Germanization of the Ukraine*, 133–34, 140.
57. Boog et al., *Germany and the Second World War*, 6:904.
58. Arimia et al., *Antonescu-Hitler*, 1:160–65.
59. Boog et al., *Germany and the Second World War*, 6:909–10.
60. Axworthy, Scafeș, and Craciunoiu, *Third Axis, Fourth Ally*, 73; Giurescu, *Romania in the Second World War*, 149.
61. Stan V. Gheorghe, *Din cercul de la Stalingrad în lagărele sovietice: Memorii 1942–1948* (Bucharest: Editura Militară, 2018), 49–50.
62. Pantazi, *Cu mareșalul până la moarte*, 122.
63. Quoted in Citino, *Death of the Wehrmacht*, 88.
64. Quoted in Bărboi et al., *Armata română în vâltoarea războiului*, 115–16.
65. AMNR, Fond Armata 3-a, dosar 511, f. 3, 8–9, 12, 23; ibid., dosar 307, f. 81.
66. Berkhoff, *Motherland in Danger*, 194.
67. Natalia Nabokova-Vasilkova, "Odesenii recunoscător fraților români liberatori," *Soldatul*, 3 February 1941, 1.
68. SIA, Fond Inspectoratul Clerului Militar, F.II.4.1575, dosar 286, c. 835–37, 766.
69. AMNR, Fond Corpul de Munte, dosar 118, f. 506–7.
70. Ibid., dosar 947, f. 655–56.

71. Scârneci, *Viața și moartea din linia întâi*, 281.
72. AMNR, Fond Armata 3-, dosar 410, f. 104, 341; AMNR, Fond Corpul de Munte, dosar 830, f. 14.
73. Quoted in Bărboi et al., *Armata română în vâltoarea războiului*, 123–24.
74. Ioanid, *Holocaust in Romania*, 186, 193; Steinhart, *Holocaust and the Germanization of the Ukraine*, 156, 131.
75. AMNR, Fond Corpul de Munte, dosar 947, f. 503.
76. AMNR, Fond Armata 3-a, dosar 888, f. 204; 223–26, 236–56; 297–98.
77. Ibid., dosar 452, f. 25–26.
78. Scârneci, *Viața și moartea din linia întâi*, 289.
79. Axworthy, Scafes, and Craciunoiu, *Third Axis, Fourth Ally*, 68.
80. Duțu, *Armata română în război*, 160–64.
81. AMNR, Fond Armata 3-a, dosar 1229, f. 15–18.
82. Ibid., dosar 888, f. 167–68, 170–71, 175–77.
83. Ibid., dosar 1229, f. 85–95.
84. Ibid., f. 106.
85. Case, *Between States*, 81.
86. Anton, *Propagandă și război*, 210.
87. AMNR, Fond Corpul de Munte, dosar 947, f. 716, 780.
88. AMNR, Fond Armata 3-a, dosar 358, f. 132, 137.
89. AMNR, Fond Armata 3-a, dosar 358, f. 13.
90. Scafeș et al., *Armata română*, 109, 118–19.
91. Axworthy, Scafes, and Craciunoiu, *Third Axis, Fourth Ally*, 75–79.
92. Arimia et al., *Antonescu-Hitler*, 1:165–66.
93. Bichir, *Cruciada diviziei de cremene*, 75–76.
94. AMNR, Fond Corpul de Munte, dosar 947, f. 758.
95. Scârneci, *Viața și moartea din linia întâi*, 297.
96. Mihalcea interview.
97. AMNR, Fond Armata 3-a, dosar 314, f. 577–78; ibid., dosar 1044, f. 33–34, 139–41.
98. Ibid., dosar 882, f. 30.
99. AMNR, Fond Corpul de Munte, dosar 499, f. 340.
100. AMNR, Fond Corpul de Cavalerie, dosar 253, f. 685–86.
101. Shepherd, *Hitler's Soldiers*, 278–79.
102. AMNR, Fond Corpul de Munte, dosar 550, f. 148; ibid., dosar 947, f. 785; ibid., dosar 914, f. 447.
103. AMNR, Fond Armata 3-a, dosar 452, f. 24.
104. Ibid., dosar 1127, f. 3, 4, 19.
105. Ibid., dosar 570, f. 261.
106. Solonari, *Satellite Empire*, 193–200.
107. AMNR, Fond Armata 3-a, dosar 1196, f. 1, 4, 10–17, 21, 27, 34, 36.
108. Ibid., dosar 1122, f. 336.
109. Ibid., dosar 1196, f. 77–78, 82.
110. Citino, *Death of the Wehrmacht*, 87, 89.
111. Axworthy, Scafes, and Craciunoiu, *Third Ally, Fourth Ally*, 70–71.
112. V. Stamati, "General-Iarnă a trecut în retragere," *Soldatul*, 5 April 1942, 2.
113. N. Trandafir, "Victoria Germaniei," *Ecoul Crimeei* (Simferopol), 8 May 1942, 1.
114. Citino, *Death of the Wehrmacht*, 69.
115. Cârlan, *Păstrați-mi amintirile!*, 13–14.

116. Ionescu, *Însemnări din război*, 88.
117. Duțu, *Armata română în război*, 146–49; Citino, *Death of the Wehrmacht*, 72–75.
118. Ionescu, *Însemnări din război*, 89.
119. Citino, *Death of the Wehrmacht*, 77; Axworthy, Scafes, and Craciunoiu, *Third Axis, Fourth Ally*, 68–69.
120. Citino, *Death of the Wehrmacht*, 94–99.
121. AMNR, Fond Armata 3-a, dosar 888, f. 236, 270–74, 354; ibid., dosar 1119, f. 153.
122. Duțu, *Armata română în război*, 167; Citino, *Death of the Wehrmacht*, 103–9.
123. He miswrote *"o victorie decisivă asupra creștinismului"*; see Ionescu, *Însemnări din război*, 94.
124. AMNR, Fond Corpul de Munte, dosar 813, f. 335.
125. "Pe urmele barbarilor," *Armata* (Bucharest), 16 May 1942, 22–23.
126. Solonari, *Purifying the Nation*, 271.
127. Ioanid, *Holocaust in Romania*, 226.
128. AMNR, Fond Corpul de Munte, dosar 852, f. 168; Feferman, *Holocaust in the Crimea and the North Caucasus*, 123.
129. AMNR, Fond Corpul de Munte, dosar 923, f. 89–90; ibid., dosar 916, f. 63–64; AMNR, Fond Armata 3-a, dosar 1498, f. 3.
130. Arad, *Holocaust in the Soviet Union*, 203–4, 211.
131. Boog et al., *Germany and the Second World War*, 6:941.
132. Citino, *Death of the Wehrmacht*, 78–79; Duțu, *Armata română în război*, 152.
133. Scârneci, *Viața și moartea din linia întâi*, 341.
134. Ibid., 345, 355–56, 367, 369.
135. Ionescu, *Însemnări din război*, 100.
136. Cârlan, *Păstrați-mi amintirile!*, 19.
137. Sebastian, *Journal*, 491.
138. David Cesarani, *Becoming Eichmann: Rethinking the Life, Crimes, and Trial of a "Desk Murderer"* (New York: Da Capo, 2004), 152.
139. AMNR, Fond Armata 4-a, dosar 1236, f. 775, 776–78.
140. Solonari, *Satellite Empire*, 168–70.
141. Citino, *Death of the Wehrmacht*, 156–65.
142. Bichir, *Cruciada diviziei de cremene*, 87–88.
143. DiNardo, *Germany and the Axis Powers*, 141.
144. Scârneci, *Viața și moartea din linia întâi*, 362.
145. Ionescu, *Însemnări din război*, 101.
146. Scârneci, *Viața și moartea din linia întâi*, 370–72, 375.
147. Ibid., 374.
148. AMNR, Fond Corpul de Munte, dosar 916, f. 96.
149. Citino, *Death of the Wehrmacht*, 80–81; Duțu, *Armata română în război*, 154–59.
150. AMNR, Fond Armata 4-a, dosar 1243, f. 68.
151. Ibid., dosar 1246, f. 1.
152. AMNR, Fond Corpul de Munte, dosar 880, f. 95, 257; AMNR, Fond Armata 3-a, dosar 1044, f. 37.
153. AMNR, Fond Corpul de Munte, dosar 855, f. 54, 208, 277, 235; ibid., dosar 856, f. 40, 114, 132, 198.
154. AMNR, Fond Armata 3-a, dosar 369, f. 399; ibid., dosar 511, f. 59.
155. AMNR, Fond Corpul de Munte, dosar 550, f. 51–53, 510, 517, 524, 668–69.

156. Teodorescu, *Mândria vânătorului de munte*, 68.
157. AMNR, Fond Comandamentul Militar al Capitalei, dosar 807, f. 464.
158. Voinescu, *Jurnal*, 1:482–83.
159. Citino, *Death of the Wehrmacht*, 224–27; Duțu, *Armata română în război*, 170.
160. "În urmăriea dușmanului dela răsărit," *Sentinela*, 26 July 1942, 1, 3.
161. Axworthy, Scafes, and Craciunoiu, *Third Axis, Fourth Ally*, 83–84; Duțu, *Armata română în război*, 167–68.
162. "Situația bolșevicilor e disperată," *Ecoul Crimeei*, 27 July 1942, 2.
163. ACNSAS, Fond Personal, dosar 7245, f. 177.
164. Ibid., f. 157–58.
165. Chirnoagă, *Istoria politică și militară a răsboiului României contra Rusiei sovietice*, 202.
166. Axworthy, Scafes, and Craciunoiu, *Third Axis, Fourth Ally*, 81–82; ACNSAS, Fond Documentar, dosar 8178, f. 48, 258.
167. AMNR, Fond Corpul de Cavalerie, dosar 639, f. 169–78, 209–15.
168. Teodorescu, *Mândria vânătorului de munte*, 72; Bichir, *Cruciada diviziei de cremene*, 132.
169. Axworthy, Scafes, and Craciunoiu, *Third Axis, Fourth Ally*, 84.
170. Citino, *Death of the Wehrmacht*, 246–47, 233–37.
171. Gheorghe, *Din cercul de la Stalingrad în lagărele sovietice*, 36–37.
172. Citino, *Death of the Wehrmacht*, 237; AMNR, Fond Armata 3-a, dosar 1299, f. 7–8, 11.
173. ACNSAS, Fond Documentar, dosar 8178, f. 16–18, 48, 352.
174. Axworthy, Scafes, and Craciunoiu, *Third Axis, Fourth Ally*, 82.
175. Citino, *Death of the Wehrmacht*, 248–51.
176. Wilhelm Filderman, *Memoirs and Diaries*, vol. 2, ed. Jean Ancel (Jerusalem: Yad Vashem, 2015), 317.
177. Solonari, *Purifying the Nation*, 296.
178. Voinescu, *Jurnal*, 1:500.
179. AMNR, Fond Corpul de Munte, dosar 951, f. 82–85.
180. Ibid., f. 153–228.
181. Duțu, *Armata română în război*, 212; Axworthy, Scafes, and Craciunoiu, *Third Axis, Fourth Ally*, 85.
182. Boog et al., *Germany and the Second World War*, 6:1083–84.
183. Ibid., 1095.
184. AMNR, Fond Corpul de Munte, dosar 888, f. 34–37.
185. Ibid., dosar 951, f. 46.
186. Păsat, *Memoriile căpitanului Dumitru Păsat*, 77–78.
187. Gheorghe Tănăsescu, *Prizonier la Cotul Donului: Jurnal de război (27.08–23.11.1942) și prizonierat (24.11.1942–20.11.1946)*, ed. Nicolae Strâmbeanu and Marius Tănăsescu (Bucharest: Editura Militară, 2017), 36–37.
188. Ibid., 40, 42.
189. Ștefanescu interview.
190. Tănăsescu, *Prizonier la Cotul Donului*, 47.
191. Duțu, *Armata română în război*, 188.
192. Axworthy, Scafes, and Craciunoiu, *Third Axis, Fourth Ally*, 86.
193. Georgescu Pion, "Odesa—Stalingrad," *Armata*, 15 October 1942, 5. Emphasis in original.

194. Tănăsescu, *Prizonier la Cotul Donului*, 43, 49–50.
195. Gheorghe, *Din cercul de la Stalingrad în lagărele sovietice*, 39.
196. Păsat, *Memoriile căpitanului Dumitru Păsat*, 93–94.
197. Rădulescu, "Pățaniile soldatului Neață," *Sentinela*, 27 September 1942, 7.
198. Păsat, *Memoriile căpitanului Dumitru Păsat*, 92–93, 103–4.
199. Petre Costea, interview with the author, Buzău, 2012.
200. Alexandru Teodorescu-Schei, *Învins și învingător: 1941–1949, Campania din est și prizonieratul* (Bucharest: Editura Allfa, 1998), 50–52.
201. Răşcănescu, *Eroul la Cotul Donului*, 126–29.
202. AMNR, Fond Armata 3-a, dosar 1046, f. 10, 74, 399.
203. Gheorghe, *Din cercul de la Stalingrad în lagărele sovietice*, 73.
204. Solonari, *Purifying the Nation*, 283.
205. Boog et al., *Germany and the Second World War*, 6:1109–10; Axworthy, Scafes, and Craciunoiu, *Third Axis, Fourth Ally*, 87.
206. Arimia et al., *Antonescu-Hitler*, 1:189–90.
207. AMNR, Fond Armata 4-a, dosar 1332, f. 70–72.
208. AMNR, Fond Armata 3-a, dosar 1299, 146–47, 163–65.
209. Ibid., f. 216–17.
210. Ibid., dosar 881, f. 6–7.
211. AMNR, Corpul de Munte, dosar 951, f. 73.
212. Ibid., dosar 1299, f. 211, 224–25.
213. Duțu, *Armata română în război*, 191.
214. SIA, Fond Inspectoratul Clerului Militar, F.II.4.1578, dosar 300, c. 203–13.
215. Costea interview.
216. Mihalcea interview.
217. Axworthy, Scafes, and Craciunoiu, *Third Axis, Fourth Ally*, 85.
218. Boog et al., *Germany and the Second World War*, 6:1120–21.
219. Cârlan, *Păstrați-mi amintirile!*, 36.
220. Tănăsescu, *Prizonier la Cotul Donului*, 60.
221. AMNR, Fond Armata 3-a, dosar 1138, f. 13.
222. Dumitru Burciu, interview with the author, Iași, 2010.
223. AMNR, Fond Armata 4-a, dosar 1273, f. 156–61, 163–67, 169.
224. AMNR, Fond Armata 3-a, dosar 881, f. 19.
225. AMNR, Fond Armata 4-a, 1273, f. 173–75.
226. Axworthy, Scafes, and Craciunoiu, *Third Axis, Fourth Ally*, 291–93.
227. Tănăsescu, *Prizonier la Cotul Donului*, 61–62.
228. Beevor, *Stalingrad*, 230–32.
229. ANIC, Fond Preşedinţia Consiliului de Miniştri: Cabinetul Militar, dosar 2–1940, f. 1, 5.

6. 1942–1944: Holy War of Defense

1. Geratimusz Morar, interview with the author, Sibiu, 2012.
2. Tănăsescu, *Prizonier la Cotul Donului*, 65–66.
3. Beevor, *Stalingrad*, 240–41; Axworthy, Scafes, and Craciunoiu, *Third Axis, Fourth Ally*, 92.
4. AMNR, Fond Armata 3-a, dosar 1094, f. 43, 60.
5. Tănăsescu, *Prizonier la Cotul Donului*, 66.

6. Beevor, *Stalingrad*, 244–45; DiNardo, *Germany and the Axis Powers*, 151–52.
7. Quoted in Bărboi et al., *Armata română în vâltoarea războiului*, 147.
8. Quoted in Beevor, *Stalingrad*, 248–49.
9. Duțu, *Armata română în război*, 214.
10. Axworthy, Scafes, and Craciunoiu, *Third Axis, Fourth Ally*, 103.
11. Crișan V. Mușețeanu, *Strigătul: Ediție definitivă* (Bucharest: Editura "Jurnalul literar," 2003), 20.
12. Beevor, *Stalingrad*, 249–50.
13. AMNR, Fond Armata 4-a, dosar 1273, f. 1.
14. AMNR, Fond Armata 3-a, dosar 1094, f. 9–10.
15. Quoted in Boog et al., *Germany and the Second World War*, 6:1123, n231.
16. Tănăsescu, *Prizonier la Cotul Donului*, 66.
17. Quoted in Bărboi, *Armata română în vâltoarea războiului*, 134.
18. Lungu, *De la Stalingrad la Gherla*, 24.
19. Răşcănescu, *Erou la Cotul Donului*, 133.
20. Citino, *Death of the Wehrmacht*, 296–97.
21. Quoted in Bărboi, *Armata română în vâltoarea războiului*, 146.
22. AMNR, Fond Armata 3-a, dosar 1152, f. 12–13.
23. Boog et al., *Germany and the Second World War*, 6:1125; Axworthy, Scafes, and Craciunoiu, *Third Axis, Fourth Ally*, 95.
24. AMNR, Fond Armata 4-a, dosar 1273, f. 22–23, 87.
25. Quoted in Bărboi et al., *Armata română în vâltoarea războiului*, 148.
26. Axworthy, Scafes, and Craciunoiu, *Third Axis, Fourth Ally*, 97.
27. Tănăsescu, *Prizonier la Cotul Donului*, 68.
28. Ibid., 69–70.
29. Burciu interview.
30. AMNR, Fond Armata 3-a, dosar 894, f. 16.
31. Păsat, *Memoriile căpitanului Dumitru Păsat*, 142.
32. Duțu, *Armata română în război*, 202–3.
33. Răşcănescu, *Erou la Cotul Donului*, 140–41.
34. AMNR, Fond Armata 3-a, dosar 894, f. 17–18.
35. Lungu, *De la Stalingrad la Gherla*, 24–25.
36. AMNR, Fond Armata 3-a, dosar 992, f. 431–32. Emphasis (underlined) in the original.
37. Tănăsescu, *Prizonier la Cotul Donului*, 70–73.
38. Ibid., 83.
39. AMNR, Fond Armata 3-a, dosar 1152, f. 17–18.
40. Axworthy, Scafes, and Craciunoiu, *Third Axis, Fourth Ally*, 97–100; Duțu, *Armata română în război*, 205.
41. AMNR, Fond Armata 3-a, dosar 838, f. 96–97.
42. Răşcănescu, *Erou la Cotul Donului*, 53.
43. Citino, *Death of the Wehrmacht*, 298.
44. Axworthy, Scafes, and Craciunoiu, *Third Axis, Fourth Ally*, 101, 109.
45. Ibid., 109–10; Museteanu, *Strigatul*, 51.
46. Robert M. Citino, *The Wehrmacht Retreats: Fighting a Lost War, 1943* (Lawrence: University Press of Kansas, 2012), 59.

47. Axworthy, Scafes, and Craciunoiu, *Third Axis, Fourth Ally*, 107–8.
48. AMNR, Fond Armata 4-a, dosar 1273, f. 270–71.
49. Ezechil, *La portile infernului*, 55.
50. Mihalcea interview.
51. AMNR, Fond Corpul de Cavalerie, dosar 928, f. 1–2.
52. AMNR, Fond Corpul de Munte, dosar 880, f. 381, 382.
53. Citino, *Death of the Wehrmacht*, 62.
54. Arimia et al., *Antonescu-Hitler*, 2:9–19, 21–23, 27–32.
55. Aly, *Hitler's Beneficiaries*, 237–43.
56. Teodorescu, *Mândria vânătorului de munte*, 147; Bichir, *Cruciada diviziei de cremene*, 191.
57. Quoted in Walter Goerlitz, *Paulus and Stalingrad: A Life of Field-Marshal Friedrich Paulus, with Notes, Correspondence, and Documents from His Papers*, trans. R. H. Stevens (London: Methuen, 1963), 156–59.
58. Gheorghe, *Din cercul de la Stalingrad în lagărele sovietice*, 42–45.
59. Lungu, *De la Stalingrad la Gherla*, 26–27.
60. Quoted in Duțu, *Armata română în război*, 230.
61. Gheorghe, *Din cercul de la Stalingrad în lagărele sovietice*, 94.
62. Axworthy, Scafes, and Craciunoiu, *Third Axis, Fourth Ally*, 111; Pantazi, *Cu mareșalul până la moarte*, 233; Duțu, *Armata română în război*, 231.
63. Gheorghe, *Din cercul de la Stalingrad în lagărele sovietice*, 108, 111.
64. Frieser et al., *Germany and the Second World War*, 8:14.
65. AMNR, Fond Armata 3-a, dosar 843, f. 152.
66. AMNR, Fond Armata 4-a, dosar 1482, f. 46, 4–14.
67. DiNardo, *Germany and the Axis Powers*, 174.
68. Frieser et al., *Germany and the Second World War*, 8:46–47.
69. Duțu, *Armata română in război*, 235; DiNardo, *Germany and the Axis Powers*, 151.
70. DiNardo, *German and the Axis Powers*, 156; Duțu, *Armata română in război*, 236–37.
71. AMNR, Fond Corpul de Munte, dosar 880, f. 418.
72. AMNR, Fond Armata 3-a, dosar 1351, f. 55–58; AMNR, Fond Corpul de Munte, dosar 933, f. 498–99.
73. Moraru, *Armata lui Stalin văzută de români*, 117.
74. Voinescu, *Jurnal*, 2:11.
75. Frieser et al., *Germany and the Second World War*, 8:232.
76. "Lupta contra comunismul," *Armata*, 1 February 1943, copertă de față.
77. "Bestialele răzbunări sovietice în Caucazul evacuat," *Ecoul Crimeei*, 21 February 1943, 2.
78. Filderman, *Memoirs and Diaries*, 2:383–84.
79. Ioanid, *Holocaust in Romania*, 218–20.
80. AMNR, Fond Armata 3-a, dosar 3032, f. 71.
81. Ioanid, *Holocaust in Romania*, 221–22.
82. Bărboi et al., *Armata română în vâltoarea războiului*, 161.
83. Citino, *Wehrmacht Retreats*, 66–70.
84. Axworthy, Scafes, and Craciunoiu, *Third Axis, Fourth Ally*, 126.
85. Bichir, *Cruciada diviziei de cremene*, 219.

86. SIA, Fond Inspectoratul Clerului, F.II.41579, dosar 300, c. 39.
87. AMNR, Fond Armata 4-a, dosar 1481, f. 23–27.
88. AMNR, Fond Corpul de Munte, dosar 933, f. 347.
89. AMNR, Fond Armata 4-a, dosar 1483, f. 101; AMNR, Fond Armata 3-a, dosar, 2759, f. 187.
90. AMNR, Fond Armata 3-a, dosar 2148, f. 85.
91. Ibid., f. 382–86; AMNR, Fond Centru de Instruție Nr. 5 Sărata, dosar 40, f. 50; dosar 856, f. 37.
92. Axworthy, Scafes, and Craciunoiu, *Third Axis, Fourth Ally*, 127.
93. AMNR, Fond Corpul de Cavalerie, dosar 1047, f. 97.
94. SIA, Fond Inspectoratul Clerului, F.II.41578, dosar 300, c. 258–59.
95. AMNR, Fond Armata 4-a, dosar 1481, f. 1–13.
96. SIA, Fond Inspectoratul Clerului, F.II.41579, dosar 300, c. 59–61. Emphasis (underlined) in the original.
97. "Bolșevicii nu vor ierta niciun popor," *Soldatul*, 25 March 1943, 1.
98. Rădulescu, "Pățaniile soldatului Neață," *Sentinela*, 25 April 1943, 13.
99. Cârlan, *Păstrați-mi amintirile!*, 75, 78, 81.
100. Filip Mihai, interview with the author, Suceava, 2011.
101. Axworthy, Scafes, and Craciunoiu, *Third Axis, Fourth Ally*, 299–301.
102. Scârneci, *Viața și moartea în linia întâi*, 408.
103. AMNR, Fond Armata 4-a, dosar 1481, f. 139, 92.
104. Scârneci, *Viața și moartea în linia întâi*, 410.
105. Citino, *Wehrmacht Retreats*, 134.
106. Scârneci, *Viața și moartea în linia întâi*, 419.
107. Cârlan, *Păstrați-mi amitirile!*, 97; Sebastian, *Journal*, 566.
108. Citino, *Wehrmacht Retreats*, 222–23.
109. AMNR, Corpul de Cavalerie, dosar 915, f. 85, 150–53.
110. AMNR, Fond Armata 3-a, dosar 2152, f. 246.
111. AMNR, Fond Corpul de Munte, dosar 1363, f. 288–89, 291.
112. Axworthy, Scafes, and Craciunoiu, *Third Axis, Fourth Ally*, 127–28.
113. Cârlan, *Păstrați-mi amitirile!*, 100.
114. Scârneci, *Viața și moartea în linia întâi*, 432.
115. SIA, Fond Inspectoratul Clerului, F.II.41579, dosar 300, c. 311–12, 491.
116. AMNR, Fond Armata 3-a, dosar 2759, f. 357.
117. Bărboi et al., *Armata română în vâltoarea războiului*, 163–64; Duțu, *Armata română în război*, 251.
118. Cârlan, *Păstrați-mi amitirile!*, 103–4.
119. Sebastian, *Journal*, 568.
120. Scârneci, *Viața și moartea în linia întâi*, 451.
121. Axworthy, Scafes, and Craciunoiu, *Third Axis, Fourth Ally*, 128.
122. Cârlan, *Păstrați-mi amitirile!*, 108.
123. AMNR, Fond Armata 3-a, dosar 2158, f. 171.
124. Duțu, *Armata română în război*, 250.
125. Citino, *Wehrmacht Retreats*, 233–34.
126. Robert Forczyk, *Where the Iron Crosses Grow: The Crimea, 1941–1944* (New York: Osprey, 2014), 243.

127. Axworthy, Scafes, and Craciunoiu, *Third Axis, Fourth Ally*, 129.
128. Scârneci, *Viața și moartea în linia întâi*, 476.
129. Cârlan, *Păstrați-mi amitirile!*, 109. Emphasis in original.
130. BMMN, Fond Manuscrise, MSS 676, f. 11–12.
131. AMNR, Fond Armata 3-a, dosar 2782, f. 76.
132. Ibid., dosar 2225, f. 68; ibid., dosar 2780, f. 149.
133. Scârneci, *Viața și moartea în linia întâi*, 472.
134. Ibid., 478.
135. Ionescu, *Însemnări din război*, 203.
136. AMNR, Fond Armata 3-a, dosar 2780, f. 67, 86.
137. AMNR, Fond Corpul de Munte, dosar 1414, f. 506. Emphasis (underlined) in the original.
138. Duțu, *Armata română in război*, 253–54; Forczyk, *Where the Iron Crosses Grow*, 250.
139. Cârlan, *Păstrați-mi amitirile!*, 126–27.
140. AMNR, Fond Corpul de Cavalerie, dosar 1256, f. 272.
141. AMNR, Fond Corpul de Munte, dosar 1407, f. 107–10.
142. AMNR, Fond Armata 3-a, dosar 2158, f. 303–5.
143. AMNR, Fond Corpul de Munte, dosar 1405, f. 56. Emphasis (underlined) in original.
144. BMMN, Fond Manuscrise, MSS 676, f. 24–25.
145. Forczyk, *Where the Iron Crosses Grow*, 260.
146. Ibid., 261, 265.
147. Ibid., 258–59.
148. Axworthy, Scafes, and Craciunoiu, *Third Axis, Fourth Ally*, 131.
149. AMNR, Fond Armata 3-a, dosar 2158, f. 404.
150. Ibid., dosar 2767, f. 144.
151. AMNR, Fond Corpul de Cavalerie, dosar 1259, f. 15; ibid., dosar 1256, f. 389.
152. "Numai Germania poate salva omenirea de bolșevism," *Ecoul Crimeei*, 20 January 1944, 1; Horia Nițulescu, "Izbândă său moarte," *Sentinela*, 6 February 1944, 6.
153. Citino, *Death of the Wehrmacht*, 235–36.
154. Axworthy, Scafes, and Craciunoiu, *Third Axis, Fourth Ally*, 156.
155. AMNR, Fond Armata 3-a, dosar 2780, f. 214–15, 237.
156. Quoted in Ioanid, *Holocaust in Romania*, 223.
157. Ibid., 255–56.
158. AMNR, Fond Armata 3-a, dosar 2281, f. 19; AMNR, Fond Corpul de Munte, dosar 1405, f. 74.
159. Duțu, *Armata română în război*, 254.
160. AMNR, Fond Corpul de Munte, dosar 1812, f. 17.
161. AMNR, Fond Armata 3-a, dosar 2282, f. 104–12.
162. AMNR, Fond Corpul de Munte, dosar 1833, f. 1–4, 7, 15.
163. Dumitru Bunescu, "'Hatmanul' Tobă," *Ecoul Crimeei*, 28 February 1943, 1.
164. Robert M. Citino, *The Wehrmacht's Last Stand: The German Campaigns of 1944–1945* (Lawrence: University Press of Kansas, 2017), 40–52.
165. Quoted in Ioanid, *Holocaust in Romania*, 256.
166. Cârlan, *Păstrați-mi amitirile!*, 142–43.

167. BMMN, Fond Manuscrise, MSS 676, f. 30.
168. ANIC, Fond Presedinția Consiliului de Ministri: Cabinetul Militar, dosar 129/1943, f. 75–79.
169. AMNR, Fond Corpul de Munte, dosar 1407, f. 3.
170. Solonari, *Satellite Empire*, 223–25.
171. AMNR, Fond Armata 4-a, dosar 1481, f. 272–73.
172. AMNR, Fond Armata 3-a, dosar 3032, f. 1–5.
173. Solonari, *Satellite Empire*, 227.
174. Duțu, *Armata română în război*, 254.
175. AMNR, Fond Corpul de Cavalerie, dosar 1211, f. 255–56.
176. Ibid., dosar 1256, f. 61–66.
177. BMMN, Fond Manuscrise, MSS 676, f. 39–40.
178. AMNR, Fond Corpul de Cavalerie, dosar 1256, f. 80.
179. Ioanid, *Holocaust in Romania*, 256.
180. AMNR, Fond Corpul de Munte, dosar 1833, f. 200–209.
181. Axworthy, Scafes, and Craciunoiu, *Third Axis, Fourth Ally*, 156.
182. Arimia et al., *Antonescu-Hitler*, 2:139–43.
183. Cornelius, *Hungary in World War II*, 269–76; Arimia et al., *Antonescu-Hitler*, 2:143–46.
184. Cârlan, *Păstrați-mi amitirile!*, 151.
185. Axworthy, Scafes, and Craciunoiu, *Third Axis, Fourth Ally*, 157–58.
186. Dorian, *Quality of Witness*, 304.
187. Klaus Schönherr, *Luptele wehrmachtului în România 1944*, 2nd ed., trans. Elena Matei (Bucharest: Editura Militară, 2015), 34.
188. AMNR, Fond Armata 3-a, dosar 2968, f. 247.
189. Ibid., dosar 3032, f. 277.
190. AMNR, Fond Armata 4-a, dosar 1533, f. 7.
191. Giurescu, *Romania in the Second World War*, 161–63.
192. David M. Glantz, *Red Storm over the Balkans: The Failed Soviet Invasion of Romania, Spring 1944* (Lawrence: University Press of Kansas, 2007), xii–xiii, 24.
193. Schönherr, *Luptele wehrmachtului în România 1944*, 37–38.
194. Axworthy, Scafes, and Craciunoiu, *Third Axis, Fourth Ally*, 157.
195. Ibid., 133; Forcyzk, *Where the Iron Crosses Grow*, 272–75.
196. Cârlan, *Păstrați-mi amitirile!*, 161.
197. Ibid., 170.
198. AMNR, Fond Armata 4-a, dosar 1596, f. 185, 187, 196–97.
199. Ibid., dosar 1533, f. 31–32.
200. Shepherd, *Hitler's Soldiers*, 472.
201. AMNR, Fond Armata 3-a, dosar 3015, f. 5.
202. Netejoru, *Și eu am luptat în est*, 68.
203. Ibid., 71.
204. Constantin Mancaș, interview with the author, Cluj, 2012.
205. Axworthy, Scafes, and Craciunoiu, *Third Axis, Fourth Ally*, 134.
206. Duțu, *Armata română în război*, 256.
207. Cârlan, *Păstrați-mi amitirile!*, 184.
208. Ibid., 186–87.

209. Dorian, *Quality of Witness*, 311.
210. AMNR, Fond Armata 4-a, dosar 1596, f. 211.
211. Ibid., dosar 1533, f. 69, 105, 111.
212. ACNSAS, Fond Personal, dosar 7245, f. 178–81.
213. AMNR, Fond Armata 4-a, dosar 1533, f. 111; AMNR, Fond Armata 3-a; dosar 2898, f. 38.
214. AMNR, Fond Armata 3-a, dosar 2877, f. 17.
215. Dorian, *Quality of Witness*, 314.
216. Duțu, *Armata română în război*, 261.
217. Only the 19th Infantry Division's depot battalions remained near its garrison on the Serbian border to fight Yugoslav partisans; see Axworthy, Scafes, and Craciunoiu, *Third Axis, Fourth Ally*, 159.
218. Mircea Ionescu-Quintus, interview with the author, Ploiești, 2012.
219. Axworthy, Scafes, and Craciunoiu, *Third Axis, Fourth Ally*, 135.
220. Duțu, *Armata română în război*, 262, 257.
221. Glantz, *Red Storm over the Balkans*, 291–304, 375.
222. AMNR, Armata 3-a, dosar 2968, f. 289; ibid., dosar 3031, f. 61, 73.
223. Ibid., dosar 3026, f. 8–11, 13, 18, 19.
224. Ioanid, *Holocaust in Romania*, 256.
225. AMNR, Fond Corpul de Munte, dosar 1814, f. 141.
226. Glantz, *Red Storm over the Balkans*, 317–18.
227. Ibid., 339–65; AMNR, Fond Armata 4-a, dosar 1666, f. 89, 96–99, 258–59, 100.
228. AMNR, Fond Armata 3-a, dosar 2898, f. 47.
229. "Ce înseamnă eliberare sovietică," *Soldatul*, 8 June 1944, 1.
230. AMNR, Fond Corpul de Munte, dosar 1814, f. 496, 509, 313–14.
231. Voinescu, *Jurnal*, 2:43.
232. Sebastian, *Journal*, 598.
233. Netejoru, *Și eu am luptat în est*, 72.
234. Axworthy, Scafes, and Craciunoiu, *Third Axis, Fourth Ally*, 159.
235. BMMN, Fond Manuscrise, MSS 625, f. 3.
236. AMNR, Armata 3-a, dosar 2968, f. 535–36.
237. Ibid., dosar 3028, f. 175.
238. Georg Grossjohann, *Five Years, Four Fronts: A German Officer's World War II Combat Memoir*, trans. Ulrich Abele (New York: Ballantine Books, 2005), 121.
239. Frieser et al., *Germany and the Second World War*, 8:733–35.
240. Friessner, *Verratene Schlachten*, 43.
241. AMNR, Fond Armata 4-a, dosar 1635, f. 35.
242. Ibid., f. 114.
243. Axworthy, Scafes, and Craciunoiu, *Third Axis, Fourth Ally*, 160.
244. Ibid., 161.
245. Scafeș et al., *Armata română*, 73.
246. Schönherr, *Luptele wehrmachtului în România*, 117.
247. Ibid., 120.
248. Luke Truxal, "Bombing the Romanian Rail Network," *Air Power History* 65, no. 1 (Spring 2018): 15–22; Duțu, *Armata română în război*, 290.
249. Frieser et al., *Germany and the Second World War*, 8:742.

250. Axworthy, Scafes, and Craciunoiu, *Third Axis, Fourth Ally*, 167–68.
251. Quoted in Bărboi et al., *Armata română în vâltoarea războiului*, 198.
252. Schönherr, *Luptele wehrmachtului în România*, 129, 132.
253. Ibid., 135–37.
254. Axworthy, Scafes, and Craciunoiu, *Third Axis, Fourth Ally*, 169–70, 174.
255. Schönherr, *Luptele wehrmachtului în România*, 156, 169–70.
256. Axworthy, Scafes, and Craciunoiu, *Third Axis, Fourth Ally*, 171.

7. Propaganda and Discipline

1. Nicolae Ureche, *Propaganda Externă a României mari, 1918–1940* (Bucharest: Editura Enciclopedică, 2015), 215.
2. Filderman, *Memoirs and Diaries*, 1:494; Bolitho, *Roumania under King Carol*, 42.
3. Hollingworth, *There's a German Just behind Me*, 188.
4. Ciucă, *Stenogramele ședințelor consiliului de miniștri guvernarea Ion Antonescu*, 1:57.
5. Anton, *Propagandă și război*, 10, 72.
6. Ibid., 199.
7. Ibid., 201.
8. AMNR, Fond Secția Propaganda, dosar 51, f. 21–22; AMNR, Fond Armata 3-a, dosar 1173, f. 16.
9. AMNR, Fond Corpul de Munte, dosar 914, f. 15.
10. AMNR, Fond Secția Propaganda, dosar 33, f. 153–54, 270–71.
11. Ibid., f. 54.
12. Anton, *Propagandă și război*, 94.
13. AMNR, Fond Corpul de Munte, dosar 921, f. 1.
14. AMNR, Fond Armata 4-a, dosar 277, f. 343–44.
15. AMNR, Fond Secția Propaganda, dosar 32, f. 13, 37–38.
16. Anton, *Propagandă și război*, 202–3.
17. AMNR, Fond Secția Propaganda, dosar 170, f. 34–35.
18. Ionescu, *Însemnări din război*, 64.
19. AMNR, Fond Secția Propaganda, dosar 14, f. 86–88.
20. Ibid., dosar 82, f. 25–27, 70–71.
21. ANIC, Fond Presedinția Consiliului de Ministri: Cabinetul Militar, dosar 124/1943, f. 166.
22. AMNR, Fond Armata 3-a, dosar 438, f. 25; AMNR, Fond Corpul de Munte, fond 947, f. 502.
23. ANIC, Fond Presedinția Consiliului de Ministri: Cabinetul Militar, dosar 137/1942, f. 109–58; AMNR, Fond Corpul de Munte, dosar 921, f. 1–2, 9.
24. USHMM, RG-25.003M, Fond Ministerul de Război: Cabinet, dosar 273, f. 59A-60A; AMNR, Fond Corpul de Munte, dosar 921, f. 24.
25. Neagu Rădulescu, "Pagina Veselă," *Sentinela*, 30 June 1940, 7.
26. Dodo Niță and Alexandru Ciubotariu, *Istoria benzii desenate românești, 1891–2010* (Bucharest: Editura Vellant, 2010), 48; "Viața soldatului Stan," *Soldatul*, 18 October 1941, 3.
27. Rădulescu, "Pățaniile soldatului Neață," *Sentinela*, 6 October 1940, 7.

28. Ibid., 10 November 1940, 7.
29. Ibid., 5 January 1941, 7.
30. Ibid., 19 January 1941, 7.
31. Ibid., 15 November 1942, 7.
32. Ibid., 6 July 1941, 7.
33. Ibid., 24 January 1943, 7.
34. Ibid., 20 June 1943, 7.
35. Ibid., 5 December 1943, 3.
36. Ibid., 7 May 1944, 3.
37. Alesandru Duțu, Florica Dobre, and Leonida Loghin, *Armata română în al doilea război mondial, 1941–1945: Dicționar enciclopedic* (Bucharest: Editura Enciclopedică, 1999), 89.
38. Ionescu-Quintus interview.
39. Reese, *Stalin's Reluctant Soldiers*, 18, 61–62; Reese, *Why Stalin's Soldiers Fought*, 162–69.
40. Bartov, *Hitler's Army*, 95–96.
41. AMNR, Fond Armata 3-a, dosar 306, f. 188.
42. AMNR, Fond Armata 4-a, dosar 766, f. 91.
43. AMNR, Fond Armata 3-a, dosar 1119, f. 7.
44. Ionescu, *Însemnări din război*, 106.
45. Ibid., 139.
46. Moraru, *Armata lui Stalin văzută de români*, 126.
47. Ștefanescu interview.
48. V. Aurel Ciornei, interview with the author, Iași, 2010.
49. Scârneci, *Viața și moartea în linia întâi*, 129.
50. ANIC, Fond Ministerul de Război: Inspectoratul General al Armatei, dosar 75, f. 73.
51. AMNR, Fond Armata 3-a, dosar 306, f. 186.
52. ANIC, Fond Ministerul de Război: Cabinetul Ministrului, dosar 210 vol. 3, f. 190; ibid., dosar 210 vol. 2, f. 60.
53. AMNR, Fond Armata 3-a, dosar 1473, f. 298.
54. Ezechil, *La porțile infernului*, 44.
55. Burciu interview.
56. ANIC, Fond Ministerul de Război: Inspectoratul General al Armatei, dosar 75, f. 116–17.
57. Charles King, *Odessa: Genius and Death in a City of Dreams* (New York: W. W. Norton, 2011), 215–16.
58. Giorgio Geddes, *Nichivó: Life, Love and Death on the Russian Front*, trans. Natalie Lowe (London: Cassell, 2001), 128–30.
59. Heinen, *Legiunea "arhanghelul Mihail,"* 491.
60. AMNR, Fond Armata 4-a, dosar 748, f. 105; ibid., dosar 793, f. 972, 981.
61. AMNR, Fond Armata 3-a, dosar 306, f. 41, 277; ibid., dosar 1351, f. 74.
62. AMNR, Fond Armata 4-a, dosar 773, f. 85.
63. AMNR, Fond Armata 3-a, dosar 358, f. 132.
64. SIA, Fond Inspectoratul Clerului Militar, F.II.41579, dosar 301, c. 638.
65. Ionescu, *Însemnări din război*, 93.

66. Scârneci, *Viața și moartea în linea întâi*, 364.
67. Ezechil, *La porțile infernului*, 48–49.
68. AMNR, Fond Centru de Instrucție Nr. 5 Sărata, dosar 108, f. 1–2.
69. Ibid., dosar 69, f. 41.
70. Ibid., f. 40.
71. Păsat, *Memoriile căpitanului Dumitru Păsat*, 54.
72. AMNR, Fond Centru de Instrucție Sărata Nr. 5, dosar 40, f. 247–48.
73. Ibid., dosar 73, f. 124.
74. Ibid., dosar 72, f. 107; Păsat, *Memoriile căpitanului Dumitru Păsat*, 55.
75. Clark, *Holy Legionary Youth*, 234.
76. AMNR, Fond Centru de Instrucție Nr. 5 Sărata, dosar 30, f. 47.
77. Ibid., dosar 40, f. 102; ibid., dosar 230, f. 192–94. Emphasis (underlined) in original.
78. Ibid., dosar 24, f. 90, 173.
79. Ibid., dosar 30, f. 66.
80. Quoted in Moraru, *Armata lui Stalin văzută de români*, 125.
81. Scârneci, *Viața și moartea în linea întâi*, 443.
82. BMMN, Fond Manuscrise, MSS 676, f. 42.
83. Scârneci, *Viața și moartea în linea întâi*, 443.
84. AMNR, Fond Armata 3-a, dosar 2968, f. 6.
85. Ibid., dosar 2873, f. 91.
86. AMNR, Fond Armata 4-a, dosar 758, f. 91.
87. Trașcă, *"Chestiunea evreiască" în documente militare române*, 161.
88. AMNR, Fond Armata 3-a, dosar 325, f. 68.
89. AMNR, Fond Corpul de Munte, dosar 639, f. 33. Emphasis (underlined) in original.
90. AMNR, Fond Armata 3-a, dosar 481, f. 88.
91. Quoted in Duțu, *Armata română în război*, 90.
92. AMNR, Fond Armata 4-a, dosar 784, f. 23, 37, 49, 81, 155, 162.
93. Ibid., f. 120.
94. AMNR, Fond Armata 3-a, dosar 992, f. 96, 183–84.
95. AMNR, Fond Corpul de Munte, dosar 933, f. 374.
96. AMNR, Fond Armata 4-a, dosar 1533, f. 31, 59.
97. Quoted in Duțu, *Armata română în război*, 296–98.
98. Ibid., 305.
99. AMNR, Fond Armata 4-a, dosar 629, f. 274; ibid., dosar 658, f. 145; ibid., dosar 860, f. 128.
100. Giurescu, *Romania in the Second World War*, 98–99.
101. Crisan, *Amazing Life*, 129.
102. Scârneci, *Viața și moartea în linea întâi*, 139.
103. ANIC, Fond Președinția Consiliului de Ministri: Cabinetul Militar, dosar 35/1944, f. 82, 84, 78.
104. Reese, *Why Stalin's Soldiers Fought*, 206–7.
105. AMNR, Fond Armata 3-a, dosar 840, f. 6–8.
106. Ibid., dosar 1299, f. 211.
107. Ibid., dosar 2152, f. 89.
108. Bartov, *Hitler's Army*, 75–76.

109. Ioanid, *Holocaust in Romania*, 147–48.
110. AMNR, Fond Armata 3-a, dosar 312, f. 211, 868; ibid., dosar 1131, f. 248.
111. AMNR, Fond Armata 4-a, dosar 1246, f. 2.
112. Aly, *Hitler's Beneficiaries*, 104–5.
113. Ionescu, *Însemnări din război*, 93.
114. Dallin, *Odessa*, 87, 119.
115. Quoted in Moraru, *Armata lui Stalin văzută de români*, 125–26.
116. Beevor, *Stalingrad*, 181; Anton, *Propagandă și război*, 13, 69, 206, 215.
117. Axworthy, Scafes, and Craciunoiu, *Third Axis, Fourth Ally*, 57–58, 71–72.

8. Women and Minorities

1. Quoted in Clark, *Holy Legionary Youth*, 227.
2. Alin Ciupală, *Bătălia lor: Femeile din România în primul război mondial* (Bucharest: Polirom, 2017), 194–223.
3. Ana Bărbulescu et al., *Munca obligatorie a evreilor din România: Documente* (Bucharest: Polirom, 2013), 73–77.
4. AMNR, Fond Asociația Surorilor de Caritate de Război, dosar 27, f. 38.
5. Similar to Russian nurses in the First World War; see Laurie S. Stoff, *Russia's Sisters of Mercy and the Great War: More Than Binding Men's Wounds* (Lawrence: University Press of Kansas, 2015), 18–19, 45–46.
6. AMNR, Fond Asociația Surorile de Caritate de Război, dosar 27, f. 2; ibid., dosar 29, f. 8.
7. Dorian, *Quality of Witness*, 163, 165.
8. Voinescu, *Jurnal*, 1:318, 322, 326.
9. ASNCRR, Fond Organizare, dosar 14/1941, f. 22–23, 38.
10. Ibid., dosar 14/1941, f. 66. Emphasis (underlined) in original.
11. Rădulescu, "Pațaniile soldatului Neață," *Sentinela*, 27 July 1941, 7.
12. AMNR, Fond Armata 4-a, dosar 1236, f. 11.
13. Ibid., dosar 629, f. 287.
14. ASNCRR, Fond Organizare, dosar 14/1941, f. 285.
15. Mihai Antonescu, "Contribuția femeii române la răsboiul sfânt," *Soldatul*, 3 March 1942, 2.
16. AMNR, Fond Armata 3-a, dosar 1126, f. 132, 134–35, 136.
17. Bărbulescu et al., *Munca obligatorie a evreilor din România*, 255, 498.
18. AMNR, Fond Armata 3-a, dosar 1732, f. 73–74.
19. AMNR, Fond Corpul de Munte, dosar 831, f. 220, 227.
20. Ibid., dosar 914, f. 382.
21. AMNR, Fond Armata 3-a, dosar 3447, f. 662.
22. Ibid., dosar 2158, f. 18.
23. AMNR, Fond Corpul Grănicerilor, dosar 3513, f. 26; USHMM, RG-25.003M, reel 15, frame 205.
24. "Mila creștină," *Soldatul*, 10 April 1943, 3.
25. AMNR, Fond Armata 3-a, dosar 2158, f. 8.
26. Like Russian soldiers in the previous war; see Stoff, *Russia's Sisters of Mercy*, 143, 267–68.
27. Scârneci, *Viața și moartea în linia întâi*, 396.

28. AMNR, Fond Corpul de Munte, dosar 1414, f. 26.
29. AMNR, Fond Armata 3-a, dosar 1130, f. 401; AMNR, Fond Corpul de Munte, dosar 933, f. 91.
30. Crucea Roşie Română, "Istoria Crucii Rosii Romane 1940–1945," Crucearosie.ro, https://crucearosie.ro/cine-suntem/istoria-crucii-rosii-romane/istoria-crucii-rosii-romane-1940-1945/.
31. Ion Munteanu, "Alţi voluntari pe front," *Soldatul*, 23 March 1944, 1.
32. Gh. I. Bejgu, "Femeile mironosiţe," *Soldatul*, 29 April 1944, 1.
33. AMNR, Fond Secţia Propaganda, dosar 115, f. 13, 20.
34. Ibid., dosar 82, f. 6–7.
35. Ion Postolache, "O voluntară a cruciadei din răsărit: Caporal Moisescu Constanţa," *Gazeta Odesei*, 9 May 1943, 3.
36. Bucur, *Heroes and Victims*, 129–30.
37. Postolache, "O voluntară a cruciadei din răsărit," 3.
38. Ion Munteanu, "Femei în lupta," *Soldatul*, 25 February 1943, 1.
39. Sebastian, *Journal*, 266.
40. AMNR, Fond Comandamentul Militar al Capitalei, dosar 84, f. 119.
41. Bărbulescu et al., *Munca obligatorie a evreilor din România*, 57–64.
42. Ibid., 70–71.
43. AMNR, Fond Armata 4-a, dosar 177, f. 17, 22, 678.
44. AMNR, Fond Corpul de Munte, dosar 377, f. 52.
45. Dorian, *Quality of Witness*, 162.
46. Ibid., 165–66.
47. Traşcă, *"Chestiunea evreiască" în documente militare române*, 42.
48. Dallas Michelbacher, *Jewish Forced Labor in Romania, 1940–1944* (Bloomington: Indiana University Press, 2020), 32–36.
49. Dorian, *Quality of Witness*, 169.
50. Bărbulescu et al., *Munca obligatorie a evreilor din România*, 171–72.
51. Michelbacher, *Jewish Forced Labor in Romania*, 47–50.
52. Dorian, *Quality of Witness*, 194.
53. Traşcă, *"Chestiunea evreiască" în documente militare române*, 459.
54. Michelbacher, *Jewish Forced Labor in Romania*, 62–65.
55. Ibid., 83.
56. Bărbulescu et al., *Munca obligatorie a evreilor din România*, 245, 249, 251.
57. Michelbacher, *Jewish Forced Labor in Romania*, 71–72.
58. AMNR, Fond Armata 4-a, dosar 779, f. 24–25.
59. Ibid., dosar 1236, f. 999.
60. Ibid., dosar 779, f. 28.
61. USHMM, RG-25.003M, reel 20, frame 91.
62. Bărbulescu et al., *Munca obligatorie a evreilor din România*, 303–4.
63. Michelbacher, *Jewish Forced Labor in Romania*, 84–85.
64. Dorian, *Quality of Witness*, 256.
65. Bărbulescu et al., *Munca obligatorie a evreilor din România*, 332–33.
66. Michelbacher, *Jewish Forced Labor in Romania*, 106.
67. Ioanid, *Holocaust in Romania*, 243.
68. Michelbacher, *Jewish Forced Labor in Romania*, 120–21.

69. Ibid., 136.
70. Ibid., 146.
71. Landau, *Goodbye, Transylvania*, vii, 5, 7.
72. AMNR, Fond Armata 4-a, dosar 16, f. 10.
73. Scafeş et al., *Armata română*, 206.
74. AMNR, Fond Armata 3-a, dosar 225, f. 108; AMNR, Fond Armata 4-a, dosar 246, f. 124; AMNR, Fond Corpul de Munte, dosar 639, f. 165.
75. Landau, *Goodbye, Transylvania*, 12.
76. Ibid., 23.
77. Vasilache Mătuşa, interview with the author, Piteşti, 2010.
78. Petre Mortun, interview with the author, Târgovişte, 2012.
79. AMNR, Fond Armata 3-a, dosar 1044, f. 355.
80. Scafeş et al., *Armata română*, 207.
81. AMNR, Fond Corpul de Munte, dosar 1393, f. 170, 177.
82. Scafeş et al., *Armata română*, 207.
83. AMNR, Fond Armata 3-a, dosar 93, f. 41.
84. Ibid., dosar 39, 310–11; ibid., dosar 225, f. 17.
85. AMNR, Fond Armata 4-a, dosar 201, f. 319.
86. AMNR, Fond Armata 3-a, dosar 306, f. 13.
87. Case, *Between States*, 84.
88. Mortun interview.
89. AMNR, Fond Armata 3-a, dosar 1486, f. 7.
90. ANIC, Fond Ministerul de Război: Cabinetul Ministrului, dosar 243, f. 17.
91. AMNR, Fond Armata 3-a, dosar 1486, f. 6.
92. USHMM, RG-25.003M, Fond Ministerul de Război: Cabinet, dosar 273, f. 69–70.
93. Livezeanu, *Cultural Politics in Interwar Romania*, 10.
94. AMNR, Fond Armata 3-a, dosar 157, f. 86; ibid., dosar 225, f. 247.
95. USHMM, RG-25.003M, reel 2, frame 202; USHMM, RG-25.004M, reel 65, frame 480.
96. AMNR, Fond Armata 4-a, dosar 781, f. 127.
97. Solonari, *Purifying the Nation*, 183–84, 318–22.
98. USHMM, RG-25.004M, reel 16, frames 243–53.
99. AMNR, Fond Armata 4-a, dosar 793, f. 455.
100. Duţu, *Armata română în război*, 10.
101. USHMM, RG-25.003M, Fond Ministerul de Război: Cabinet, dosar 272, f. 25.
102. Viorel Achim, ed., *Politica regimului Antonescu faţă de cultele neoprotestante: Documente* (Bucharest: Editura Institutului Naţional pentru Studierea Holocaustului din România "Elie Weisel), 12.
103. SIA, Fond Inspectoratul Clerului Militar, F.II.4.1568, dosar 260, c. 79.
104. AMNR, Fond Armata 3-a, dosar 225, f. 60.
105. SIA, Fond Inspectoratul Clerului Militar, F.II.4.1568, dosar 260, c. 91, 77.
106. Gusti, *Enciclopedia României*, 441.
107. ANIC, Fond Ministerul de Război: Inspectoratul General al Armatei, dosar 131, f. 7; ibid., dosar 133, f. 44; AMNR, Fond Corpul de Munte, dosar 888, f. 2; AMNR, Fond Armata 4-a, dosar 789, f. 2.

108. Crisan, *Amazing Life*, 114, 122.
109. AMNR, Fond Corpul de Cavalerie, dosar 308, f. 398.
110. Păsat, *Memoriile căpitanului Dumitru Păsat*, 67.
111. Deletant, *Hitler's Forgotten Ally*, 73.
112. ANIC, Fond Ministerul de Război: Inspectoratul General al Armatei, dosar 134, f. 73.
113. SIA, Fond Inspectoratul Clerului Militar, F.II.41579, dosar 301, f. 678–79.
114. Crisan, *Amazing Life*, 142.
115. David Crowe, *A History of the Gypsies of Eastern Europe* (New York: St. Martin's Griffin, 1996), 107–21.
116. M. Benjamin Thorne, "Assimilation, Invisibility, and the Eugenic Turn in the 'Gypsy Question' in Romanian Society, 1938–1942," *Romani Studies* 21, no. 2 (Winter 2011): 182.
117. Viorel Achim, ed., *Documente privind deportarea țiganilor în Transnistria*, vol. 1 (Bucharest: Editura Enciclopedică, 2004), 163–64.
118. Scârneci, *Viața și moartea în linia întâi*, 212.
119. Costea interview.
120. Ionescu-Quintus interview.
121. Luminița Mihai Cioabă, ed., *Lacrimi rome / Romane asva* (Bucharest: Ro Media, 2006), 7.
122. Ibid., 8–9.
123. AMNR, Fond Armata 4-a, dosar 779, f. 28.
124. Solonari, *Purifying the Nation*, 273–78.
125. Achim, *Documente privind deportarea țiganilor în Transnistria*, 1:245–46.
126. USHMM, RG-25.003M, reel 148, frame 9.
127. Ibid., frame 10.
128. AMNR, Fond Corpul de Munte, dosar 951, f. 170.
129. AMNR, Fond Centru de Instrucție Nr. 5 Sărata, dosar 72, f. 32.
130. Ibid., dosar 110, f. 362.
131. Ibid., dosar 72, f. 170, 176.
132. AMNR, Fond Armata 3-a, dosar 992, f. 20.
133. Ibid., f. 85–86.
134. Cioabă, *Lacrimi rome / Romane asva*, 10.
135. AMNR, Fond Comandamentul Militar al Capitalei, dosar 810, f. 243.
136. USHMM, RG-31.004M, reel 13, frame 245.
137. AMNR, Fond Armata 4-a, dosar 1481, f. 317.
138. Ioanid, *Holocaust in Romania*, 236.
139. Ezechil, *La porțile infernului*, 124.

Epilogue

1. Quoted in Ivor Porter, *Michael of Romania: The King and the Country* (Gloucestershire, UK: Sutton, 2005), 105–10.
2. Quoted ibid., 112, 115.
3. Guderian, *Panzer Leader*, 367.
4. Axworthy, Scafes, and Craciunoiu, *Third Axis, Fourth Ally*, 177, 180.

5. AMNR, Fond Armata 3-a, dosar 3065, f. 284–87.
6. Quoted in Bărboi et al., *Armata română în vâltoarea războiului*, 200.
7. Duțu, *Armata română în război*, 347.
8. BMMN, Fond Manuscrise, MSS 625, f. 24–31.
9. Armă, *București sub bombardamente*, 202.
10. AMNR, Fond Corpul de Munte, dosar 1814, f. 418.
11. Frieser et al., *Germany and the Second World War*, 8:775.
12. Schönherr, *Luptele wehrmachtului în România*, 186–87.
13. Axworthy, Scafes, and Craciunoiu, *Third Axis, Fourth Ally*, 188–93.
14. Cârlan, *Păstrați-mi amintirile!*, 196–201.
15. Schönher, *Luptele wehrmachtului în România*, 231–32.
16. Ezechil, *La porțile infernului*, 84.
17. Sebastian, *Journal*, 610.
18. BMMN, Fond Manuscrise, MSS 625, f. 34, 39.
19. Rășănescu, *Erou la Cotul Donului*, 191–93.
20. Citino, *Wehrmacht's Last Stand*, 311–12.
21. Axworthy, Scafes, and Craciunoiu, *Third Axis, Fourth Ally*, 185.
22. Ibid., 119–20.
23. Bossy, *Recollections of a Romanian Diplomat*, 455–56.
24. Giurescu, *Romania in the Second World War*, 286–88, 300–301.
25. Crisan, *Amazing Life*, 143.
26. Giurescu, *Romania in the Second World War*, 326–28.
27. Ibid., 308–9; Porter, *Michael of Romania*, 75–76.
28. Ibid., 83.
29. Ibid., 100.
30. Giurescu, *Romania in the Second World War*, 320.
31. Sebastian, *Journal*, 614.
32. "The Armistice Agreement with Romania; September 12, 1944," Avalon Project, http://avalon.law.yale.edu/wwii/rumania.asp.
33. AMNR, Fond Armata 3-a, dosar 3047, f. 5.
34. Rădulescu, "Pățaniile soldatului Neață," *Sentinela*, 10 September 1944, 3.
35. BMMN, Fond Manuscrise, MSS 625, f. 49–50.
36. Ezekial, *La porțile infernului*, 93–94.
37. AMNR, Fond Centru de Instrucție Nr. 5 Sărata, dosar 376, f. 2, 56–57.
38. Crisan, *Amazing Life*, 143–46.
39. Florin Șperlea, *De la armata regală la armata populară: Sovietizarea armatei române, 1948–1955* (Bucharest: Editura Ziua, 2003), 48.
40. Ibid., 48, 257n106.
41. Teodorescu, *Mândria vânătorului de munte*, 185.
42. AMNR, Fond Corpul de Cavalerie, dosar 266, f. 105, 121.
43. AMNR, Fond Centru de Instrucție Nr. 5 Sărata, dosar 376, f. 116, 139–41.
44. Ibid., f. 65.
45. Trașcă, *"Chestiunea evreiască" în documente militare române*, 880–82.
46. Axworthy, Scafes, and Craciunoiu, *Third Axis, Fourth Ally*, 200–202.
47. Csaba Békés et al., eds., *Soviet Occupation of Romania, Hungary, and Austria, 1944/45–1948/49* (Budapest: Central European University Press, 2015), 15–17.

hy, Scafes, and Craciunoiu, *Third Axis, Fourth Ally*, 203.
Michael of Romania, 126–27, 129.
et al., *Soviet Occupation of Romania, Hungary, and Austria*, 31–38.
ş et al., *Armata română*, 92, 127.
orthy, Scafes, and Craciunoiu, *Third Axis, Fourth Ally*, 206.

53. Ibid., 214.
54. Teodorescu, *Mândria vânătorului de munte*, 197–98.
55. Duțu, *Armata română în război*, 446.
56. Quoted ibid., 511.
57. AMNR, Fond Centru de Instrucție Nr. 5 Sărata, dosar 378, f. 42, 43, 83–84.
58. Heinen, *Legiunea "arhanghelul Mihail,"* 432–34.
59. Scafeș et al., *Armata română*, 208–10.
60. Axworthy, Scafes, and Craciunoiu, *Third Axis, Fourth Ally*, 208.
61. Alesandru Duțu and Florica Dobre, *Drama generalilor români: 1944–1964* (Bucharest: Editura Enciclopedică, 1997), 50–54; "General Gheorghe Avramescu," WorldWar2.ro, http://worldwar2.ro/generali/?language=en&article=97.
62. Axworthy, Scafes, and Craciunoiu, *Third Axis, Fourth Ally*, 207.
63. Giurescu, *Romania in the Second World War*, 394.
64. Cârlan, *Păstrați-mi amintirile!*, 211, 243, 247–48.
65. Axworthy, Scafes, and Craciunoiu, *Third Axis, Fourth Ally*, 212–14.
66. Giurescu, *Romania in the Second World War*, 395.
67. Cârlan, *Păstrați-mi amintirile!*, 258–59.
68. Duțu, *Armata română în război*, 9.
69. Vittalie Văratie, coord., *Prizonieri de război români în Uniunea Sovietică: Documente, 1941–1956* (Bucharest: Eitura Monitorului Oficial, 2013), xx–xxi.
70. Ioanid, *Holocaust in Romania*, 224.
71. Ibid., 236.
72. Duțu, *Armata română în război*, 12.
73. Ibid., 242.
74. Minority Rights Information System, *Final Report of the International Commission on the Holocaust in Romania*, 248–49, http://miris.eurac.edu/mugs2/do/blob.pdf?type=pdf&serial=1117716572750.
75. Porter, *Michael of Romania*, 158–59.
76. Deletant, *Hitler's Forgotten Ally*, 259.
77. ACNSAS, Fond Personal, dosar 8434, vol. 1, f. 114, 148–50; ACNSAS, Fond Informativ, dosar 138870, f. 8.

Bibliography

Archives

Arhiva Consiliului Național pentru Studierea Arhivelor Securității (ACNSAS), Bucharest
Arhiva Societății Naționale de Crucea Roșie Română (ASNCRR), Bucharest
Arhivele Militare Naționale Române (AMNR), Pitești
Arhivele Naționale Istorice Centrale (ANIC), Bucharest
Biblioteca Muzeului Militar Național (BMMN), Bucharest
Serviciul Istoric al Armatei (SIA), Bucharest
United States Holocaust Memorial Museum (USHMM), Washington, DC

Oral Interviews

Burciu, Dumitru. Interview with the author. Iași, 2010
Buzea, Bartu. Interview with the author. Brăila, 2012
Ciornei, V. Aurel. Interview with the author. Iași, 2010
Costea, Petre. Interview with the author. Buzău, 2012
Halic, Teodor, and Iuliu Dobrin. Interview with the author. Bucharest, 2009
Ionescu-Quinitus, Mircea. Interview by the author. Ploiești, 2012
Mancaș, Constantin. Interview with the author. Cluj, 2012
Mătușa, Vasilache. Interview with the author. Pitești, 2010
Mihalcea, Constantin. Interview with the author. Brăila, 2012
Mihai, Filip. Interview with the author. Suceava, 2011
Morar, Geratimusz. Interview with the author. Sibiu, 2012
Mortun, Petre. Interview with the author. Târgoviște, 2012
Staicu, Nicolae. Interview with the author. Constanța, 2012
Ștefanescu, Marin. Interview with the author. Târgu Mureș, 2012

Periodicals

Arma Cuvântului: Organ oficial al episcopiei militare, 1940–1944, Bucharest
Armata: Revista oficială a marelui stat major, 1942–1944, Bucharest
Cuvinte către ostași, 1940–1944, Bucharest
Ecoul Crimeei: Ziar săptămânal de informații pentru ostași, 1942–1944, Simferopol
România militară: Revista generală lunară, 1921–1946, Bucharest
Sentinela: Gazeta ostășească a națiunii, 1939–1945, Bucharest
Soldatul: Foaie de lămuriri și informații pentru ostași, 1941–1944, Bucharest

Primary Sources

Achim, Viorel, ed. *Documente privind deportarea țiganilor în Transnistria*. Vols. 1 and 2. Bucharest: Editura Enciclopedică, 2004.

——. *Politica regimului Antonescu față de cultele neoprotestante: Documente*. Bucharest: Editura Institutului Național pentru Studierea Holocaustului din România "Elie Weisel," 2013.

Alexandru, J., L. Benjamin, D. Brumfeld, A. Florea, P. Litma, and S. Stanciu, eds. *Martiriul evreilor din România, 1940–1944: Documente și mărturii*. Bucharest: Editura Hasefer, 1991.

Ancel, Jean, ed. *Documents concerning the Fate of Romanian Jewry during the Holocaust*. New York: Beate Klarsfeld Foundation, 1986.

Arad, Yitzhak, Shmuel Krakowski, and Shmuel Spector, eds. *The Einsatzgruppen Reports: Selections from the Dispatches of the Nazi Death Squads' Campaign against the Jews, July 1941–January 1943*. New York: Holocaust Library, 1989.

Arimia, Vasile, Ion Ardelanu, Ștefan Lache, and Florin Constantiniu, eds. *Antonescu-Hitler: Corespondență și întîlniri inedite (1940–1944)*. Vols. 1 and 2. Bucharest: Cozia, 1991.

Athanasescu, Gheorghe. *Jurnal, 1926–1940*. Bucharest: Editura Vremea, 2018.

Bacalbașa, Anton. *Moș teacă—Din viața militară*. Iași: Editura Junimea, 1989.

Bălaj, Mihai. *Jurnal de front (1942–1943)*. Baia Mare: Editura Gutinul, 1999.

Bărboi, Vasile, Gheroghe Ioniță, Victor Atanasiu, and Alesandru Duțu, eds. *Armata română în vâltoarea războiului*. Bucharest: Editura "Vasile Cârlova," 2002.

Bărbulescu, Ana, Alexanru Florian, Alexandru Climescu, and Laura Degeratu, eds. *Munca obligatorie a evreilor din România: Documente*. Bucharest: Polirom, 2013.

Békés, Csaba, László Borhi, Peter Ruggenthaler, and Ottmar Trașca, eds. *Soviet Occupation of Romania, Hungary, and Austria, 1944/45–1948/49*. Budapest: Central European University Press, 2015.

Bichir, Florian, ed. *Cruciada diviziei de cremene cu tricolorul în Caucaz: Viața și memoriile generalului Ioan Dumitrache, cavaler al "crucii de fier."* Bucharest: Editura Militară, 2018.

Bolitho, Hector. *Roumania under King Carol*. New York: Longmans, Green, 1940.

Bossy, Raul. *Recollections of a Romanian Diplomat, 1918–1969: Diaries and Memoirs of Raoul V. Bossy*. Edited and translated by G. H. Bossy and M.-A. Bossy. Stanford, CA: Hoover Institution, 2003.

Cârlan, Ștefan. *Păstrați-mi amintirile! Jurnal de război (1942–1945)*. Bucharest: Editura Militară, 2007.

Carp, Matatias. *Holocaust in Rumania: Facts and Documents on the Annihilation of Rumania's Jews—1940–1944*. Translated by Seán Murphy. Budapest: Primor, 1994.

Chirnoagă, Platon. *Istoria politică și militară a răsboiului României contra Rusiei sovietice, 22 iunie 1941–23 august 1944*. 2nd ed. Madrid: Editura Carpatii, 1986.

Cioabă, Luminița Mihai, ed. *Lacrimi rome / Romane asva*. Bucharest: Ro Media, 2006.

Ciucă, Marcel-Dumitru, Aurelian Teodorescu, and Bogdan Florin Popovici, eds. *Steonogramele ședințelor consiliului de miniștri guvernarea Ion Antonescu*. Vols. 1–9. Bucharest: Arhivele Naționale ale României, 1997.

Codreanu, Corneliu Zelea. *For My Legionaries*. York, SC: Liberty Bell, 1990.
Cretzianu, Alexandru. *Relapse into Bondage: Political Memories of a Romanian Diplomat*. Iași: Center for Romanian Studies, 1998.
Crisan, George. *An Amazing Life: Escape from Romania*. New York: Vantage, 1990.
Dobre, Florica, Vasilica Manea, and Lenuța Nicolescu, eds. *Anul 1940: Armata română de la ultimatum la dictat, Documente*. Vols 1–3. Bucharest: Editura Europa Nova, 2000.
Dorian, Emil. *The Quality of Witness: A Romanian Diary, 1937–1944*. Edited by Marguerite Dorian. Translated by Mara Soceanu Vamos. Philadelphia: Jewish Publication Society of America, 1982.
Easterman, A. L. *King Carol, Hitler and Lupescu*. London: Victor Gollancz, 1942.
Emrich, Rebecca A. *In Search of the Lost Ones: The German Soldiers of Transylvania in the Second World War and Their Stories*. Vancouver: For the Love of Books, 2011.
Ezechil, Emilian. *La porțile infernului: 1941–1945*. Bucharest: Tritonic, 2008.
Filderman, Wilhelm. *Memoirs and Diaries*. Vols. 1 and 2. Edited by Jean Ancel. Jerusalem: Yad Vashem, 2004, 2015.
Fontaine, Marcel. *Jurnal de război: Misiune în România, noiembrie 1916–aprilie 1918*. Translated by Micaela Ghițescu. Bucharest: Humanitas, 2016.
Friessner, Johannes. *Verratene Schlachten: Die Tragödie der deutschen Wehrmacht in Rumänien und Ungarn*. Hamburg: Holsten-Verlag, 1956.
Geddes, Giorgio. *Nichivó: Life, Love and Death on the Russian Front*. Translated by Natalie Lowe. London: Cassell, 2001.
Gheorghe, Stan V. *Din cercul de la Stalingrad în lagărele sovietice: Memorii 1942–1948*. Bucharest: Editura Militară, 2018.
Grossjohan, Georg. *Five Years, Four Fronts: A German Officer's World War II Combat Memoir*. Translated by Ulrich Abele. Ballantine Books: New York, 1999.
Grosu, Ion. *Memoriile unui ofițer de informații*. Bucharest: Editura Militară, 2009.
Guderian, Heinz. *Panzer Leader*. Translated by Constantin Fitzgibbon. Cambridge, MA: Da Capo, 1996.
Hall, Donald. *Romanian Furrow*. London: Bene Factum, 2007.
Hollingworth, Clare. *There's a German Just behind Me*. London: Right Book Club, 1943.
Iancu, Constantin. *Să te împaci cu . . . tine*. Edited by Alexandru Birou. Constanța: Editura "Neliniști metafizice," 2009.
Ionescu, Evsevie M. *Însemnări din război: Jurnalul unui sergent (1941–1944)*. Bucharest: Editura Militară, 2005.
Knittel, Marjorie. *The Last Bridge: Her Own True Story, Elvera Ziebart Reuer*. Aberdeen, SD: Midstates Printing, 1984.
Landau, Sigmund Heinz. *Goodbye Transylvania: A Romanian Waffen-SS Soldier in WWII*. Mechanicsburg, PA: Stackpole Books, 1985.
League of Nations. *Armaments Year-Book:* First–Fifteenth Year. Geneva: League of Nations, 1924–1939.
Lungu, Ioan T. *De la Stalingrad la Gherla: Roman document*. Timișoara: Editura de Vest, 1993.
Manolescu, John. *Permitted to Land: An Autobiography*. London: Staples, 1950.
Manstein, Erich. *Lost Victories*. Edited and translated by Anthony G. Powell. St. Paul, MN: Zenith, 2004.

Mărdărescu, Gheorghe. *Campania pentru dezrobirea Ardealului și ocuparea Budapestei, 1919.* Baia Mare: Editura Marist, 2009.
Mușețeanu, Crișan V. *Strigătul: Ediție definitivă.* Bucharest: Editura "Jurnalul literar," 2003.
Netejoru, Gheorghe. *Și eu am luptat în est: Spovedania unui fost prizonier de război.* Bucharest: Editura Militară, 2010.
Nicolescu, Gheorghe, Gheorghe Dobrescu, and Andrei Nicolescu, eds. *Preoți în tranșee: 1941–1945.* Bucharest: Fundația General Ștefan Gușă, 1999.
Nimigeanu, Dumitru. *Însemnările unui țăran deportat din Bucovina.* Bucharest: Editura Vestala, 2015.
Pantazi, Constantin. *Cu mareșalul până la moarte: Memorii.* Bucharest: Editura Publiferom, 1999.
Scârneci, Vasile. *Viața și moartea în linia întâi: Jurnal și însemnări de război, 1916–1920, 1941–1943.* Bucharest: Editura Militară, 2013.
Scurtu, Ioan, ed. *Pe marginea prăpastiei: 21–23 ianuarie 1941.* Vols. 1 and 2. Bucharest: Editura Scripia, 1992.
Sebastian, Mihail. *Journal, 1935–1944: The Fascist Years.* Translated by Patrick Camiller. Chicago: Ivan R. Dee, 2000.
Stivelman, Michael. *The Death March.* Rio de Janeiro: Editora Nova Frontiera, 1997.
Sturdza, Michel. *The Suicide of Europe: Memoirs of Prince Michel Sturdza, Former Foreign Minister of Rumania.* Belmont, MA: Western Islands, 1968.
Tănăsescu, Gheorghe. *Prizonier la Cotul Donului: Jurnal de război (27.08–23.11.1942) și prizonierat (24.11.1942–20.11.1946).* Edited by Nicolae Strâmbeanu and Marius Tănăsescu. Bucharest: Editura Militară, 2017.
Teodorescu, Dumitru. *Mândria vânătorului de munte.* Baia Mare: Editura Marist, 2013.
Teodorescu-Schei, Alexandru. *Învins și învingător: 1941–1949, Campania din est și prizonieratul.* Bucharest: Editura Allfa, 1998.
Trașcă, Ottmar, ed. *"Chestiunea evreiască" în documente militare române, 1941–1944.* Iași: Institutul European, 2010.
Văratie, Vittalie, coord. *Prizonieri de război români în Uniunea Sovietică: Documente, 1941–1956.* Bucharest: Eitura Monitorului Oficial, 2013.
Waldeck, R. G. *Athene Palace: Hitler's "New Order" Comes to Romania.* Chicago: University of Chicago Press, 2013.
Wieland, George F. *Bessarabian Knight: A Peasant Caught between the Red Star and the Swastika; Immanuel Weiss's True Story.* Lincoln, NE: American Historical Society of Germans from Russia, 1991.

Secondary Sources

Aly, Götz. *Hitler's Beneficiaries: Plunder, Racial War, and the Nazi Welfare State.* New York: Holt Paperback, 2006.
Ancel, Jean. *The History of the Holocaust in Romania.* Lincoln: University of Nebraska Press, 2011.
———. *Prelude to Mass Murder: The Pogrom in Iași, Romania, June 29, 1941 and Thereafter.* Translated by Fern Seckbach. Jerusalem: Yad Vashem, 2013.

BIBLIOGRAPHY

——. *Transnistria*. Vols. 1–3. Bucharest: Editura Atlas, 1998.
Anderson, Benedict. *Imagined Communities: Reflections on the Origin and Spread of Nationalism*. Rev. ed. London: Verso, 2006.
Anton, Mioara. *Propagandă și război, 1941–1944*. Bucharest: Tritonic, 2007.
Arad, Yitzhak. *The Holocaust in the Soviet Union*. Lincoln: University of Nebraska Press, 2009.
Armă, Alexandru. *București sub bombardamente (1941–1944)*. Bucharest: Editura Militară, 2015.
Axworthy, Mark. "Peasant Scapegoat to Industrial Slaughter: The Romanian Soldier at the Siege of Odessa." In *Time to Kill: The Soldier's Experience of War in the West, 1939–1945*, edited by Paul Addison and Angus Calder, 221–32. London: Pimlico, 1997.
——. *The Romanian Army of World War II*. Oxford: Osprey, 1991.
Axworthy, Mark, Cornel Scafes, and Christian Craciunoiu. *Third Axis, Fourth Ally: Romanian Armed Forces in the European War, 1941–1945*. St. Petersburg, FL: Hailer, 1995.
Bărbulescu, Constantin. *România medicilor: Medici, țărani și igienă rurală în România de la 1860 la 1910*. Bucharest: Humanitas, 2015.
Bartov, Omer. *Hitler's Army: Soldiers, Nazis, and War in the Third Reich*. New York: Oxford University Press, 1992.
Beevor, Antony. *Stalingrad, the Fateful Siege: 1942–1943*. New York: Penguin Books, 1998.
Beldiman, Dana. *Armata și mișcarea legionară, 1927–1947*. Bucharest: Institutul Național Pentru Studiul Totalitarismului, 2002.
Bell, David. *The First Total War: Napoleon's Europe and the Birth of Warfare as We Know It*. New York: Houghton Mifflin, 2007.
Bellamy, Chris. *Absolute War: Soviet Russia in the Second World War*. New York: Vintage Books, 2008.
Beorn, Waitman Wade. *The Wehrmacht and the Holocaust in Belarus*. Cambridge, MA: Harvard University Press, 2014.
Berkhoff, Karel C. *Motherland in Danger: Soviet Propaganda during World War II*. Cambridge, MA: Harvard University Press, 2012.
Bernád, Dénes. *Rumanian Aces of World War 2*. Oxford: Osprey, 2003.
Boog, Horst, Jürgen Förster, Joachim Hoffmann, Ernst Klink, Rolf-Dieter Müller, and Gerd R. Ueberschär. *Germany and the Second World War*. Vol. 4, *The Attack on the Soviet Union*. Translated by Dean S. McMurry, Ewald Osers, and Louise Willmot. Oxford: Clarendon, 1996.
Boog, Horst, Werner Rahn, Reinhard Stumpf, and Bernd Wegner. *Germany and the Second World War*. Vol. 6, *The Global War: Widening of the Conflict into a World War and the Shift of the Initiative 1941–1943*. Translated by Ewald Osers, John Brownjohn, Patricia Crampton, and Louise Willmot. Oxford: Clarendon, 2001.
Bowd, Gavin. *Memoria războiului, 1941–1945*. Bucharest: Editura Pro Historia, 2006.
Bozdoghină, Horia. *Antisemitismul lui A. C. Cuza în politica românească*. Bucharest: Curtea Veche, 2012.
Browning, Christopher. *Ordinary Men: Reserve Police Battalion 101 and the Final Solution in Poland*. New York: Harper Perennial, 1998.

BIBLIOGRAPHY

———. *The Origins of the Final Solution: The Evolution of the Nazi Jewish Policy, September 1939–March 1942*. Lincoln: University of Nebraska Press, 2004.
Bucur, Bogdan. "Budgetary Austerity Measures Taken by Romania during the Great Recession of 1929–1933 and Reflected in the Specialized Press of the Time." *Revista română de jurnalism și comunicare* 6, no. 3 (2011): 34–41.
Bucur, Maria. *Eugenics and Modernization in Interwar Romania*. Pittsburgh: University of Pittsburg Press, 2002.
———. *Heroes and Victims: Remembering War in Twentieth-Century Romania*. Bloomington: Indiana University Press, 2009.
Case, Holly. *Between States: The Transylvanian Question and the European Idea during World War II*. Stanford, CA: Stanford University Press, 2009.
Cesarani, David. *Becoming Eichmann: Rethinking the Life, Crimes, and Trial of a "Desk Murderer."* New York: Da Capo, 2004.
Chiper, Mihai. *Pe câmpul de onoare: O istorie a duelui la români*. Bucharest: Humanitas, 2016.
Citino, Robert M. *Death of the Wehrmacht: The German Campaigns of 1942*. Lawrence: University Press of Kansas, 2007.
———. *The Wehrmacht Retreats: Fighting a Lost War, 1943*. Lawrence: University Press of Kansas, 2012.
———. *The Wehrmacht's Last Stand: The German Campaigns of 1944–1945*. Lawrence: University Press of Kansas, 2017.
Ciupală, Alin. *Bătălia lor: Femeile din România în primul război mondial*. Bucharest: Polirom, 2017.
Clark, Charles Upson. *Greater Romania*. New York: Dodd, Mead, 1922.
Clark, Roland. "Fascists and Soldiers: Ambivalent Loyalties and Genocidal Violence in Wartime Romania." *Holocaust and Genocide Studies* 31, no. 3 (Winter 2017): 408–32.
———. *Holy Legionary Youth: Fascist Activism in Interwar Romania*. Ithaca, NY: Cornell University Press, 2015.
———. "Nationalism, Ethnotheology, and Mysticism in Interwar Romania." *Carl Beck Papers*, no. 2002 (September 2009): 1–47.
Cornelius, Deborah S. *Hungary in World War II: Caught in the Cauldron*. New York: Fordham University Press, 2011.
Crîşmaru, Dumitru-Dan. *Elita militară românească în timpul lui Carol I (1866–1914)*. Bucharest: Editura Militară, 2017.
Crowe, David. *A History of the Gypsies of Eastern Europe*. New York: St. Martin's Griffin, 1996.
Dallin, Alexander. *Odessa, 1941–1944: A Case Study of Soviet Territory under Foreign Rule*. Iași: Center for Romanian Studies, 1998.
Dăscălescu, Nicolae. *General Nicolae Dăscălescu: Sacrificiu, glorie și supliciu*. Bucharest: Editura Militară, 2014.
Deletant, Dennis. *Hitler's Forgotten Ally: Ion Antonescu and His Regime, Romania 1940–1944*. New York: Palgrave Macmillan, 2006.
———. *Romania under Communist Rule*. Iași: Center for Romanian Studies, 1999.
DiNardo, Richard L. *Germany and the Axis Powers: From Coalition to Collapse*. Lawrence: University Press of Kansas, 2005.
Doughty, Robert A. *Pyrrhic Victory: French Strategy and Operations in the Great War*. Cambridge, MA: Belknap Press of Harvard University Press, 2005.

Drace-Francis, Alex. *The Making of Modern Romanian Culture: Literacy and the Development of National Identity*. London: Tauris Academic Studies, 2006.
Dumitru, Diana. *The State, Antisemitism, and Collaboration in the Holocaust: The Borderlands of Romania and the Soviet Union*. New York: Cambridge University Press, 2016.
Duțu, Alesandru. *Armata română în război, 1941–1945*. Bucharest: Editura Enciclopedică, 2016.
Duțu, Alesandru, and Florica Dobre. *Drama generalilor români: 1944–1964*. Bucharest: Editura Enciclopedică, 1997.
Duțu, Alesandru, Florica Dobre, and Leonida Loghin. *Armata română în al doilea război mondial, 1941–1945: Dicționar enciclopedic*. Bucharest: Editura Enciclopedică, 1999.
Dwork, Debórah, and Robert Jan van Pelt. *Holocaust: A History*. New York: W. W. Norton, 2002.
Eaton, Henry. *The Origins and Onset of the Romanian Holocaust*. Detroit: Wayne State University Press, 2013.
Engelstein, Laura. *Russia in Flames: War, Revolution, Civil War, 1914–1921*. New York: Oxford University Press, 2018.
Feferman, Kiril. *The Holocaust in the Crimea and the North Caucasus*. Jerusalem: Yad Vashem, 2016.
Fink, Carole. *Defending the Rights of Others: The Great Powers, the Jews, and International Minority Protection, 1878–1938*. Cambridge: Cambridge University Press, 2004.
Florescu, Radu R. *General Ioan Emanoil Florescu: Organizer of the Romanian Army*. Boulder, CO: East European Monographs, 2007.
———. *The Struggle against Russia in the Romanian Principalities, 1821–1854*. Iași: Center for Romanian Studies, 1997.
Forczyk, Robert. *Where the Iron Crosses Grow: The Crimea, 1941–1944*. New York: Osprey, 2014.
Frieser, Karl-Heinz, Klaus Schmider, Klaus Schönherr, Gerhard Schreiber, Krisztián Ungváry, and Bernd Wegner. *Germany and the Second World War*. Vol. 8, *The Eastern Front 1943–1944: The War in the East and on the Neighbouring Fronts*. Translated by Barry Smerin and Barbara Wilson. Oxford: Clarendon, 2007.
Geissbühler, Simon. *Iulie însângerat: România și holocaustul din vara lui 1941*. Translated by Ioana Rostoș. Bucharest: Curtea Veche, 2015.
Giurescu, Dinu C. *Romania in the Second World War (1939–1945)*. Translated by Eugenia Elena Popescu. New York: Columbia University Press, 2000.
Glantz, David M. *Red Storm over the Balkans: The Failed Soviet Invasion of Romania, Spring 1944*. Lawrence: University Press of Kansas, 2007.
Glenny, Misha. *The Balkans: Nationalism, War, and the Great Powers, 1804–1999*. New York: Penguin, 1999.
Goerlitz, Walter. *Paulus and Stalingrad: A Life of Field-Marshal Friedrich Paulus, with Notes, Correspondence, and Documents from His Papers*. Translated by R. H. Stevens. London: Methuen, 1963.
Gusti, Dimitrie, ed. *Enciclopedia României*. Vol. 1. Bucharest: Imprimeria Națională, 1938.
Hanebrink, Paul. *A Specter Haunting Europe: The Myth of Judeo-Bolshevism*. Cambridge, MA: Belknap Press of Harvard University Press, 2018.

Harward, Grant. "First among Un-equals: Challenging German Stereotypes of the Romanian Army during the Second World War." *Journal of Slavic Military Studies* 24, no. 3 (July 2011): 439–80.

———. "Purifying the Ranks: Ethnic and Minority Policy in the Romanian Armed Forces during the Second World War." *Studies in Ethnicity & Nationalism* 13, no. 2 (October 2013): 158–78.

Haynes, Rebecca. "Germany and the Establishment of the Romanian National Legionary State, September 1940." *Slavonic and East European Review* 77, no. 4 (October 1999): 700–725.

———. "Reluctant Allies? Iuliu Maniu and Corneliu Zelea Codreanu against King Carol II of Romania." *Slavonic and East European Review* 85, no. 1 (January 2007): 105–34.

———. *Romanian Policy towards Germany, 1936–1940*. New York: St. Martin's, 2000.

Hehn, Paul N. *A Low Dishonest Decade: The Great Powers, Eastern Europe, and the Economic Origins of World War II, 1930–1941*. New York: Continuum, 2002.

Heinen, Armin. *Legiunea "arhanghelul Mihail": Mișcare socială și organizație politică*. Translated by Cornelia Eșianu and Delia Eșianu. Bucharest: Humanitas, 2006.

Hentea, Călin. *Brief Romanian Military History*. Translated by Cristina Bordianu. Lanham, MD: Scarecrow, 2007.

Hillgruber, Andreas. *Hitler, regele Carol și mareșalul Antonescu: Relațiile germane-române (1938–1944)*. 2nd ed. Translated by Maria Alexe. Bucharest: Humanitas, 2007.

Hitchins, Keith. *The Romanians, 1774–1866*. Oxford: Clarendon, 1996.

———. *Rumania, 1866–1947*. Oxford: Clarendon, 1994.

Horne, John, and Alan Kramer. *German Atrocities: A History of Denial*. New Haven, CT: Yale University Press, 2001.

Hull, Isabel. *Absolute Destruction: Military Culture and the Practices of War in Imperial Germany*. Ithaca, NY: Cornell University Press, 2005.

Iancu, Carol. *Evreii din România: De la excludere la emancipare*. Bucharest: Hasefer, 2009.

Ilie, Mihaela Camelia. "Processing the Political Image of a King: An Overview of the Interwar and Communist Discourse about Carol II of Romania." *Revista de științe Politice* 47 (2015), 206–15.

Ioanid, Radu. *The Holocaust in Romania: The Destruction of Jews and Gypsies under the Antonescu Regime, 1940–1944*. Chicago: Ivan R. Dee, 2000.

Ionescu, Ștefan Cristian. *Jewish Resistance to "Romanianization," 1940–44*. New York: Palgrave Macmillan, 2015.

Jeican, Ionuț Isaia, Florin Ovidiu Botiș, and Dan Gheban. "Typhus Exanthematicus in Romania during the Second World War (1940–1945) Reflected by Romanian Medical Journals of the Time." *Clujul Medical* 88, no. 1 (2015): 83–90.

Kaplan, Robert D. *Balkan Ghosts: A Journey through History*. New ed. New York: Picador, 2005.

Karamanou, M., I. Liappas, Ch. Antoniou, G. Androutsos, and E. Lykouras. "Julius Wagner-Jauregg (1857–1940): Introducing Fever Therapy in the Treatment of Neurosyphilis." *Psychiatriki* 24, no. 3 (July–September 2013): 208–12.

Karețki, Aurel, and Maria Covaci. *Zile însângerate la Iași (28–30 iunie 1941)*. Bucharest: Editura Politică, 1978.

King, Charles. *The Moldovans: Romania, Russia, and the Politics of Culture*. Stanford, CA: Hoover Institution, 1999.

———. *Odessa: Genius and Death in a City of Dreams*. New York: W. W. Norton, 2011.
Klier, John Doyle. *Russians, Jews, and the Pogroms of 1881–1882*. Cambridge: Cambridge University Press, 2011.
Kochanski, Halik. *The Eagle Unbowed: Poland and the Poles in the Second World War*. Cambridge, MA: Harvard University Press, 2012.
Leustean, Lucian. "'For the Glory of Romanians': Orthodoxy and Nationalism in Greater Romania, 1918–1945." *Journal of Nationalism and Ethnicity* 35, no. 4 (August 2007): 717–42.
———. *Orthodoxy and the Cold War: Religion and Political Power in Romania, 1947–65*. New York: Palgrave Macmillan, 2009.
Levin, Don. *The Lesser of Two Evils: Eastern European Jewry under Soviet Rule, 1939–1941*. Translated by Naftali Greenwood. Philadelphia: Jewish Publication Society, 1995.
Livezeanu, Irina. *Cultural Politics in Greater Romania: Regionalism, Nation Building, and Ethnic Struggle, 1918–1930*. Ithaca, NY: Cornell University Press, 1995.
Luca, Victor, Mihai V. Zodian, and Cătălin Radu, eds. *Războiul ofiților de rezervă (1941–1944, fragmente)*. Bucharest: Socitatea Scriitorilor Militari, 2003.
Lynn, John. *Bayonets of the Republic: Motivation and Tactics in the Army of Revolutionary France, 1791–1794*. Boulder, CO: Westview, 1996.
Manole, Ilie, ed. *Armata și biserica*. Bucharest: Colecția "Revista de Istorie Militară," 1996.
Megargee, Geoffrey P. *War of Annihilation: Combat and Genocide on the Eastern Front, 1941*. Plymouth, UK: Rowman & Littlefield, 2006.
Mendelsohn, Erza. *The Jews of East Central Europe between the World Wars*. Bloomington: Indiana University Press, 1983.
Messenger, Charles. *The Last Prussian: A Biography of Field Marshal Gerd von Rundstedt, 1875–1953*. London: Brassey's, 1991.
Michelbacher, Dallas. *Jewish Forced Labor in Romania, 1940–1944*. Bloomington: Indiana University Press, 2020.
Midan, Christophe. *Carol al II-lea și teroarea istoriei, 1930–1940*. Translated by Daniela Codruța Midan. Bucharest: Editura Militară, 2008.
Millett, Allan, and Williamson Murray, eds. *Military Effectiveness*. 2nd ed. Vol. 1, *The First World War*. Cambridge: Cambridge University Press, 2010.
Miron, Ovidiu Marius. *Jandarmeria română în perioada interbelică, 1919–1941: Mit și realitate*. Lugoj: Editura Dacia Europa Nova, 2003.
Mironov, Alexandru-Murad. "And Quiet Flows the Dniester: Life and Death on the Romanian-Soviet Border, 1918–1940." *Arhivele Totalitarismului* 19, no. 3 (2011): 32–58.
Mishkova, Diana, Balázs Trencsényi, and Marja Jalava, eds. *"Regimes of Historicity" in Southeastern and Northern Europe, 1890–1945: Discourses of Identity and Temporality*. New York: Palgrave Macmillan, 2014.
Moraru, Pavel. *Armata lui Stalin văzută de români*. Bucharest: Editura Militară, 2006.
———. *La hotarul românesc al Europei: Din istoria siguranței generale în Basarabia, 1918–1940*. Bucharest: Institutul Național Pentru Studiul Totalitarismului, 2008.
Moșneagu, Marian, Petrișor Florea, and Dan Prisăcaru, coords. *Armata română și cultele*. Brăila: Editura Istros, 2014.

Nagy-Talavera, Nicholas M. *The Green Shirts and the Others*. Iași: Center for Romanian Studies, 2001.

Nastasa-Kovacs, Lucian, ed. *Pogromul itinerant sau decembrie antisemit: Oradea, 1927*. Bucharest: Curtea Veche, 2014.

Niță, Dodo, and Alexandru Ciubotariu. *Istoria benzii desenate românești, 1891–2010*. Bucharest: Editura Vellant, 2010.

Oișteanu, Andrei. *Inventing the Jew: Antisemitic Stereotypes in Romanian and Other Central-East European Cultures*. Lincoln: University of Nebraska Press, 2009.

Otu, Petre. *Mareșalul Alexandru Averescu: Militarul, omul politic, legenda*. Bucharest: Editura Militară, 2009.

——. *Mareșalul Constantin Prezan: Vocația datoriei*. Bucharest: Editura Militară, 2008.

Paxton, Robert O. *The Anatomy of Fascism*. New York: Knopf, 2004.

Pelin, Mihai. *Săptămîna patimilor (23–28 iunie 1940): Cedarea Basarabiei și a nordului Bucovinei*. Bucharest: Compania, 2008.

Petrescu, Nicolae. *Regina Maria și vânătorii de munte în războiul întregirii neamului*. Bucharest: Editura Oscar Print, 2008.

Pleshoyano, Dan V. *Colonel Nicolae Pleșoianu and the National Regeneration Movement in Wallachia*. Translated by Kathe Lieber. Boulder, CO: East European Monographs, 1991.

Popa, Ion. *The Romanian Orthodox Church and the Holocaust*. Bloomington: Indiana University Press, 2017.

Porter, Ivor. *Michael of Romania: The King and the Country*. Gloucestershire, UK: Sutton, 2005.

Prisăcaru, Dan. *În avanpostul luptei pentru supraviețuire: Apărarea națională României și frontul secret în vâltoarea anilor 1938–1940*. Bucharest: Editura Militară, 2014.

Quinlan, Paul D. *The Playboy King: Carol II of Romania*. Westport, CT: Greenwood, 1995.

Ralston, David B. *The Army of the Republic: The Place of the Military in the Political Evolution of France, 1871–1914*. Cambridge, MA: MIT Press, 1967.

Rășcănescu, Gheorghe. *Erou la Cotul Donului: Însemări din război, 1941–1944*. Bucharest: Editura Militară, 2017.

Reese, Roger R. *Red Commanders: A Social History of the Soviet Army Officer Corps, 1918–1991*. Lawrence: University Press of Kansas, 2005.

——. *Stalin's Reluctant Soldiers: A Social History of the Red Army, 1925–1941*. Lawrence: University Press of Kansas, 1996.

Roberts, Henry L. *Rumania: Political Problems of an Agrarian State*. New Haven, CT: Yale University Press; London: Geoffrey Cumberlege, Oxford University Press, 1951.

Savu, Gh. Al., ed. *The Army and the Romanian Society*. Bucharest: Military Publishing House, 1980.

Scafeș, Cornel, Horia Vladimir Șerbănescu, Ioan I. Scafeș, Cornel Andonie, Ioan Dănilă, and Romeo Avram. *Armata română, 1941–1945*. Bucharest: Editura RAI, 1996.

Schönherr, Klaus. *Luptele wehrmachtului în România 1944*. 2nd ed. Translated by Elena Matei. Bucharest: Editura Militară, 2015.

Scurtu, Ioan. *Istoria românilor în timpul celor patru regi*. Vols. 1–4. Bucharest: Editura Enciclopedică, 2011.

Șerbănescu, Horia Vladimir. "Caricatura militară în presa umoristică românească de la unire până la războiul cel mare." *Studii și cercetări de istoria artei, Artă plastică* 47, no. 3 (2013): 9–48.

Shapiro, Paul A. "Faith, Murder, Resurrection: The Iron Guard and the Romanian Orthodox Church." In *Antisemitism, Christian Ambivalence, and the Holocaust*, edited by Kevin P. Spicer, 136–70. Bloomington: Indiana University Press, 2007.

———. *The Kishinev Ghetto, 1941–1942: A Documentary History of the Holocaust in Romania's Contested Borderlands*. Tuscaloosa: University of Alabama Press, 2015.

Sheffield, Gary. *Command and Morale: The British Army on the Western Front, 1914–1918*. South Yorkshire, UK: Praetorian, 2014.

Shepherd, Ben. *Hitler's Soldiers: The German Army in the Third Reich*. New Haven, CT: Yale University Press, 2016.

Showalter, Dennis. "Army and Society in Imperial Germany: The Pains of Modernization." *Journal of Contemporary History* 18, no. 4 (October 1983): 583–618.

Smith, Helmut Walser. *The Butcher's Tale: Murder and Anti-Semitism in a German Town*. New York: W. W. Norton, 2002.

Snyder, Timothy. *Bloodlands: Europe between Hitler and Stalin*. New York: Basic Books, 2010.

Solonari, Vladimir. *Purifying the Nation: Population Exchange and Ethnic Cleansing in Nazi-Allied Romania*. Washington, DC: Woodrow Wilson Center, 2010.

———. *A Satellite Empire: Romanian Rule in Southwestern Ukraine, 1941–1944*. Ithaca, NY: Cornell University Press, 2019.

Șperlea, Florin. *De la armata regală la armata populară: Sovietizarea armatei române, 1948–1955*. Bucharest: Editura Ziua, 2003.

Stahel, David. *Kiev 1941: Hitler's Battle for Supremacy in the East*. Cambridge: Cambridge University Press, 2012.

———. *Operation Barbarossa and Germany's Defeat in the East*. Cambridge: Cambridge University Press, 2009.

———. *Operation Typhoon: Hitler's March on Moscow, October 1941*. Cambridge: Cambridge University Press, 2013.

Stănescu, Marin C. *Armata română și unirea Basarabiei și Bucovinei cu România, 1917–1919*. Constanța: Ex Ponto, 1999.

Statiev, Alexander. "The Ugly Duckling of the Armed Forces: Romanian Armor, 1919–1941." *Journal of Slavic Military Studies* 12, no. 2 (1999): 220–44.

———. "When an Army Becomes 'Merely a Burden': Romanian Defense Policy and Strategy (1918–1941)." *Journal of Slavic Military Studies* 13, no. 2 (2000): 67–85.

Steiner, Zara. *The Triumph of the Dark: European International History, 1933–1939*. Oxford: Oxford University Press, 2011.

Steinhart, Eric C. *The Holocaust and the Germanization of the Ukraine*. New York: Cambridge University Press, 2015.

Stoenescu, Alex Mihai. *Armata, mareșalul și evreii*. Bucharest: Editura RAO, 2010.

Stoff, Laurie S. *Russia's Sisters of Mercy and the Great War: More Than Binding Men's Wounds*. Lawrence: University Press of Kansas, 2015.

Thomas, Martin. "To Arm an Ally: French Arms Sales to Romania, 1926–1940." *Journal of Strategic Studies* 19, no. 2 (1996): 231–59.

Thorne, Benjamin M. "Assimilation, Invisibility, and the Eugenic Turn in the 'Gypsy Question' in Romanian Society, 1938–1942." *Romani Studies* 21, no. 2 (Winter 2011): 177–205.

Torrey, Glenn E., ed. *Romania and World War I*. Iași: Center for Romanian Studies, 1999.

——. *The Romanian Battlefront in World War I*. Lawrence: University Press of Kansas, 2011.

Truxal, Luke. "Bombing the Romanian Rail Network." *Air Power History* 65, no. 1 (Spring 2018): 15–22.

Ureche, Nicolae. *Propaganda externă a României mari, 1918–1940*. Bucharest: Editura Enciclopedică, 2015.

Voinescu, Alice. *Jurnal*. Vols. 1 and 2. Bucharest: Polirom, 2013.

Watson, Alexander. *Enduring the Great War: Combat, Morale and the Collapse in the German and British Armies, 1914–1918*. Cambridge: Cambridge University Press, 2008.

Watts, Larry L. *Romanian Cassandra: Ion Antonescu and the Struggle for Reform, 1916–1941*. Boulder, CO: East European Monographs, 1993.

Weinberg, Gerhard. "Hitler and the Beginning of the Holocaust." In *Lessons and Legacies*, vol. 10, *Back to the Sources: Reexamining Perpetrators, Victims, and Bystanders*, edited by Sara R. Horowitz, 5–12. Evanston, IL: Northwestern University Press, 2012.

Westermann, Edward B. *Hitler's Police Battalions: Enforcing Racial War in the East*. Leavenworth: University Press of Kansas, 2005.

Zagoroff, S. D., Jenö Végh, and Alexander D. Bilimovich. *The Agricultural Economy of the Danubian Countries, 1935–1945*. Stanford, CA: Stanford University Press, 1955.

Internet

Avalon Project. "The Armistice Agreement with Romania; September 12, 1944." Accessed 4 May 2018. http://avalon.law.yale.edu/wwii/rumania.asp.

Crucea Roșie Română. "Istoria Crucii Rosii Romane 1940–1945." Accessed 2 February 2018. https://crucearosie.ro/cine-suntem/istoria-crucii-rosii-romane/istoria-crucii-rosii-romane-1940–1945/.

Minority Rights Information System. *Final Report of the International Commission on the Holocaust in Romania*. Accessed 9 April 2016. http://miris.eurac.edu/mugs2/do/blob.pdf?type=pdf&serial=1117716572750.

WorldWar2.ro. "General Gheorghe Avramescu." Accessed 29 March 2016. http://worldwar2.ro/generali/?language=en&article=97.

Index

1st Armored Division, 89, 104, 109–10, 113, 118–19, 147, 170–74, 202–3, 256
8th Cavalry Brigade / 8th Cavalry Division, 125, 134, 136, 139, 147, 150, 175
1st Cavalry Division, 147, 172, 177
2nd Cavalry Division, 71
3rd Cavalry Division, 71
5th Cavalry Division, 147, 160–62
6th Cavalry Division, 147, 181, 186, 188–89
7th Cavalry Division, 147, 171
9th Cavalry Division, 147, 149, 160, 181, 187–89
1st Fortification Division, 158, 246
110th Infantry Brigade, 198
1st Infantry Division, 141–43, 146–47, 150, 153
2nd Infantry Division, 146–47, 150, 261
3rd Infantry Division, 141
4th Infantry Division, 188, 261, 263
5th Infantry Division, 85, 147
6th Infantry Division, 85, 147, 157, 172, 198
7th Infantry Division, 147, 157
8th Infantry Division, 91, 147, 150
9th Infantry Division, 147, 256, 305n217
10th Infantry Division, 126–29, 143–44, 147, 181, 186, 209, 213
11th Infantry Division, 85, 147, 157
13th Infantry Division, 147, 157, 172
14th Infantry Division, 98–99, 147, 157, 172, 178, 201
15th Infantry Division, 147, 171–74
18th Infantry Division, 144, 147, 155, 157
19th Infantry Division, 147, 150, 181, 185–89, 195, 220
20th Infantry Division, 147, 150, 171, 177–78
24th Infantry Division, 186, 188, 219. See also 4th / 24th Infantry Division

1st Mixed Mountain Brigade / 1st Mountain Division, 134–36, 142, 144, 147–48, 155, 157, 184, 187, 189, 193, 199
2nd Mixed Mountain Brigade / 2nd Mountain Division, 116, 135, 147, 157, 159–60, 167, 176–77, 181–83, 187, 189–90, 199, 243, 262
4th Mixed Mountain Brigade / 4th Mountain Division, 125, 135, 139, 147, 151, 155, 157, 183, 186–88, 201. *See also* 4th / 24th Infantry Division
101st-104th Mountain Commands, 198
3rd Mountain Division, 147, 157, 162, 181, 184, 186, 189
35th Reserve Infantry Division, 103
3rd Security Division, 239, 251
4th / 24th Infantry Division, 188, 190, 220. *See also* 4th Mountain and 24th Infantry Divisions

Acmecetca, 138, 140, 143
Adâncata, 104
air raids, 100, 197, 199–200, 255; association with Jews of, 74, 96, 198; fostering of panic by, 96–98, 156; weak air defense against, 96. *See also* strategic bombing
Aksay River, 145, 160, 175
Albița, 107
Aldea, Aurel, 258
Alexianu, Gheorghe: deportation of Jews from Odessa by, 138, 140; as governor of Transnistria, 156, 181, 192; trial and execution of, 265–66
Alushta, 134
amalgamation, 124, 155, 169, 194–96, 205, 267; breaking up of Romanian divisions for, 181, 188; with German "corset stays," 186, 189
Anapa, 145, 161
Angelescu, Paul, 54–55
anti-Bolshevism. *See* anticommunism

327

anti-Carlism, 53, 57–58, 80
anticommunism: as basis for holy war, 2, 17–18, 35, 56, 266; origins of, 30–31; pervasiveness of, 6, 229; as propaganda theme, 14; reinforcement after invasion of, 13. *See also* anti-Bolshevism
anti-Gypsy racism, 10, 18, 118, 154, 210, 225, 236, 249–51
anti-Hitlerite war, 3, 257, 265; overemphasis of, 4; unpopularity of, 259, 261, 267
antipartisan warfare, 134–35, 191–93, 197; divide and conquer strategy of, 148; as Jew hunting, 154, 156, 163; mass reprisals as practice of, 3, 8, 128, 165, 190, 192
antisemitism: fanning by press of, 27, 72; intensification by First World War of, 27–28; as linchpin of holy war, 13, 65, 162, 181, 260–61; origins of, 26–27; racial ideas of, 18, 29
anti-Slavism, 2, 18–19
Anton, Mioara, 13
Antonescu, Ion: antisemitism and xenophobia of, 18, 44, 54; arrest, trial and execution of, 254, 265–66; belief in final victory of, 83, 119; bribing by Hitler of, 117, 140; as chief of staff, 54–55; conflict with Carol II of, 54, 57, 79; conflict with Legionary movement of, 56, 84; conflict with Mihai I of, 257–58; courting of far right of, 57–58, 65, 87; decision to double down on German victory of, 140–41; early career of, 53–54; maneuvers to obtain Transnistria by, 120; with MCG at the front, 90, 105; meetings with Hitler of, 84, 90, 117, 176, 194, 203; messianic view of, 83, 87, 98; as minister of defense, 57, 82, 123; as nationalist martyr, 4, 266; opposition to an armistice of, 254, 257; order to "cleanse the terrain" of, 95, 103, 108–10; personality of, 39, 54, 55; reputation for incorruptibility of, 54, 80, 83; role in Iași pogrom of, 99, 102–3; role in Odessa massacre of, 128–29; as scapegoat for the war, 1, 3, 111; seizure of power by, 80–82, 86–87
Antonescu, Maria, 54, 230, 232
Antonescu, Mihai: arrest, trial, and execution of, 254, 265–66; propaganda efforts of, 146, 207; push for ethnic cleansing by, 94, 104, 246; as vice prime minister, 87, 90, 92, 165, 257
Antonescu regime: continued popular support for, 169–70, 195, 202; decision to "cleanse the terrain" of Jews of, 108–9; decision to delay repatriation of Gypsies by, 253; decision to deport Gypsies of, 154; decision to deport Inochentiști of, 248–49; decision to repatriate Jews of, 190–93; desire for war of, 65, 85; disillusionment about victory of, 165; economic challenges of, 88–90; labor service law of, 230; limited repressive nature of, 223; moves toward a military welfare state of, 158; negotiations to deport Jews to Poland of, 155–56; orders to halt to deportations of, 162, 165; plans for Romanianization of Transnistria of, 120–21, 130; plans to dump Jews into Ukraine of, 114, 117, 127, 129, 137–38; plebiscites of, 88, 134; preparations for war of, 90, 93–94; relaxation of policies against Jews of, 180–81, 199; remobilization of Romanian society by, 146–47, 192; sowing myth of Romania as reluctant Axis by, 257; strategy to fight in Ukraine for northern Transylvania of, 111
Arad, 62, 83, 259
Arbore, Ioan, 160, 215
Arciz, 69–70, 217
ardeleni, 21–22, 24, 58, 80–81
Army Group Antonescu, 246; attack by, 103–4; bridgehead battles of, 95–97; dissolving of, 115; Einsatzgruppe D assigned to, 109; talk of reestablishing of, 160, 163; von Schobert actual commander of, 94. *See also* Don Staff
Army Group Dumitrescu, 194
Army Group No. 1, 59, 76; deployment of, 60, 66; losses during withdrawal, 77; retreat of, 66–68
army intelligence, 84, 89, 98, 120, 125, 127, 154, 156, 207, 243, 244
artillery regiments: 3rd Horse, 148; 7th, 163; 8th, 62, 73; 16th, 69; 24th, 98; 53rd, 9
Astrakhan, 163
Atachi, 30
Athanasescu, Gheorghe, 43, 52, 69, 72
atrocities: "hot-blooded" versus "cold-blooded," 93; influence of commander's character on, 2, 93; time required to commit, 104, 106, 115; use of alcohol in, 107, 127; waves of, 110. *See also* war crimes
Aurelian, Petre S., 27
Auschwitz, 17, 243, 265
Austria-Hungary, 9, 27, 37

INDEX

Averescu, Alexandru, 48, 50, 52, 53
Avramescu, Gheorghe: arrest and mysterious death of, 263; as Fourth Army commander, 202, 204; good relationship with von Manstein of, 149; as Mountain Corps commander, 118, 123, 134, 139, 142, 163; skepticism about *francs-tireurs* of, 106; as III Corps commander, 187
Axis: competition between Romanian and Hungary in, 140–41, 147, 160, 176, 194; holding together by anticommunism of, 6, 180; importance of Romania to, 176; Romania's joining of, 79–80, 85; weakening of, 169, 178, 185–86, 200
Axworthy, Mark, 4, 13

Bacalbaşa, Anton, 38, 45, 46
Băgulescu, Gheorghe, 86
Bakhchysaray, 136
Balta, 118, 137, 143, 181
Bălţi, 68, 71, 107–9, 154, 194, 231
Bârlad, 232
Bartov, Omer, 14
Bârzotescu, Emanoil, 143, 146
basarabeni, 22, 58, 70–72, 94, 106, 121, 194, 196, 201, 259
Berlin, 34–35, 165
Berşad, 144
Bessarabia, 21, 23, 29, 31, 60, 62, 65, 77, 81, 113, 115, 123, 192, 207, 245, 259
Bilyaivka, 120
Birzula, 232
Bistriţa, 79
Black Sea, 68, 95, 161, 190
Blue Line, 183, 185
Bock, Fedor von, 150, 153
Bogdanovca, 138, 140
Bolgrad, 69, 71–72, 73
Bolsheviks, 23, 30–31, 123–24, 131, 183, 211. *See also* communists
Bolshoy, 170–72
Botoşani, 95, 239
boyars, 19–20, 34, 45. *See also* large landowning class
Brăila, 203, 232, 256
Braşov, 9, 50, 80, 187, 232, 235, 241–43, 256
Brătianu, Constantin I. C., 162
Brătianu, Gheorghe I., 51, 78, 82, 111
Brătianu, Ion, 26
Brătianu, Ion I. C., 48, 50–51
Brătianu, Vintilă I. C., 51
Brno, 264

Bucharest, 19, 27, 53, 59, 80, 96, 232; declaring of war celebration in, 92; fighting around, 255–56; pogrom in, 86; victory parade in, 134
bucovineni, 22, 106, 201, 259
Bug River, 116, 119, 129, 140, 182
Buhai, 121
Bukovina, 21, 24, 29, 59, 68, 191–92, 245
Bulgaria, 24, 37, 55, 80, 88; ceding of southern Dobruja to, 12, 81, 266; population exchange in Dobruja with, 82, 245–46
Bulgarian Army, 51, 60, 90
Buşteni, 235
Buzău, 110, 232
Byelorussia, 202–3

Cahul, 107
Calafat, 103
Călăraşi, 103, 246
călăraşi regiments: 2nd, 215; 3rd, 70, 96; 11th, 71; 13th, 187–88, 191–93, 220
Călinescu, Armand, 58, 59
Cantacuzino, Gheorghe, 56
Capital Military Command, 80, 82, 86, 258
capitalism, 30, 32, 200
Captaru, Dumitru, 97–98, 100
Caracal, 103
Carlaonţ, Dimitru, 103, 110
Carlism, 50–52, 57–58, 83
Carol I: criticism of the army's performance by, 42; expansion and "Prussianization" of military under, 37, 39; recruiting of, 20
Carol II: antisemitic laws of, 25–26, 58, 79, 236; courting of minorities by, 58, 243; as crown prince, 50; decisions to cede territory without fighting by, 64, 66, 80; exile of, 80; reputation for corruption of, 52, 83; restoration of, 51–52; royal dictatorship of, 57, 207; rumors on the front about, 176, 202; suppression of the Legionary movement by, 34, 57–58, 59
Carol Line, 60–61
Carpathian Mountains, 17, 196, 254
Case, Holly, 12
Case Blue, 145, 147, 151; changes to plans of, 159; influence on Holocaust of, 156; optimism in, 152, 153, 159; reliance on Axis allies' of, 140
Caspian Sea, 163
Caucasus, 5, 157–63, 167, 169, 176–78, 180–81, 209, 218–19
Caucasus Mountains, 145, 162

INDEX

Cavalry Corps: attack into Bessarabia of, 104, 107; in Caucasus, 157, 159–62, 167; in Crimea, 188, 193; disbanding of, 261; guarding Azov Sea coast by, 137, 139; in Kuban bridgehead, 176, 181; retreat from Bessarabia of, 69–71, 76; in Ukraine, 110, 113, 116, 124–25
Cernăuți, 53, 66, 180, 226, 232, 249; ghetto in, 114, 127, 156; liberation of, 104, 106; occupation of, 68, 194
Cernavodă, 94
Cetatea Albă, 66, 232; liberation of, 104, 114–17; (re-)occupation of, 68, 204
chaplains, 12–13, 24, 41, 49, 122, 217, 247; as missionaries, 121, 154, 163, 185, 200, 249; as propagandists, 83, 142, 166, 182–83, 234; recruiting of, 25, 142, 212, 247–48
Chersonese Peninsula, 157–58, 197
Chilia Nouă, 117
Chirilovici, Constantin, 97–98
Chirnoagă, Platon, 3, 263
Chir River, 172, 174–75, 219
Chișinău, 33, 64, 66, 154, 180, 195–96, 199–201, 216, 232; capture of, 104, 110–11, 113, 116–17; ghetto in, 114, 127; occupation of, 69
Cialâk, Gheorghe, 176, 187, 192–93, 263
Ciopron, Partenie, 25, 212, 247
Ciudei, 74, 106
Ciupercă, Nicolae, 66, 69, 71–73, 76, 93, 109, 116–22, 266
civilians: Romanian, willingness to join in mass reprisals of Jews of, 97–102, 106, 110; Soviet, abuse of, 104, 115, 120, 126–27, 132, 135, 139, 142, 160, 222; Soviet, disinclination to join in mass reprisals of Jews of, 115
Cluj, 80–81, 261, 265
Codreanu, Corneliu: arrest, trials, and assassination of, 57–58; as "Captain" of Legionary movement, 17, 34, 56; as Iași student, 29; reburial of, 84–85
Coman, Simion, 219
Comănești, 74, 76
communism, 4, 13, 32, 51, 77, 88, 115, 183, 200
communists, 24, 32–33, 71, 84, 90, 93, 106, 109, 128, 157. *See also* Bolsheviks
Constanța, 92, 96, 102, 147, 195, 197, 256
Constantinescu-Claps, Constantin, 167, 172, 175–76, 180, 266
Coroamă, Dumitru, 80
courts-martial, 8, 61, 108, 148, 185, 187, 215–17, 222–23, 226, 251

Craiova, 38, 53, 103
Crimean Peninsula: Axis conquest of, 123–25, 132–35, 151–53; Axis evacuation of, 169, 196–97; Hitler's determination to hold onto, 188–89, 192, 198; Soviet reconquest of, 195, 199; Soviet winter counteroffensive against, 136, 138–41, 144; as unsinkable aircraft carrier, 118
Crimean War, 19, 155
Cristea, Miron, 24, 25–26, 30, 57, 58
Cretzianu, Alexandru, 3, 60, 86
Cuza, Alexandru C., 29, 34, 57–58, 207
Cuza, Alexandru Ioan, 19–20, 23, 37, 39
Czech Protectorate, 264
Czechoslovakia, 55, 56, 57–59

Dalnik, 123–24, 128–29
Danube River, 69, 72, 96–97, 114, 203, 220, 246
Dămăceanu, Dumitru, 258
Dăscălescu, Nicolae, 38, 40, 141, 166, 263, 265–66
Davidescu, Gheorghe, 65–66, 71
deportation: of Gypsies to Transnistria, 154, 250–52; of Inochentiști to Transnistria, 248; of Jews from Moldavia to Wallachia, 91, 94, 98, 103, 110; of Jews from Bukovina and Bessarabia to Transnistria, 110, 114, 121, 127, 156, 226, 239; of Jews in Transnistria to the Bug, 129, 149; of Lipovans from Dobruja to Wallachia, 103, 246; of Poles and Ukrainians from Bukovina and Bessarabia to Transnistria, 246
deserters: to enemy, 77, 188, 220, 263; formation of bandit groups by, 146, 188, 216; minority, 241–42, 244, 247, 248; punishment of, 139, 148, 166, 180, 193, 196, 199, 215; to rear, 182, 200; rounding up of, 146–47, 154; Soviet encouraging of, 177, 187; from Transnistria to Crimea, 158–59. *See also* rehabilitation
Deva, 159
DiNardo, Richard, 11
discipline, 6–7, 25, 48, 56, 83, 212–13, 261; by blocking detachments, 14, 119, 213, 222–23; by capital punishment, 177, 188, 196, 221–23; concern about, 75–76, 103–4, 115–16, 168, 198; by corporal punishment, 119, 213–15, 260; by financial punishment, 223–27; of minorities, 222, 244; by penal

INDEX 331

punishment, 181, 215–21; selective enforcing of, 14, 95. *See also* flogging
Dnepropetrovsk, 141, 143, 182
Dniester River, 23, 60, 68, 106, 111, 113, 117, 187, 193, 196, 199, 204
Dobruja, 21, 28, 80–83, 95, 245, 247
Domanovca, 138, 140, 143–44
Donets River, 156, 178, 181, 183
Don River, 159–66, 168, 170–74, 176
Don Staff, 165, 171. *See also* Army Group Antonescu
dorobanți regiments: 2nd, 72; 6th, 119; 11th, 109; 13th, 98; 15th, 125
Dorohoi, 72, 95, 190; pogrom in, 73–74, 75
Dragalina, Corneliu, 135, 143, 153
Dragomir, Nicolae, 176, 178, 223, 263
Dubossary, 114, 117
Duca, Ion, 53
Dumitrache, Ioan, 116, 125, 177, 181
Dumitrescu, Petre: arrest and release of, 265–66; as commander of the Third Army, 94, 119, 133, 157, 164–67, 190, 232, 255; commitment to final victory of, 146, 174; conflict with other generals of, 148, 160; as strict disciplinarian, 115, 174–75, 194, 199, 214–15, 222
Dumitru, Diana, 5
Duțu, Alesandru, 5
Dzhankoy, 142, 233

Edineț, 107,
effectiveness, 14–5, 47, 104, 165, 169, 205, 261, 264, 267
Eltigen, 188–89
Eminescu, Mihai, 20
enlisted men: conscripting of, 37, 46; conditions for, 45–46; misuse of, 47, 52; treatment of, 8, 45, 62
Einsatzgruppe D, 108–10, 117, 133, 135–36, 142, 154, 158, 226; cooperation with SSI of, 109; more active in Bessarabia than Bukovina, 114; use of Romanians by, 154. *See also* SS
ethnic minorities: Bulgarians, 44–45, 60, 245–47; Germans, 9, 44, 46, 69–70, 83, 88, 137–43, 218, 222, 229, 235–36, 240–43, 255; Hungarians, 17, 44, 219, 243–45, 260; Russians, 44, 69, 113, 219, 245–47; Ukrainians, 45, 113, 245–27
eugenics, 18, 29, 249
Eupatoria, 131, 136, 139, 143

fascism, 17, 33–34, 36, 57, 62, 88, 260
Fălciu, 107, 109, 232
Fălticeni, 108
Fântână Albă, 106
female volunteers, 229–30; as entertainers, 234; as nurses, 230–34; officers' wives among, 232–33; as soldiers, 255
Feodosia, 136, 138–41, 182–83, 233
Ferdinand I: 21, 25, 43, 50–51
Filderman, Wilhelm, 133, 180, 193
Final Solution, 65, 137, 266. *See also* Holocaust
Finland, 60, 62, 66, 126, 258
First Army: in Hungary, 259–63; initial mobilization of, 59; in reserve during campaign in east, 94
First Vienna Award, 58
First World War, 17, 22, 24, 27, 38, 48, 230, 235; crushing of "Red Budapest by Romania," 31; French military mission to Romania, 62; Paris Peace Conference, 28; Russian Revolution, 13, 21, 37; typhus epidemic in Moldavia, 37
flogging, 10, 46, 165, 178, 188, 199, 239; bottom-up pressure to reinstate, 76, 115; re-banning of, 260; regulations for, 214–15; reintroduction of, 14, 119, 213–14. *See also* discipline
FNB Line, 203–4, 240, 254, 256
Fourth Army: in battle of Odessa, 118–26, 222; in battle of Stalingrad, 166–68, 171–76; demobilization of, 132–34, 182; evacuation from Bessarabia of, 68–72, 75–76; Hitler's request to cross Dniester of, 116; in Hungary and Slovakia, 262–64; on Iași front, 193–94, 198–204, 223, 256; mobilization of, 59; reconquest of central Bessarabia by, 95, 104, 107–9, 113–14; reconquest of northern Transylvania by, 261; remobilization of, 163, 193
France, 48, 50, 58–59, 62–63, 65, 87
francs-tireurs: equating with Jews of, 93, 113–14; execution of, 105–6, 110. *See also* partisans
French Army, 42, 55
Fretter-Pico, Maximilian, 204
Friessner, Johannes, 3, 202, 204, 255

Galați, 26, 53, 69, 221, 232; massacre in, 72–73
Găiești, 231, 237
Gelendzhik, 162

INDEX

gendarmes: as civilian law enforcers, 46, 74, 94; conferences to "cleanse the terrain" for, 108; conflict with SS over deporting Jews of, 117; crimes by, 73–74, 96, 99–102, 113, 127, 129, 138, 140, 143–44, 226, 250; as military police, 59, 61, 98, 116, 148, 177, 182, 185–86, 192, 222, 226; as more murderous in Bessarabia, 113–14; successive waves of, 93, 110

General Staff, 15, 37, 39, 83, 94, 133, 185, 192–93, 198, 200, 204, 219, 226, 232–33, 259; anti-Gypsy bias of, 252; antisemitism of, 154, 199, 236, 260–61; as brake on antisemitic violence, 64, 75; creation of rehabilitation policy by, 147, 182, 216–18; efforts to bolster troops' morale by, 70, 136–37, 143, 183, 189, 200, 207–9; efforts to preserve Romanian neutrality by, 58–62; fears about Soviet landings in Transnistria of, 138; forming of labor detachments by, 60–61, 148, 238–40, 246–47; improvised deployment of forces to Russia by, 159–60; order to abandon northern Bukovina and Bessarabia of, 66; order to deport Jews of, 127; preparations for war of, 85, 89; shifting blame onto Jews by, 71, 77; suspicion of minority soldiers of, 229, 235–36, 243, 247; removal of generals deemed lacking in toughness by, 146; reorganization of army by, 83, 147; replacement of leadership of, 140–41; request to use poison gas of, 150. *See also* MCG

German Army, 2–3, 10, 85, 111, 123, 131, 147, 178, 181, 184, 213, 241, 258; 13th Motorized Infantry Division, 83; 6th Panzer Division, 175; 16th Panzer Division, 85, 88; 17th Panzer Division, 175; 22nd Panzer Division, 150–51, 170–74; 23rd Panzer Division, 175; Army Group A, 159–62, 167, 176–77, 181, 185–86, 188–95; Army Group B, 159–65, 167–68, 170, 172; Army Group Center, 103, 136, 167, 202; Army Group Don, 175, 177, 181; Army Group North, 103, 202; Army Group South, 94, 103–4, 111, 115–19, 132, 141, 144, 150–51, 156–59, 181, 183, 185–86, 190–91, 193; Army Group South Ukraine, 195–99, 202–4, 257; Army Group Wöhler, 194; aura of invincibility of, 90, 92, 153; crediting Antonescu for the Romanian Army's performance by, 111, 127, 202; First Panzer Army, 116, 153, 160, 167, 176; Fourth Panzer Army, 160–61, 166, 168, 171; German Eleventh Army, 90, 95, 104, 107–11, 114–16, 123–25, 132–36, 140–42, 144, 148, 151, 153–55, 157, 208–9, 222, 241; Grodeck Motorized Brigade, 139, 151; Koch Group, 153; liaison staffs of, 11, 111, 157, 170, 201; LVII Corps, 204; opinion about the Romanian Army of, 11, 88, 111–12, 132, 177, 201–2; Panzer Group Kleist, 125; Seventeenth Army, 115, 141, 143, 146, 150, 153, 156, 161–62, 167, 177, 181, 183, 185–86, 188–90, 195–97; Sixth Army, 160–61, 163, 167–68, 170–75, 177–78, 186–87, 194–95, 199, 204–5, 256; "war of annihilation" by, 2; XXXXVIII Panzer Corps, 167, 170–72, 178; Ziegler Motorized Brigade, 133–34

German Ethnic Group in Romania, 241–42

German Luftwaffe, 94, 241, 255; Luftflotte, 4, 96, 121, 150–51, 153, 155, 166

German Military Mission to Romania, 79, 83, 85–89, 118, 120, 126, 254, 256

Germany: annexing of Austria by, 57; annexing of Sudetenland by, 58; delay allying with Romania of, 70; as lessor evil than Soviet Union, 35, 59, 84, 87, 180; Nazi takeover of, 54; rearming of, 55; Romania's fate bound to, 2, 135, 141; Romania's "turning of arms" against, 255–56; as trade partner with Romania, 56, 140, 176

Ghineraru, Nicolae, 146, 129, 246

Gigurtu, Ion, 78, 89

Giurgiu, 232

Giurgiulești, 75

Glogojanu, Ionel, 126, 128–29

Goga, Octavian, 57–58, 207

Golovsky, 172–73

grănicieri, 40–41, 61, 73, 75, 115, 246

Grăniceri Division, 221

grăniceri regiments: 2nd, 115–16; 3rd, 73, 75–76; 5th, 216

Great Britain, 58–59, 62, 83, 133, 257

Greece, 24, 56, 59, 88, 90

Grodeck, Karl von, 151

Gromky, 170–72

Groza, Petru, 263–64, 266

Grozny, 167

Guard Division, 40, 261

Gudarevici, I. I., 69, 72

Guderian, Heinz, 3, 255

Gypsies: bravery of, 225, 250; deportation of, 154; effect of deportations on, 250–52; elite protest against deporting of, 162; presence at Sărata Training Center of, 251–52; popular support for deporting of, 154; repatriation of, 265

Hansen, Erik, 85, 87, 89–90, 120
Hauffe, Arthur, 120, 123, 140
Helen, 50, 83, 162, 230, 232, 258
Herța, 68, 73, 77
Himmler, Heinrich, 108, 137
historiography, 3–6
Hitler, Adolf, 2, 57, 80, 85, 136, 155, 176, 184, 189, 194, 241, 256
Holocaust: in Crimea, 135–35, 142, 154–55; in Romania and Transnistria, 5, 127, 149, 265. *See also* Final Solution
honor: elite units more concerned with, 40, 107, 157; influence on discipline of, 7, 220; as motivation, 65, 76–77, 91, 153, 173, 178, 180; officers' obsession with, 39, 41, 70, 81, 95, 178, 216, 223
Horthy, Miklós, 31
Horthy regime, 194, 265
hostages, 93, 100, 102, 110, 116, 128, 135, 192, 200
Hotin, 68, 104, 106, 194, 239; uprising at, 30–31
Hube, Hans, 88
Hull, Isabel, 8
Hungarian Army, 31, 81, 140–41, 178, 243–44, 259; Rapid Corps, 118; Second Army, 150, 178
Hungary: claims on Transylvania of, 79; German occupation of, 194; as lesser threat to Romania, 81; as more passive than Romania, 202, 258; Romania's fear of war with, 56; territorial aggrandizement of, 58–59, 80

Iacobici, Iosif: arrests and death of, 265–66; as chief of staff, 124, 222; as Fourth Army commander, 121, 126, 231; as minister of defense, 90, 213–15; opposition to max support for Case Blue of, 140; resignation of, 141; role in Odessa massacre of, 126, 128; as Third Army commander, 68
Iași, 19, 38, 53, 72, 95, 110, 195–97, 199–204, 232; averted pogrom in, 75–76; as center of right-wing student activism, 27–29; "death trains" of, 100–102, 246; pogrom in, 5, 13, 97–100, 102–3

I Corps, 172, 176
ideology: alleged Romanian lack of, 1, 3, 18, 135, 227; as primary foundation of motivation, 11–13, 18, 168, 170, 181, 205; reinforcing by propaganda of, 6, 13, 212; similarity with Nazi's of, 2, 35; soldiers' worldview of, 41, 48, 65, 95, 206
II Corps: in battle of Stalingrad, 170–71; reconquest of southern Bessarabia by, 95–96, 104, 113–14; responsibility for coastal defense in Transnistria of, 150, 190; temporary responsibility for military and police forces in Odessa of, 141
III Corps, 58, 66, 70, 120, 187, 190
Ilcuș, Ioan, 66
infanterie regiments: 13th, 123; 14th, 74; 16th, 74, 106; 29th, 73–74; 38th, 9, 131, 195; 56th, 62; 85th, 153; 93rd, 153; 111th, 220; 112th, 220
Inhul River, 184, 193
interwar politics: 1923 constitution, 29, 44, 47–48; 1933 election, 30, 56; 1937 election, 57; 1938 constitution, 57; Conservative Party, 20–21, 27, 48; Everything for the Country Party, 56–57; Front of National Rebirth, 57–58, 85; "Generation of 1922," 28; Great Depression, 30, 42, 47, 51; LANC, 29, 34, 56–57, 73, 106, 284n63; Liberal Party, 20–21, 27, 29, 48–51, 53, 55, 57, 65, 162, 254, 258, 261; Peasant Party, 48; People's Party, 48, 50–51; Ploughman's Front, 263; National Agrarian Party, 57; National Christian Party, 57; National Peasant Party, 29–30, 51, 53, 57, 65, 254, 258, 261; regency, 25, 50, 51; Romanian National Party, 48; Škoda scandal, 53; Social Democratic Party, 32
Ioanițiu, Alexandru: accidental death of, 123; as chief of staff, 89, 102, 105, 119, 123, 222, 244; personality of, 123–24
Ionescu, Nae, 25
Iorga, Nicolae, 84
Iron Guard. *See* Legion of the Archangel Michael
Ismail, 66, 70, 97, 114, 246
Isopescu, Modest, 137–38, 265
Italian Army, 11, 90, 111, 140, 167, 184, 211; Eighth Army, 163, 175–76, 178
Italy, 34, 80, 147, 178, 184–85, 200, 207, 228, 258
IV Corps, 104, 164, 166, 170–71, 193, 203
Izyum, 141, 143–46, 150–51, 153, 158

Jaenecke, Erwin, 185–86, 188, 190–92, 196, 198
Jean, Ancel, 4–5
Jewish Central Office, 156, 180, 239–40
Jewish communism: de facto start of war against, 65; fear of future vengeance of, 13, 180, 195; origins of myth of, 33; reinforcement by alleged Jewish treachery of, 12–13, 28, 71, 73, 75, 96–99; supposed threat of, 1–2, 34, 77, 91, 248; as target during invasion, 71, 90, 93, 104–5, 124, 151.
Jewish labor detachments: disbanding of, 260; efforts to increase productivity of, 237–39; increased reliance on, 229; at Sărata, 219; used to build fortifications, 60–61, 96, 240
Jews: as *arendași*, 20–21; conditions in Romania versus Transnistria for, 156, 181; deportation of, 121, 127; diversity of, 28; ghettoization of, 110, 120, 137–38, 149; interwar persecution of, 28–29, 30, 56–58; massacres in Transnistria of, 144; in military, 43, 85, 236–37; pogroms in northern Bukovina and Bessarabia of, 117; population growth of, 26–28; prominence in cities of, 22; repatriation from Transnistria of, 190–93, 199
Jijia Valley, 203
Jilava, 58, 84
Judeo-Bolshevism. *See* Jewish communism

Kalach, 160
Kalmyk Steppe, 161, 163–67, 171–73, 177, 215, 217
Karasubazar, 134, 142, 154
Karpovka River, 174
Keitel, Wilhelm, 85, 147
Kerch, 136, 158, 189, 233; battle of, 134, 138–39, 142, 144, 148, 151–53; Soviet landings on peninsula of, 131, 188; straits of, 160–61
Kherson, 134–35, 187, 233, 241
Kiev, 85, 123, 126, 132, 223
Kirovograd, 135, 141, 146, 191
Kiselyov, Pavel, 19, 37
Kitzinger, Karl, 135
Kleist, Paul von, 125, 192
Kletskaya, 164, 170
Korne, Radu, 151, 202, 263, 266
Korne Detachment, 133, 136, 151, 160, 171
Kotelnikovo, 166, 171–73, 175
Krasnodar, 177, 181

Kuban bridgehead, 176, 181–87, 205, 222, 257, 267
Kuban River, 160–61, 177
Kursk, 183, 228, 267; battle of, 184

labor battalions, 60–62, 148, 219–20, 229, 236, 244, 246–47, 253, 260
large landowning class, 24, 27, 32, 38, 48. *See also* boyars
Lascăr, Mihail: as 1st Mixed Mountain Brigade commander, 104, 135–36, 142–43; as 6th Infantry Division commander, 172–73, 178; as Horia, Cloșca, and Crișan Division commander, 264
Lascăr Group, 172–74, 219
League of Nations, 23, 30, 32, 34–35, 56, 78, 111
Lecca, Radu, 156, 162, 238–40
Legion of the Archangel Michael: bringing to power (National Legionary State) of, 82; Carlist suppression of, 58; origins of, 34; puppet regime of, 257, 263; uprising of, 86; views of, 25, 56; violence of, 53, 59, 84. *See also* Iron Guard
Lemberg, 232
Lenin, Vladimir, 30
Leningrad, 132
looting, 68–69, 74, 98–99, 104, 106–7, 110, 115–16, 127, 134, 142, 196, 213–14, 216–17, 219, 221, 223, 226–27
Lozovaya, 146
Lugoj, 103
Lupescu, Elena, 50–52, 54–55, 80, 83
Lupu, Constantin, 97–100, 102–3
Lynn, John, 6–8

Macici, Nicolae: arrest and trial of, 265; as First Army commander, 263; as II Corps commander, 128; role in Odessa massacre of, 128–29
Madgearu, Virgil, 84
Maikop, 160
Malinovsky, Rodion, 261, 264
Mânecuța, Ioan, 114
Maniu, Iuliu, 48, 51–52, 57, 78, 82, 111, 257, 265
Manoliu, Gheorghe, 139, 157
Manstein, Erich von, 3, 124–25, 132–36, 139, 144, 149–51, 153, 155, 157, 175–76, 178, 181
Mărășești, 232
Marcu, Alexandru, 207
Mărculești, 108

Mărdărescu, Gheorghe, 31
Marie, 43, 224, 230
Mariupol, 134–35, 143, 157, 182, 184, 216, 219, 222
massacres: after defeating Soviet amphibious landings in Crimea, 142; in northern Bukovina and Bessarabia, 96–97, 104; in Transnistria, 138, 140, 143. *See also* pogroms
Matieş, Ermil, 97, 108
Mazarini, Nicolae, 140–41, 172–73
MCG: belief in final victory of, 132–33; dissolving of, 133, 182; doubts about final victory of, 161, 165; effect of Iaşi pogrom on, 102–3; efforts to boost morale of, 124, 166; establishment of, 90, 160; feeding paranoia of Jewish fifth column by, 94, 96; negotiations for Transnistria of, 120; at Odessa, 118, 120; opposition to amalgamation of, 181; order about deporting Jews of, 127; orders to evacuate civilians behind front by, 94, 96, 197; order intensifying propaganda east of Dniester of, 111; at Stalingrad, 166, 172, 178; weaknesses of, 15. *See also* General Staff
Mechanized Corps, 261
Meculescu, Teodor, 114
medals: land grant with, 41, 132, 224, 294n6; as motivation, 135, 153, 158, 164, 223–25, 250
Melitopol, 125, 134–35, 182, 186
middle class, 19–22, 24, 26–27, 32, 36, 38–40, 42–43, 45–46, 48, 52, 84, 230, 249
Mihai I: coup of, 254–56, 258; as figurehead king, 65, 80, 83, 92, 120, 257; opposition to treatment of Jews by, 162, 258; regency of, 50–51; role in war crimes trials of, 265
Mihail, Gheorghe, 258, 261
Mihai the Brave, 24
Military Bishopric, 25, 142, 247
military system, 7–8, 15
Millett, Allan, 14
Mindszent, 261
Ministry of Air and Navy, 55
Ministry of Defense, 9, 146, 153–54, 216–17, 237, 244–45, 250–52
Ministry of External Affairs, 86
Ministry of Internal Affairs, 61, 94, 108, 110, 237–38, 250–53, 255
Ministry of Propaganda, 207
Mius River, 183

Mogilev, 68, 104, 107, 113–14, 117, 149, 193
Moldavia, 19–20, 23, 26, 28–29, 37, 59, 72, 89, 103, 192
Molotov, Vyacheslav, 60, 65–66, 17
monarchism, 35, 48, 56, 83
morale, 3, 7–8, 11–12; blaming of Jews for undermining of, 110, 184; blaming of rehabilitation soldiers for weaking of, 184, 193; efforts to bolster, 76, 96, 113, 119, 124, 137, 142–43, 158, 183, 188–90, 208, 212, 234; fluctuations of, 62, 92, 125–26, 166, 176, 181–82, 208, 227–28; of Gypsy soldiers, 250, 252; permanent eroding of, 200, 202, 262; of rehabilitation soldiers, 218–19; resilience of, 147–48, 153
moral education, 7, 22, 36, 48
Morozowskaya, 164
Moscow, 23, 32, 35, 60, 132, 136, 176, 187, 263
motivation, 3–8, 11, 18, 36, 70, 90, 92–93, 95, 131, 166, 169, 202, 205–6, 212, 227, 229, 234, 239, 262, 267
motivational system, 7, 15
Mountain Corps: in battle of Crimea, 134–36, 139–40, 142–43; in battle of Sevastopol, 144, 147, 155, 157–58; defense of Crimea by, 186–91, 196–97; elite, 41, 235; liberation of northern Bukovina by, 106–7; near skirmish with Hungarian Rapid Corps of, 118; as Mountain Corps and Romanian Troops in Crimea Command, 148–49, 154, 158, 163; piercing of Stalin line by, 113, 116
Mureş River, 260
Murray, Williamson, 14

Nalchik, 167
Nămoloasa, 203
National Democratic Bloc, 258
National Democratic Front, 261
nationalism: First World War as catalyst for, 21; as foundation of anti-fascist crusade, 259; as foundation of holy war, 2, 11–12; lack of resonance among minorities of, 229; literacy enabling spread of, 19–20; origins of, 19; peasant uprising of 1907 as nadir of, 20–21
NCOs: abuses by, 45; Jews restricted from being, 43; lack of professionalism of, 44; as more abusive than officers, 47; *reangajaţi*, 44–45, 226

INDEX

Nikolaev, 123, 133, 135, 146, 241
Nikopol, 190, 192
Njecajanoje, 232
NKVD, 114, 128, 133, 149, 223, 263
Nogay Steppe, 124–25
North Africa, 155, 159, 168
Novorossiysk, 161–62, 167, 181–82, 186
nurses: association with sex workers of, 233; on front, 231–33; as "sisters of charity" versus female medical assistants, 230; qualities of, 231

occupation: of northern Bukovina and Bessarabia, 81, 94, 106; Romanian, of Transnistria, 120, 192, 194; Soviet, of northeastern Romania, 194, 197; Soviet, of Romania, 258–59, 261–62
Odessa: battle of, 118–26; black market in, 227; deporting of Jews from, 129, 138, 140, 143, 150; ghetto in, 129, 139; as Jewish-communist nest, 124, 126; liberation of, 195; massacre in, 128–29; partisans in catacombs of, 127–28, 149–50, 156, 194; as supply point for Crimea, 191
Odessa Military Command, 126–28, 150, 156
Odobești, 90
Obodovca, 144
officer corps: aristocratic ethos of, 36; dominated by boyars or military sons, 39; difficulty expanding of, 62; dislike of Legionary egalitarianism of, 57; ethnic Germans in, 44; levels of prestige in, 40–41; lifestyle of, 39–40, 50; middle-class aversion to, 36, 39; official restriction of Jews from, 43; old-fashioned man management of, 45, 47; Old Man Scabbard stereotype of, 38; opening to non-nobles of, 37; politics of, 4, 48, 51, 57, 87, 90, 146; professionalism of, 41–42; purging of, 264; "salon generals" in, 43; schools for military sons/military high schools for, 38; sympathy toward Legionary movement of, 35–36, 58, 80; training of, 42–43, 164; unofficial restriction of Gypsies from, 44
oil, 56, 85, 88, 94, 140, 155–56, 167, 176, 185, 203
OKH, 85, 115, 118–19, 124–25, 141, 148, 150–51, 153, 156, 159, 161, 163, 165–67, 172, 178, 181, 184–86, 189, 193–94, 202–4, 213, 227
OKW, 85, 89, 140, 150, 153, 242

Operation Barbarossa: Antonescu learns start date of, 94; failure of, 137; planning of, 85, 90–91; signs of, 88–90; start of, 95
Operation Citadel, 184
Operation Winter Storm, 175
Oradea, 17, 29, 80–81

Panaite, Mitica, 200, 255–56, 259
Pantazi, Constantin: as 3rd Cavalry Division commander, 71; arrest and trial of, 254, 265; as minister of defense, 141, 146, 159–60, 168, 177, 180, 183–84, 187, 215, 227, 233; as sub-secretary to minister of defense, 82
Pântea, Gherman, 128–29
partisans: capture of, 143, 150, 190–91, 193; equating with Jews of, 134, 163; execution of, 127, 135, 154, 191, 266; female, 135, 154; as loosely applied label, 133–34; origins of, 133. See also *francs-tireurs*
Patronage Council of Social Works, 230, 232, 234, 240
Paulescu, Nicolae, 29
Paulus, Friedrich, 161, 163, 177–78
peasant class, 10, 20–22, 24, 27, 32, 38, 45, 47, 50, 70, 106, 230
Perekop Isthmus, 124–25, 132, 134, 188–89, 191, 195
Petala, Marcela, 117
Petrovicescu, Constantin, 82, 86
Piatra Neamț, 26, 90, 108
Pitești, 9, 53
Ploiești, 53, 94, 96, 110, 185, 241, 256
Podu Iloaiei, 102
Poenaru, Alexandru, 218, 251
pogroms: absence in Ukraine of, 115; during advance into northern Bukovina and Bessarabia, 106; during withdrawal from northern Bukovina and Bessarabia, 73–76; history in Romania of, 26, 27, 29. See also massacres
Poland, 24, 58, 103, 156, 162, 166, 180, 203, 218, 258; Anglo-French guarantee to, 59; anti-Soviet alliance with Romania of, 56; partition of, 59, 87; refugees from, 166; Soviet justification for occupation of, 75
policemen: accused of being corrupt ("Judaized"), 98, 149, 156; Cossacks recruited as in southern Russia, 165, 216; in Romania, 97–103, 243, 246; Tatars recruited as in Crimea, 142;

in Transnistria, 137–38; Ukrainians recruited as in Transnistria, 137, 140, 143–44
Popescu, Dumitru, 53
Popescu, Dumitru I., 154
Popescu Cavalry Group, 175
Potopeanu, Gheorghe, 192
Praetoral Service, 61, 110, 137, 215
praetors, 61, 96, 98, 108, 117
Prague, 264
Predeal, 232, 235
prefects, 89, 96–97, 137, 141, 184, 254, 265; replacement with Legionaries of, 82; replacement with officers of, 87
pre-military training, 51, 55
Prezan, Constantin, 31, 43, 52, 54
primary group, 7, 18, 83, 219, 266
prisoners of war: German, taken after armistice, 255–56; Romanian, survival rate of, 264–65; Soviet, murder of, 135, 151–53, 157, 161; Soviet, parole of, 247
propaganda: about defense of Christian civilization, 1, 12, 14, 91–92, 154, 200, 206, 248; about final victory, 132, 146, 155, 159, 174, 200, 206, 212; about German-Romanian comradeship, 14, 206, 208, 211; about holy war, 2, 142, 159, 166, 200, 208, 234, 260; about Judeo-Bolshevism, 77, 104, 124, 126, 183; about Soviet atrocities, 72, 79, 114, 124, 146, 180; in *The Misadventures of Private Neață*, 13, 77, 87, 127, 135, 164, 183, 209–12, 231, 234, 259
propaganda missionaries, 13, 189, 200, 212
Propaganda Section, 207–9, 212, 234
Prut River, 2, 60, 66, 68, 70–72, 75–77, 92, 94–96, 104, 106–7, 109, 194, 196, 204, 208, 226, 256

Racoviță, I. Mihail: as 2nd Cavalry Division commander, 71; arrest and imprisonment of, 266; as Cavalry Corps commander, 160, 162, 176; dereliction of duty of, 202, 255; as Fourth Army commander, 194, 196–97, 223; as minister of defense, 260; support for mass reprisals of, 110, 113
Rădăuți, 68, 72, 95
Rădescu, Nicolae, 262
rape, 2, 7–8, 10, 14, 86, 97, 104, 107, 110, 127, 129, 197, 214, 218, 222, 260–61
Red Army, 2, 51–52, 94, 111, 119, 123, 131, 168, 181, 258; atrocities in Romania of, 106, 261; Gudarevici detachment, 69; Horia, Cloșca, and Crișan Division, 264; Independent Coastal Army, 118, 121, 123–26, 134, 136, 144, 155; Kiev Military District, 66–68, 76; Odessa Military District, 96, 103, 114; political commissars of, 10, 90, 120, 124; poor reputation of, 60, 77, 92; scorched-earth tactics of, 114, 148; Second Ukrainian Front, 259, 261–64; Tudor Vladimirescu Division, 256, 260, 264
refugees: Polish, 63, 166; Romanian, 68–69, 72–73, 75, 77, 82, 98, 193–95, 198–99; Russian, 28, 31; Soviet, 32, 109–10, 113, 118, 129
rehabilitation: in battalions, 150, 163, 186, 218–19, 259–60; in companies/squadrons, 185; of criminals, 150, 199, 217–18, 251; expansion (General Order No. 240) of, 147, 217; decline of, 220; of individuals, 148, 187, 193, 226; of Legionaries, 216–20, 262; origins of, 216; retraining at Sărata Training Center for, 182, 218–21, 248; retraining at Tiraspol Training Center for, 182, 220; retraining at Tirol Training Center for, 220, 259–60, 262. *See also* deserters
Reichskommissariat Ukraine, 18, 135, 181, 182, 192, 226
religion: centrality to national identity of, 24–25; commonality between Romanians and Soviets of, 115; evangelical fervor resulting from, 121, 162–63; as ideology uniting Romanian and minority soldiers, 229; legitimizing of anti-fascist crusade of, 259; legitimizing of holy war of, 12, 92, 159; nationalization of, 23–24
religious minority groups: Adventists, 25, 247–49, 253; Baptists, 62, 137, 247–49; Calvinists, 243; Catholics, 24–26, 41; Evangelists, 248; Greek Catholics (Uniates), 19, 24–25; Inochentiști, 248, 253; Jehovah's Witnesses, 248; Lipovans, 96, 103, 174, 246; Muslims, 25, 247–48; Pentecostals, 248; Stiliști, 248
Reni, 73
Richter, Gustav, 156, 162
Riga, 180
Roman, 108, 232
Românești, 232
Romania: 1866 constitution of, 27, 48; expansion to Greater Romania of, 21; independent kingdom of, 20; socialist republic of, 266; as United Principalities of Moldavia and Wallachia, 19, 37

INDEX

Romanian Aeronautical Industry, 50, 55
Romanian Air Force, 94, 231; 108th Light Transport Squadron, 231; GAL, 95, 121, 166; I Air Corps, 184
Romanian Army: casualties of, 77, 120, 126, 153, 158, 178, 185, 199–200, 257, 265; doctrine of, 42–43; Echelon I versus Echelon II divisions of, 147–48, 153, 157, 159–62, 166, 228, 242, 244; equipment of, 4, 15, 165, 182; financial aid for soldiers' families of, 88, 119, 158, 167, 182, 193, 226, 239; interwar budget of, 50–52, 55; Legionaries in, 88, 97, 216, 263; "model divisions" of, 15, 85, 104; origins of, 37–38; poor training of, 47; rations of, 158–59; rearmament of, 54, 55, 62, 80; size of, 52, 60, 61, 88, 94, 168, 203; strict discipline of, 14, 46; support for investment in industry of, 50; use to crush worker demonstrations of, 53
Romanian Communist Party, 3–4, 12, 32–33, 99, 258, 263, 266
Romanianization: Antonescu regime's legal version of, 191; interwar policies of, 22; Legionaries' violent version of, 34, 84, 88; officers' concerns about missing out on spoils of, 226–27
Romanian Orthodox Church, 12, 17, 23–26, 34, 41, 64, 121, 154, 249
Romanian Red Cross, 227, 229–34, 253
Rosenberg, Alfred, 57
roșiori regiments: 3rd, 192; 4th, 141; 6th / 6th Motorized, 70–71, 133; 7th, 95, 107, 162; 10th Motorized, 182
Rostov, 159–60, 165, 167, 176, 178, 180, 182
Rotta Ski Detachment, 141
Rozdilna, 232
Rundstedt, Gerd von, 111
Russia, 5, 15, 21, 24, 26–27, 31, 70, 109, 132, 137, 156, 159, 161, 167, 205, 209, 234, 257, 267
Russian Army, 19, 21, 37
Russian Civil War, 13, 23, 28, 31–32, 44
Russo-Turkish War of 1877–1878, 20, 24, 37, 40, 246

Sănătescu, Constantin: as chief of staff, 262, 264; as chief of the military household, 254, 258; as prime minister, 259–62; as VII Corps commander, 76
Sanitary Service, 231–32, 236–37
Sărata, 150, 182, 218, 256
Schobert, Eugen von, 90, 94, 109–10, 117, 119, 123, 222

Schörner, Ferdinand, 194, 196, 198–99, 200
Schwab, Hugo, 187–91, 196, 242, 255
Sculeni, 68, 96–97, 104
Second Army, 59; as nickname for Romanian Railways, 195
Second Balkan War, 21, 37, 81
Second Vienna Award, 80, 82–83, 90, 111, 119, 184, 241, 243
Second World War: Anglo-American landings in France, 200; Anglo-American landings in North Africa, 168; German blitzkrieg into France, 63; German invasion of Poland, 59; German surrender, 264; Italian capitulation, 186; Soviet-Finnish "Winter War," 60; Soviet reconquest of Byelorussia, 202
Secureni, 107
Seletzki, Bruno, 54
Serafimovich, 164, 170
Serbia, 24, 241, 305n217
Sevastopol, 124, 139, 150–51, 154, 169, 180, 190, 193, 217, 250; battle of, 134–36, 144, 147, 155, 157–58; defense of, 195–97, 199; massacre in, 155, 158
Severnaya Bay, 155, 157, 196
Sheffield, Gary, 8
Sibiu, 41, 59
Sicily, 184, 247
Sighișoara, 80
Sima, Horia, 78, 82, 84, 86, 263
Simferopol, 136, 141–42, 154, 188, 190, 208–9, 232–33, 241
Sinaia, 232, 233
Sion, Ioan, 172–74
Siret, 96
Siret River, 72
Sivash Sea, 134, 188–89, 191, 193, 195
Slănic, 202, 204
Slovak Army, 111, 188, 190, 198
Slovakia, 59, 262, 264, 267
Smochină, Nichita, 32
Smolensk, 154, 180
Solonari, Vladimir, 5
Soroca, 66, 69, 110
Soviet Black Sea Fleet, 118, 203
Soviet Moldavians, 23, 121, 154, 156, 182, 191
Soviet-Romanian Armistice: announcing of, 255; demand for Romanian divisions of, 259; enforcement of Allied (Soviet) Control Commission by, 260–61; propaganda by, 260; requirement to prosecute war criminals (People's Tribunals) of, 263, 265–66; shuttering of

INDEX

Romanian signing of, 257–58; territorial revisions of, 259
SS: distrust of Romanian soldiers of, 135; exclusive claim on Jews in Reichskommissariat Ukraine by, 135; recruitment of ethnic Germans in Romania by, 241–43; recruitment of Romanian prisoners of war by, 263; Sonderkommando R of, 138, 140. *See also* Einsatzgruppe D
SSI: agents in Iași of, 98; calls to create a ministry of propaganda of, 207; chief of, 254; drawing up lists of Jews and communists to be arrested by, 94; Operational Echelon of, 109, 117; reports of, 125, 129, 149, 190, 220, 227
Stavka, 118, 125, 133, 150, 153, 157, 163, 166–67, 170–71, 175, 177, 181, 184–86, 189, 191, 193, 195, 198–99, 202–3, 205, 213, 261
Stalin, Joseph, 51, 60, 96, 136, 180, 258, 260–61, 263
Stalingrad: battle of, 159–61, 164, 167, 170–73, 175; effect on morale of, 4, 16, 187, 212, 228; logistical crisis at, 163; pocket in, 174, 176–78
Stalin Line, 111, 113, 208, 222
Stânca Roznovanu, massacre at, 97
Stănescu, Traian, 173–74
starvation: of Axis troops in Stalingrad pocket, 117; of Gypsies in Transnistria, 252; of Jews in Transnistria, 114, 118, 143–44; of Soviet civilians in Crimea, 149
Stavrescu, Gheorghe, 99–100
Șteflea, Ilie: arrest of, 263; attempted resignations of, 159–60, 198; as chief of staff, 141, 146–47, 154, 158, 161, 167, 174, 177, 193–94; effort to end corruption of exemptions for Jews of, 239; as Fourth Army commander, 204, 223
Stere, Constantin, 48, 51
Stoenescu, Alex Mihai, 4
Storojineț, 74, 105
strategic bombing: Anglo-American, 155, 185, 195, 198, 200, 203; Soviet, 96. *See also* air raids
Sturdza, Mihail, 4, 263
Sudak, 134, 139, 142

Taganrog, 133, 135
Taman, 161, 181, 183–84, 233
tank regiments: 2nd, 264
Târgoviște, 38
Târgu Frumos, 102, 203
Târgu Jiu, 94, 103, 197, 219, 235, 262
Târgu Mureș, 260
Târgu Neamț, 26
Tătăranu, Nicolae: as 20th Infantry Division commander, 177–78; as deputy chief of staff, 140–41; negotiation of Tighina Agreement by, 120; push for more death sentences by, 222
Tătărași, 117
Tatarbunar, uprising in, 31–32
Tatars, 142, 149, 187, 197, 233
Tecuci, 87, 232
Temryuk, 160
Țenescu, Florea, 66, 75–76
Teodorescu, Iosif, 254
Third Army: advances farther east after German requests of, 119–20, 132; in battle of Azov Sea, 123–25; in battle of Stalingrad, 162, 164–68, 170–73, 175–76, 178; in battle of Uman, 115–18; crossing Dniester of, 111, 113; disbanding of, 261; on Dniester front, 194, 204; German Eleventh Army's operational control of, 94; mobilization of, 59; order to create "citizen committees" to welcome Germans of, 89; as rear echelon headquarters, 133–34, 143, 146, 148, 157, 160, 182, 187, 190; reconquest of northern Bukovina by, 95–96, 103–7; withdrawal from northern Bukovina of, 68
Țigancă, 109, 115, 257
Tighina, 104, 113, 116, 120, 123, 137, 147, 187, 196, 232, 241
Tighina Agreement, 120, 132, 137
Timișoara, 53, 232, 249
Tinguta, 160
Tiraspol, 133, 198–99, 204, 215, 232
Tirol, 220
Tisa River, 22, 31, 260–62
Todt Organization, 85, 98–99, 243
Topor, Ioan, 108, 110, 113, 121, 265
Trajan Line, 203–4
Transcarpathia, 59
Transnistria: Axis retreat from, 196; black market in, 137, 149; conditions for deported Gypsies in, 252; as dumping ground for Jews, 121, 133, 137, 144; German takeover of, 193; Governorate of, 127, 143; military's distrust of civilian rule in, 156; Romanian takeover of, 120; security by Third Army in, 149–50, 156, 192; size of occupying force in, 132, 138; transition to Military Administration of the Territory between the Dniester and Bug Rivers of, 192

transnistrieni, 23, 32, 111, 130
Transylvania, 11, 19, 21, 24, 31, 41, 56, 59, 74, 80, 123, 159, 207, 240, 247, 259
Treaty of Berlin, 27
Treaty of Bucharest, 21
Treaty of Trianon, 31
Trestioreanu, Constantin: arrest and trial of, 263, 265; as Odessa Military Command commander, 150; role in Odessa massacre, 128
Tudose, Dumitru, 116
Tulcea, 246
Turda, 17
Turkey, 56, 257
Turnu Severin, 103

Uman, 115–18, 193
Ungheni, 75, 232
United States, 162, 168, 257
US Fifteenth Air Force, 195
USSR, 18, 56, 62, 75, 198; alliance with, 259; as greatest threat to Romania, 23, 31, 65, 84; as "Jewish" homeland, 33–34; Moldavian Autonomous SSR of, 32; negotiations with, 257; rapid industrialization of, 51

Vaida-Voevod, Alexandru, 52–53
vânători regiments: 3rd Motorized, 256; 5th, 143; 6th, 97–98, 108; 10th, 70, 198
Vasiliu, Constantin: arrest, trial, and execution of, 254, 265; opposition to repatriation of Jews of, 193; orders to "cleanse the terrain" of Jews of, 108; pressure to deport more Gypsies of, 251
Vasiliu-Rășcanu, Constantin, 147, 264
Vatra Dornei, 76
V Corps, 167, 170–71, 202, 261
Vertujeni, 121
VI Corps: assignment to rear area security between Bug and Dnieper of, 135; in battle of Stalingrad, 160–61, 163–67, 171–72; in Case Blue, 156, 159; in second battle of Kharkov, 153; transferred to lead Romanian soldiers at Izyum salient, 150
VII Corps: in battle of Kerch, 150–51, 155; in battle of Stalingrad, 166–68, 171; in Case Blue, 157, 162; on Iași front, 255; redirection to southern Russia of, 162; in siege of Budapest, 262
VIII Corps, 76
Vladimirescu, Tudor, 19
Voiculescu, Constantin, 87, 113
Voikovstat, rural ghetto in, 136, 139
Volga River, 159–61, 163, 174
Voznesensk, 118

Wallachia, 19, 21, 24, 26, 37, 91, 103, 203, 246, 249
war crimes: fear of punishment for as motivation, 3, 130; post-war trials for, 9–10, 95, 265–66; turn from primarily against Jews to also non-Jews of, 132. *See also* atrocities
Watson, Alexander, 8
Weichs, Maximilian von, 164–65, 17
working class, 29, 30, 32, 45, 230
Wöhler, Otto, 204

XI Corps, 120, 246

Yaila Mountains, 134, 169
Yalta, 134
Yampol, 68
Yugoslavia: as cautionary tale to Romania, 90; German invasion of, 88–89; as member of Little Entente and Balkan Pact, 56

Zaharești, 76
Zaporozhye, 182, 186
Zeitzler, Kurt, 193